Software Studies

LEONARDO

Roger F. Malina, Executive Editor
Sean Cubitt, Editor-in-Chief

A complete list of books published in the Leonardo series appears at the back of this book.

Software Studies

A Lexicon

edited by Matthew Fuller

The MIT Press
Cambridge, Massachusetts
London, England

For information about special quantity discounts, please email special_sales@mitpress.mit.edu

This book was set in Garamond 3 and Bell Gothic by Graphic Composition, Inc.

Printed and bound in the United States of America.

Library of Congress Cataloging-in-Publication Data
Software studies : a lexicon / edited by Matthew Fuller.
      p. cm.—(Leonardo books)
   Includes bibliographical references and index.
   ISBN 978-0-262-06274-9 (hbk. : alk. paper) 1. Computer software. 2. Computers and civilization—Encyclopedias. 3. Programming languages (Electronic computers)—Lexicography. 4. Technology and the arts. I. Fuller, Matthew.
QA76.754.S64723 2008
005.1—dc22

                                                     2007039724

10 9 8 7 6 5 4 3 2 1

Contents

Contents

Series Foreword

The arts, science, and technology are experiencing a period of profound change. Explosive challenges to the institutions and practices of engineering, art making, and scientific research raise urgent questions of ethics, craft, and care for the planet and its inhabitants. Unforeseen forms of beauty and understanding are possible, but so too are unexpected risks and threats. A newly global connectivity creates new arenas for interaction between science, art, and technology but also creates the preconditions for global crises. The Leonardo Book series, published by the MIT Press, aims to consider these opportunities, changes, and challenges in books that are both timely and of enduring value.

Leonardo books provide a public forum for research and debate; they contribute to the archive of art-science-technology interactions; they contribute to understandings of emergent historical processes; and they point toward future practices in creativity, research, scholarship, and enterprise.

To find more information about Leonardo/ISAST and to order our publications, go to Leonardo Online at http://lbs.mit.edu/ or e-mail leonardobooks@mitpress.mit.edu.

Sean Cubitt
Editor-in-Chief, Leonardo Book series

Leonardo Book Series Advisory Committee: Sean Cubitt, *Chair*; Michael Punt; Eugene Thacker; Anna Munster; Laura Marks; Sundar Sarrukai; Annick Bureaud

Doug Sery, Acquiring Editor
Joel Slayton, Editorial Consultant

Leonardo/International Society for the Arts, Sciences, and Technology (ISAST)

Leonardo, the International Society for the Arts, Sciences, and Technology, and the affiliated French organization Association Leonardo have two very simple goals:

1. to document and make known the work of artists, researchers, and scholars interested in the ways that the contemporary arts interact with science and technology, and
2. to create a forum and meeting places where artists, scientists, and engineers can meet, exchange ideas, and, where appropriate, collaborate.

When the journal *Leonardo* was started some forty years ago, these creative disciplines existed in segregated institutional and social networks, a situation dramatized at that time by the "Two Cultures" debates initiated by C. P. Snow. Today we live in a different time of cross-disciplinary ferment, collaboration, and intellectual confrontation enabled by new hybrid organizations, new funding sponsors, and the shared tools of computers and the Internet. Above all, new generations of artist-researchers and researcher-artists are now at work individually and in collaborative teams bridging the art, science, and technology disciplines. Perhaps in our lifetime we will see the emergence of "new Leonardos," creative individuals or teams that will not only develop a meaningful art for our times but also drive new agendas in science and stimulate technological innovation that addresses today's human needs.

For more information on the activities of the Leonardo organizations and networks, please visit our Web sites at <http://www.leonardo.info/> and <http://www.olats.org>.

Roger F. Malina
Chair, Leonardo/ISAST

ISAST Governing Board of Directors: Martin Anderson, Michael Joaquin Grey, Larry Larson, Roger Malina, Sonya Rapoport, Beverly Reiser, Christian Simm, Joel Slayton, Tami Spector, Darlene Tong, Stephen Wilson

Acknowledgments

This volume is the result of a collaborative working process that leaves the editor largely a timepiece, squawking about deadlines here and there. All of the authors have contributed not just their own text or texts, but their generous engagement in and attention to a project that has emerged out of their interactions.

This project was initiated through the Media Design Research programme at the Piet Zwart Institute of the Willem de Kooning Academie Hogeschool Rotterdam. Richard Ouwerkerk, the Director of the Institute, gave immediate and generous support for the work. Leslie Robbins co-organized the workshop out of which most of this work was produced. Michael Murtaugh made the content management system which provided the working environment for the texts to develop and provided instant reviews of drafts on the train between Amsterdam and Rotterdam. Femke Snelting and Calum Selkirk provided insightful feedback on the project as it developed. The students of the Master of Arts in Media Design at Piet Zwart Institute spurred us on to get the thing done. Beatrice DaCosta, Phoebe Sengers, Volker Grassmuck, and Peter Geble helped with suggesting and contacting contributors to the book. Thom Morrison provided sharp and speedy translation. Florian Cramer, Rolf Pixley, Søren Pold, Dragana Antić (the book's indexer), and Graham Harwood provided useful feedback at key points. Thanks to Mandie, Leon, Milo, Rosa, and Felix for making time for me to get the manuscript finished up. Doug Sery, Valerie Geary, Alyssa Larose, and other staff at MIT Press provided excellent advice and collaboration throughout.

Friedrich Kittler's text "Code," which appears here in English for the first time, originally appeared in German as *Code, oder wie sich etwas anders schreiben lässt* in the catalogue to Ars Electronica 2003, "Code—the language of our time" (Gerfried Stocker and Christian Schöpf, eds., Hatje Cantz Verlag Osterfildern-Ruit, 2003).

Ron Eglash and Matti Tedre's entry on *Ethnocomputing* is based upon work supported by (1) the National Science Foundation under Grant No. 0119880, and (2) the Korean Government, Ministry of Education and Human Resources (National Institute for International Education Development).

Software Studies

Introduction, the Stuff of Software

Matthew Fuller

This project is entitled software studies[1] for two reasons. First, it takes the form of a series of short studies: speculative, expository, and critical texts on particular digital objects, languages, and logical structures. Additional terms touch on some of the qualities software is supposed to possess and ideas by which to approach it. Together, at certain scales of interpretation, these constitute the "stuff" of software. Software structures and makes possible much of the contemporary world. This collection proposes an exercise in the rapid prototyping of transversal and critical approaches to such stuff.

What is covered here includes: algorithms; logical functions so fundamental that they may be imperceptible to most users; ways of thinking and doing that leak out of the domain of logic and into everyday life; the judgments of value and aesthetics that are built into computing; programming's own subcultures and its implicit or explicit politics; or the tightly formulated building blocks working to make, name, multiply, control, and interrelate reality. Does *Software Studies* offer a pair of super X-ray specs for the standardized user, allowing them to see behind the screen, through the many layers of software, logic, visualization, and ordering, right down to the electrons bugging out in the microcircuitry and on, into the political, cultural and conceptual formations of their software, and out again, down the wires into the world, where software migrates into and modifies everything it touches? Does it offer even a diagram of such a vision? Not quite. That would take a second volume. What we can achieve though, is to show the stuff of software in some of the many ways that it exists, in which it is experienced and thought through, and to show, by the interplay of concrete examples and multiple kinds of accounts, the conditions of possibility that software establishes.

Secondly, *Software Studies* proposes that software can be seen as an object of study and an area of practice for kinds of thinking and areas of work that have not historically "owned" software, or indeed often had much of use to say about it. Such areas include those that are currently concerned with culture and media from the perspectives of politics, society, and systems of thought and aesthetics or those that renew themselves via criticism, speculation, and precise attention to events and to matter among others. In a famous anecdote, computing pioneer Alan Kay is said to have said of the first Macintosh that despite its limitations it was the first computer really worthy of criticism.[2] By this, one imagines he means a computer that deserves a reciprocation of the richness of thought that went into it, with the care to pay attention to what it says and what it makes palpable or possible, and the commitment to extend such attention into its continuing development. The texts written for this volume suggest their use as a handbook of supplements to some of the key standard objects of computer science, programming, and software culture. As such, our question here is: Where is the rest of that criticism? Indeed, criticism with its undertones of morality or imperious knowledge might be better phrased as a questioning or setting in play. Yes, there is plenty of studiousness being dished up about what people do with software; there are big, fat, and rapidly remaindered books about how to write or use software. But we can't find much of it that takes things at more than face value, or not nearly enough of it to understand the world as it is. There's only one thing to do in such a situation: get on and write what you need to read.

Software's Roots and Reverberations

Recent etymological research[3] credits John W. Tukey with the first published use of the term "software." In a 1958 article for *American Mathematical Monthly* he described how the mathematical and logical instructions for electronic calculators had become increasingly important, "Today the 'software' comprising the carefully planned interpretive routines, compilers, and other aspects of automative programming are at least as important to the modern electronic calculator as its 'hardware' of tubes, transistors, wires, tapes and the like."[4]

Another crucial moment was the decision by IBM in 1968, prompted in no small part by antitrust court actions, to split its software section off from its hardware section. Software was no longer to be bundled as a service or gratuity. As a result, according to Martin Campbell-Kelly, "IBM liberated the industry by unbundling."[5] At the point of software's legal reordering as a separate kind of entity, it became a commodity, an entity the prime or sole motive for the production of which is to generate a monetary profit for those who own the entities, such as companies, by which it is made.[6] This description allows it to circulate in different ways, such as markets, while occluding others. For various reasons, software has always had a parallel geneology including the amateur, academic, gratuitous, experimental, and free. This lexicon, it is hoped, provides useful access to all of these trajectories.

Beyond these beginnings, as software becomes a putatively mature part of societal formations (or at least enters a phase where, in the global north, generations are now born into it as an infrastructural element of daily life), we need to gather and make palpable a range of associations and interpretations of software to be understood and experimented with. While applied computer science and related disciplines such as those working on computer-human interface have now accreted around half a century of work on this domain, software is often a blind spot in the wider, broadly cultural theorization and study of computational and networked digital media. This is not simply because the disciplinary cookie-cutter for the arts and humanities is incompetent with the daily fabric of contemporary working lives, which includes word processors, websites, search engines, email, databases, image editors, sound software and so on; software as a field is largely seen as a question of realized instrumentality. As viewed through the optic of applied logic, software exists as something that has gone through a "threshold of formalization"[7] and now exists only in terms devoid of any reference other than itself. Software is seen as a tool, something that you do something with. It is neutral, grey, or optimistically blue. On the one hand, this ostensive neutrality can be taken as its ideological layer, as deserving of critique as any such myth. But this interpretation itself one that emphasizes only critique can block a more inventive engagement with software's particular qualities and propensities. Working with the specificities of software at the multiple scales at which it occurs is a way to get past this dichotomy.

Recognition of the synthetic power of computing should not block the understanding that much software comprises simply and grimly of a social relation made systematic and unalterable.[8] (Consider, for instance, the ultimately abitrary informational regimes governing who is inside or outside of a national population.) It may not work or offer a rich field of bugs and loopholes of course, but this structuration is often imperceptible,[9] actuated with little public debate or even platforms capable of achieving such debate with meaningful effect. or in a way that is culturally rich enough to bother taking part in. Technologisation of the senses and structuring of relations by technology is often carried out by naturalized means, lessening our ability to understand and engage with such changes. Many accounts have been made of how such naturalization occurs through the technologization of a problem. The optimal solution becomes the one that is most amenable to technical description, usually a description that is only in terms of certain already normalized precursors. By contrast, when technology is used in a way that is interrogable or hackable,[10] it allows and encourages those networked or enmeshed within it to gain traction on its multiple scales of operation. Hackability is not in itself a magic bullet; it relies on skills, knowledge, and access, of making such things public and changing them in the process. Gathering together forms of knowledge that couple software with other kinds of thinking is hopefully a way of enlarging the capacity of hackability itself to be hacked from all directions.

Another theoretical blockage that this collection seeks to overcome is the supposed "immateriality" of software. While this formulation has been deployed by many writers to explain software's distinction from things that have a straightforward physicality at the scale of human visual perception, or the way in which its production differs from industrial or craft forms of fabrication the idea of software's "immateriality" is ultimately trivializing and debilitating.[11]

The new lexicon relies upon an understanding of the materiality of software being operative at many scales: the particular characteristics of a language or other form of interface—how it describes or enables certain kinds of programmability or use; how its compositional terms inflect and produce certain kinds of effects such as glitches, cross-platform compatibility, or ease of sharing and distribution; how, through both artifact and intent, events can occur at the level of models of user subjectivity or forms of computational power, that exceed those of pre-existing social formatting or demand new figures of knowledge.

Whereas much work published in the area of new media largely adopts an Information and Communications Technology model (the shunting of 'content' from point A to point B) for its understanding of phenomena such as the internet or even games, and aims its critical faculties at what happens around or through software, this project differs by, among other things, emphasizing the neglected aspect of *computation*, which involves the possibilities of virtuality, simulation, abstraction, feedback, and autonomous processes.

The purpose of this lexicon then is not to stage some revelation of a supposed hidden technical truth of software, to unmask its esoteric reality, but to see what it is, what it does and what it can be coupled with. In doing so we hope also to construct multiple entry points into the field. Rather than simply watch and make notes on the humans lit by the glow of their monitors it aims to map a rich seam of conjunctions in which the speed and rationality, or slowness and irrationality, of computation meets with its ostensible outside (users, culture, aesthetics) but is not epistemically subordinated by it.

At the same time, the contents of this lexicon acknowledge that software exists at many scales. It is increasingly distributed as an embedded part of sociotechnical infrastructures; manifest as the "semantic sugar" and operational constraints of user-friendly interface elements or higher level languages; integrated into patterns of work and communication so thoroughly that it is desirable to describe all of these in order to account for any; and operative at a low level in interaction with the physical properties of conductive and nonconductive materials. Finding a way of accounting for, understanding, and crucially, working with this multiscalar reality is an important challenge requiring new tools for thought, and ways of holding different kinds of account together.

Software marks another of its beginnings in Alan Turing's desire to chart the computable, arising as a response to David Hilbert's assertion that all mathematical problems are decidable (solvable by means of a definite universal method) within the terms of mathematics.[12] Computation establishes a toy world in conformity with its axioms, but at the same time, when it becomes software, it must, by and large (except for autonomous processes, such as Cron, the demon to execute commands to a schedule in a Unix system, or as exemplified in work such as *Artificial Paradises*[13]) come into combination with what lies outside of code. Just as science, under the admirably empirical plan drawn up by Karl Popper,[14] is a 'Pataphysical machine driven by the accumulation of finer and finer grained errors, which are in turn surpassed by better and better miscomprehensions, software is computation, which, whether it is as useful and mundane as a word-processor, or as brilliant and simple as a cellular automaton, gains its power as a social or cultural artifact and process by means of a better and better accommodation to behaviors and bodies which happen on its outside. Whether these are writing or evolutionary models, the terms by which they are understood have to be grafted, and hence modified and filtered, back into the limited but paradoxical domain of computation. And it is this paradox, the ability to mix the formalized with the more messy—non-mathematical formalisms, linguistic, and visual objects and codes, events occurring at every scale from the ecological to the erotic and political—which gives computation its powerful effects, and which folds back into software in its existence as culture. This folding in does not only happen to software, but with which it couples. Hardware, with its rich panoply of sensors and triggering devices, its mixture of the analog and digital, is perhaps still the finest purveyor of messiness, but as several texts here attest, it finds its complement in software. Once things have become modeled, replicated, and reified, they can be intensified, copied, multiplied, and stretched or subject to a host of other functions that have become familiar from the basic grammars of applications.[15]

The development of software is in many cases simply not subject to the rigor of the requirement for the "better and better" typical of technologies aimed at consumers. Its self-sufficiency, which has allowed computer science to maintain its status as a closed world,[16] allows the plainly dysfunctional and imaginary to roam free. This freedom applies as much to the bizarre fruits of business plans gorged on the tragedy of imagined or "intellectual" property as to the whimsical, inventive, or deranging entities stored in software art repositories. (A whole separate volume of the vocabulary of the anxious, deluded, and mendacious could be drawn up for large-scale private or governmental software projects.) The rise of software and of computational and networked digital media in general has in many ways depended upon massive amounts of investment in institutions, training, and the support of certain kinds of actors. One other strand of the development of software over its history has often depended upon individuals or small groups of people finding a breathable pocket of time and resources in the intestines of larger hierarchically ordered organizations, or acting on their own cobbled-together means. Since the development of computer networks, such pockets of differentiated pressure have been able to be assembled across space, in smaller chunks, and asynchronously. Since the massification of computing they have in some small ways also been able to construct themselves in relation to other forms of life. (In the sense that Ludwig Wittgenstein means when he says, "To imagine a language is to imagine a form of life."[17]) This "self-sufficiency" of software, in such a context, allows (in much the same way as it allows a programmer to think he or she is working on the formulation of a particularly interesting and chewy algorithm when working at another scale, perhaps more determining, on an insurance program to more finely exclude the poor from public services) a certain distance from social or cultural norms. Things can be done in software that don't require much dependence on other factors. The range of articulation software allows due to the nature of the joints it forms with other layers of reality means that this freedom (that of a closed world), while somewhat paralyzing, has also guaranteed it a space for profound and unfinishable imagination.

Parallels and Precursors

While this book proposes a set of approaches to thinking about software, it is not alone in this work. It comes out of a wider set of interlocking areas of activity in digital cultures, but two other key areas, historical research into the genesis of computing and the discourse associated with free and open source software, have provided a context for the work here.

Computing is beginning to be recognized as something having a history, rather than just being permanently in a state of improvement. Computing history thus becomes discursive, and opens computing in the present day up to the consideration of palpable alternatives. Several of the key texts in the history of computing are called upon here and it is an area from which one anticipates further revealing developments.

Of special interest for this lexicon is the way in which free software, and associated currents such as open source have set off ripples in the way people talk and think about software. This discussion has often taken place on blogs, mailing lists, and in the opinion pieces of industry pundits.[18] While it is often short on historical memory or connection to thought outside of its own domain, this discussion can be lively and insightful. Neal Stephenson suggests that, "Linux per se is not a specific set of ones and zeroes, but a self-organizing net subculture."[19] Because free and open source software opens up the process of writing software in certain ways its also opens up the process of talking and thinking about it.

Two other currents have also fed into this project. While art and design have for a reasonably long period had something of an inkling that objects, devices, and other material entities have a politic—that they engage in the arrangement and composition of energies, allow, encourage or block certain kinds of actions—these concerns have also more recently been scrutinized by the inter-disciplinary area of science and technology studies. Shifting from an emphasis on epistemologies to also encompass the way in which things are embedded with and produce certain kinds of knowledge and possibility of interaction with the world (and indeed make worlds) has been extremely fruitful. Such work has also contributed to this book because, among other things, it provides a means of talking about the materiality of abstraction, the interplay between formalization and the heterogenous stuff it mobilizes.

The area that has become known as software art[20] is perhaps the most direct feed into this lexicon. This current of work, along with hacker culture, provides a means for bringing the generative, reflexive, and anarchist intelligence of art into compositional entanglement with the ostensibly ordered and self-sufficiently technical language, working patterns, and material of software. Art understands that the style of thought is crucial—style not simply as a metric for the deposition of flourishes and tricks, but as a way of accessing multiple universes of reference. *Software Studies* also proposes another set of potential interactions between art and other inventive cultural practices and domains such as mathematics and logic. Significant work has been done in the overlap between the two fields utilizing conceptual figures such as "beauty" or "symmetry." Other, non-idealist interactions are also possible, and indeed, necessary. The project provides a space for interactions between art and mathematics outside of clean-room purity in dirtier interactions with cultures, economies, hardware, and life. Mathematics becomes applied, not to the cleanly delineated sets of problems set it by productivity and efficiency goals in software projects, but to the task of inventing and laughing with its own goofily serene self and in doing so regaining its "pure" task of establishing systems and paroxysms of understanding.

What Is a Lexicon?

Finding a mode of writing capable of inducing experiment is tricky. In what way does a lexicon provide a useful structure for this form of software study? A lexicon is a vocabulary of terms used in a particular subject. Rather than an encyclopedia, which is too universal, or a dictionary or glossary, which offer too short descriptions or readings of terms, a lexicon can be provisional and is scalable enough a form to adapt to any number of terms and lengths of text. In producing a lexicon for an area that is as wide, deep, and fast moving as software, one can easily make a virtue out of the necessary incompleteness of the work. Indeed, *Software Studies* cannot claim to be a summa of terms, objects, structures, and ideas. Although we refer often to monumental works such as Donald Knuth's *Art of Computer Programming*,[21] a systematic and good humored survey and exposition of algorithms and data structures, other forms of encyclopedia and glossary also influenced the adoption of this structure. *The Jargon File*[22] is a lengthy and wry catalogue of early North American hackers' argot displaying readily the way in which something can be at once both technically informative, enjoying word-play or double, if not infinitely recursive, meaning, and also reflexive upon its own working culture. Another strand of work that informs *Software Studies* is the trajectory of dictionaries and folios of terms and keywords, which recognize the ridiculousness of attempting to catalogue, name, and explain reality. These supplementary explanations investigate our culture as if it requires an interpretative account. They try to capture the language of a possible future, actual language at the cusp of where it intersects the possible and the unspeakable. These works, among them such dark jewels as the "Dictionary" supplements to the magazine *Documents* edited by Georges Bataille, capture through their many facets a pattern out of which an approach to life can be sensed and articulated.[23] Rather more hopeful of the possibility of lucid communication is Raymond Williams's *Keywords*, a book established as a personal "enquiry into a vocabulary."[24] Both of these use the way in which a lexicon can establish alliances between words, texts, and ideas without necessarily agglutinating them as a whole, thus effacing a more complex reality. A normal dictionary comes to a point of momentary stability when it defines all the words which it uses to define all the words that it contains. Each definition, then, reaches out to all the terms used to establish its meaning in a beautiful, recursively interwoven networking of language. *Software Studies* is not quite so mature, but an astute reader will find many pathways between the different texts.

Words bind thinking and acting together, providing a means for the conjunction and differentiation of work and other dynamics between persons, across groups of ideas, and ways of doing things. Collections of words build up a consistency, becoming a population teeming with the qualities that Ronald Sukenick ascribes to narrative: "agonistic, sophistic, sophisticated, fluid, unpredictable, rhizomatic, affective, inconsistent and even contradictory, improvisational and provisional."[25] At the same time, in the case of software studies, words work in relation to another set of dynamics, a technical language that is determined by its relation to constants that are themselves underpinned by a commitment to an adequately working or improved description. That is, at a certain, software demands an engagement with its technicity and the tools of realist description. As software becomes an increasingly significant factor in life, it is important to recognize this tension and to find the means for doing so.

Stuff behind Stuff

One rule of thumb for the production of this book is that the contributors had to be involved in some way in the production of software as well as being engaged in thinking about it in wider terms. It is perhaps a sign of an underlying shift that this project is possible now, that this many people who can work within this format and topic could be brought together.

Part of this underlying shift is that software is now, unevenly, a part of mass and popular cultures. It forms a component, if not the largest part, of more and more kinds of work. Knowledge about how to make it, to engage with programming and how to use software more generally, circulates by an increasing number of formal and informal means. The experience and understanding of software is undergoing a change in both quantity and quality. This book aims to make available some of the mixed intelligences thinking through these conditions. The authors are artists, computer scientists, designers, philosophers, cultural theorists, programmers, historians, media archaeologists, mathematicians, curators, feminists, musicians, educators, radio hams, and other fine things, and most straddle more than one discipline. The voices collected here bring more than one kind of intelligence to software because software makes more sense understood transversally.

There's another rule of thumb: In order to program, you have to understand something so well that you can explain it to something as stonily stupid as a computer. While there is some painful truth in this, programming is also the result of a live process of engagement between thinking with and working on materials and the problem space that emerges. Intelligence arises out of interaction and the interaction of computational and networked digital media with other forms of life conjugate new forms of intelligence and new requirements for intelligence to unfold. As a result, a number of authors collected in this book have called for a renewed understanding of what literacy should mean contemporarily. Amongst others, Michael Mateas has made an important call for what he describes as Procedural Literacy.[26] Those whose working practice involves education, and the need to address the tension between education and knowledge,[27] know that the question of what such a literacy might be returns always as a question, and not as a program. In order to ask that question well, however, it is useful to have access to vocabularies which allow one to do so.

Returning to the question of the lexicon, the investigation of such a problem space requires an adequate form of description for computational processes and digital objects. For this, we look at what is most familiar.[28] There is a dual danger here: What is more pretentious than an attempt to interpret the banal, to see in the stuff of everyday life something more than what is seen by those who made it, use it, or live it? Do we just offer up a banality from another field of work (say, those that have currently and partially settled out as economics, philosophy or art) plonking it down as a reference to software, stating that the subject is now "complex" and somehow therefore familiarly sublime in its difficulty?[29] On the other hand, should we limit ourselves to repeating, using, and abjectly loving that which is given, or limit ourselves only to the language of specialists where "questions and differences about words"[30] are erased and terminologies are owned?

What is important is not to settle for either of these traps. Friedrich Nietzsche suggests that the need for knowledge is often founded on the fear of the unfamiliar, and the refusal to face the familiar, that which we are the most habituated to, as the most potentially unknown or disturbing. He suggests that when we look at what seems strange, and then find behind it something "that is unfortunately quite familiar to us, such as our multiplication tables or our logic, or our willing and desiring,"[31] we are doing so as a way of avoiding more difficult processes of questioning and revaluation. Software has become our familiar. The stuff of software is what excites the writers gathered here. I hope that in setting out a few terms for discussion that we have not left either the unfamiliar or the familiar in the same state and that we enhance for the users of these texts the capacity, by any means, to become strange.

Notes

1. "Software studies" is a conjunction of words describing a possible field of activity in Lev Manovich's *The Language of New Media* and is further commented upon in N. Katherine Hayles's *My Mother was a Computer*. A useful follow-up text to Manovich is Matthew G. Kirschenbaum, "Virtuality and VRML: Software Studies After Manovich," *Electronic Book Review*, 8/29/2003, available at http://www.electronicbookreview .com/thread/technocapitalism/morememory. Software Studies itself, and the various components it draws from, is a wide field with a history, and perhaps a counter-history, running back to the various beginnings of computing.

2. Alan Kay, "Would you buy a Honda with a one-gallon gas tank?" memo, 1984, cited in Steven Levy, *Insanely Great*, 192.

3. Fred R. Shapiro, "Origin of the Term Software: Evidence from the JSTOR Electronic Journal Archive."

4. John W. Tukey, "The Teaching of Concrete Mathematics."

5. Martin Campbell-Kelly, *From Airline Reservations to Sonic the Hedgehog*, 13. See pp. 109–114 of that volume for a detailed account.

6. See Ellen Meiskins Wood, *The Origins of Capitalism: A Longer View.*

7. Michel Foucault, *The Archaeology of Knowledge.* For commentary on this formulation, see Gilles Deleuze, *Foucault*, 90.

8. For instance, see the accounts of Call Centre "masks," software that prescribes the use of the computer to a certain set of delimited task sequences, in Kolinko, *Hotlines: Call Centre Inquiry Communism.*

9. A simple example: When booking your next flight, try selecting "Palestine" as your country of citizenship in the scrollable, alphabetical menu provided by the website.

10. See the panel description for "Design for Hackability" at ACM SIG-CHI conference, 2004, including Jonah Brucker-Cohen, Anne Galloway, Layla Gaye, Elizabeth Goodman, and Dan Hill, available at http://www.sigchi.org/DIS2004/Documents/Panels/DIS2004_Design_for_Hackability.pdf/.

11. For one account of why this is so, see Ursula Huws, "Material World: The Myth of the Weightless Economy," in *The Making of a Cybertariat: Virtual Work in a Real World.*

12. For an accessible account, see Andrew Hodges and Alan Turing, *The Enigma of Intelligence.*

13. Artificial Paradises, available at http://www.1010.co.uk/ap0202.html/.

14. As succinctly stated in the lecture, "Science as Falsification," in Karl Popper, *Conjectures and Refutations*, pp. 33–39. See also Karl Popper, *The Logic of Scientific Discovery.*

15. See Matthew Fuller, *Softness, Interrogability, General Intellect: Art Methodologies in Software.*

16. Paul Edwards, *The Closed World: Computers and the Politics of Discourse in Cold War America.*

17. Ludwig Wittgenstein, *Philosophical Investigations,* §19.

18. See, for instance, Joel Spolsky, ed., *The Best Software Writing 1: Selected and Introduced by Joel Spolsky.*

19. Neal Stephenson, *In the Beginning was the Command Line*, 93. See also, http://www.spack.org/wiki/InTheBeginningWasTheCommandLine.

20. For numerous texts, scripts, applications, and sites, see the RunMe.org repository of software art, available at http://www.runme.org/, and the catalogs for the Read_Me festivals, edited by Olga Goriunova and Alexei Shulgin.

21. Donald Knuth, *The Art of Computer Programming.*

22. *The Jargon File*, available at http://www.dourish.com/goodies/jargon.html/.

23. These texts and others are collected as Georges Bataille, Isabelle Waldberg, and Iain White, *Encyclopaedia Acephalica.*

24. Raymond Williams, *Keywords: A Vocabulary of Culture and Society*, 15.

25. Ronald Sukenick, *Narralogues: Truth in Fiction*, 1.

26. Michael Mateas, "Procedural Literacy: Educating the New Media Practitioner," also available at http://www.lcc.gatech.edu/~mateas/publications/MateasOTH2005.pdf/.

27. McKenzie Wark, *A Hacker Manifesto.*

28. Friedrich Nietzsche, *The Gay Science*, §355.

29. For a call to go beyond such a lazy acceptance of "complexity," see the introduction to John Law and Annemarie Mol, eds., *Complexities: Social Studies of Knowledge Practices.*

30. Francis Bacon, *The Advancement of Learning, Second Book.*

31. Nietzsche, *The Gay Science*, §355.

Algorithm

Andrew Goffey

Algorithm = Logic + Control[1]

The importance of the algorithm for software studies is indicated with admirable succinctness by Les Goldschlager and Andrew Lister in their textbook, *Computer Science: A Modern Introduction*. The algorithm "is the unifying concept for all the activities which computer scientists engage in." Provisionally a "description of the method by which a task is to be accomplished," the algorithm is thus the fundamental entity with which computer scientists operate.[2] It is independent of programming languages and independent of the machines that execute the programs composed from these algorithms. An algorithm is an abstraction, having an autonomous existence independent of what computer scientists like to refer to as "implementation details," that is, its embodiment in a particular programming language for a particular machine architecture (which particularities are thus considered irrelevant).

But the algorithm is not simply the theoretical entity studied by computer scientists. Algorithms have a real existence embodied in the class libraries of programming languages, in the software used to render web pages in a browser (indeed, in the code used to render a browser itself on a screen), in the sorting of entries in a spreadsheet and so on. Specialized fields of research, such as artificial life or connectionism in cognitive science, utilize genetic algorithms, backpropagation algorithms, least mean square algorithms for the construction of models to simulate evolutionary processes or the learning capacities of neural networks. Algorithms have material effects on end users—and not just when a commercial website uses data-mining techniques to predict your shopping preferences.

In short, both theoretically and practically, ideally and materially, algorithms have a crucial role in software. But none of this tells us much about the social, cultural, and political role algorithms play, if anything. Nor does it tell us much about the strata of material reality algorithmic abstractions might be correlated with: glowing configurations of pixels on a screen? mouse movements? the flow of electrons around an integrated circuit? Locating itself squarely on the side of the reductionist strategies of the exact sciences, society, culture, and politics are very much marginal to the concerns of computing

Algorithm

15

science. Software engineering, on the other hand, concerned as it is with the pragmatic efficacy of building software for particular purposes, might appear to offer a better starting point for factoring culture back into software. However, it is unlikely that software engineering will allow us to view culture as anything other than something that software plugs into, as long as we fail to arrive at a better understanding of some of its basic building blocks. The key question then is what, if anything, a study of algorithms as such can tell us about the place of culture in software.

Historically, the algorithm occupies the central position in computing science because of the way that it encapsulates the basic logic behind the Turing machine. Alan Turing's concept of a machine that could be used to determine whether any particular problem is susceptible to being solved mechanically was a highly original interpretation of the aim of David Hilbert's famous project of formally deciding whether or not any mathematical proposition can be proved true. The algorithm, which Turing understood as an effective process for solving a problem, is merely the set of instructions fed into the machine to solve that problem.[3] Without the algorithm then, there would be no computing.

Although computer scientists work with them as if they were purely formal beings of reason (with a little bit of basic mathematical notation, it is possible to reason about algorithms, their properties and so on, the way one can reason about other mathematical entities), algorithms bear a crucial, if problematic, relationship to material reality. This was tacit in the way that the Turing machine was envisaged in terms of effective processes: A computer is a machine, after all, and while the Turing machine is an imaginative abstraction, its connotations of materiality are entirely real. Robert Rosen has suggested that the temptation to extrapolate from formal procedures to material processes was practically inherent in the enterprise of the early computing scientists.[4] Such a temptation implies a confusion between the mathematics of algorithms and the physics of real processes, of which Stephen Wolfram's bold speculation that the universe is itself a giant computer is one possible outcome.[5] The rest of this article explores another possibility, equally speculative but perhaps more mundane.

One of the implications of characterizing the algorithm as a sum of logic and control is that it is suggestive of a link between algorithms and action. Despite the formal-logical framework of the theory of algorithms and the fact that programming languages are syntactic artifacts, the construction of algorithms as a precisely controlled series of steps in the accomplishment of a task is a clear indication of what might be called the pragmatic dimension of

Algorithm

16

programming. Algorithms do things, and their syntax embodies a command structure to enable this to happen. After all, the Turing machine as an imaginative abstraction had as a material correlate a series of real computers. And dumb though they may be, missile guidance systems, intelligence databases, and biometric testing are all perfectly real. Without this effective existence in concrete machinery, algorithms would only ever have a paper reality as the artifacts of a formal language.

In the field of linguistics, the existence of a pragmatic dimension to language—the fact that words do things—has created enormous problems for attempts to formalize the structure of natural language. Because pragmatics connects language to extrinsic factors, it becomes impossible to conceptualize a language as a self-sufficient system closed in on itself. Perhaps attempting to conceptualize the pragmatic dimension of the algorithm might yield a similar result? However, while formalization comes afterwards with natural languages, with algorithms, formalization comes first, the express aim being to divorce (formal) expression from (material) content completely. Understandably then, the study of computation has tended to concentrate on issues of syntax and semantics, the assumption being that what algorithms do can be appropriately grasped within such a framework. This has tended to result in making the leap from the theoretical world to the practical world a difficult one to accomplish. Always the trivia of implementation details.

A conception of the algorithm as a *statement* as Michel Foucault used the term might allow us to understand this approach a little better. For Foucault, the statement is not analytically reducible to the syntactic or semantic features of a language; it refers instead to its historical existence and the way that this historical existence accomplishes particular actions. The statement is a sort of diagonal line tracing out a function of the existence of language, which is in excess of its syntactic and semantic properties. In this way, the concept of the statement acts as a reminder that the categorical distinction between form and content is, paradoxically, insufficiently abstract to grasp the intelligence of concretely singular constellations of language in their effective existence. As Foucault puts it in *The Archaeology of Knowledge,* "to speak is to do something—something other than to express what one thinks, to translate what one knows, and something other than to play with the structure of language."[6] For Foucault, these actions are restricted to the human sphere, as is only to be expected from an analysis which focuses on the historical existence of natural languages. Appropriately translated into the field of software studies, however,

Algorithm

17

focusing on the development and deployment of algorithms and an analysis of the actions they accomplish both within software and externally might lead us to view the latter as a sort of machinic discourse, which addresses the ways in which algorithms operate transversally, on themselves, on machines, and on humans. (Alternatively, we might want to start to think about cultural analysis as a process of software engineering.)

Viewing algorithms in this way as statements within a machinic discourse would problematize their existence in a way which undercuts the "pure/applied" or "theory/practice" dichotomies which crop up when the distinction between computing science and software engineering is too hastily made. The formalist aim at complete abstraction from content not only relays the theory/practice divide, it also tends to preclude an analysis of the link between the crucial entities of computing science and historical context. Just because the development of an algorithm requires a level of de facto formal abstraction, which then allows that algorithm to be applied to other kinds of content, does not mean that we have exhausted everything that we need to know to understand the processes of which it is a part. To borrow an expression from Gilles Deleuze and Félix Guattari, whose analysis of the place of pragmatics in language is part of the inspiration for this discussion, the problem with the purely formal conception of the algorithm as an abstract machine is not that it is abstract. It is that it is not abstract enough. That is to say, it is not capable of understanding the place of the algorithm in a process which traverses machine and human.[7]

Algorithms obviously do not execute their actions in a void. It is difficult to understand the way they work without the simultaneous existence of data structures, which is also to say data. Even the simplest algorithm for sorting a list of numbers supposes an unsorted list as input and a sorted list as output (assuming the algorithm is correct). Although computer scientists reason about algorithms independendently of data structures, the one is pretty near useless without the other. In other words, the distinction between the two is formal. However, from a practical point of view, the prerequisite that structured data actually exist in order for algorithms to be operable is quite fundamental, because it is indicative of a critical operation of translation that is required for a problem to be tractable within software. That operation of translation might be better understood as an incorporeal transformation, a transformation that, by recoding things, actions, or processes as information, fundamentally changes their status. This operation can be accomplished in myriad ways, but generally requires a structuring of data, whether by something as innocuous as the use of

Algorithm

18

a form on a web page or by social processes of a more complex form: the knowledge extraction practiced by the developers of expert systems, the restructuring of an organization by management consultants, and so on.

It would be easy to leave the analysis of algorithms at this point: We are back on familiar territory for cultural analysis, that of the critique of abstraction. Within cultural studies and many other fields of research in the human sciences, abstraction is often thought of as the enemy. Many movements of philosophical thought, literary and artistic endeavor, and human-scientific research set themselves up against the perceived dehumanizing and destructive consequences of the reductionism of mathematics, physics, and allied disciplines, as the perennial debates about the differences between the human and the exact sciences suggests. We could even understand major elements of the concept of culture as a response to the abstract machinery of industrial capitalism and the bifurcated nature modern rationality is built upon. Understanding things, activities, tasks, and events in algorithmic terms appears only to exacerbate this situation. What is an algorithm if not the conceptual embodiment of instrumental rationality within real machines?

However, to simply negate abstraction by an appeal to some other value supposedly able to mitigate the dehumanizing consequences of reductionism misses a crucial point. It fails to adequately question the terms by which the algorithm, as a putatively self-sufficient theoretical construct, maintains its hierarchizing power. In questioning the self-sufficiency of the algorithm as a formal notion by drawing attention to its pragmatic functioning, however, it becomes possible to consider the way that algorithms work as part of a broader set of processes. Algorithms act, but they do so as part of an ill-defined network of actions upon actions, part of a complex of power-knowledge relations, in which unintended consequences, like the side effects of a program's behavior, can become critically important.[8] Certainly the formal quality of the algorithm as a logically consistent construction bears with it an enormous power—particularly in a techno-scientific universe—but there is sufficient equivocation about the purely formal nature of this construct to allow us to understand that there is more to the algorithm than logically consistent form.

Lessig has suggested that "code is law," but if code is law it is law as a "management of infractions."[9] Formal logics are inherently incomplete and indiscernibles exist. Machines break down, programs are buggy, projects are abandoned and systems hacked. And, as the philosopher Alfred North Whitehead has shown, humans are literally infected by abstractions.[10] This no bad

Algorithm

19

thing, because like the virus which produced variegated tulips of a rare beauty, infection can be creative too.

Notes

1. Robert Kowalski, "Algorithm = logic + control."

2. Les Goldschlager and Andrew Lister, *Computer Science: A Modern Introduction*, 2nd ed., 12.

3. See Rolf Herken, ed., *The Universal Turing Machine: A Half-Century Survey* for an excellent collection of appraisals of the Turing machine.

4. Robert Rosen, "Effective Processes and Natural Law" in Herken, ibid.

5. Stephen Wolfram, *A New Kind of Science*.

6. Replace the word "speak" with the word "program" and one might begin to get a sense of what is being suggested here. See Michel Foucault, *The Archaeology of Knowledge*.

7. Gilles Deleuze and Félix Guattari, "November 20, 1923: Postulates of Linguistics," in *A Thousand Plateaus*.

8. See Philip Agre, *Computation and Human Experience* on the crucial role of side effects in software. Max Weber's essay *The Protestant Ethic and the Spirit of Capitalism* is the classic text on the fundamental role of unintended consequences in human action.

9. Gilles Deleuze, *Foucault*, p. 39.

10. See for example, Alfred North Whitehead, *Science and the Modern World*, and the extended commentary by Isabelle Stengers, *Penser avec Whitehead*.

Algorithm

20

■

Analog

Derek Robinson

> Now the analogy between reasons, causes, forces, principles, and
> moral rules is glaring, but dazzling.
> —JAMES CLERK MAXWELL[1]

The term "analog" has come to mean smoothly varying, of a piece with the apparent seamless and inviolable veracity of space and time; like space and time admitting infinite subdivision, and by association with them connoting something authentic and natural, against the artificial, arbitrarily truncated precision of the digital (e.g., vinyl records vs. CDs). This twist in the traditional meaning of "analog" is a linguistic relic of a short-lived and now little-remembered blip in the history of technology.

Electronic analog computers, based on technologies developed in the 1930s–1940s and sold commercially from the mid-1950s onward, were used by scientists and engineers to create and explore simulation models, hence their name: A model is something standing in analogical relationship to the thing being modeled. The medium of the analogy was voltage, the electromotive force flowing and varying continuously through a circuit. Electronic amplifiers would allow any varying quantity sensed by instruments to be input to and transformed through an analog computer's "program" (i.e., its circuit), fitting it for use in ballistics computations and real time process control.

General purpose analog computers were anticipated in certain exotic mechanical devices dating from the 1870s, but these were costly specialized machines, never widely deployed. Only twenty or so Bush Differential Analyzers were ever built, and a similar number of Kelvin's Tidal Predictor and Harmonic Analysers installed worldwide. The final iteration of the Bush Differential Analyzer was operational by 1942; it had 2000 vacuum tubes, 200 miles of wire, 150 electric motors, thousands of relays, and weighed 100 tons.[2] Of the mechanical analog computers (barring the slide rule) the Norden bombsight probably saw widest service, being used in U.S. bombers from World War II until the end of the Vietnam War. Given airspeed and altitude, the bombsight calculated a bomb's trajectory through a complex assembly of electric motors, gyros, levels, gears, and optical parts.

Much of the early work on electronic computing, both analog and digital, was carried out under the shroud of wartime secrecy, and it would be decades before detailed accounts of projects like the Colossus computers used by British codebreakers began to emerge. It turns out that the first general purpose analog electronic computer was built in 1941 at Peenemunde, the German military's top-secret rocket facility. Helmut Hoelzer's "Mischgerat" was used as an onboard flight controller in V-2 ballistic missiles and as a programmable launch dynamics simulator on the ground. At the war's close, Hoelzer was one of the German scientists spirited away by Operation Paperclip to develop guided missiles for the U.S. military. He became head of the Marshall Space Flight Center Computation Lab and contributed to the Saturn V rocket used in the Apollo and Skylab missions.[3]

In the decade following World War II, a number of American, English, Dutch, and German electronics firms got into the business of manufacturing analog computers. These were large handsome objects in enameled sheetmetal cases, sporting delicate vernier dials, glowing nixie tubes, rows of black bakelite knobs and colorful patch-cords hanging in braids—an epitome of the modern instrument-maker's art. Rapidly adopted by research labs due to their versatility and relatively modest cost, by the end of the 1960s they had been replaced in most areas by digital software. One noteworthy exception was computers made for music synthesis. Analog synthesizers, a special breed of analog computer, didn't yield to digital synths like the Yamaha DX-7 until the 1980s.[4] And similarly to realtime video synthesizers used by avant garde cineastes, their palette wouldn't be reproducible in software until the 2000s (whence came the laptop VJ).[5] Certain kinds of embedded analog controllers might also be seen as special purpose analog computers, however analog control system design is its own branch of engineering, which both contributed to and outlasted the brief apogee of analog computing.

It might have been initially unclear which type of giant electronic brain would prevail, but with the advent of mainframes (the Remington-Rand typewriter company began commercial development of the UNIVAC in 1951) the balance tipped in favor of digital machines for general purpose number crunching. Analog computers by their nature were unsuited to the preparation of the National Census; almost before getting underway the analog era entered a lengthy decline into its present obscurity.

Analogies and Amplifications

The term "analog," as indicated above, was an allusion to a body of physical and geometric "analogies" and their corresponding systems of equations, established by mathematicians from Newton's time forward. The differential equations of physics represent, in a bristlingly arcane syntax, common spatio-temporal patterns occurring across the panoply of chemical, hydraulic, thermal, mechanical, acoustic, electrical, and biological phenomena. Electronic analog computers, arriving as and when they did, imbued the standard physical analogs with a new concreteness and gravitas, and made tangible the abstract dynamics hidden behind the mathematics. Researchers could quickly construct a working system (indeed a system of equations, but now "in the metal") whose transient and long-term behaviors they could observe and record oscillographically and freely tweak with sliders and knobs. An analog computer was functionally an oversize, precision manufactured, rocket-age version of the home circuit hobbyist's electronic breadboard.

The basic unit of analog computing was the operational amplifier, so named because it could be configured to mimic, by changing the values of resistors and capacitors attached to its inputs, all the basic operations of mathematics (negation, addition, subtraction, multiplication, division, differentiation, integration) and so emulate in circuitry virtually anything that could be modeled in a system of equations. Unlike a digital CPU, whose speed is limited by a fixed clock cycle and the efficiency or otherwise of the code being executed, and which operates on binary 1s and 0s rather than continuous voltages and can execute only one instruction at a time, analog computation takes place effectively instantaneously, at every point in a circuit at once.

The op amp was a refinement and elaboration of the negative feedback amplifier developed by Harold Black, and patented in his name by Bell Labs in 1937. It is in large part owed to Black's invention, placed in the hands of wartime electronics engineers, that the term "feedback" entered into common use. Black's negative feedback amplifier revolutionized scientific instrumentation in the 1940s, and a generation of scientists (at the time scientists were necessarily also analog hackers, just as today's scientists are trained to be fluent in Unix, C programming, and LaTEX) were exposed to the sometimes startling consequences attendant on feeding a system's outputs back as its inputs.[6]

Mapped into electronic engineering schematics and circuit symbols, the scientist's analogies formed a highly compressed picture language of systems in general, applicable to very nearly any focus of scientific inquiry. What made electronic analog computation possible is that circuits and circuit elements intrinsically embody a common mathematics and physicogeometrical metaphor of force, flow, and circular feedback. The root metaphor and lasting legacy of the analog era is therefore this concept of "system" itself, as an assembly of elements in relations of interdependence, altogether constituting a complex organized whole.[7]

Owing to the connective tissue of intervening dependencies, in a system every part ultimately depends upon every other part, and the temporal linear chain of causes and effects is made circular. It becomes a "circuit." The snake swallows its tail, the world is round. Effects fed back become the causes of their own causes, and the mutual constraint of part upon part ensures that any imbalance or error (which physicists term the "energy") is immediately relayed to adjacent parts, and by these to the parts adjoining and being acted upon by them, driving the entire system to equilibrium, an energy minimum. It might not be the lowest such minimum, and the system might never stabilize. Instead it may endlessly oscillate (oscillators are handy things to engineers) or jitter and career about madly in so-called mathematical chaos. Without corrective negative feedback, amplifier circuits immediately saturate, solutions take off for infinity, speaker-cones and eardrums are easily blown.

Feedback

This picture of circularly dependent systems, bound together in dynamic feedback loops, in many ways marked a return to ideas current two centuries before. The image of electricity as a strangely sexed fluid circulating endlessly in closed loops had been advanced by Volta, Franklin, Ampere, and other late-eighteenth-century natural philosophers.[8] A hydraulic or pneumatic analogy was already present in Descartes's diagrams of fiery ethers conveying sensation and volition by nerves going to and from the brain, and in Harvey's famous demonstration of the circulation of blood by the action of the heart. Simon Stevin, a Flemish contemporary of Galileo, had revived Archimedean hydrostatics, framed the parallelogram law of forces, and advised the use of double-entry bookkeeping for national accounts. By 1760 the Physiocrats were proposing a circulatory model of the French economy: Quesnay's Tableau Economique was the prototype "spreadsheet model," with money and goods charted as reciprocal flows through the demographic sectors of pre-revolutionary France. The scientific enlightenment of the Early Modern period thus saw the union of a philosophical apperception of universal cyclical flow, with precise new laboratory procedures and instruments, and a rigorous, newly minted accounting system where input and output quantities must necessarily balance.

Philosopher-scientists in the time of Leibniz and Newton were readier to see in the laws of dynamics evidence for a divine or even panpsychical[9] purpose that with seeming prescience is able to discern paths of least resistance to achieve its ends using the least action, the least effort, the greatest economy of means. With the discovery of the "conservation laws" or "action principles," as they later came to be known, it seemed to savants like Fermat, Maupertuis, Leibniz, and Euler as though all physical phenomena could be explained as the unfolding consequences of one universal necessity. We should have to return to pre-Socratic philosophy, or to Lao-Tzu's mysterious "valley spirit"[10] to find as like an image of the entire cosmos as a living, questing, even a cognizant being: fluid, active, elastic, responsive, self-regulating, self-repairing, optimizing.

"All equations equal zero" is the cardinal rule of mathematics. It is equally and profoundly true of physics, and one needn't look further to find reasons for what Eugene Wigner called the "unreasonable effectiveness of mathematics" in modeling nature.[11] A corollary is this: whenever in nature we see an object or a substance moving or flowing from one place to another, the motion can be interpreted as an attempt to return to a state of balance, or "zero difference." Any displacement from equilibrium elicits an equivalent compensating motion and force. Bodies at rest will spontaneously adopt a configuration that minimizes the total potential energy. The trajectory of a body subject to external forces is that for which its kinetic energy over the duration of the motion is minimal. The energy expended pumping water up a hill is paid back when the water is released to flow down a channel to turn a wheel and grind the corn. Even the small but perplexing differences between the energies paid and reclaimed, observed once there were instruments to measure things finely enough, were at the close of the nineteenth century finally resolved into a common accountancy of heat, work, and statistical entropy.

Feedback Everywhere

By the 1950s researchers in a growing number of fields had tripped over the now suddenly ubiquitous feedback loop, and were seeking opportunities to share their discoveries with other scholars. Thus were enjoined the new, syncretistic sciences of cybernetics and systems theory, which were to enjoy a couple of decades' vogue before losing their lustre. (They wouldn't remain lost for long however. In the 1980s and 1990s, remarkably similar investigations were being presented under the banners of mathematical chaos, artificial neural nets, nonlinear dynamics, and complexity theory, even if some of their authors seemed unaware of precedent studies scarcely a generation removed.)

Feedback is one of the grand unifying concepts of intellectual history. Once it had been named and witnessed and felt in fingers and elbows it became possible to apprehend earlier appearances of the same idea: Elmer Sperry's autopilot of 1912, Claude Bernard and Walter B. Cannon's notions of biological "homeostasis," James Watt's 1788 development of the centrifugal steam governor, the unknown inventor of the float valves found in ancient Greek water clocks, Rene Descartes's canny elucidation of the reflex arc, even the bimetallic "brain" inside the humble household thermostat. James Clerk Maxwell had, in 1868, written a mathematical analysis of Watt's governor, which failed to find readers able to appreciate the scope and subtlety of the idea. But once the notion had gelled and circulated widely enough, anyone could readily see in Darwin's theory of evolution, for example, a cybernetic feedback loop linking organisms and their environments. Cybernetics made what takes place at the laboratory bench philosophically interesting again, and reaffirmed science's relevance to the life-world.[12]

The difficulty of designing electronic circuits and devices that will exhibit specified behaviors attests to the vastly greater complexity observed in the interdependent cycles and flows in natural systems. The classic ecosystem model is the tidal pool; marine biologists are still searching for its bottom. We living creatures apparently weren't made with a purpose in mind (evolutionary theory offers an elegant account of how we could have arisen spontaneously) but living matter is distinguished from the nonliving by a future-directed "telos" or purposiveness. The cyclic-AMP motor inside every cell is an electrochemical "ratchet-and-pawl" for storing energy against future need, in a way similar to though far more complex than how the windmill exploits fickle winds to pump water into a reservoir from which its motive force may later, at human discretion, be tapped.

The icons and circuit diagrams of the analog engineers were in fairly short order picked up by ecologists and planners to aid in visualizing the complex loops of energy, matter, and information flowing through ecological, economic, and industrial systems. Bill Phillips's famous hydraulic analog computer, the "MONIAC," was an extraordinary example of analog model building built in 1949 while he was a student at the London School of Economics. Circular flows of money through the UK economy (household and government expenditures, business investments, export revenues, losses due to imports, all tweaked via policy measures aimed at controlling unemployment and stimulating growth, e.g., through setting tax rates or issuing new currency) were physically embodied in tanks and streams of water of various colors, their levels charted by felt-tipped pens as the system attempted to restore equilibrium following economic shocks and corrections. With each change, the impacts could be traced kinetically through the coupled lags and loops of its nine differential equations. Even hardened mathematical economists were surprised and at times dismayed to see the system demonstrating consequences unanticipated in their favorite theories.[13]

In the 1960s, an emergent systems ecology[14] used the graphic language of analog computing to synoptically map the interlinking systems of feedbacks upon which industrial civilization depends. Simulation programming languages like MIT's Dynamo (used to program the World Dynamics models of the influential "Limits to Growth" report,[15] helping fuel the environmental battles of the 1970s) were expressly created to emulate analog computers in the more flexible medium of software. The simulation languages would in turn give way, except in specialized areas like circuit design, to electronic spreadsheets running on desktop computers, so completing and democritizing a cycle begun with the Tableau Economique.

Analog Again

Systems modeling has for the most part retired from the public's gaze, back to the university and industrial laboratories from whence it came. And while op amps are the trusty mainstay of analog IC design, nowadays it would be unusual to use or describe them as "computing elements." One area in which the old-style systems models continue to play a role behind the scenes is in computer games like "Age of Empires,"[16] which are basically system dynamics simulations recast in historical fantasy worlds, where functional relations between variables of state (the "stocks and flows" of ecological and economics modeling) are hardwired by the game's designers. (An earlier incarnation of the genre, which readers of a certain age may recall fondly, is the game "Lemonade Stand."[17])

Recently, there have been intriguing reports of new excitement stirring up the cold grey ashes of the analog. Carver Mead, the distinguished CalTech physicist who in 1980 established the rules for silicon compiling of VLSI (Very Large Scale Integrated) digital circuits, has been turning his hand to bending and breaking those very rules to engineer a new generation of analog circuits from the same VLSI technology used to manufacture ultra high density CPUs and memory chips. Mead and his students have in effect been building analog computers on a silicon substrate with digital technology.[18] They have built and tested an artificial cochlea, analog neural networks, and several varieties of synthetic retina (one of which has been incorporated into a high-end electronic camera).

Following Mead's lead, a number of small initiatives were undertaken in the 1990s to create flexible hybrid arrays of field-programmable analog blocks within a digital interconnection matrix on a single chip. While uptake by system designers and manufacturers hasn't yet lived up to expectations, it seems that fifty years after its brief golden age, analog computing has at least to this extent returned. And while it is probably too early to say, its revival might be an occasion to reevaluate our concepts of what "computation" is, or might in time become.

Notes

1. J. C. Maxwell, "Are There Real Analogies in Nature?" (Essay read to the Apostles Club in Cambridge, 1856; the entire text is given in: L. Campell and W. Garnet, *Life of James Clerk Maxwell.*)

2. The Tidal Predictor and Harmonic Analyzer machines were based on the wheel-and-disc integrator invented by Lord Kelvin's brother, James Thomson, in 1876, which could mechanically solve a first order linear differential equation. Kelvin saw that a second integrator linked to the first might solve equations of second order by an iterative process, where results obtained from passing through the dual mechanism could be manually copied as inputs for another iteration, thus generating a series of functions, each closer to an exact solution than its predecessor. Some time later he realized that if the second integrator's output were mechanically fed back to drive the first integrator, convergence would take place "rigorously, continuously, and in a single process." As it happened, the disc integrator's torque was too weak; his plan would be realized only fifty years later with Vannevar Bush's Differential Analyzer, completed 1930. (All credit was owed to its electric Torque Amplifier, which would find its way into big American cars as "power steering.") Where digital computers can simulate feedback processes through stepwise iteration (comparable to Kelvin's first scheme) electronic analog computers embody dynamic feedback intrinsically (as in Kelvin's second).

3. The story is told by Thomas Lange, "Helmut Hoelzer, Inventor of the Electronic Analog Computer." As for the interesting question of which side actually won World War II, see Thomas Pynchon, *Gravity's Rainbow* and Philip K. Dick, *The Man in the High Castle*, and Hawthorne Abendsen, *The Grasshopper Lies Heavy*, (n.d.).

4. Digital music synthesis was realized in 1957 by Max Matthews at Bell Labs on an IBM 704 mainframe. Despite its theoretical virtues, the technique would for decades be limited to lugubrious and painstakingly assembled tape-based studio compositions. Realtime digital music premiered with a 1977 concert by David Behrman and the League of Automated Music Composers, using networked $200 KIM-1 single board microcomputers.

5. Gene Youngblood, *Expanded Cinema*. As of this writing, a PDF file is available online from ubuweb http://www.ubu.com/ and elsewhere (highly recommended). Also see the "Radical Software" archives hosted at http://www.radicalsoftware.org/—published by the New York–based Raindance Collective, this was the print organ of American experimental video art in the 1970s.

6. Henry Paynter, ed., *A Palimpsest on the Electronic Analog Art*. (In 1937 George Philbrick had built an electronic Automatic Control Analyzer for process-control simulation, but it was hardwired. After the war Philbrick went into business making electronic flight control computers for military aircraft, and in 1952 the Philbrick company produced the first (tube-based) stand-alone op amp component for electronic design. Within a decade op amps were solid-state (i.e., transistor-based) and their price had dropped to a small fraction of what the original vacuum tube models cost.)

7. Harry F. Olson, *Dynamical Analogies*; also see Olson's, Music, *Physics and Engineering*.

8. J. H. Heilbron, *Electricity in the 17th and 18th Centuries*. Also see Hankins and Silverman, *Instruments and the Imagination* for a lively and inspiring history of the sometimes porous boundary separating scientific demonstration and theatrical spectacle.

9. Panpsychism: the philosophical doctrine that all matter is in some degree conscious. Among its subscribers are Leibniz, Spinoza, Berkeley, Gustav Fechner, William James, Ernst Haeckel, A. N. Whitehead and J. A. Wheeler.

10. Compare Heraclitus: "The concord of the universe is like that of a lyre or bow, resilient if disturbed" with Lao-Tzu: "Is not the way of heaven like the stretching of a bow? The high it presses down, the low it lifts up; the excessive it takes from, the deficient it gives to."

11. E. P. Wigner, "The Unreasonable Effectiveness of Mathematics in the Natural Sciences."

12. The manifesto is Norbert Wiener, *Cybernetics, or Control and Communication in Animals and Machines*. A rather more practical and reliable guide is W. Ross Ashby's

Introduction to Cybernetics, which is available online at Principia Cybernetica: http://pespmc1.vub.ac.be/ASHBBOOK.html/.

13. Bill Phillips' MONIAC or "Financephalograph" was constructed largely from scrounged parts (including bits of a war surplus Lancaster bomber) in his landlady's garage, for about 400 GBP. Upwards of a dozen were built and sold; a recently refurbished MONIAC, on loan from the New Zealand Institute of Economics, was featured in an installation by artist Michael Stevenson at the 2003 Venice Biennale and one is on display at the Science Museum in London.

14. Systems Ecology got underway with the 1953 publication of E. P. and H. T. Odum's *Fundamentals of Ecology*. Howard Odum's *Systems Ecology* is the most in-depth account of graphical model construction; Robert Ulanowicz *Ecosystems Phenomenology* is a contemporary treatment based on information theory principles. Robert Axelrod's *Structure of Decision* in the area of political science, developed a similar approach to modelmaking with simple feedback diagrams.

15. Donella Meadows, Dennis L. Meadows, and Jørgens Randers, *The Limits to Growth*. (Also see Meadows, Meadows, and Randers, *Limits to Growth: The 30 Year Update.*) The Systems Dynamics approach was developed by MIT professor Jay Forrester between 1961 and 1973 in a series of books on Industrial Dynamics, Urban Dynamics and World Dynamics. Forrester also invented random access magnetic core memory, used before the introduction of semiconductor RAM.

16. "Age of Empires," first published in 1997, developed by Ensemble Studios and published by Microsoft; AOE is now its own empire with several popular sequels, add-ons, and spinoffs. A sense of the continuity between system dynamics modeling and video games is developed by Chris Crawford in *The Art of Computer Game Design*. The following passage touches on the complex modeling decisions which inform the design of a so-called "God Game":

> To help keep the system balanced, each differential equation should have a damping factor that must be empirically adjusted:
>
> ```
> new value = old value + (driving factor / damping factor)
> ```
>
> A small damping factor produces lively systems that bounce around wildly. A large damping factor yields sluggish systems that change slowly. Unfortunately, recourse to simple damping factors can backfire when a relationship of negative feedback exists between the "new value" and the "driving force." In this case, large damping inhibits the negative feedback, and one of the variables goes wild.

17. "Lemonade Stand," a text game created by Bob Jamison in 1973 for use on time-shared teletype terminals, ported to the Apple II computer in 1979. A copy of "Lemonade Stand" was included with every Apple system sold throughout most of the 1980s.

18. Carver Mead, *Analog VLSI and Neural Systems*.

■

Button

Søren Pold

Buttons are everywhere in software interfaces, they "initiate an immediate action" and are an essential part of the controls in the modern graphical user interface (GUI). An intensive design effort has gone into the sculpting of buttons, they have become sonified, texturized, sculpted, and various kinds are developed with distinct functionality and signification: push buttons, metal buttons, bevel buttons, round buttons, help buttons, and radio buttons.[1] They appeared from the moment of the earliest graphical user interfaces such as in Xerox's SmallTalk and the Xerox Star computer from the 1970s and early 1980s.[2] Buttons are a cornerstone in contemporary software interfaces. But why and what do they signify, and why are buttons so important and seductive?

Buttons signify a potential for interaction. When the mouse was invented by Douglas Engelbart's team in the 1960s, it was used to click on text and hypertext links. These gradually changed into buttons when the GUI became established. Already ASCII interfaces like DOS shells and the notorious Norton Commander (figure 1) had button-like text boxes to click on when the mouse became a standard interface with PCs. The GUI introduced icons and its buttons gradually became reactive, inverting the black and white colors when they were clicked. Later, in the 1990s, they became increasingly three-dimensional in style as the available screen resolution increased. The interface designer Susan Kare, who had earlier worked on the Macintosh, worked for Microsoft in the late 1980s on what was to become Windows 3.0 (1990), where she replaced "black rectangles with images that looked like three-dimensional 'pressable' buttons."[3] By the mid-1990s 3–D buttons were a fully fledged standard in, for example, Windows 95 (1995) and Mac OS 8.0 (1997).

A button indicates a functional control; something well defined and predictable will happen as a result of the user pressing it. The fact that it is often rendered in 3–D simulates a physical, mechanical cause-and-effect relationship

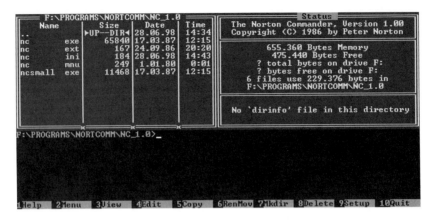

Figure 1 *Norton Commander* (1986)

which is often emphasized by the system event sound of a mechanical button being pressed. This is a simulation of how we know buttons from old machinery and electronics, where the buttons are in fact the mechanical interface, which might switch a relay through a mechanical lever, followed by an audible click and noise from the machinery and electronics. Since the connection is mechanical and not symbolic, such buttons are trustworthy, and one can feel them working tactilely. They do not change functionality; they always precipitate the same action. There is an analog connection between pressing the button and, by the force of one's finger transmitted through a lever, changing the state of the apparatus—as in old tape recorders, where one actually pushed the tape head into place with the button. The computer interface does away with the analog mechanical functionality, but the function of buttons here is to signify the same stable denotation, even though its material basis is gone. That is, interface buttons disguise the symbolic arbitrariness of the digital mediation as something solid and mechanical in order to make it appear as if the functionality were hardwired: they aim to bring the old solid analog machine into the interface. In this sense buttons are a part of a remediation[4] of the machine in the computer interface, a way of dressing it up as something well known and well understood, but there is more to it than this. It points directly to our limited understanding of the computer as a machine and as a medium and how it functions in culture and society.

One pioneer of computer graphics, computer art, and semiotics, Frieder Nake, has described the computer as an instrumental medium that we use instrumentally as a tool while communicating with it as a medium, thus it is both machine and mediation simultaneously.[5] Following Nake's concept of the instrumental medium, the computer is a new kind of media-machine that mediates the instrumental or functional and functionalizes the representational medium. That is, function becomes mediated and the mediated representation becomes functional. This chimerical quality, though difficult to grasp from both a functional perspective (e.g., engineering) and from a media perspective (e.g., postmodern media studies and aesthetic theory) has become a standard mode of expression in software interfaces, with the button as a central element of expression.

When pushing a button in an interface—that is, by movement of the mouse, directing the representation of one's hand onto the representation of a button in the interface and activating a script by clicking or double-clicking—we somehow know we are in fact manipulating several layers of symbolic representation and, as such, interacting with a complex mediation of a functional expression, engaging with what Steven Johnson characterizes as the "strange paradoxical quality" of direct manipulation.[6] But we nevertheless see and interpret it as something that triggers a function—and for good reason, since it is designed to perform in this way. It is a software simulation of a function, and this simulation aims to hide its mediated character and acts as if the function were natural or mechanical in a straight cause-and-effect relation. Yet it is anything but this: it is conventional, coded, arbitrary, and representational, and as such also related to the cultural.

Just think about how many codes and values—from programming, commerce, and ideology—are mobilized when you click "buy," pay with your credit card, and download a tune in a proprietary file format with technically and juridically imposed restrictions on how you can use, play, and copy it. The cultural, conventional, and representational elements are disguised or "blackboxed" as pure technical functionality; you do not even realize the consequences of the copy protection technology, the money transfer via your credit card company, or the way the music is produced, commercialized, and regulated by the recording company, the outlet, and the artist. The functional spell is only broken when the software crashes, or when the software becomes reflexive: either through artistic means as in net- and software art, in order to surprise, criticize, or inform; or through juridical necessities such as when submitting to licenses, etc. The installation screens where, before installing the software, one has to accept a lot of restrictions and modes of conduct by pressing a button are perhaps some of the most perverse examples of using buttons in software. The long intricate message and the easy accept button seem contradictory, and even though you are asked in capitals to read the agreement carefully before using the software, it only seems symptomatically to point to the contradiction. For example when installing Apple's iTunes player, it states that by clicking the button you accept a 4000-word contract stating that you are only licensing the software, that you may only use it to reproduce material which is not in violation of copyright, that you will not use iTunes to develop nuclear missiles, chemical or biological weapons(!), and, among other things, that you will be solely responsible for any damages to your computer or data.

This example highlights how buttons force decisions into binary choices. There is no way of answering that one partially agrees, has not realized the consequences of accepting, or does not care, even though these would probably be franker answers from most users. Buttons are verbs that rule out tenses other than present tense, and rule out modal auxiliary, subjunctive, and other more sophisticated ways in which our language expresses activity. Buttons also designate you as a masterful subject in full control of the situation, which obviously is problematic in many cases, such as the one above, where one cannot oversee, predict, or even understand the consequences of clicking "I accept," or in other examples where the buttons effectively hide the scripts enacted by pressing it, such as in the "buy" example.

But as manufacturers of technological consumer goods from cars and hi-fi equipment to computer hardware and software know, buttons have seductive aesthetic qualities and should provide a satisfying response to the desire to push them. They should evoke confidence by returning a smooth response, not plastickey or cheap, even though it might have nothing to do with functionality. Buttons are tempting—just watch kids in technical museums. Their magnetism may reflect a desire for control or for the capacity to have an effect, and this is combined with a tactile desire that is emphasized by the adding of simulated textures (e.g., metal, shadows, lighting, grooves, 3-D, etc., shown in figure 2), as in the *Mac OS 7.5.3 CD-Player*. That buttons still are important for the success of a product is demonstrated by the iPod's *Apple ClickWheel*, which is the tactical icon for the extremely successful iPod.

In fact the *ClickWheel* points out how software buttons have increasingly become hardware. The *ClickWheel* is a button on the iPod hardware designed to control specific functions of the software, thus materializing the software into the hardware. Other and older examples of software buttons migrating

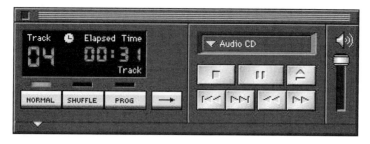

Figure 2 CD-player from *Mac OS System 7.5.3* (1996)

back to hardware are the mouse itself, buttons on a computer for controlling sound volume or various functions of the operating system (home, end, search) or the function buttons (F1–F12) on the computer keyboard. These kind of soft-hardware buttons are often seen when the universal computer is customized for special use, such as in mobile phones, iPods, game consoles, etc., and they seem to be flourishing currently as seductive branding on fashionable electronic gadgets. A special case is touch screens, where one interacts with the interface by touching the screen and tapping its buttons. Here the interface becomes directly touchable though it is only an illusion which does not exactly feel right—instead of actually touching the interface it feels as if one's finger becomes a mouse. Still, even if next generation touch screen producers feel tempted to produce screens that could automatically sculpt 3-D buttons with a tactile feel to them, it would not solve the paradox of the button as an expression of the interface's mediation of the functional and instrumentation of the representational, as pointed out previously. Software buttons incarnate this paradox. As exemplified by the function buttons, software buttons turned into hardware are often reconfigurable, programmable, and, as such, they reverse the logic of mechanical buttons from giving the interface a hardwired functional trustworthiness to softening the buttons on the box. This both leads to frustration (as when your keyboard layout is accidentally changed) and an at least momentary frisson (e.g., playing computer games or handling SMS's).

Powerful buttons have an unmistakably "trigger happy" feel to them. They make the world feel controllable, accessible, and conquerable, providing "Information at your fingertips" as the slogan goes, or, more broadly, the reduction of society, culture, knowledge, its complexity, countless mediations, and transformations to a "double-click" information society,[7] where everything becomes packaged in manageable and functional scripts activated by buttons offering easy rewards. From this perspective, the interface button becomes an emblem of our strong desire to handle the increasingly complex issues of our societies by efficient technical means—what one may call the "buttonization" of culture, in which our reality becomes clickable.

In Adrian Ward's artistic software, *Signwave Auto-Illustrator,*[8] there is a big, tempting button in the preferences palette with the caption "Don't push this button," which paradoxically pinpoints and heightens the desire to push it. One could say that by its apparent denial of functional purpose the button self-consciously tempts our desire for the functional experience of tactical control and mastery—a strong ingredient in the aesthetics of the functional interface, even when denied.[9]

Notes

1. Apple Computer, Apple Human Interface Guidelines, Cupertino, CA, Apple Computer, Inc. Retrieved March 20, 2006 from http://developer.apple.com/documentation/UserExperience/Conceptual/OSXHIGuidelines/.

2. See Steven Johnson, *Interface Culture: How New Technology Transforms the Way We Create and Communicate*; N. Lineback, "GUI Gallery"; J. Petersen and J. H. Hansen, "MacLab Danmark"; M. Wichary, "GUIdebook, Graphical User Interface Gallery"; M. Tuck, "The Real History of the GUI"; J. Reimer, "A History of the GUI."

3. Susan Kare, "Design Biography." http://www.kare.com/design_bio.html/.

4. J. David Bolter and R. Grusin, *Remediation: Understanding New Media.*

5. Frieder Nake, *Der Computer als Automat, Werkzeug und Medium und unser Verhältnis zu ihm.*

6. Johnson, *Interface Culture.*

7. Bruno Latour, E. Hermant, et al. *Paris Ville Invisible.*

8. Adrian Ward, *Signwave Auto-Illustrator.*

9. Søren Pold, "Interface Realisms: The Interface as Aesthetic Form," in *Postmodern Culture,* vol. 15 no. 2, January 2005.

Class Library

Graham Harwood

```perl
use Poetic::Violence;

# Software for the aggressive assault on society.
# Thank GOD It's all right now — we all want equality —
use constant EQUALITY_FOR_ALL
=>
"the money to be in the right place at the right time";
use constant NEVER = 'for;;';
use constant SATISFIED => NEVER;
# It's time to liposuck the fat from the thighs of the bloated
# bloke society—smear it on ourselves and become invisible.
# We are left with no option but to construct code that
# concretizes its opposition to this meagre lifestyle.

    package DON'T::CARE;
    use strict; use warnings;
    sub aspire {
        my $class            = POOR;
        my $requested_type   = GET_RICHER;
        my $aspiration       = "$requested_type.pm";
        my $class            = "POOR::$requested_type";
        require $aspiration;
        return $class->new(@_);
    }
    1;


# bought off with $40 dvd players

sub bought_off{
    my $self = shift;
    $self->{gain} = shift;
    for( $me = 0;
```

```perl
        $me <= SATISFIED;
        $me += EQUALITY_FOR_ALL ){

        $Exploit
        =
        push(@poverty_on_someone_else,$self->{gain});
        die "poor" if $Exploit
        =~ m/ 'I feel better about $me'/g;
    }
    foreach my $self_worth ( @poverty_on_someone_else){
        wait 10;
        &Environmental_catastrophe (CHINA,$self_worth)
    }
}
# TODO: we need to seek algorithmic grit
# for the finely oiled wheels of capital.
# Perl Routines for the redistribution of the world's wealth
# Take the cash from the rich and turn it into clean
# drinking water

# Constants
use constant SKINT => 0;
use constant TO_MUCH => SKINT + 1;
# This is an anonymous hash record to be filled with
# the Names and Cash of the rich

%{The_Rich} = {
    0 => {
            Name => '???',
            Cash => '???',
    },
}

# This is an anonymous hash record to be filled
# with the Price Of Clean Water
# for any number of people without clean water
```

```perl
%{The_Poor} = {
    0 =>{
        #the place name were to build a well
        PlaceName          => '???',
        PriceOfCleanWater  => '???',
        Cash               => '???',
    },
}


# for each of the rich, process them one at a time passing
#them by reference to RedistributeCash.

  foreach my $RichBastardIndex (keys %{The_Rich}){
      &ReDisdributeCash(\%{The_Rich->{$RichBastardIndex}});
 }


# This is the core subroutine designed to give away
# cash as fast as possible.

sub ReDisdributeCash {
    my $RichBastard_REFERENCE = @_;


    # go through each on the poor list
    # giving away Cash until each group
    # can afford clean drinking water
    while($RichBastard_REFERENCE ->{CASH} >= TO_MUCH){
        foreach my $Index (keys @{Poor}){
        $RichBastard_REFERENCE->{CASH}—;
        $Poor->{$Index}->{Cash}++;
        if( $Poor->{$Index}->{Cash}
            =>
            $Poor->{$Index}->{PriceOfCleanWater} ){
            &BuildWell($Poor->{$Index}->{PlaceName});
            }
        }
    }
}
```

■

Code (or, How You Can Write Something Differently)

Friedrich Kittler

Codes—by name and by matter—are what determine us today, and what we must articulate if only to avoid disappearing under them completely. They are the language of our time precisely because the word and the matter code are much older, as I will demonstrate with a brief historical regression. And have no fear: I promise to arrive back at the present.

Imperium Romanum

Codes materialize in processes of encryption, which is, according to Wolfgang Coy's elegant definition, "from a mathematical perspective a mapping of a finite set of symbols of an alphabet onto a suitable signal sequence."[1] This definition clarifies two facts. Contrary to current opinion, codes are not a peculiarity of computer technology or genetic engineering; as sequences of signals over time they are part of every communications technology, every transmission medium. On the other hand, much evidence suggests that codes became conceivable and feasible only after true alphabets, as opposed to mere ideograms or logograms, had become available for the codification of natural languages. Those alphabets are systems of identically recurring signs of a countable quantity, which map speech sounds onto letters more or less one-to-one and, hopefully, completely. A vocalic alphabet of a type such as Greek,[2] justly praised for being the "first total analysis of a language,"[3] does appear to be a prerequisite for the emergence of codes, and yet, not a sufficient one. For what the Greeks lacked (leaving out of consideration sporadic allusions in the work of Aischylos, Aenas, Tacticus, and Plutarch to the use of secret writing[4] was that second prerequisite of all coding, namely, developed communications technology. It is anything but coincidental that our reports of the first secret message systems coincide with the rise of the Roman Empire. In his *Lives of the Caesars*, Suetonius—who himself served as secret scribe to a great emperor—recounts discovering encrypted letters among the personal files left behind by both the divine Caesar and the divine Augustus. Caesar contented himself with moving all the letters of the Latin alphabet by four places, thus writing D instead of A, E instead of B, and so forth. His adoptive son Augustus, by contrast, is reported to have merely skipped one letter, but a lack of mathematical discernment led him to replace the letter X, the last in his alphabet, by a double A.[5] The purpose was obvious: When read aloud by those not called upon to do so (and Romans were hardly the most literate of people), a stodgy jumble of consonants resulted. And as if such innovations in matters of encryption were not sufficient, Suetonius attributes to Caesar another invention immediately beforehand—that of having written in several columns, or even separate pages, reports to the Roman Senate on the Gallic campaign. Augustus is credited with the illustrious deed of creating, with riders and relay posts, Europe's first strictly military express-mail system.[6] In other words, the basis on which command, code, and communications technology coincided was the Empire, as opposed to merely the Roman Republic or shorthand writers like Cicero. Imperium is the name of both the command and its effect: the world empire. "Command, control, communications, intelligence" was also the Pentagon's imperial motto until very recently, when, due to the coincidence of communication technologies and Turing machines it was swapped for C[4]—"command, control, communication, computers"—from Orontes to the Scottish headland, from Baghdad to Kabul.

It was the case, however, that imperia, the orders of the Emperor, were also known as codicilla, the word referring to the small tablets of stripped wood coated with wax in which letters could be inscribed. The etymon codex for its part—*caudex* in Old Latin and related to the German verb *hauen* (to hew)—in the early days of the Empire assumed the meaning of "book," whose pages could, unlike papyrus scrolls, for the first time be leafed through. And that was how the word that interests us here embarked on its winding journey to the French and English languages. From Imperator Theodosius to Empereur Napoleon, "code" was simply the name of the bound book of law, and codification became the word for the judicial-bureaucratic act needed to arrest in a single collection of laws the torrents of imperial dispatches or commands that for centuries had rushed along the express routes of the Empire. Message transmission turned into data storage,[7] pure events into serial order. And even today the Codex Theodosius and Codex Iustinianus continue to bear a code of ancient European rights and obligations in those countries where Anglo-American common law does not happen to be sweeping the board. In the Corpus Iuris, after all, copyrights and trademarks are simply meaningless, regardless of whether they protect a codex or a code.

Nation-States

The question that remains is why the technical meaning of the word "code" was able to obscure the legal meaning to such a degree. As we know, contemporary legal systems regularly fail to grasp codes in the first place and, in consequence, to protect them, be it from robbers and purchasers or, conversely, from their discoverers and writers. The answer seems to be simple. What we have been calling a code since the secret writings of Roman emperors to the arcana imperii of the modern age was known as a "cipher" from the late Middle Ages onward. For a long time the term code was understood to refer to very different cryptographic methods whereby words could still be pronounced, but obscure or innocuous words simply replaced the secret ones. Cipher, by contrast, was another name for the zero, which at that time reached Europe from India via Baghdad and put sifr (Arabic: "emptiness") into mathematical-technical power. Since that time, completely different sets of characters have been devised (in sharp contrast to the invention of Greek for speech sounds and numbers: on one side of language the alphabet of the people, on the other the numbers of the bearers of secrets—the name of which spelled the Arabic sifr once again. Separate character sets, however, are productive. Together they brew wondrous creatures that would never have occurred to the Greeks or Romans. Without modern algebra there would be no encoding; without Gutenberg's printing press, no modern cryptology. In 1462 or 1463, Battista Leone Alberti, the inventor of linear perspective, was struck by two plain facts. First, that the frequency of occurrence of phonemes or letters varies from language to language, a fact which is proved, according to Alberti, by Gutenberg's letter case. From the frequency of shifted letters as they were written by Caesar and Augustus, cryptanalysis can heuristically derive the clear text of the encrypted message. Second, it is therefore insufficient to encrypt a message by shifting all the letters by the same number of places. Alberti's proposal that every new letter in the clear text be accompanied by an additional place-shift in the secret alphabet was followed up until World War II.[8] One century after Alberti, François Viète, the founder of modern algebra, and also a cryptologist in the service of Henry IV, intertwined number and letter more closely still. Only since Viète have there been equations containing unknowns and universal coefficients written with numbers encoded as letters.[9] This is still the work method of anybody who writes in a high-level programming language that likewise allocates variables (in a mathematically more or less correct manner) to alphanumeric signs, as in equations. On this basis—Alberti's polyalphabetic code, Viète's algebra, and Leibniz' differential calculus—the nation-states of the modern age were able to technically approach modernity.

Global Message Traffic

Modernity began, however, with Napoleon. As of 1794, messengers on horseback were replaced by an optical telegraph which remote-controlled France's armies with secret codes. In 1806, the laws and privileges surviving from the old days were replaced by the cohesive Code Napoléon. In 1838, Samuel Morse is said to have inspected a printing plant in New York in order—taking a leaf from Alberti's book—to learn from the letter case which letters occurred most frequently and therefore required the shortest Morse signals.[10] For the first time a system of writing had been optimized according to technical criteria—that is, with no regard to semantics—but the product was not yet known as Morse code. The name was bestowed subsequently in books known as Universal Code Condensers, which offered lists of words that could be abbreviated for global cable communications, thus reducing the length, and cost, of telegrams, and thereby encrypting the sender's clear text for a second time. What used to be called deciphering and enciphering has since then been referred to as decoding and encoding. All code processed by computers nowadays is therefore subject to Kolmogorov's test: Input is bad if it is longer than its output; both are equally long in the case of white noise; and a code is called elegant if its output is much longer than itself. The twentieth century thus turned a thoroughly capitalist money-saving device called "code condenser" into highest mathematical stringency.

The Present Day — Turing

All that remains to ask is how the status quo came about or, in other words, how mathematics and encryption entered that inseparable union that rules our lives. That the answer is Alan Turing should be well known today. The Turing machine of 1936, as the principle controller of any computer, solved a basic problem of the modern age: how to note with finitely long and ultimately whole numbers the real, and therefore typically infinitely long, numbers on which technology and engineering have been based since Viète's time. Turing's machine proved that although this task could not be accomplished for all real numbers, it was achievable for a crucial subset, which he dubbed computable numbers.[11] Since then a finite quantity of signs belonging to a numbered alphabet which can, as we know, be reduced to zero and one, has banished the infinity of numbers.

No sooner had Turing found his solution than war demanded its cryptanalytical application. As of spring 1941 in Britannia's Code and Cipher School, Turing's proto-computers almost decided the outcome of the war by successfully cracking the secret codes of the German Wehrmacht, which, to its own detriment, had remained faithful to Alberti. Today, at a time when computers are not far short of unravelling the secrets of the weather or the genome—physical secrets, that is to say, and increasingly often biological ones, too—we all too often forget that their primary task is something different. Turing himself raised the question of the purpose for which computers were actually created, and initially stated as the primary goal the decoding of plain human language:

Of the above possible fields the learning of languages would be the most impressive, since it is the most human of these activities. This field seems, however, to depend rather too much on sense organs and locomotion to be feasible. The field of cryptography will perhaps be the most rewarding. There is a remarkably close parallel between the problems of the physicist and those of the cryptographer. The system on which a message is enciphered corresponds to the laws of the universe, the intercepted messages to the evidence available, the keys for a day or a message to important constants which have to be determined. The correspondence is very close, but the subject matter of cryptography is very easily dealt with by discrete machinery, physics not so easily.[12]

Conclusions

Condensed into telegraphic style, Turing's statement thus reads: Whether everything in the world can be encoded is written in the stars. The fact that computers, since they too run on codes, can decipher alien codes is seemingly guaranteed from the outset. For the past three-and-a-half millennia, alphabets have been the prototype of everything that is discrete. But it has by no means been proven that physics, despite its quantum theory, is to be computed solely as a quantity of particles and not as a layering of waves. And the question remains whether it is possible to model as codes, down to syntax and semantics, all the languages that make us human and from which our alphabet once emerged in the land of the Greeks.

This means that the notion of code is as overused as it is questionable. If every historical epoch is governed by a leading philosophy, then the philosophy of code is what governs our own, and so code—harking back to its root, "codex"—lays down the law for one and all, thus aspiring to a function that was, according to the leading philosophy of the Greeks, exercised exclusively by Aphrodite.[13] But perhaps code means nothing more than codex did at one time: the law of precisely that empire which holds us in subjection and forbids us even to articulate this sentence. At all events, the major research institutions that stand to profit most from such announcements proclaim with triumphant certainty that there is nothing in the universe, from the virus to the Big Bang, which is not code. One should therefore be wary of metaphors that dilute the legitimate concept of code, such as when, for instance, in the case of DNS, it was not possible to find a one-to-one correspondence between material elements and information units as Lily Ray discovered in the case of bioengineering. As a word that in its early history meant "displacement" or "transferral"—from letter to letter, from digit to letters, or vice versa—code is the most susceptible of all to faulty communication. Shining in the aura of the word code one now finds sciences that do not even master their basic arithmetic or alphabet, let alone cause something to turn into something different as opposed to merely, as in the case of metaphors, go by a different name. Therefore, only alphabets in the literal sense of modern mathematics should be known as codes, namely one-to-one, finite sequences of symbols, kept as short as possible but gifted, thanks to a grammar, with the incredible ability to infinitely reproduce themselves: Semi-Thue groups, Markov chains,[14] Backus-Naur forms, and so forth. That, and that alone, distinguishes such modern alphabets from the familiar one that admittedly spelled out our languages and gave us Homer's poetry[15] but cannot get the technological world up and running the way computer code now does. For while Turing's machine was able to generate real numbers from whole numbers as required, its successors have—in line with Turing's daring prediction—taken command.[16] Today, technology puts code into the practice of realities, that is to say: it encodes the world.

I cannot say whether this means that language has already been vacated as the House of Existence. Turing himself, when he explored the technical feasibility of machines learning to speak, assumed that this highest art, speech, would be learned not by mere computers but by robots equipped with sensors, effectors, that is to say, with some knowledge of the environment. However, this new and adaptable environmental knowledge in robots would remain obscure and hidden to the programmers who started them up with initial codes. The so-called "hidden layers" in today's neuronal networks present a good, if still trifling, example of how far computing procedures can stray from their design engineers, even if everything works out well in the end. Thus, either we write code that in the manner of natural constants reveals the determinations of the matter itself, but at the same time pay the price of millions of lines of code and billions of dollars for digital hardware; or else we leave the task up to machines that derive code from their own environment, although we then cannot read—that is to say: articulate—this code. Ultimately, the dilemma between code and language seems insoluble. And anybody who has written code even only once, be it in a high-level programming language or assembly, knows two very simple things from personal experience. For one, all words from which the program was by necessity produced and developed only lead to copious errors and bugs; for another, the program will suddenly run properly when the programmer's head is emptied of words. And in regard to interpersonal communications, that can only mean that self-written code can scarcely be passed on with spoken words. May myself and my audience have been spared such a fate in the course of this essay.

Translated by Tom Morrison, with Florian Cramer

Notes

1. Wolfgang Coy, *Aufbau und Arbeitsweise von Rechenanlagen: Eine Einführung in Rechnerarchitektur und Rechnerorganisation für das Grundstudium der Informatik*, p. 5.

2. On the latest research developments, see Barry B. Powell, *Homer and the Origin of the Greek Alphabet*.

3. Johannes Lohmann.

4. See, Wolfgang Riepl, *Das Nachrichtenwesen des Altertums: Mit besonderer Rücksicht auf die Römer*.

5. See, Caius Suetonius Tranquillus, *Vitae Caesarum,* I 56, 6 and II 86.

6. See Suetonius, I 56, 6 and II 49, 3. On the cursus publicus, in which Augustus himself recorded passes, orders, and letters dated with the exact time of day or night

(Suetonius, II 50), see Bernhard Siegert, "Der Untergang des römischen Reiches," in Hans Ulrich Gumbrecht and K. Ludwig Pfeiffer, eds., Paradoxien, Dissonanzen, Zusammenbrüche: Situationen offener Epistemologie, 495–514.

7. On the subject of temporal and spatial media and the process of adjustment from the empire to the monastic early Middle Ages, see Harold A. Innis, *Empire and Communications,* 104–120.

8. On the subject of Alberti, see David Kahn, *The Codebreakers: The Story of Secret Writing.* On the Enigma of the German Wehrmacht, see Andrew Hodges, *Alan Turing, The Enigma of Intelligence.*

9. Viète himself chose vowels for unknowns, and consonants for coefficients. Since Descartes' *Géométrie* (1637), the coefficients proceed from the beginning of the alphabet and the unknowns from the end (a, b, c . . . x, y, z). Since then, $x^n + y^n = z^n$ has been the classical example of a mathematical equation with no numbers at all, and thus one that would have been inconceivable to the Greeks, Indians, and Arabs.

10. See Coy, *Aufbau,* 6.

11. See Alan M. Turing, *Intelligence Service: Schriften,* 19–60.

12. Ibid, 98. ("Intelligent machinery," in *Machine Intelligence* 5, or in *The Essential Turing.*

13. "daímohn hê pánta kubernâi" ("God, who [feminine form!] controls all") is what Aphrodite called Parmenides (DK 8, B 12, 3).

14. On the subject of Markov chains, see Claude E. Shannon, *Ein/Aus: Ausgewählte Schriften zur Kommunikations- und Nachrichtentheorie,* 21–25.

15. On the subject of Homer and the vocalic alphabet, see Barry B. Powell, *Homer and the Origin of the Greek Alphabet.*

16. See, Turing, *Intelligence Service,* 15.

■

Codecs

Adrian Mackenzie

Codecs (coder-decoders) perform encoding and decoding on a data stream or signal, usually in the interest of compressing video, speech, or music. They scale, reorder, decompose, and reconstitute perceptible images and sounds so that they can get through information networks and electronic media. Codecs are intimately associated with changes in the "spectral density," the distribution of energy, radiated by sound and image in electronic media.

Software such as codecs poses several analytical problems. Firstly, they are monstrously complicated. Methodologically speaking, coming to grips with them as technical processes may entail long excursions into labryinths of mathematical formalism and machine architecture, and then finding ways of backing out of them bringing the most relevant features. In relation to video codecs, this probably means making sense of how transform compression and motion estimation work together. Second, at a phenomenological level, they deeply influence the very texture, flow, and materiality of sounds and images. Yet the processes and parameters at work in codecs are quite counterintuitive. Originating in problems of audiovisual perception, codecs actually lie quite a long way away from commonsense understandings of perception. Third, from the perspective of political economy, codecs structure contemporary media economies and cultures in important ways. This may come to light occasionally, usually in the form of an error message saying that something is missing: the right codec has not been installed and the file cannot be played. Despite or perhaps because of their convoluted obscurity, codecs catalyze new relations between people, things, spaces, and times in events and forms.

Patent Pools and Codec Floods

Video codecs such as MPEG-1, MPEG-2, MPEG-4, H.261, H.263, the important H.264, theora, dirac, DivX, XviD, MJPEG, WMV, RealVideo, etc., are strewn across networked electronic media. Roughly a hundred different audio and video codecs are currently in use, some in multiple implementations. Because codecs often borrow techniques and strategies of processing sound and image, they have tangled geneologies.

Leaving aside the snarled relations between different codecs and video technologies, even one codec, the well-established and uncontentious MPEG-2 coding standard, is extraordinarily complex in its treatment of images. MPEG-2 (a.k.a. H.262) designates a well-established set of encoding and decoding procedures for digital video formalized as a standard.[1] The standards for MPEG-2 are widely described. Many diagrams, definitions, and explanations of coding and decoding the bitstream are available in print and online.[2] Open source software implementations of the MPEG-2 standard offer a concrete path into its implementation. For instance, ffmpeg, "is a complete solution to record, convert and stream audio and video."[3] It handles many different video and audio codecs, and is widely used by many other video and audio projects (VLC, mplayer, etc.).

Economically, MPEG-2 is a mosaic of intellectual property claims (640 patents held by entertainment, telecommunications, government, academic, and military owners according to Wikipedia.[4] The large patent pool attests to the economic significance of MPEG-2 codecs. As the basis of commercial DVDs, the transmission format for satellite and cable digital television (DVB and ATSC), as the platform for HDTV as well as the foundation for many internet streaming formats such as RealMedia and Windows Media, MPEG-2 forms a primary technical component of contemporary audiovisual culture. It participates in geopolitical codec wars (e.g., China's AVC codec, versus the increasingly popular H.264, versus other versions such as Microsoft Windows VC-1—Windows Media 9).

Many salient events in the development of information and digital cultures (for instance, MP3-based file-swapping, or JPEG-based photography) derive from the same technological lineage as MPEG-2 (lossy compression using transforms). At a perceptual level, what appears on screen is colored by the techniques of "lossy compression" that MPEG-2 epitomizes. Codecs affect at a deep level contemporary sensations of movement, color, light, and time.

Trading Space and Time in Transforms

The MPEG standard is complex. Digital signal processing textbooks caution against trying to program it at home (which immediately suggests the desirability of doing so). They suggest buying someone else's implementation of the standard.[5] Where does this complexity come from? The purpose of the MPEG-2 standard developed in the early 1990s is generic:

This part of this specification was developed in response to the growing need for a generic coding method of moving pictures and of associated sound for various applications such as digital storage media, television broadcasting and communication. The use of this specification means that motion video can be manipulated as a form of computer data.[6]

How does a "generic coding method" end up being so complex that "it is one of the most complicated algorithms in DSP [digital signal processing]"?[7] MPEG-2 defines a bitstream that tries to reconcile the complicated psycho-physical, technocultural, and political-economic processes of seeing. MPEG-2 puts more pictures, more often, in more places. It moves images further and faster in media networks than they would otherwise.

To do that, the code in MPEG-2 codecs reorganizes images at many scales. The code works to reorganize relations within and between images. Algorithmically, MPEG-2 combines several distinct compression techniques (converting signals from time domain to frequency domain using discrete cosine transforms, quantization, Huffman and Run Length Encoding, block motion compensation), timing and multiplexing mechanisms, retrieval and sequencing techniques, many of which are borrowed from the earlier, low-bitrate standard, MPEG-1.[8]

From the standpoint of software studies, how can these different algorithms be discussed without assuming a technical background knowledge? The technical intricacies of these compression techniques are rarely discussed outside signal processing textbooks and research literature. Yet these techniques deeply affect the life of images and media today. One strategy is to begin by describing the most distinctive algorithmic processes present, and then ask to what constraints or problems these processes respond. From there we can start to explore how software transforms relations.

For instance, we could concentrate on what happens at the lowest levels of the picture, the "block" (8 × 8 pixels). Digital video typically arrives at the codec as a series of frames (from a camera, from a film or television source). Each frame or static digital image comprises arrays of pixels defined by color (chrominance) and brightness (luminance) values. Each frame then undergoes several phases of cutting and reassembling. These phases probe and re-structure the image quite deeply, almost to the pixel level. Digital video pictures are composed of arrays of pixels that have much spatial redundancy. Many adjacent pixels in an image of a landscape will be very similar, and it wastes storage space (on a DVD) or bandwidth (on satellite transmitters or internet) to repeat the same pixel over and over. A sky could be mostly blue. Rather than transmit an exact replica of the sky, why not use an algorithmic process that transforms the blue sky into a quasi-statistical summary of the spatial distribution of blueness?

The so-called I-Picture or Intra-Picture is the product of one phase of encoding, *transform compression*. It is applied to selected frames. The I-Pictures effectively become key-frames in the MPEG videostream. This phase relies on spectral analysis carried out using Fourier transforms. What does spectral analysis do? Broadly speaking, it breaks a complex waveform into a set of component waveforms of different amplitude or energy. Many computational processes today rely on Fourier Transforms or on a particular variant of the Fourier Transform, the Discrete Cosine Transform (DCT). The DCT, implemented in silicon or C code, encodes complex signals that vary over time or space into a series of discrete component frequencies. They can be added together to reconstitute the original signal during decoding. Nearly all video codecs transform spatially extended images into sets of simple frequencies. This allows them to isolate those components of an image that are most perceptually salient to human eyes. These would include the brightest or most colorful components.

There is something quite counter-intuitive in transform compression applied to images. In what way can a videoframe be seen as a waveform? The notion of the transform is mathematical: It is a function that takes an arbitrary waveform and expresses it as a series of simple sine waves of different frequencies and amplitudes. Added together, these sine or cosine waves reconstitute the original signal. Practically, in encoding a given frame of video, the MPEG-2 code divides the 720×576 pixel DVD image into 8×8 pixel blocks. So application of the transform compression is not general or global. The image has been turned into in an array of small blocks that can be quickly transformed separately. This can be seen by freeze-framing a complex visual scene on a DVD. It will appear "blocky." The DCT sees each of these blocks as spatial distribution of brightness and color. It delivers a series of coefficients (or multiplicative factors) of different frequency cosine waves.

The decomposition of a spatial or temporal signal into a series of different frequency components allows correlation with the neurophysiological measurements of human hearing and sight. For instance, because the transform treats blocks as spectra of values, some of which are more significant to human eyes than others, it converts the spectrum values into a sequence in which the most important come first. Components of the series that have small coefficients can be discarded because they will not be visually salient. In this way, a block can be compressed, transmitted or stored, and decompressed without ever sending any information about individual pixels. The cosine wave coefficients represent amplitudes of different frequency cosine waves. When the block is decoded (for instance, during display of a video frame on screen), the coefficients are reattached to corresponding cosine waves, and these are summed together to reconstitute arrays of color and brightness values comprising the block.

What stands out in transform compression is decomposition of the framed images through densely complex matrix manipulations occurring on the thousands of blocks. In contrast to film's use of linear sequences of whole frames, or television and video's interlacing of scan-lines to compose images, transforms such as DCT deal with grids of blocks in highly counterintuitive spectral analysis that has little to do with space. Blocks themselves are not fragments of pictures, but rather distributions of luminosity and chrominance that are packed into the bit stream.

Motion Prediction — Forward and Backward in Time

What does it mean to say that codecs catalyze new relations between people, things, spaces, and times in events and forms? Software has long been understood as closely linked to ideation or thought, particularly mathematical thought. Despite the mathematical character of the DCT compression just discussed, the thinking present in software cannot be reduced to mathematical thought, or not to mathematical thought as it is usually conceived. Codecs perhaps challenge cinematic and televisual perception even as they participate in making the world more cinematic or televisual. They deviate radically from the normal cinematic or televisual production of frames in a linear sequence. Video codecs are very preoccupied with reordering relations between frames rather than just keeping a series of frames in order. Indeed just as frames themselves are individually reconfigured as blocks of luminance and chrominance, the relation between frames is subject to calculated reordering in the interests of accelerated or compressed transport.

In order to gain purchase on the relation between frames, the MPEG codec again breaks the frame into an array of discrete "macroblocks" (usually four blocks put together). It compares successive frames to see how a specific macroblock shifts between frames. The working assumption behind the motion-predicted encoding of video in MPEG-2 is that nothing much happens between successive frames that can't be understood as macroblocks undergoing geometric manipulations (translation, rotation, skewing, etc.). The fact that nothing much happens between frames apart from spatial transformation is the basis of the interframe compression and the generation of P and B pictures (forward and backward motion prediction, respectively). P (Predicted) and B (Backward) pictures, the pictures that accompany the I-Picture in a MPEG-2 bitstream are, therefore, really nothing like film frames. There will never be a flicker in an MPEG video because the boundaries between pictures are not constructed in the same way they are in film or even in television with its interlaced scanned images.

If intrapicture compression is the first major component of MPEG-2, motion prediction between frames is the second. Interpicture motion prediction compression relies on forward and backward correlations, and in particular on the calculation of motion vectors for blocks. In the process of encoding a video sequence, the MPEG-2 codec analyzes for each picture how blocks have moved, and only transmits lists of motion vectors describing the movement of blocks in relation to a reference picture or keyframe, itself coded using DCT transform compression. This fundamentally alters the framing of images. We have already seen that rather than the raw pixel being the elementary material of the image, the block becomes the elementary component. Here the picture itself is no longer the elementary component of the sequence, but an object to be analyzed in terms of sets of motion vectors describing relative movements of blocks and then discarded. The P and I pictures, after encoding, are nothing but a series of vectors describing how and where macroblocks move. Decoding the MPEG stream means turning these vectors back into arrangements of blocks animated across frames.

Motion prediction takes time to work out, but heavily compresses the videostream. Transform compression is fast to calculate, but yields quite a large amount of data. Hence, the actual ratio of intraframe and interframe pictures in a given bitstream is heavily weighted toward motion prediction. In an MPEG datastream, the precise mixture of different frame-types (I, P-forward, and B-backward) is defined at encoding time in the Group of Pictures (GOP) structure. It is usually 12 or 15 frames in a sequence such as I_BB_P_BB_ P_BB_P_BB_P_BB_. One intracoded frame is followed by a dozen or so block motion-compensation frames. The combination of forward-prediction and backward-prediction found in the GOP means that the MPEG bitstream effectively treats the video stream as a massive doubly linked list.[9] Each item in the list is itself a list describing where and how (rotated, translated, skewed) each block should be placed on screen.

The ratio of different frame types to each other affects the encoding time because motion compensation is much slower to encode than the highly optimized block transforms. Codecs must make direct tradeoffs between computational time and space. The tradeoffs sometimes result in artifacts visible on screen as, for example, blocking and mosaic effects. At times, motion prediction does not work. A change in camera shot, the effect of an edit, might mean that no blocks are shared between adjacent frames. In that case, a well-designed codec falls back on intraframe encoding.

From Complicated to Composite

Many of the complications and counterintuitive orderings of the MPEG-2 codecs arise because they try to negotiate a fit between network bandwidth constraints (a commercially marketed service), viewing conventions (the rectangular frame of cinema and television), embodied perception (sensations of motion, light, and color), and cultural forms (fast-moving images or action). They respond to the economic and technical need to reduce the bandwidth required to circulate high-resolution digital pictures and sounds. As a convention, the MPEG-2 standard refers implicitly to a great number of material entities ranging from screen dimensions through network and transmission infrastructures to semiconductor and data storage technologies. The generic method of encoding and decoding images for transmission relates very closely to the constraints and conditions of telecommunications and media networks. And the codec more or less performs the function of displaying light, color, and sound on screen within calibrated psycho-perceptual parameters.

However, the way the MPEG-2 codec pulls apart and reorganizes moving images goes further than simply transporting images. Transform compression and motion estimation profoundly alter the materiality of images, all the while preserving much of their familiar cinematic or televisual appearance. Like so much software it institutes a relational ordering that articulates realities together that previously lay further apart.

Notes

1. ISO/IEC 13818-1, I. I. (1995). "Information technology—Generic coding of moving pictures and associated audio information: Systems." ISO/IEC 13818-2 (1995). "Information technology—Generic coding of moving pictures and associated audio information: Video."

2. S. W. Smith, *The Scientist and Engineer's Guide to Digital Signal Processing*, p. 225; Wikipedia, 2006, MPEG-2, available at http://en.wikipedia.org/wiki/MPEG-2/ (accessed Jan. 12, 2006).

3. ffmpeg, *FFMPEG Multimedia System, 2006.*

4. Wikipedia, "MPEG-2," 2006.

5. S. W. Smith, *The Scientist and Engineer's Guide to Digital Signal Processing,* p. 225.

6. ISO/IEC 13818-2 (1995) (E), vi.

7. S. W. Smith, *The Scientist and Engineer's Guide to Digital Signal Processing,* 225.

8. ISO/IEC 11172-1 (1993).

9. Donald Knuth, *The Art of Computer Programming*, p. 280.

■

Computing Power

Ron Eglash

Computational power plays an accelerating role in many powerful social locations. Simulation models, for example, sneak into our medical decisions, speak loudly in the global warming debate, invisibly determine the rates we pay for insurance, locate the position of a new bridge in our city, plot the course of our nation's wars, and testify in the courtroom both for and against the defense. Other applications in which computing power matters are molecular biology, communication surveillance, and nanotechnology. Social scientists concerned with the relations of power and society commonly examine who has money, who owns property, and who owns the means of production. But the ownership of computing power is more evasive, and far less probed. This paper will out-line some of the ways in which we might begin to examine the relations between computing power and social authority.

The Need for Alternatives to the Realist Critique

One of the most common analyses of the relations between computing power and social power is what I call the "realist critique." This analysis goes something like the following: The computer representation of X is used to substitute for the real X, but since it's an artificial version it has certain bad effects (prevents us from seeing injustice, from being in touch with people or nature, etc.). There are indeed moments in which some form of such realist critiques are applicable. But the critique has been overused in ways that are quite problematic.

When we blindly start putting categories of the Real on the ethical side, and categories of the Unreal on the unethical side, we imply a system of morality which mimics the Christian story of the fall from the Garden, or Rousseau's dichotomy between nobility of the natural and the evils of artifice. We imply that computer simulations are unethical simply because they are unnatural. Similar moral assumptions have been used in attacks on the civil rights of gays and lesbians ("unnatural sex" is a violation of God's plan), or arguments used for purging Germany of its Jews (because they were not "natural" to Germany), or denying citizens the right to birth control. Notions of the Real or Authentic have been used in colonialism to differentiate between the "real natives" who stayed on their reservation, versus "inauthentic natives" who could thus be imprisoned for their disruptions (seen again in recent times during the American Indian Movement of the 1960s, when activists were criticized as being "urban indians"). Thus, when we read critiques that condemn digital activities as "masturbation,"[1] we need to think not about artificial worlds as pathologies, but rather about how innocent sexual activity has been used to pathologize and control individuals.

Even in cases where scholars of computing have been very aware of the suspect ethics of realism, it can creep in. Take, for example, computer graphics representations of the human body, such as the Visible Man project. Investigations of such anatomical simulations are immediately queried for all the right reasons: how the social construction of the technical happened, who benefits, how it influences the viewer's experience, and so on. But inevitably there rises what Wahneema Lubiano calls "the ghost of the real"; we are haunted by some element of the pre-virtual past (almost literally in this case by the donor of the body, a 39-year-old prisoner who was executed by lethal injection in Texas).[2] Despite the best intentions of the writers, in the end simulation critiques often imply an ethics of the Real. Even Sandy Stone, well known for her commitment to virtual communities and identities, ends her oft-cited essay with the line, "No refigured virtual body, no matter how beautiful, will slow the death of a cyberpunk with AIDS."[3] Again the real haunts us; critiques of simulation accuracy or realism tend to move us toward an organicist framework.

Even when a realism critique is warranted—in the case, for example, of a corporate sponsored simulation that attempts to dupe the public into a false sense of environmental or health security—exclusive concern with issues of accuracy can be problematic in that they focus on symptom rather than cause. Ostensibly one could correct the inaccuracy, and then we would have nothing to complain about. But most critics have a loftier goal in mind: They are really trying to show how social elites have managed to manipulate the power of computing to support their own interests. By focusing on the accuracy or realism of the simulation, we lose sight of the original goal: We focus on getting the American Petroleum Institute to use the right equations rather than asking how they managed to control the truthmaking abilities of computing in the first place. How can we get at a more fundamental understanding of the relationship between social power and computing power, and how might we change those relations?

Three Dimensions of Computing Power:
Speed, Interactivity, and Memory

Let us begin with the technical definitions for computing power. On the one hand, the mathematical theory of computation has precisely defined what we mean by saying that one system is computationally more powerful than another. The least powerful system is a finite state automaton, the greatest in power is a Turing machine, and in between we find machines such as the push-down automaton. But such formal definitions for computing power, collectively termed the Chomsky hierarchy, are essentially absent in the world of commercial computing. There are two reasons for this disconnection. First, there is the quite sensible and responsible distinction that real-world computing systems have multiple physical constraints that are poorly represented by such abstract assessment; in fact features that matter a great deal for the real world, such as the amount of time it takes to complete a calculation, are absent in the traditional computational models of the Chomsky hierarchy.[4] But there is also the rather suspect way in which the social authority of computing power requires an unfettered ability to make its claims. Let us now look at three categories for this slippage: speed, interactivity, and memory.

Speed

Consider the simulations which produce special effects for Hollywood movies and television commercials. Computing power here is almost entirely a question of processing speed, due to the computational requirements of high-resolution graphic simulation. Movies like *Terminator II* and *Jurassic Park* were milestones in visual simulations of physical movement, so much so that they are treated like NASA projects whose "spin-offs" are for the general benefit of humanity. Special effects wizards have now become frequent speakers at mathematics conferences; for example, the creator of the wave in the movie *Titanic* was a featured speaker for National Mathematics Awareness Week. Often the visual spectacle of their virtual realism is a much greater audience selling point than plots or acting; in fact, it is precisely this uncanny ability to (apparently) manipulate reality that becomes the proof of computing power. When the Coca-Cola corporation spends 1.6 million dollars on thirty seconds of airtime during the super bowl, it is no surprise that supercomputing is at the center of their message. Like the Marxist observation that "money is congealed labor,"[5] special effects are congealed computing. The power to command reality to do your bidding is sexy, even if it is only a virtual reality. Marshal McLuhan's theme that "the medium is the message" was always too deterministic for my taste, but I am willing to make an exception in the case of computational advertising, where the cliché that "sex sells" has been augmented by the sexiness of simulacra.

Interactivity

We can find a similar account of simulation's sex appeal in the rise of multimedia computing, particularly for websites. Here the measure of computing power is most often presented in terms of "interactivity." Yet formal assessments for interactivity, as could be produced through the Chomsky hierarchy, are never brought to bear. To understand this, it is useful to first examine similar questions about the assessment of intricate behavior in simple biological organisms. Spiders are not taught how to spin a web; the behavior is genetically programmed. Even semi-learned behaviors such as bird songs are often characterized as the result of a "serial pattern generator." Tightly sequenced behaviors such as spider webs and bird songs can be modeled as finite state automata,[6] because they require little adaptive interaction with their environment. They may appear to be complicated but they are in fact a "preprogrammed" sequence of actions. This stands in strong contrast to animal behaviors that require spontaneous interaction, as we see for example in the social cooperation of certain mammals (wolves, orca, primates, etc.). Even lone animals can show this kind of deep interactivity: A raccoon learning to raid lidded trash cans is clearly not clocking through a sequence of prepared movements.

In the same way, our interactions with websites can vary from "canned" interactions with a limited number of possible responses—pressing on various buttons resulting in various image or sound changes—to truly interactive experiences in which the user explores constructions in a design space or engages in other experiences with near-infinite variety. Such deep interactivity does not depend on the sophistication of the media. The 1970s video game of Pong, with its primitive low-resolution graphics, has far greater interactivity than a website in which a button press launches the most sophisticated 3-D fly-though animation. As Fleischmann[7] points out in his analysis of web media, rather than measure interactivity in terms of two-way mutual dependencies, commercial claims for interactivity depend on an "interrealism effect" that substitutes flashy video streaming or other one-way gimmicks for user control of the simulation. Such multimedia attempts to create the effect of interactive experience without relinquishing the producer's control over the simulation. At least speed, for all its elitist ownership, has a quantitative measure that allows us to compare machines; for interactivity we have only the rhetoric of public relations. Even in cases in which we are not duped by this interrealism effect, and strive for deep interactivity, the informational limits of interactive computing power (the bandwidth of the two-way communication pipeline) is carefully doled out in accordance to social standing, with the most powerful using high-speed fiberoptic conduits of Internet II, lesser citizens using cable connections on Internet I, and the poorest segments of society making do with copper telephone wires—truly a "trickle-down" economy of interactivity.

Memory

Third and finally, we must evaluate computing power in terms of access to memory. Increasingly the users' local hard drive memory has become augmented or even superfluous as internet companies such as MySpace or YouTube shift to the "Web 2.0" theme of internet as operating system. In terms of individual use this is a move toward democratization through lay access, but in terms of business ownership it is a move toward monopolization, as only large scale corporations such as Google can afford the economy of scale that such memory demands place on hardware.[8] Memory also plays a constraining/enabling role in the professional utilization of large databases. Consider, for example, the agent-based simulations that allow massively parallel interactions, such as genetic algorithms based on Darwinian or Lamarckian evolution. The epicenter for this activity has been the Santa Fe Institute, where mathematicians like James Crutchfield have been admonishing researchers in the field of Artificial Life for their supposed willingness to put public acclaim over formal results.[9] Crutchfield is on the losing side of the battle: He is forgetting that science is a social construction, and thus those who are able to best exploit computing power—in this case the artificial life folks—will be able to exploit the social power that can define the contours of the field. To take another example, science historian Donna Haraway expressed great surprise when she learned that critical sections of the Human Genome Project were being run out of Los Alamos Labs: What in the world was the modernist location for transuranic elements doing with the postmodern quest for trans-species organisms? The answer was computing power: Whether modeling nuclear reactions or nucleic acid, the social authority of science requires the computational authority of machines. From the MySpace of layusers to the gene space of molecular biologists, memory matters.

In sum, these three factors—computing speed, computing interactivity, and computing memory—both define the technical dimensions of simulation's computing power, as well as its social counterparts. Indeed, we can think about them in terms of information equivalents: Computing memory is comparable to social memory, interactivity is comparable to social discourse, and computing speed is comparable to social rhetoric. Thus we see the rhetorical power of special effects, the discursive power of interactive websites, and the mnemonic power of large-scale lay constructions and professional simulations.

Elite versus Lay Public Access to Computing Power

What can be done about this alliance between computing power and social authority? Looking at the changes in computing power over time, we can see both stable and unstable elements. For example, the public face of computing power is typically portrayed as the steady increase in computing speed per dollar, often encapsulated in Moore's Law, which posits that the number of components (i.e., transistors) on a chip will double every eighteen months. But privately chip manufacturing companies agonize over strategies to maintain this pace.[10]

Contrasting elite versus lay public access to computing power through time makes this precarious stability even more apparent. The earlier modeling efforts secured elite access through expertise: Even if laypersons were offered access to a timesharing system, they preferred the shallow learning curve of a wordprocessor—it was the user-unfriendly interface of text-based UNIX that separated the hackers from the hacks. This barrier did not become compromised until the advent of the graphical user interface (GUI) in the late 1970s. During the mid-1980s this sparked an unusual moment of lay access; thus the creation of popular "toy" simulations such as SimCity during that time. But by the early 1990s a gradient of computing power began to resolidify in which the "cutting edge" of elite computer simulations could leverage truth claims in ways unavailable to the "trailing shadow" of the lay public's computer power (figure 3). The introduction of techniques such as agent-based modeling and genetic algorithms have established trajectories which tend to restabilize this relation between the cutting edge and trailing shadow. Yet new technological opportunities continue to arise. We have recently seen the birth of the Free and Open Source Software movement, of Napster's challenge to the recording

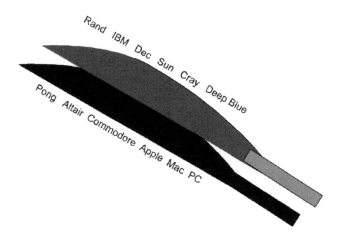

Figure 3 The Cutting Edge and the Trailing Shadow

industry, Wikipedia, and other quasi-popular appropriations. How might similar challenges to the social authority of the cutting edge take place in the domain of computing power?

In the early 1990s I had lunch one day with some graduate students in computational mathematics at the University of California at Santa Cruz. They were abuzz with excitement over the use of supercomputers for the design of a yacht that might win the Americas Cup. For them, this was an exciting "popular" application; one that was neither military nor academic big science. But I was struck by the ways in which computing power and financial power had managed to stick together, even in this ostensibly nonprofessional exception. What did the yacht owners have that made their problem more attractive than poverty, racism, sexism, and other pressing humanitarian problems? The answer, I believe, is that they had good problem definition. Yes it is true that the people associated with the Yachting Club of America are generally more flush with cash than, say, those of the Southern Poverty Law Center, but half the challenge is getting problems defined in ways that high-end computing power can address. We need organizations like the National Science Foundation to support research specifically directed to the challenge of problem definition in the application of supercomputing power to nonelite humanitarian causes.[11]

The other half of the challenge is computing access. A breakthrough in access to supercomputing power came as a result of the Berkeley Open Infrastructure for Network Computing (BOINC). The system was originally created for SETI@home, which analyzed data from the Arecibo radio telescope in hopes of finding evidence of radio transmissions from extraterrestrial intelligence. Ordinary lay users installed software that allows the BOINC system to run in the background, or run while their computer is not in use, providing spectral analysis for small chunks of the 35 gigabyte daily tapes from Arecibo, and uploading the results back to BOINC where they are integrated together. With over five million participants worldwide, the project is the world's largest distributed computing system to date. In upgrading to the BOINC system the programmers also called for broadening applications to include humanitarian projects. However none of the current projects seem directed at humanitarian causes for specifically nonelite groups, with the possible exception of Africa@home's Malaria Control Project, which makes use of stochastic modeling of the clinical epidemiology and natural history of *Plasmodium falciparum malaria.*

What other kinds of problem definition might allow greater computing power to be applied to the challenges of survival and sustainability for those at the margins of social power? Consider, for example, flexible economic networks (FENs). First observed in the revitalization of regional European economies,[12] FENs allow small-scale businesses to collaborate in the manufacture of products and services that they could not produce independently. These networks rapidly form and re-form in response to market variations, creating spinoff businesses in the process, which then give rise to further FEN growth. More recently the Appalachian Center for Economic Networks (ACENet) has demonstrated that this approach can be successfully applied in a low-income area of the US. But ACENet found that they were hampered by lack of information about both the resources of potential participants and the potential market niches to be exploited. Similar problems in establishing "virtual enterprise" cooperatives for large-scale industrial production—collaboration between multiple organizations and companies for the design and manufacture of large, complex, mechanical systems such as airframes, automobiles, and ships—has been addressed through the application of cutting-edge computing.[13] Why not apply similar techniques to generate FENs for low-income areas in either first or third world contexts?

In conclusion, the social authority of computing power follows the gradient of cutting edge and trailing shadow, stabilizing what might be gains for popular use by always putting that promise for equality in the near future. But we can also see ruptures in both technical and social dimensions of these relations, which create new opportunities to reconfigure both social and computational power.

Notes

1. For example, Sally L. Hacker, *Doing it the Hard Way.*

2. Catherine Waldby, *The Visible Human Project: Informatic Bodies and Posthuman Medicine.*

3. Stone, Allucquére Rosanne, "Will The Real Body Please Stand Up?: Boundary Stories About Virtual Cultures."

4. See Sloman, Aaron, "The Irrelevance of Turing Machines to AI," in Matthias Scheutz, ed., *Computationalism: New Directions*, 87–127.

5. Donna Haraway, Lecture, UCSC, 1992.

6. Kazuo Okanoya, "Finite-State Syntax in Bengalese Finch Song: From Birdsong to the Origin of Language." Third Conference on Evolution of Language, April 3–4, Paris 2000. Available online at http://www.infres.enst.fr/confs/evolang/actes/_actes52.html/.

7. Kenneth R. Fleischmann, "Exploring the Design-Use Interface: The Agency of Boundary Objects in Educational Technology," Doctoral dissertation, dept of STS, Rensselaer Polytechnic Institute, 2004.

8. See George Gilder, "The Information Factories," *Wired*, vol. 14, no. 10, pp. 178–202, October 2006.

9. Stefan Helmreich, Personal communication, 1999.

10. Aart J. de Geus, "To the Rescue of Moore's Law." Keynote address, 20th annual Custom Integrated Circuits Conference, Santa Clara, CA. May 11–14, 2000.

11. I've qualified this as non-elite because to simply say "humanitarian" often allows the loophole of limiting the studies to those humanitarian causes that elites themselves benefit from, such as the development of expensive medical treatments, expensive new prosthetics, solutions to types of pollution that affect affluent suburbs, etc.

12. Charles Sabel and Michael Piore, *Dialog on Flexible Manufacturing Networks*.

13. M. Hardwick, D. Spooner, T. Rando and K. Morris, "Sharing Manufacturing Information in Virtual Enterprises," *Communications of the ACM,* Vol. 39, No. 2, (February 1996).

■

Concurrent Versions System

Simon Yuill

The highest perfection of software is found in the union of order and anarchy.
—PIERRE-JOSEPH PROUDHON (patched)[1]

Concurrent Versions System (CVS) is a tool for managing collaborative software development. It enables groups of coders working on the same set of source files to coordinate and integrate the changes they make to the code, and acts as a repository to store all those changes. If, for example, two different programmers alter the same section of code, CVS can compare both versions and show that there is a difference between them (known as a "conflict" in CVS) that needs resolved or "merged." Another feature of the system is to keep an historical record of the project's development over time, enabling people to retrieve earlier versions. It also supports the possibility of the code "branching," meaning that alternative versions of the same code can be split off from the main project and maintained in parallel without causing conflicts. If someone wants to experiment with re-writing a certain section of a project, they can do so in a new branch while everyone else continues to use the main branch unaffected by the experiment.

The repository is a set of files in a directory structure that is maintained by the CVS server. Programmers submit updates and new files to the repository through a CVS client. This enables them to work remotely, with the CVS server acting as a central coordination point. Each entry in the CVS repository is represented by an individual file that maintains a record of both its content and changes. Other information relating to the project's development within the repository is stored as metadata. These enable logs of who has done what to be retrieved from the repository.

CVS was originally developed as a set of UNIX shell scripts by Dick Grune in 1984 as part of the Amsterdam Compiler Kit (ACK), a cross-platform C compiler developed at the Free University in Amsterdam. It was made public in 1986 and converted into C by Brian Berliner, from whose code the current version of CVS derives.[2] Other tools providing similar functionality, such as BitKeeper, also exist, and the new Subversion system is emerging as a possible replacement for CVS; however, CVS is currently the most widely used code management system.[3] In many ways CVS has been essential to the success of FLOSS (Free/Libre Open Source Software), as it facilitates the collaboration of the widely dispersed individuals who contribute to such projects. This facilitation, however, is restricted solely to the archiving of the code and its changes. Other aspects of development, such as communication between developers, are managed through tools such as mailing lists and IRC (Internet Relay Chat, or other online chat systems). Savane, used by the GNU project's Savannah repository, and Trac, are examples of larger toolsets that have been developed to pull these different components together.[4] Because CVS focuses on cohering code implementations, it is arguably not well suited to facilitating discussion of more abstract, conceptual aspects of a particular project. While mailing lists and IRC are often the forums for such discussions, they do not, by the very temporality of their nature, allow for such discussions to be built into identifiable documents. Similarly, comments in source code, while also facilitating this, can become too diffuse to gather such ideas together. The Wiki emerged as a response to this need, adapting the version control of CVS into a simpler web-based system in which the more conceptual modeling of projects could be developed and archived, exemplified in the very first Wiki, the Portland Pattern Repository, which gathered different programming "design patterns" together.[5] CVS, nevertheless, remains a central plenum within which the material origination of software is performed.[6]

Code creation is an inherently social act. It involves processes of collaboration, consensus, and conflict resolution, and embodies social processes such as normalization and differentiation. Software development tools such as CVS implicitly formalize such processes and, in doing so, potentially provide means of tracking them. As a result of this, forms of sociological analysis have developed based around "archaeological" studies of CVS repositories.[7] These studies revolve around questions of how FLOSS development actually works, especially given that it runs counter to many conventional models of product creation and production management. There is, for example, a lack of clearly delineated team structures in FLOSS projects; people can choose what they work on rather than being assigned jobs, there are frequently no project roadmaps or contractual deadlines, and you have a mixture of professional and amateur contributors, some working from within a paid capacity (such as in commercially or institutionally supported projects), others in their spare time.

Rather than following predefined managerial models, the practices and tools of FLOSS development facilitate emergent organizational structures. These can vary from one project to another, and may reflect aspects of the social situatedness of a given project, such as whether it is driven by institutional research, commercial development, or people with shared interests but no official affiliation. One recurrent form is described as an "onion structure,"[8] in which a reasonably stable core team of developers who are the main contributors and maintainers for a project is surrounded by layers of more occasional contributors and users. In some projects this may give a highly centralized shape to the overall social structure of the project, but in others there may be several such "core nodes" with an organizational form that is characterized by multiple interacting clusters. This latter formation is particularly evident in large-scale projects with many subareas, such as the KDE or GNOME desktop systems, or those that are largely driven by shared interest rather than institutional or commercial bodies.[9] Other studies describe a kind of guild structure, in which newcomers to a project have to serve a kind of apprenticeship and prove their capabilities before becoming accepted within the core development group.[10] Shadow networks might also influence the social structures of a project, such as secondary affiliations constructed through ideological, institutional or corporate links.[11] These kinds of studies provide an understanding of agency and governance within FLOSS, and clarify how software development operates as a form of discursive formation.

As Foucault describes it, a discursive formation arises through the relations "established between institutions, economic and social processes, behavioural patterns, systems of norms, techniques, types of classification, modes of characterization"[12] that are not inherent within an object of discourse or practice itself, such as a piece of software, but is that which "enables it to appear, to juxtapose itself with other objects, to situate itself in relation to them."[13] All software is inherently discursive, it exists not as a set of discrete, stable artifacts, but rather as interrelated components, entering into various combinations with one another. This is evident both in the user experience of software and in how software is constructed. At a user level we can see this in the way in which a web browser, for example, will interact with various web server systems and the content tools they support, which may in turn feed into other pieces of software or computer-mediated processes. If I buy an air ticket online this will connect with other processes such as the management of my bank account and that of the airline company, and then in making my journey, the check-in process and management of the airport and air flight itself will utilize various software systems, all of which construct and articulate different relations "between institutions, economic and social processes, behavioural patterns . . ." etc. Similarly, no piece of software is a singular entity. The simple act of writing a piece of code involves the use of multiple software tools, such as text editors and compilers, but also issues such as which specific language the code is written in, whether it uses external code libraries and, if so, which choice of libraries, and what design patterns are followed in its construction. These derive not solely from pragmatic issues of functionality but also factors such as institutional alignment, the distribution and use of the final software, whether it operates by itself or as part of a larger system, and whether or not the source code will be made available for others to develop into and upon. Numerous decisions underlie the development of a software project: which language to develop in—whether to use Python, C or Microsoft's .Net, for example; what external code libraries to use (e.g., Apple's QuickTime library or the open source Simple Direct Media library); what kind of license to use—to distribute the code under an open source license that prohibits any commercial use, or one that allows the code to be used but not altered by others; and issues such as what file formats the software will support and what protocols it uses to interact with other software—will these be based on open standards such as SVG and HTTP, or on closed systems? The outcomes of such decisions are all influenced by the wider relations in which the production of the software is situated. The ways in which tools such as CVS are used will carry a residue of these factors, and the CVS repository can become a territory in which these issues and debates are inscribed. CVS is not simply a tool to manage the production of code therefore, but as "the space in which code emerges and is continuously transformed" (to paraphrase Foucault), also an embodiment and instrument of its discursive nature.

Notes

1. Proudhon's original statement was: "The highest perfection of society is found in the union of order and anarchy." Pierre-Joseph Proudhon, *What Is Property? An Inquiry into the Principle of Right and of Government,* 286, translated from the French by Benjamin R. Tucker. The translation in the Dover edition has a slightly different phrasing from that used here.

2. For historical documents on the development of CVS see: Wikipedia, Concurrent Versions System, available at http://en.wikipedia.org/wiki/Concurrent_Versions_System (accessed March 31, 2006), and Dick Grune, "Concurrent Versions System CVS." http://www.cs.vu.nl/~dick/CVS.html (accessed March 31, 2006).

3. The main websites for the different tools are http://www.cvshome.org, http://www.bitkeeper.com, http://subversion.tigris.org.

4. For information on Savane see https://gna.org/projects/savane (accessed April 11, 2007). Savannah is the GNU project's main repository for free software development: http://savannah.gnu.org (accessed April 11, 2007). Trac is documented at http://trac.edgewall.org (accessed April 11, 2007).

5. The Portland Pattern Repository is available at http://c2.com/ppr (accessed April 11, 2007). Design Patterns are high-level descriptions of how particular structures of code can be built, or problems in the design of software systems addressed. The notion of design patterns was derived from the architect Christopher Alexander's work on pat-

tern languages in building design, see Christopher Alexander, et al., *A Pattern Language: Towns, Buildings, Construction.*

6. A plenum can be a "fully attended meeting" or a "space filled with material." In relation to CVS it carries both meanings: the gathering point of developers, and the space in which code is most evident in its material form.

7. Examples of such studies include Kevin Crowston and James Howison, "The Social Structure of Open Source Software development teams," available at http://crowston .syr.edu/papers/icis2003sna.pdf, 2003; Stefan Koch and Georg Schneider, "Results from Software Engineering Research into Open Source Development Projects Using Public Data" in H. R. Hansen and W. H. Janko, eds., *Dikussionspapiere zum Tatigkeits-feld Informationsverarbeitung unde Informationswirtschaft*; Gregory Madey, Vincent Freeh, and Renee Tynan, "Modeling the Free/Open Source Software Community: A Quantitative Investigation," in Stefan Koch, ed., Free/Open Source Software Development, 203–220; Christopher R. Myers, "Software Systems as Complex Networks: Structure, Function, and Evolvability of Software Collaboration Graphs," *Physical Revue E*; and Rishab Aiyer Ghosh, "Clustering and Dependencies in Free/Open Source Software Development: Methodology and Tools," *First Monday,* 8(4), April 2003.

8. Crowston and Howison, "The Social Structure" p. 3.

9. KDE and GNOME are two of the desktop environments available for the Linux operating system. For an analysis of the relationship between institutional interests and Open Source project development see Gilberto Camara, "Open Source Software Production: Fact and Fiction," in *MUTE,* volume 1, issue 27, Winter/Spring 2004, 74–79.

10. For a discussion of such issues see Biella Coleman, "The Politics of Survival and Prestige: Hacker Identity and the Global Production of an Operating System," available at http://healthhacker.org/biella/masterslongversion.html, Masters Thesis, University of Chicago, 1999; Biella Colemann, "High-Tech Guilds in the Era of Global Capital," available at http://www.healthhacker.org/biella/aaapaper.html, undated; Warren Sack, "Aesthetics of Information Visualization."

11. Madey, Freeh and Tynan, "Modeling the Free/Open Source Software Community," 13–14.

12. Michel Foucault, *The Archaeology of Knowledge*, p. 45.

13. Foucault, ibid.

■

Copy

Jussi Parikka

The process of copying is a key cultural technique of modernity. The mechanization of *imitatio* awed even the hailed Renaissance artist Leon Battista Alberti at the dawn of the Gutenberg era: "Dato and I were strolling in the Supreme Pontiff's gardens at the Vatican and we got talking about literature as we so often do, and we found ourselves greatly admiring the German inventor who today can take up to three original works of an author and, by means of movable type characters, can within 100 days turn out more than 200 copies. In a single contact of his press he can reproduce a copy of an entire page of a large manuscript."[1] In Alberti's time, the spiritual concept of *imitatio* (Latin) or mimesis (remediated from the philosophy of Ancient Greece) became the cornerstone of art theory, which lasted for hundreds of years, but also turned at the same time into a material process of copying: especially the texts of the ancients.

From the printing press that replaced the meticulous work of monks copying texts to the technique of mass production of photographs and other technical media objects, "copy" has become a central command routine of modernity. Modern media can be understood as products of a culture of the copy as Walter Benjamin has analyzed in relation to film. Paraphrasing Benjamin, mechanical reproduction is an internal condition for mass distribution. In contrast to literature and painting, film production is about mechanical reproduction, which Benjamin claims "virtually causes mass distribution."[2] This coupling of copying and mass distribution is not, however, restricted to the media technology of cinema, but also characterizes networked and programmable media such as computers. I will return to this point at the end of the text.

Nineteenth-century enthusiasm for the copy was tied to the possibility of producing low-cost photographs and films, and the commercial prospects of such a process. Similarly the mass production and distribution of printed material was inherently connected to material principles of production, notably the rotation press, and other factors such as the cheapening of paper. Even the Gutenberg printing machine is fundamentally a copy machine, ingenious in its use of standardized modular parts for individualized signs. During the nineteenth century the first copy machines entered offices due to the rising need for archiving and distributing documents. Such machines slowly replaced the work done by scribes, or copy clerks, such as Bob Cratchit in Charles Dickens's

A Christmas Carol from 1843 or the dysfunctional copy-man in Herman Melville's *Bartleby the Scrivener* from 1853 (who would "rather not" do his work).[3]

To guarantee obedience and efficiency, the copy routine was technologically automated and also integrated as part of computing systems fairly early on. The early punch card machines used standardized copy processes in the form of special reproducing punch-machines (i.e., the IBM 514) to copy the cards used as templates for further data processing purposes. Some reproduction machines apparently also incorporated special control programs. The data fields of the specific cards to be copied were fed to a control panel, and were then duplicated onto blank cards.[4] In other words, the instructions for making copies were in themselves part of the mass-production of copies: recursive algorithms are at the heart of modernity. With digital computers, the mechanical process is substituted for the informationalization of modular entities and creation of abstract mathematical patterns that are the focus of copying and reproduction.[5] This in itself has eased the copying of cultural products and consequently led to new techniques of copy protection and consumer surveillance.

In digital software culture "copy" is used in two different ways (1) in the context of file-management and as a new phase of cultural reproduction and (2) as part of copy/paste—a cultural technique and aesthetic principle. The two lineages constantly overlap in the modern history of media technologies, where copying, the verb, designates a shift in the cultural techniques of reproduction from humans to machines, and copy, as a noun, presents itself as the key mode of becoming-object of digital culture—as easily reproducible and distributed packages of cultural memory.

With the early computers that used core memory, copy routines were a source of maintenance as well as amusement. The cleaning programs used copying routines to move themselves from one memory location to the next one. This was to fill the memory space with a known value, allowing it to be programmed with a new application.[6] As Ken Thompson recollects, the FORTRAN language was employed for the competitive fun of a "three-legged race of the programming community": to write the shortest program that "when compiled and executed, will produce as output an exact copy of its source."[7] Several kinds of "rabbit" and "bacteria" programs were used to clog up systems with multiple copies of the original program code. The general idea was to make the program spread to as many user accounts as possible on the IBM 360 system. This "constipated" the system. The rabbit program could input itself back into the jobstream over and over again.[8] Such self-referential procedures connect with recursive algorithms, which are part of every major programming language. Recursion can be understood as a subroutine that calls (or invokes) itself. The very basic memory functions of a computer involve copying in the sense of data being continuously copied between memory registers (from cache memory to core storage, for example.) Such operations can be termed "copying" but can equally justifiably be given names such as "read" and "write" or "load" and "store register" operations.[9]

With the move from the mechanical programming of computers to informational patterns, the copy command became integrated as an organic part of file management and programming languages in the 1960s.[10] The UNIX system, developed at Bell Labs, was one of the pioneers with its "CP" command. The CP command was a very basic file management tool, similar to, for instance, the use of the "copy" command in the later DOS environment.

The emerging trends and demands of network computing underlined the centrality of the copy command. Instead of mere solitary number crunchers, computers became networked and communicatory devices where resource sharing was one of the key visions driving the design of, among other things, the ARPANET.[11] During the same time as the early computer operating systems for wider popular use were developed, meme theory, originally conceived by Richard Dawkins in the mid-1970s, depicted the whole of culture as based on the copy routine. Memes as replicators are by definition abstract copy machines "whose activity can be recognized across a range of material instantiations."[12] Informatics is coupled with meme copying; media technological evolution can be seen as moving toward more precise copy procedures, as Susan Blackmore suggested. Copying the product (mechanical reproduction technologies of modernity) evolves into copying the instructions for manufacturing (computer programs as such recipes of production).[13] In other words, not only copying copies, but more fundamentally copying copying itself. What makes meme theory interesting is not whether or not it is ultimately an accurate description of the basic processes of the world, but that it expresses well this "cult of the copy" of the digital era while it abstracts "copying" from its material contexts into a universal principle.

During the 1990s, copy routines gained ground with the Internet being the key platform for copying and distributing audiovisual cultural products. Of course, such techniques were already present in early fax machines. Since the latter half of the nineteenth century, these routines allowed for the transmission of ones "own handwriting" over distances. Soon images also followed. (Technically, mid-nineteenth-century phototelegraphy already allowed the encoding of data into patterns and the transmission of this copy via telegraph lines.) Hence, facsimile, factum simile, should be seen as "a copy of anything made, either so as to be deceptive or so to give every part and detail of the original; an exact copy likeness."[14] Of course, no copy is an exact reproduction of the original but an approximation that satisfies, for example, the expectations of the consumer. To guarantee such consumer satisfaction, especially since the 1970s, with the help of engineers at Philips and Sony, digital optical archiving techniques have presented us with a material memetic technology of cultural reproduction that happens via a simple command routine: copy.

The material processes of copy routines have often been neglected in cultural analysis, but the juridical issue of copyright has had its fair share of attention. Yet the issues are intimately tied, both being part of the same key thematics of modernization that spring from the fact that automated machines can reproduce culture (a major change of the mode of cultural reproduction when compared to, e.g., the nineteenth-century emphasis on civilization). Copy routines that originated with medieval monks are integrated in special copy/ripper programs with easy point-click routines and CSS interpretation possibilities. Hermeneutic questions of meaning are put aside and attention is paid to the minuscule routines of reproduction: "Thus, it was only after the fall of the Roman Empire that writing fell as an obligation on monks, nuns, and finally male students. Of all forms of manual labor, mechanical copying, just as in present day computers, most closely corresponded to Saint Benedict's dictum: *ora et labora*. Even if the writer, simply because his tongue knew only some vernacular dialect, had no understanding of the Latin or even Greek words he was supposed to preserve, his handicap augmented the monastery library."[15]

The difference between such earlier forms of preserving and reproducing cultural memory and contemporary digital archiving techniques has to be emphasized. Contemporary forms of copy are intimately tied to the consumer market and the commercial milieu of the digital culture (especially the internet), whereas the work done by monks was part of the theological networks where God, in theory, played the key mediator (and the final guarantor of mimesis) instead of, for example, Sony BMG or Microsoft. Theological issues defined the importance of what was copied and preserved, whereas nowadays the right to copy and to reproduce culture is to a large extent owned by global media companies. This illustrates how copying is an issue of politics in the sense that by control of copying (especially with technical and juridical power) cultural production is also hierarchized and controlled.

The high fidelities of consumer production connect to the other key area of copy within computer programming: the copy/paste routine that is part and parcel of graphic user interfaces (GUI). Aptly, the Xerox Company, now a kind of cultural symbol of the modern culture of copy, and especially its Palo Alto research center (PARC), are responsible for the original ideas of graphic user interfaces and point-click user control using the mouse. The Gypsy graphical interface system from 1974/1975 was probably the first to incorporate the cut and paste command as part of its repertoire (although Douglas Engelbart and the "Augmentation Research Center" had introduced the idea in 1968). The command was designed as a remediation of the paper-and-scissors era, keeping nonprofessionals especially in mind. The interface was designed for efficient office work, where adjustments could be done on screen while always having a clean copy in store for backup. The idea at PARC was to create an office workstation that would seem as invisible to the lay user as possible. This was effected by providing a set of generic commands.[16]

The Xerox Star (1981) was hailed as the software system of the future, designed as a personal workspace for networks. The Star office system incorporated key commands (Move, Copy, Open, Delete, Show Properties, and Same [Copy Properties]) as routines applicable "to nearly all the objects on the system: text, graphics, file folders and file drawers, records files, printers, in and out baskets, etc."[17] Being generic, such commands were not tied to specific objects. In addition, the commands were accessible using special function keys on Star's keyboard. Star's design transferred, then, responsibilities from the user to the machine. The user no longer had to remember commands, but could find them either in special function keys or in menus.[18] The desktop became for the first time the individualized Gutenberg machine, or the hard-working and pious medieval monk that followed the simple commands universalized as generic.

The very familiar point-click copy-paste routine originates from those systems, and is now integrated into everyday consumer culture. This, as Lev Manovich suggests, is perhaps how Fredric Jameson's ideas of postmodernization should be understood: Copy production as the dominant mode of cultural production culminated in the digital production techniques of GUI operating systems that originated in 1980s. Manovich notes that "[E]ndless recycling and quoting of past media content, artistic styles and forms became the new 'international style' and the new cultural logic of modern society. Rather than assembling more media recordings of reality, culture is now busy reworking, recombining, and analyzing already accumulated media material."[19] In addition, recycling is also incorporated as part of the actual work routines of programming in the sense of reusing already existing bits and pieces of code, and pasting them into novel collages (so-called copy and paste programming). Since the 1960s, copying has been elevated into an art practice but it is more likely to be articulated in monotonous office work context or as pirate activity.[20]

In general, "CTRL + C" functions as one of the key algorithmic order-words piloting the practices of digital culture. This returns focus on the key economic-political point: who owns and controls the archives from which content is quoted and remediated? The question does not only concern the software producers who are in a key position to define the computer environment but also the large media conglomerates, which have increasingly purchased rights to the audiovisual archives of cultural memory. Purchasing such rights means also purchasing the right to copying (as a source of production) and the right to the copy as an object of commercial distribution. The archive functions as the key node in the cultural politics of digital culture. One alarming trend is how such key nodes are being defined in commercial interests, such as in the 1996 Copy Protection Technical Working Group, in which technical manufacturers (Panasonic, Thomson, Philips), content producers (Warners Bros, Sony Pictures), Digital Rights Management (Macrovision, Secure Media), telecommunications (Viacom, Echostar Communications) and the computer industry (Intel, IBM, Microsoft) are represented.[21] The issue under consideration is not only about content that is archived in private corporate collections but about how copying is subject to technical, commercial, and political restrictions.

"Postmodernization" should be understood as a media technological condition. Aesthetic and consumer principles have been intimately intermingled with the engineering and programming routines of modern operating systems that are part of the genealogy of modern technical media. For Friedrich Kittler, the Turing machine as the foundation of digital culture acts as a digital version of the medieval student, "a copying machine at almost no cost, but a perfect one." Similarly for Kittler, "The internet is a point-to-point transmission system copying almost infallibly not from men to men, but, quite to the contrary, from machine to machine."[22] Hence we move from the error-prone techniques of monks to the celluloid-based cut and paste of film, and on to the copy machines of contemporary culture, in which digitally archived routines replace and remediate the analog equivalents of prior discourse networks. With computers, copying becomes an algorithm and a mode of discrete-state processing. Digital copying is much more facile (if not totally error-free) than mechanical copying, and copies are more easily produced as mass-distribution global consumer products. In digital products the tracking and control of the objects of copying is easier, and there is the added capability to tag the copies as copyright of the producer or the distributor. The novelty of the digital copy system is in the capability to create such copy management systems or digital rights management (DRM) techniques, which act as microcontrollers of user behavior: Data is endowed with an inherent control system, which tracks the paths of software (for example, restricting the amount of media players a digitally packed audiovision product can be played on).

In addition, copying is intimately entwined with communication as a central mode of action of network culture. Such sociotechnological innovations as nineteenth-century magnetic recording, the modem (1958), the c-cassette (1962), the CD-disc (1965), the Ethernet local network (1973), and Napster (1999) and subsequent file-sharing networks can be read from the viewpoint of the social order words, "copy" and "distribution." The act of copying includes in a virtual sphere the idea of the copy being shared and distributed. What happens in copying is first the identification or framing of the object to be copied, followed by the reproduction of a similar object whose mode of existance is predicated upon its being distributed. There is no point in making copies without distributing them. Copying is not merely reproducing the same as discrete objects, but coding cultural products into discrete data and communicating such coded copies across networks: seeding and culturing. Similar to how Benjamin saw mechanical reproduction and distribution as inherent to the media technology of cinema, copy routines and distribution channels are intimate parts of the digital network paradigm: connecting people, but also copying machines.

Notes

1. Quoted in David Kahn, *The Codebreakers: The Story of Secret Writing,* 125.

2. Walter Benjamin, *Illuminations: Essays and Reflections,* 244 fn. 7.

3. See the online Early Office Museum pages for copying machines, available at http://www.officemuseum.com/copy_machines.htm.

4. See the Waalsdorp museum online page at http://www.museumwaalsdorp.nl/computer/en/punchcards.html. Thanks also to Jaakko Suominen for his notes.

5. As Hillel Schwartz notes in his thought-provoking *The Culture of the Copy,* two modes, or philosophies, of copying were early rivals: copying discretely bit by bit, or analogically copying an entirety, as with chemical copying. Hence the cultural origins of computerized scanning and the calculation of, for example, images, and the copying of these images in the form of bits spans further in time than actual digital machines. See Hillel Schwartz, *The Culture of the Copy: Striking Likenesses, Unreasonable Facsimiles,* 223.

6. Robert Slade, "History of Computer Viruses," 1992, available at http://www.cknow.com/articles/6/1/Robert-Slade&%2339%3Bs-Computer-Virus-History.

7. Ken Thompson, "Reflections of Trusting Trust," *Communications of the ACM,* vol. 27, issue 8 (August 1984), 761.

8. Bill Kennedy, "Two Old Viruses," *The Risks Digest,* Vol. 6, Issue 53 (March 1988), available at http://catless.ncl.ac.uk/risks. Another similar observation is dated to 1973, which shows that several programmers thought about the same ideas. See "Old Viruses," *The Risks Digest,* vol. 6, issue 54 (April 1988), available at http://catless.ncl.ac.uk/risks. Another example are the "bacteria" programs that have been listed as one of the oldest forms of programmed threats. A bacterium is another name used for rabbit programs. It does not explicitly damage any files, its only purpose is to reproduce exponentially, but can thus take up all the processor capacity, memory, or disk space. See Thomas R. Peltier, "The Virus Threat," *Computer Fraud & Security Bulletin,* June 1993, p. 15.

9. Thank you to Professor Timo Järvi for pointing this out to me.

10. See B. I. Blum, "Free-Text Inputs to Utility Routines," *Communications of the ACM,* vol. 9, issue 7 (July 1966), 525–526.

11. See Janet Abbate, *Inventing the Internet,* 96–106.

12. Matthew Fuller, *Media Ecologies: Materialist Energies in Art and Technoculture,* 111.

13. Susan Blackmore, *The Meme Machine,* 214.

14. See the "Facsimile & SSTV History," available at http://www.hffax.de/html/hauptteil_faxhistory.htm.

15. Friedrich Kittler, "Universities: Wet, Hard, Soft, and Harder," *Critical Inquiry,* vol. 31, issue 1 (Autumn 2004), 245.

16. Michael Hiltzik, *Dealers of Lightning: Xerox PARC and the Dawn of the Computer Age,* 209–210.

17. Butler W. Lampson, "Hints for Computer System Design," *Proceedings of the Ninth ACM Symposium on Operating Systems Principles* (1983), 39.

18. See Jeff Johnson and Teresa L. Roberts, "The Xerox Star: A Retrospective," *IEEE Computer* (September 1989), 11–29.

19. Lev Manovich, *The Language of New Media,* 131.

20. Schwartz, *The Culture of the Copy,* 238–239.

21. See Volker Grassmuck, "Das Ende der Universalmaschine," in *Zukunfte des Computers,* ed. Claus Pias, 251.

22. Kittler, "Universities," 252.

■

Data Visualization

Richard Wright

Any transformation of digital material into a visual rendering can arguably be called a visualization, even the typographic treatment of text in a terminal window. Conventionally, however, "data visualization" is understood as a mapping of digital data onto a visual image. The need for visualization was first recognized in the sciences during the late 1980s as the increasing power of computing and the decreasing cost of digital storage created a surge in the amount and complexity of data needing to be managed, processed, and understood. In 1987 the US National Science Foundation published their "Visualization in Scientific Computing" report (ViSC) that warned about the "firehose of data" that was resulting from computational experiments and electronic sensing.[1] The solution proposed by the ViSC report was to use visualization to quickly spot patterns in the data that could then be used to guide investigations toward hypotheses more likely to yield results. By using these "intuitive perceptual qualities as a basis for evaluation, verification and understanding," the ViSC panelists intended to put "the neurological machinery of the visual cortex to work."

In a book published in 2000, visualization scientist Colin Ware concisely summed up the main advantages of modern visualization techniques.[2] As mentioned above, visualization permits the apprehension of large amounts of data. The flexibility of human vision can perceive emergent properties such as subtle patterns and structures. It can compare small scale and large scale features at the same time. It can also help with the discernment of artifacts or mistakes in the gathering of the data itself. Yet despite these observations being at the intuitive level it is still possible to use them to suggest more formal hypotheses about the data in question. The early criticism that "pictures don't prove anything" has gradually been mitigated by the promise that apparent relationships can be later confirmed by applying more exact analytical methods.

Visualizations are created for people rather than for machines—they imply that not all computational processes can be fully automated and left to run themselves. Somewhere along the line a human being will need to evaluate or monitor the progress of the computation and make decisions about what to do next. Yet despite the fact that the material operations of software and data processing are perfectly objective and describable, they are rarely directly accessible to us. One of the fundamental properties of software is that once it is being executed it takes place on such a fine temporal and symbolic scale and across such a vast range of quantities of data that it has an intrinsically different materiality than that with which we are able to deal with unaided. Visualization is one of the few techniques available for overcoming this distance. In the visualization process, the transformations that lead from data to digital image are defined through software, often in a direct or "live" relationship with it, yet aim to be apprehended at a level of human sensibility far beyond it. A visualization is therefore distinguished by its algorithmic dependence on its source data and its perceptual independence from it.

Early writers on visualization such as Edward Tufte developed guidelines and examples for how to design information graphics that are still influential today. Tufte's main concern is now referred to as the principle of being "expressive": to remove all unnecessary graphical ornamentation and show as much data as possible; to "let the data speak for itself."[3] To some extent, when we use computer graphics we can often "express" so much data that we do not have to choose which is the most significant. But even if we are *able* to show everything we may still not know *how* to show it—how do we order the variables into an image in a way that expresses their interrelationships? The semiologist Jacques Bertin did important early work during the 1970s on how to organize a "visual structure" that reflects the features and relations between the data.[4] The usual approach is to start from some basic knowledge about the data's internal structure. In theory the data we start with is raw and uninterpreted, but in practice there is always some additional information about its composition, usually derived from the means by which it was gathered. For instance, if the data has up to three variables it can be directly mapped into a three-dimensional graph of x, y, z values (or by transforming it using an intermediate stage called a "data table"). Ware provides a typical example of such a visualization from oceanography—a multibeam echo sounder scanning of the tides at Passamoquoddy Bay in Canada, which produces a three-dimensional array of height fields, rendered as a color image (figure 4).[5] This data used to be sampled and rendered as a set of contour lines, but the continuous computer-generated image allows us to clearly see the more subtle features, textures, and artifacts in all the millions of measurements made. Of course, we do not have to render it in this way—if we chose to we could unravel the array into a one-dimensional sequence of values, interpret each one as a frequency and "play" the data as a series of tones. But this would be to ignore the variables' positional structure and we would almost certainly not be able to "see" the ripples and pockmark patterns that we can in the image. Ordering the values into a linear sequence might also imply precedence or ranking not in the original data. The internal structure of the data is spatial rather than temporal.

If we are using visualization to forage for particular known pieces of information such as which stocks are rising most steeply or in creating a graphic notation for structuring conceptual propositions, then we are dealing with more explicit functions of data catered to by specialized fields of information visualization, "data mining," or knowledge visualization. These disciplines are often closer to interface design, employing popular techniques such as interactive "fisheye" views, "table lens" document graphs, or spatial "mind mapping" tools.[6] But in a more general context, if the properties of the data are yet to be discovered, then visualization has less to do with retrieval, monitoring, or communication and is more of an experimental technique. In contrast to a diagram that is constructed on the basis of a preestablished set of significances, a visualization is about finding connections (or disconnections) between dataset attributes like amounts, classes, or intervals that were previously unknown.

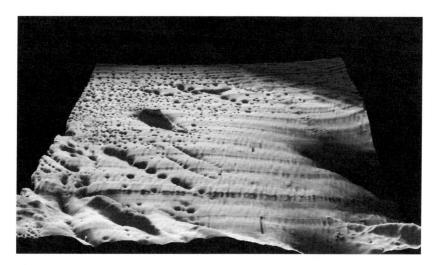

Figure 4   Three dimensional array of height fields from a multibeam echo sounder scanning of tides at Passamoquoddy Bay, Canada.

Visualizations are always partial and provisional and they may entail the application of a number of different methods until the data gives up its secrets. The images frequently exhibit the continuous qualities of the familiar visual world despite the fact that they are utterly constructed. It is these implicit visual properties that are valued for their openness to perceptual inference—a continuous interplay of surface features rather than discrete graphic elements or symbols. At this end of the spectrum, visualization is nonrepresentational because it is speculatively mapped from the raw, isolated data or equations and not with respect to an already validated representational relation. A visualization is not a representation but a means to a representation.

As recently as 2004, visualization scientist Chaomei Chen described visualization as still being an art rather than a science.[7] There is still no taxonomy of techniques that might help designers select one that is more effective for their requirements, and no generic criteria with which to assess the value of a visualization once they have. In the absence of guidance, there has been a tendency by some scientists to seize upon the underlying code of a successful visualization and make it a de facto standard. Colin Ware has tried to remedy this by grounding visualization as a specifically scientific discipline by combining the fields of physiology, human perception, and cognitive studies.[8] This feeds into a desire among many scientists to conform visualization to scientific method by treating visual perception and cognition in terms of computation itself, to be harnessed as an instrumental resource. For instance, the ability of the eye to instantly see that one visual feature is bigger than another is referred to as "computational offloading" in some places: "a diagram may allow users to avoid having to explicitly compute information because users can extract information 'at a glance.'"[9] There is now a push to try to streamline visualization by designing it for the faster "automatic processing" stage of human vision that deals with the unconscious detection of light, pattern, orientation, and movement. If the abilities of this retinal level of processing can be defined and standardized then the hope is that visualization can be freed of the inefficiencies and contingencies of learned visual conventions, that it can promise a fast and universal "understanding without training" that crosses all cultural boundaries.[10]

In the literature there is little emphasis on how to see visualizations, only on how they are seen. Despite the fact that low level perceptual mechanics may not be formally learned, they can still be exercised, sensitized, tuned, and focused as an acquired skill. The editor of a film can see a hair on an individual frame that appears far too briefly for his audience to be conscious of it. Visualization as a practice is not just a question of designing for human perception but of being perceptive. In fact, some people's eyes have been "retrained" by visualization itself until it has altered their apprehension of the world. Some of the earliest and most ubiquitous forms of scientific visualization were images of fractals, chaos theory, and complex systems of the late 1980s.[11] Despite the fact that, as media theorists such as Vilém Flusser pointed out, these pictures were "images of equations" rather than "images of the world," they were frequently used to model the appearance of natural phenomena such as mountains, plants, and marble textures.[12] Some scientists working with fractal modeling, such as Michael Barnsley, found that after a while they began to "see" the rivers, trees, and clouds around them in terms of fractal mathematics,[13] internalizing concepts of self-similarity and strange attractors until they had become a way of thinking and perceiving itself, as though turning the whole world into a "natural" visualization. Both algorithm and sensory vision are thus finally reunited in the cortex, in an endless circularity of computation and perception.

Visualization is usually separated out as a tool for knowledge formation rather than a visual form of knowledge itself. Although forms such as "analogical representation" (which preserves some structural features of the object such as visual resemblance) or "enactive knowledge" (which is bound to actions such as a certain skill) are recognized as valid forms of knowledge, scientists still mainly characterize their aims in terms of "conceptual knowledge": that which can be symbolically represented or discursively expressed.[14] This causes some uncertainty in the status of visuality; the literature frequently switches between statements like "using vision to think," "using visual computation to think," and "visual sense making."[15] Michel Foucault described a similar situation in his study of the origins of modern systems of knowledge at the end of the Renaissance.[16] He pointed out how the principle of "resemblance," which had previously been so important, became relegated to a preliminary stage on the borders of knowledge during the Enlightenment. This was despite the fact that at the dawn of representational knowledge, as now, no order could be established between two things until a visual similarity had occasioned their comparison. The use of memory and imagination in the discovery of a latent resemblance is what makes the creation of knowledge possible. Whether such visual relations will continue to be restricted to the rudimentary status of perceptual pre-processing under the reign of visualization will define one of the most important characteristics of knowledge in the age of computer software.

Although initially applied to imagery, visualization has now become a more generic term that covers the sensory presentation of data and processing using interactive techniques, animation, sonics, haptics, and multi-user VR environments. Over the course of the 1990s, visualization has spread from the sciences into engineering disciplines, marketing, law, policy making, and art and entertainment, indeed to any field that has found its object of interest replaced by datasets or computer models. It helps make visible the fluctuations in the international money market, defends the innocent through accident reconstruction, discloses network traffic in order to detect telephone fraud, and reports the proportion of files consolidated by one's disk defragmenter.

These new fields obviously exceed the original scientific aims of visualization, yet even in art and design applications some form of cognitive knowledge may still be the intention. Christian Nold is an artist who has been building "bio maps" of communities using a mixture of consciously and unconsciously recorded data.[17] For the "Greenwich Emotion Map" (figure 5), groups of local residents each received a Galvanic Skin Response unit which measured their emotional arousal as they went for a walk around the neighbourhood. Every four seconds their level of excitation was recorded along with their geographical location as they reacted or failed to react to whatever coincidence of encounters, sights, and smells the city channelled to them that day. When they

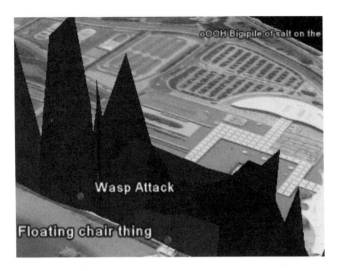

Figure 5   Christian Nold, detail from *Greenwich Emotion Map,* 2006.

returned, their data was uploaded and plotted onto a map of Greenwich and annotated with written notes and photos they made at the time. When uploaded and rendered as an overlay of nervous peaks and troughs, markers, and pop-ups over a Google Earth satellite image, we are able to pick apart Google's naturalistic photographic image of Greenwich in terms of a mass of individual responses and rejoinders. "BioMapping" recreates the urban crowd using data visualization to become a dynamic object of fluctuating emotional intensities, informal commentaries, and subjective trajectories.

There also exist many noncognitive "visualizations" in common use. In some cases this is because they move so far from their source data that the data disappear from relevance entirely. For example, it is easy to take any arbitrary data including random, unstructured data and contrive a rich pattern from it using elaborate visualization tools. Noise functions are widely used in media production software as the starting point for synthetic image generation. By repeatedly applying a barrage of frequency filters, scalings, and interpolation methods it is routinely possible to design the convincing appearance of natural phenomena such as marble, wood, smoke, or fire, or the vertiginous synaesthetic abstractions familiar to users of the Windows Media Player. In these cases we move away from "data visualization" as such to the more general category of computer generated "visualization."

Figure 6 Graham Harwood, *Lungs: Slave Labour,* 2005.

But there are other noncognitive visualizations whose power is derived from the very strain of stretching yet maintaining a connection to their original database. "Lungs: Slave Labour," (figure 6), by Graham Harwood, is an acoustic, affective visualization based on Nazi records of the foreign laborers that were forced to work in the ex-munitions factory that now houses the Centre for Media Art in Karlsruhe.[18] By interrogating their age, sex, and height, "Lungs" is able to calculate their vital lung capacity and emit a "breath" of air for each worker through a speaker system. The general aim of the "Lungs" project is to take computer records of local events or communities that have been reduced or demeaned to the status of information and to allow people to re-experience and recover their own value. This attempt to give a database a pair of lungs reconnects people with a political atrocity in a very visceral way that seems to belie the muteness of the bureaucratic records themselves.

This last example might be seen as highly tendentious, but it factually elaborates the politics involved in any representation of data. It still meets the central requirement for data visualization of algorithmically deriving a sensory expression from the structures implicit in digital data, even when, and especially when, that expression takes us far from the realm of computer code. The greatest material distance between human senses and computer code, when compared to the simplest material connections between them, delineates the imaginative possibilities of data visualization. Within this area we can explore the most extreme perspectives that software can create of itself. It is its ability to put cognitive and affective modes of perception into creative tension with data structures and with each other, and to articulate the gap between the processing of data, social life, and sensory experience, that will allow visualization to reach its full potential, both as a scientific and as an artistic technique.

Notes

1. Bill H. McCormick, Tom A. DeFanti, and Maxine D. Brown, "Visualization in Scientific Computing," *Computer Graphics, 21, no. 6* (November 1987).

2. Colin Ware, *Information Visualization: Perception for Design*, 2.

3. Edward Tufte, *Visual Explanations*, 45.

4. Jacques Bertin, *Graphics and Graphic Information Processing*.

5. Ware, *Information Visualization*, 2.

6. Sigmar-Olaf Tergan and Tanja Keller, eds., *Knowledge and Information Visualization: Searching for Synergies (Lecture Notes in Computer Science)*, 5.

7. Chaomei Chen, *Information Visualization*, 2nd edition, 1.

8. Ware, *Information Visualization*, 5.

9. Mike Scaife and Yvonne Rogers, "External Cognition how do graphical representations work?," *International Journal of Human-Computer Studies*, vol. 45, no. 2, 185–213.

10. Ware, *Information Visualization*, 10.

11. Hans Otto Peitgen and Peter Richter, *The Beauty of Fractals: Images of Complex Dynamical Systems*.

12. Vilém Flusser, "Curie's Children: Vilém Flusser on an Unspeakable Future," *Artforum* (March 1990).

13. Michael Barnsley, *Fractals Everywhere: The First Course in Deterministic Fractal Geometry*, 1.

14. Tergan and Keller, *Knowledge and Information Visualization*, 4.

15. Stuart Card, Jock Mackinlay, and Ben Schneiderman, eds., *Readings in Information Visualization: Using Vision to Think,* 33, 34, 579.

16. Michel Foucault, *The Order of Things,* 67–68.

17. Christian Nold, "Greenwich Emotion Map," 2006, available at http://www.emotion map.net.

18. Graham Harwood, "Lungs: Slave Labour," 2005. Permanent collection, ZKM, Karlsruhe, Germany, available at http://www.mongrel.org.uk/lungs.

■

Elegance

Matthew Fuller

In *Literate Programming*,[1] Donald Knuth suggests that the best programs can be said to possess the quality of elegance. Elegance is defined by four criteria: the leanness of the code; the clarity with which the problem is defined; spareness of use of resources such as time and processor cycles; and, implementation in the most suitable language on the most suitable system for its execution. Such a definition of elegance shares a common vocabulary with design and engineering, where, in order to achieve elegance, use of materials should be the barest and cleverest. The combination is essential—too much emphasis on one of the criteria leads to clunkiness or overcomplication.

Such a view of elegance is supported by Gregory Chaitin's formulation of program-size definition of complexity: A measure of the complexity of an answer to a question is the size of the smallest program required to compute it. The resulting drive to terse programs produces a definition of elegance being found in a program "with the property that no program written in the same programming language that produces the same output is smaller than it is."[2]

The benefit of these criteria of elegance in programming is that they establish a clear grounding for the evaluation of approaches to a problem. This set of criteria emerging from programming as a self-referent discipline it works on the level of disciplinary formalization, as a set of metrics that allow for a scale of abstraction. This formalization can also be politically crucial as a rhetorical and intellectual device that allows programmers to stake their ground in contexts where they might be asked to compromise the integrity of their work, and something that allows them to derive satisfaction from work that might otherwise be banal.

When writing code to test compilers, Knuth takes the opposite route. He writes test programs that are, "Intended to break the system, to push it to its extreme limits, to pile complication on complication, in ways that the system programmer never consciously anticipated." He continues, "To prepare such test data, I get into the meanest, nastiest frame of mind that I can manage, and I write the cruelest code I can think of; then I turn round and embed that and embed it in even nastier constructions that are almost obscene."[3] There is a clear counter-position between code that contains as much vileness as one could want and model code that is good. For users of software configured as consumers such "metaphysical" questions aren't often the most immediately apparent, although questions of elegance, as will be suggested below are also recapitulated at the scale of interface.

To return to the politics of elegance at the level of programming practice it is also useful to think about those contexts where paradoxically, in order to become more adequately self-referent, the process of writing software finds itself constituted in combination with other elements. In working conditions where programmers might be concerned with conserving elegance against other imperatives, such as the cutting of costs, the criteria are often posed in terms of benign engineering common sense, or the ethics of satisfying the needs of the user in the clearest way possible, or the onus of clarity to one's collaborators. Elegance is often invoked defensively. In each case however, elegance remains a set of parameters against which a program can be measured.

In the four criteria proposed by Knuth, elegance is constructed between the machine and the talents of the programmer, with the context of the program occurring as something already filtered into a problem definition. Elegance in this sense is defined by its containment within programming as a practice that is internally self-referent and stable.

Knuth's criteria for elegance are immensely powerful when evaluating programming as an activity in and of itself. It might be useful, however, to think about the terms against which they might be modifiable, or for the context of elegance to be allowed to roam, to make obscene couplings, to find other centers of gravity. In such cases, software is not simply software, and it in turn conjugates those other realities with which it mixes with computation. Different criteria for elegance pour into the domain of software, and those of software begin to manifest in combination with other scales of reality.

At the same time, something interesting happens to stability at the level of software. Further work by Gregory Chaitin has revealed that the decision as to whether a program is the shortest possible is complicated by a fundamental incompleteness.[4] As a program's complexity increases, and concomitantly that of the problem it deals with, there is an increasing difficulty in accurately stating the most concise means of answering it. At a certain threshold, the possibility of stating the tersest formula for arriving at an answer is undecidable. The elegance of software then, by at least one of the above criteria, is not absolutely definable at a mathematical level. This is not the same as saying, as of software debugging, "If you don't have an automated test for a feature, that feature doesn't really exist."[5] Elegance, because it cannot be proven, comes down to a rule of thumb, something that emerges out of the interplay of such constraints, or as something more intuitively achievable as style (in Knuth's terminology, an "art"). Like William Burroughs' proposal for an informal self-discipline of movement, "Do Easy,"[6] it is something that can be practiced and learned, the dimensions, weights, capacities of objects dancing in an endless dynamic geometry incorporating the body of the adept and the repositories of heuristics that have gone before in the form of languages, institutions, archives, books, and techniques. Eventually, a certain effortlessness is achieved.

Effortlessness is offered straight out of the box in the vision of computing which sees interaction with information as being best achieved through simple appliances that are easy to use and which operate with defined, comprehensible scopes. At this point, elegance gives way to another set of criteria, which provide powerful, occasionally even fundamental constraints. Such constraints act as limiting devices that force a piece of software toward elegance. A condition of elegance, however, is that it charts a trajectory, often an unlikely one, through possible conditions of failure. Finding a way of aligning one's capacities and powers in a way that arcs through the interlocking sets of constraints and criteria, the material qualities of software, and the context in which it is forged and exists is key to elegance.

Achieving striking effects with an economy of means has been crucial to formulating elegance within software, particularly within the domain of graphic interaction. To produce a convincing animated sprite within a tiny cluster of pixels, to develop a bitmapped font working at multiple scales, or to develop a format allowing for the fast transfer and calculation of vector graphics over limited bandwidth requires a variation in criteria from those Knuth set for elegance at the level of programming. (For instance, one might be working for a predefined platform or a range of them, or within a particular protocol.) Equally, at the level of the operating system, a language, a data-structure, or within a program, defining the core grammars of conjunction and differentiation of digital objects each provide scalar layers wherein elegance might be achieved or made difficult. In such cases, elegance can be found in the solutions that allow a user to get as close to the bare bones of the underlying layer of the system, without necessarily having to go a layer deeper. In proprietary software, a good example of such elegance is the formulation of the Tool Kit, built into the ROM of the early Macintoshes, which defined the available vocabulary of actions, such as cut, paste, save, copy, and so on that were able to work powerfully across many different applications.[7] Such work builds upon the particularity of digital and computational materials. Crucially, however, it also abstracts from the many potential kinds of interaction with data that might be desirable to produce a limited range of operations that can be deployed across many different kinds of information. While the range of such a vocabulary of functions might be constrained, the concrete power that arises from the conjoint and recursive use of these operations elegantly directs the power of computation in a trajectory toward its conjugation with its outside. The outside in this case consists of the multiple uses of these functions in programs aimed at the handling of multiple kinds of data. Elegance then is also the capacity to make leaps from one set of material qualities and constraints to another in order to set off a combinatorial explosion generated by the interplay between their previously discrete powers.

Elegance can also be seen in the way in which a trajectory can be extended, developing the reach of an abstraction, or by finding connections with domains previously understood as being "outside" of computation or software. A fine example of such elegance would be achieved if a way was found to conjoin the criteria of elegance in programming with constraints on hardware design consonant with ecological principles of nonpollution, minimal energy usage, recyclability or reusability, and the health requirements of hardware fabrication and disposal workers.[8] Good design increasingly demands that elegance follows or at least makes itself open to such a trajectory. The criteria of minimal use of processor cycles already has ecological implications.

While elegance, then, demands that we step outside of software, keep combining it with other centers of gravity, computation also suggests a means by which we can think it through, prior to its formulation. The virtual has become an increasingly significant domain for philosophical thought, but it is also one that is always simultaneously mathematical. Steven Wolfram's figure of the "computational universe"[9] suggests that it is possible to map out every possible algorithm, and every possible result of every algorithm. A concept of the virtual reminiscent of Linneas's attempts to graph the entirety of speciation, this is a decisive imaginal figure, if not quite a mapping, of the constraint of computability itself. It follows from Emile Borel's idea that it would be possible to construct a table containing every possible statement in the French language, and indeed from Turing's formalization of all possible computations. Needless to say, Borel's table did not account for irony, that multiple semantic layers can be embedded in the same string of characters. If an ironic computational universe is not the one we currently inhabit, it will inevitably occur as soon as computation snuggles up to its outside. The condensation of multiple meanings into one phrase or statement turns elegance from a set of criteria into a, necessarily skewed, way of life.

Here we can see a further clue to elegance within multiscalar domains, that is to say, how it is produced in most actual computing work. The transversal leap or arc characteristic of elegance does not necessarily depend on a structural, ethical, or aesthetic homomorphy between code, the problem it treats, and the materials it allies itself with (such as hardware, language and people). Elegance also manifests by means of disequilibrium, the tiny doses of poison, doping, required to make a chip functional, to make it hum: a hack can be elegant, a good hack is inherently so. Elegance exists in the precision madness of axioms that cross categories, in software that observes terseness and clarity of design, and in the leaping cracks and shudders that zigzag scales and domains together.

Notes

1. Donald Knuth, *Literate Programming.*

2. Gregory Chaitin, *Epistemology as Information Theory: From Leibniz to Omega.* See also Gregory Chaitin, *MetaMaths! The Quest for Omega.*

3. Donald Knuth, *Literate Programming,* 266–267.

4. Gregory Chaitin, "Elegant LISP Programs" in Cristian Calude, *People and Ideas in Theoretical Computer Science,* 35–52.

5. Eric Kidd, "More Debugging Tips."

6. William S. Burroughs, "The Discipline of DE."

7. The Mac ToolKit was programmed by Andy Hertzfeld; see his *Revolution in the Valley.*

8. See Basel Action Network, available at http://www.ban.org/; Silicon Valley Toxics Coalition, available at http://www.svtc.org/; Greenpeace, *Green My Apple Campaign,* available at http://www.greenmyapple.org/.

9. See Steven Wolfram, *A New Kind of Science.*

■

Ethnocomputing

Matti Tedre and Ron Eglash

Social studies of the relations between culture and knowledge in science and technology have in general been approached from three directions. First, in the ethnosciences approach, the study of the knowledge of indigenous societies has been given terms such as ethnobotany, ethnomathematics, and ethno-astronomy.[1] Second, in the social constructionist approach, the cultural dimensions of contemporary science and technology have been analyzed as a "seamless web" of both social and natural constraining and enabling factors.[2] Third, in the interactionist approach, the researchers take into account that after technology has been designed and produced, its use may vary depending on cultural context, adaptation, appropriation, and reinvention.[3] Ethnocomputing is an umbrella term that encompasses all three of these approaches to examine the relations between computing and culture.

The technical elements of ethnocomputational practices include (formal or non-formal) (a) data structures: organized structures and models that are used to represent information, (b) algorithms: ways of systematically manipulating organized information, and (c) physical and linguistic realizations of data structures and algorithms: devices, tools, games, art, or other kinds of realizations of computational processes.[4] Non-Western examples of the first element can be found in, for instance, Inca Quipu[5]; examples of the second element include techniques for calculating textile lengths and costs[6]; examples of the third element can be found in, for instance, the Owari game.[7]

The foregoing examples are manifestations of computational ideas in indigenous cultures, and they exemplify the diversity of computational ideas. There are two central arguments in ethnocomputing: a design/social justice argument and a theoretical/academic argument. The first argument is that a better understanding of the cultural dimensions of computing can improve the design of computational devices and practices in disadvantaged groups and third world populations. The second argument is that an understanding of the cultural dimensions of computing can enrich the disciplinary self-understanding of computer science at large.

Theory: Conceptual Starting Points

One of the most difficult barriers to the research of ethnocomputational ideas is the unequal assessment of knowledge in locations of high social power (e.g., Western, first-world, high-tech) and knowledge at the margins of social power (e.g., indigenous, third-world, vernacular). By using the term ethnocomputing to encompass both domains, the tendency to privilege the Western version as the universal, singularly correct answer is avoided: all computing can be seen as equally cultural, and cultural variation should be seen as a resource for diversity in theory, design, and modeling.

Stressing the sociocultural construction of computing does not mean advocating ontological or epistemological relativism, that is, it does not mean questioning the existence of the real world or its underlying principles of physics and mathematics. However, all human attempts to derive these laws and exploit them through technology are done through cultural lenses. Computing is a field in which sociocultural factors play a big role. Unlike the natural sciences, where most theoretical and practical problems arise from the complexity of the physical world, in computer science the difficulties usually stem from computer scientists' earlier work—computer scientists have created the complexity of their own discipline. Earlier design choices in control structures, architectures, languages, techniques, data structures, syntax, semantics, etc., affect future design choices.

However, the sociocultural influences in computing—whether in the first world or third world—should not be considered to be a problem, but rather means for the design and understanding of effective computing technologies and practices. For instance, Andrew Pickering[8] has argued that science proceeds by accommodations, not by replacement. He argued that scientists accommodate for whatever anomalies experiments may reveal, by reconfiguring various elements of a model's technical, social, and natural relations. There are undoubtedly universal physical laws that govern the operation of computational devices, but only through a multiplicity of experiments—whether carried out by silicon chips, carved African game boards, or the generation of theorems and proofs—can one learn those principles.

Research Directions

As an umbrella term, ethnocomputing entails a number of active research directions, of which three examples are presented here. Firstly, there is the project that focuses on the history of computer science. Compared to the millennia-long history of mathematics, the standard history of computer science is very short. As a discipline, computer science is typically thought of as having arisen only with the advent of electronic computers. From the small group of countries that have led the computer revolution, an even smaller segment of people have set the development trends of Information and Communication Technology (ICT). The early development of computer science was mostly determined by military and industrial priorities. Not surprisingly, home computers are also designed for the Western knowledge worker.[9]

Computers are cultural artifacts in which a Western understanding of logic, inference, quantification, comparison, representation, measurement, and concepts of time and space are embedded at a variety of levels. That is not to say that all aspects of the computer should be redesigned to aid its cultural fit but that one needs to be aware of the underlying viewpoints of computing. Because of a lack of knowledge about the sociocultural history of computing, the lack of cultural diversity in its teaching material, literature, and problems are more easily overlooked. One project of ethnocomputing is to reassess the history of computer science,[10] just as ethnomathematics has inspired a reconsideration of the influence of non-Western cultures in mathematics.

Secondly, there is the project of ethnocomputing that focuses on cultural issues in human-computer interaction. It has been argued that there is an ongoing shift from computer-centered computer science to user-centered computer science.[11] At the same time, computers, ICT in general, and the internet are spreading to the developing countries. The ongoing diffusion of computing technology in developing countries is increasingly diversifying the user base.[12] Consequently, there is a clear motivation for learning more about users rather than thinking of them as superficial "cultural markers," and to take more responsibility for the effects modern ICT may have on people's everyday lives.

Thirdly, there is the project of ethnocomputing that focuses on translations between indigenous/vernacular and high-tech representations of computing. For example, Ron Eglash describes a project that began with modeling traditional African architecture using fractal geometry. Field work in Africa showed that these architectural fractals result from intentional designs, not simply unconscious social dynamics, and that such iterative scaling structures can be found in other areas of African material culture—art, adornment, religion, construction, games, and so forth—often as a result of geometric algorithms known (implicitly or explicitly) by the artisans.

Computational models of these fractals have been developed into a suite of interactive tools in which grade 4–12 students could control simulation parameters (such as geometric transformations and iterative levels) and create not only simulations of the original indigenous designs, but also new creations of their own making. The tools also include modeling computational aspects of Native American design (such as iterative patterns in beadwork, basketry, and weaving), Latino design (such as least common multiple relations in traditional drumming patterns and the iterative construction of pyramids), and youth subculture designs (linear and nonlinear curves in graffiti). The collective website, titled "Culturally Situated Design Tools"[13] has been successfully used in math, art, and technology education classes, primarily with minority students from African American, Native American, and Latino cultures (figure 7).

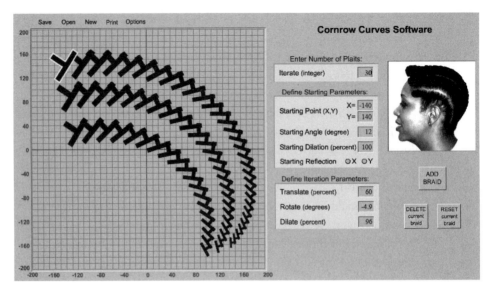

Figure 7 Cornrow curves design tool.

Applications in ICT Education

Information and Communication Technology research has created many gains for majority populations in Western countries. But both students from disadvantaged groups in the West and the general population in non-Western nations have had substantially fewer gains from ICT research. Some of this is attributable to economic factors. Schools with concentrations of disadvantaged groups in Western nations tend to have fewer ICT resources, and non-Western general populations have much less computer access. There are also cultural factors that hinder ICT education and its use in developing countries. ICTs are not culturally-neutral objects and concepts.

The cultural specificity of ICTs is perhaps most evident in the case of pedagogy. Different kinds of curricula, textbooks and other study material, the examples used, the choice of pedagogical approaches, and even what is considered a "valid problem" in ICT education often have a heavy Western bias. This bias sets expectations that only the students with a Western cultural background can meet without extra cognitive overhead. Students from other cultures experience more difficulties than Western students when trying to adapt to culturally specific examples and applications that the current ICT education exhibits, and when the non-Western students' own mental imagery is not supported. The problem with the cultural specificity of ICT education in developing countries has been addressed on a number of levels ranging from mere importing of technology, to technology transfer, application, and contextualization.[14]

Applications in Innovation and Diffusion

Technological decisions are often made on grounds other than technical limitations: for instance, on economic, political, ideological, or cultural grounds.[15] Several motivations can be attributed, for example, to the development of GNU/Linux and its introduction into use.[16] Arguably, GNU/Linux is advanced (technical motivation), free of initial investment (economical motivation), its roots are in hacker ethics and the free software movement (ideological and social motivations), and sometimes it can emphasize a cultural or political message (e.g., IMPI Linux in South Africa and RedFlag Linux in China). If one wants to really understand why GNU/Linux has developed as it has, these motivations cannot be ignored, and the same applies to all other computational systems.

Modern ICT tools are not detached from other technologies, but because complete systems are bound to and based on the design decisions of pre-existing tools,[17] they have to be relevant to the existing infrastructure.[18] ICT can be implemented in highly variable situations, as long as the local infrastructure (e.g., electricity, phone lines, or OSI layers) is known. Second, the ICT systems have to be relevant to local needs. Technologies that are not advantageous from the viewpoint of the users are not easily taken into use, no matter how great their "objective" advantage is.[19] Third, ICT systems have to be relevant to the local users. Systems that are hard to use are adopted more slowly than those that are easy to use, or they may be rejected altogether. Fourth, ICT systems have to be relevant to the local culture and society. The structure of a social system may facilitate or impede the diffusion of technologies. Technology transfer from Western countries to developing countries often ignores aspects of relevance.

Other Ethnocomputing Exemplars

Examples of ethnocomputational phenomena are numerous and they range from social to technical, from theoretical to practical, from low-tech to high-tech, and so forth. A number of different ethnocomputing projects are presented below.

Cellular Automata Model for Owari

Aspects of the Ghanaian game Owari have been modeled in computational terms such as one-dimensional cellular automata.[20] But cellular automata have their own history and cultural dimensions. For example, John von Neumann, the founder of cellular automata, was motivated by his interest in self-reproducing robots; his interest has been attributed to the uncertain environment of his childhood as a Jew in Eastern Europe.[21] The particular form of cellular automata that von Neumann chose—two-dimensional cells with only four nearest-neighbors that are oriented vertically and horizontally—was a result of the computational restrictions of his day. Later models utilized eight nearest-neighbors (the additional four at each corner), hexagonal cells, one-dimensional and three-dimensional arrays, and even (e.g., in the case of Sugarscape, one of the first artificial society models) a return to von Neumann's four nearest-neighbor configuration. Each of the varieties of cellular automata, including the Ghanaian game Owari, is the result of a combination of technical and social features.

Simputer and the $100 Laptop

The famous Simputer project provides an example of the hardware side of ethnocomputing. Conceived during the organization of the International Seminar on Information Technology for Developing Countries (Bangalore, October 1998), the original Simputer (simple, inexpensive, multilingual computer) plan discussed the need for a low-cost device that will bring local-language IT to the masses. Another technology-oriented project, the OLPC (one laptop per child) project (also dubbed "the $100 laptop"), developed by researchers at MIT, uses open-source software focused on education, and is connected with several industrial partners. However, at a UN conference in Tunisia, several African officials were suspicious of the motives of the project, suggesting it was excessively influenced by an American framework for development. The important point here is not the outcomes of Simputer and OLPC projects, but that such designs must be considered from a wide range of socio-technical intersections.

IAAEC Alternative to the Desktop Metaphor Project

Brian Smith from MIT Media Lab and Juan Gilbert from Auburn University have explored culturally-specific alternatives to the desktop metaphor. They note that prior attempts to redesign the graphical user interface (GUI) by replacing the desktop with spatial metaphors (e.g., rooms, buildings, villages) had largely failed—they were more cumbersome than the desktop metaphor.

The aim of Smith and Gilbert is to focus on African-American populations and to explore the various approaches to information manipulation that are already in use in these communities. While replacing the desktop GUI is one possible outcome, it is not necessarily the ultimate goal. Rather the aim is to use the metaphor research as a spring board for broader research that aims to capture aspects of use that have been neglected by the dominance of the desktop metaphor.

Culturally Embedded Computing Group

Headed by computer scientist Phoebe Sengers, this Cornell University group has been generating collaborations between the Department of Information Sciences and the Department of Science and Technology Studies. They emphasize critical technical practice (a term coined by Phil Agre) as a means of integrating IT design with cultural, philosophical, and social analysis. Many of their projects make use of culturally and individually unique home environments, fusing various IT devices with new modes of communication and self-reflection. For example, a mailbox that responds to the affective content of postcards (via a hidden barcode) becomes a social probe for various human interactions.

Native American Language Acquisition Toys

With the support of the Cherokee Nation tribal council, filmmaker Don Thorton teamed with the Neurosmith Corporation to create a version of their educational toy for Native American languages. Neurosmith provided the proprietary software, and Thorton himself digitized the script. The resulting toy, "Little Linguist," became commercially available in 2001. It is physically the same toy used for all the languages; the only difference is the cartridge containing the digitized script. A similar project is planned for the Cree language from an MIT team headed by Vinay Prabhakar and Carlos French, with the aim of providing a more culturally-specific physical device as well as its digital scripting.

Conclusion

The multidimensional approach that ethnocomputing promotes encourages a partnership between computer science and social science. The common goal is to bring the historical and societal constructions of the computational practices of different cultural groups to bear on technological design and practice.

Notes

1. See, C. M. Cotton, *Ethnobotany: Principles and Applications.*

2. For example, Wiebe E. Bijker, Thomas P. Hughes, and Trevor Pinch, eds., *The Social Construction of Technological Systems: New Directions in the Sociology and History of Technology;* Donald MacKenzie and Judy Wajcman, eds., *The Social Shaping of Technology,* 2nd ed.

3. For example, Nelly Oudshoorn and Trevor Pinch, eds., *How Users Matter;* Ron Eglash, Jennifer L. Croissant, Giovanna Di Chiro, and Rayvon Fouche, eds., *Appropriating Technology: Vernacular Science and Social Power.*

4. Matti Tedre et al., "Ethnocomputing: ICT in Social and Cultural Context," in *Communication of the ACM,* vol. 49 no. 1.

5. Marcia Ascher and Robert Ascher, *Code of the Quipu: A Study in Media, Mathematics, and Culture.*

6. Claudia Zaslavsky, *Africa Counts: Number and Pattern in Africa Culture.*

7. Ron Eglash, *African Fractals: Modern Computing and Indigenous Design.*

8. Andrew Pickering, *The Mangle of Practice: Time, Agency, and Science.*

9. See Ron Eglash and J. Bleecker, "The Race for Cyberspace: Information Technology in the Black Diaspora." *Science as Culture,* vol. 10, no. 3.

10. Matti Tedre et al., "Is Universal Usability Universal Only to Us?"

11. Ben Shneiderman, *Leonardo's Laptop: Human Needs and the New Computing Technologies.*

12. Minna Kamppuri, Matti Tedre, and Markku Tukiainen, "Towards the Sixth Level in Interface Design: Understanding Culture."

13. "Culturally Situated Design Tools," available at http://www.rpi.edu/~eglash/csdt.html.

14. Mikko Vesisenaho et al. "Contextualizing ICT in Africa: The Development of the CATI Model in Tanzanian Higher Education," *African Journal of Information and Communication Technology* 2(2) (June 2006) 88–109.

15. See, for example, MacKenzie & Wajcman, *The Social Shaping of Technology.*

16. Matti Tedre et al., "Ethnocomputing: ICT in Social and Cultural Context."

17. MacKenzie & Wajcman, *The Social Shaping of Technology.*

18. Everett M. Rogers, *Diffusion of Innovations.*

19. Ibid.

20. See Ron Eglash, "Geometric Algorithms in Mangbetu Design," and Henning Bruhn, "Periodical States and Marching Groups in a Closed Owari."

21. Steve Heims, *The Cybernetics Group.*

■

Function

Derek Robinson

> A word is a box containing words.
> —GERTRUDE STEIN[1]

A function in programming is a self-contained section of code (one still comes across the term "subroutine," which is the same thing) that is laid out in a standard way to enable deployment and re-use at any number of different points within a program. It's a way of minimizing the duplication of intellectual effort, of making things routine, and as Alfred North Whitehead remarked, "Civilization advances by extending the number of important operations which we can perform without thinking about them."[2]

Functions are usually small and limited to performing a single task. They are active, they do things to things. Some typical examples of functions would be arithmetic operators like "plus," "times," and "square root," which can be combined with other arithmetic operations to compose expressions. If they might be useful in the future, these expressions can be named and turned into functions. Programmers will often keep personal files of utility functions for importing into projects; collections of greater breadth and size are made into libraries and maintained in repositories for use by other coders. It wasn't so long ago that libraries of machine code subroutines, with a light dusting of syntactic sugar, formed the basis of the first high level computer languages.[3]

Programming is a civic-minded activity. Politeness counts. Intense thought is expended in the hope that others, including most importantly one's future self, will not have to keep repeating the same tired phrases again and again. We try to be smart about parameterizing and abstracting, about dignifying as Variables those parts of things that vary, and as Functions the parts that do not, and which are to this degree redundant, vulnerable to automation, ripe for refactoring or removal. The activity of programming, like Jean Tinguely's famous self-destroying automaton ("Homage to New York," 1960), occupies the peculiar position, part teleological and part topological, of existing, ultimately, to obviate its own existence. (Q: "If computers are so smart, why don't they program themselves?" A: "Somebody would first have to write the program, and no-one has yet been that smart.")

When defining a function, there is some sort of preamble establishing its identity (usually a name, although sometimes not) and declaring any arguments or parameters that it will require. Something like "`function defunknose (x,y)`"—`defunknose` here being the name and x and y the arguments—followed by the function's "body," the block of code that actually carries out the computation the function was designed to perform. When later this function is called (by invoking "`defunknose (5,6)`" for example) each instance of an argument found in the function's body gets replaced by its corresponding value. In general, calling a function with different argument values produces different results. In the more sophisticated languages like Lisp or JavaScript, functions can be passed as arguments to functions (it might well be an anonymous "lambda" function that is passed). Finally it is customary (but not obligatory) for functions to return results to their callers. The code that invokes a function should have no reason to care how the result was produced.

A function's definition is a symbolic expression built up recursively from previously defined functions. The regressus of expressions composed of functions whose definitions are expressions composed of functions ultimately bottoms out in a small and irreducible set of atomic elements, which we may call the "axioms" or "ground truths" of the symbol system. In a computer these are the CPU's op-codes, its hardwired instruction set. In the system of arithmetic they would be the primitives "identity" and "successor," from which the four basic arithmetic operations can be derived and back into which they can be reduced. Such radical atomism was a favorite pastime of analytical philosophers of the mid-twentieth century, prefiguring the development of electronic giant brains designed to tirelessly carry out just this sort of task (which our little human brains have difficulty keeping straight). (This is why writing software is so hard.)

Functional Programming

Functional Programming is an approach to programming and programming language design that uses only functions. It abjures any assignment of values to variables on the grounds that this can lead to unexpected side effects and thus compromise correct execution of programs. A function ought not, according to this philosophy, affect anything outside its scope; consequences shall owe only to results returned, and the only proper way to interact with a function is by means of the values passed to it as arguments when the function is invoked.

The first functional programming language was GEORGE, created in 1957 by Charles Hamblin for use on DEUCE, an early Australian computer. (Everything was upper case in those days.) The design was termed a zero-address architecture, because no memory was allocated for named, persistent variables; thus no symbol table was needed either. Any argument values needed by a function were accessed though a special dynamically growing and shrinking range of addresses called the "stack." (Imagine a stack of plates: the last plate added is the first removed.) A function could count on its arguments having been the last things pushed onto the stack before it was called; a stack pointer kept track of the current "top" cell as data were added to and removed from it. All calculations used the stack to store intermediate results, and the final result would be left on top of the stack as an argument for the next function in line. GEORGE programs used Reverse Polish Notation, a strange-looking syntax where operands precede their operators. Today's programming languages will often translate their code into RPN internally, and use a data stack for expression evaluation. Again, functions are recursively constructed symbolic expressions, and stacks are essential to their unraveling.[4]

Purely functional programs, despite or because of their elegant construction, are rarely found outside computer science textbooks. Most programming jobs involve states of affairs and making changes thereto conditional thereupon, but functions of the purer stripe don't acknowledge the concept of "memory"—for them there is only a continual process of transformation. It's very Zen, very committed, very macrobiotic. A function-ish style of programming, on the other hand, is encouraged in languages like Lisp, Forth, or JavaScript; it is empirically, programmer-lines-of-code-measurably a very productive way to realize interesting and useful things in software. It's about writing many little functions that you then get to reuse inside the definitions of not yet defined little functions, and so on, and so on, bootstrapping one's way up a personal tower of metalinguistic abstraction until at the very top there is perched one final function: the program itself. (Think of a bathtub full of mousetraps, and yourself poised there, ping-pong ball in hand. Think cascades, fusillades, think detonations of denotations. Now let go, let fly.)

Functions as Mappings

But real mathematical functions aren't executable subroutines. A function is an ideal abstract consensual cerebration, and the code a programmer commits is only one out of indefinitely many possible materializations, each a pale sublunary reflection of the ideal. A function proper is propaedeutic, telling how the thing should behave, giving the theory but not concerning itself with how it is to be implemented. The "real" sine function, for example, defined over the real numbers, would require infinite-precision arithmetic—demanding an infinite supply of memory to inscribe its unscrolling digits, and asking all eternity for its satisfaction.

Our familiarity with functions like the sine curve shouldn't get in the way of a more general, modern conception of functions as mappings. Functions as understood by programmers are pretty close to the modern idea. That computers can't represent continuous values isn't really a big deal; human mathematicians, after all, share the same limitation. (Even if by dint of drill and long contemplation they learn to conceive in themselves a supple, subtle, logical intuition of the infinitely great and the vanishingly small, to the point where they may indeed come to see their occult fictions as Reality. As actually the realer Reality. As indeed, gone far and deep enough into their cups, the very thoughts of God.)[5]

A function can be regarded as a look-up table (often enough it may be implemented as one too) which is to say a mapping from a certain symbol, the look-up key, to a value associated with this key. Modern scripting languages typically include as a native data type the "associative array" (also known as hash table, dictionary, or map) for managing look-up tables of arbitrary complexity. In JavaScript associative arrays are at the same time "objects," the main building blocks (as "lists" are in Lisp) out of which all other entities are constructed. Associative arrays, as the name suggests, can, with a bit of coding cleverness, give software an associative capability, permitting programmers to emulate (after a fashion) the more flexible, soft-edged categories of natural cognition,[6] against the all-or-nothing, true-or-false Boolean logic, which many people still seem to think is all that computers are capable of.

To briefly pursue the organic analogy: individual neurons, while glacially slow by comparison with CPU switching speeds, in their imprecise massively parallel way still vastly "outcompute" (buying the theory that computations are what brains do) the swiftest supercomputers. It's a version of the classic algorithmic trade-off between processing time and memory space, first essayed by the nineteenth-century computing pioneer Charles Babbage.[7] It may often be advantageous to precompute a function and save having to recalculate it later by compiling the results into a table of key-value pairs (with its argument vector as the look-up key and the result returned as the key's value), perhaps with a rule for interpolating (or "connecting the dots") between tabulated data values at look-up time. In cases where all one has is a collection of discrete samples—where the function that generated the data isn't known a priori, for example measurements of things and events taking place in the world—a look-up table and a rule for smoothing the data belonging to nearby or similar points is hard to beat. (Many of the techniques used in statistics and neural network modeling can be seen as wrinkles on this "nearest neighbors" idea.) Such numerical methods date back to the Ptolemys, when trigonometric tables were first compiled for use by astronomers, navigators, and builders.

Functions and Logic

A function is an abstract replica of causality. It's what it is to be a simple, deterministic machine: the same input must always map to the same output. This intuition is at the heart of logic. If repeating the same operation with the same input gives a different output, you know without a doubt that something changed: it isn't the function you thought it was, it isn't a simple machine. Or perhaps one's measuring instrument was faulty; maybe you blinked. Still you will know for certain that something went sideways since (it is of our humanness to believe) nothing happens without a reason. This inferential form was anciently termed "modus tollens." It says that "A implies B; but not B; hence not A." In other words, there is some theory "A" with testable consequence "B," but when the experiment is performed the predicted outcome wasn't observed, so we must conclude (assuming that the twin constancies of nature and reason haven't failed us) that the theory was wrong.[8]

There's a one-wayness to functions, an asymmetry. They can be one-to-one, where a single input value (which could be an argument list or vector made up of several values) is associated with a single output value. Or they can go from many-to-one: two or more inputs arrive at the same output. But they can never go from one-to-many. The same input must always—if this thing is rational, if it's a machine—produce the same result. One can't in general simply replace a function's inputs by its outputs, run the function backwards and expect to get the inputs back as the result; that isn't deterministic, it's not a function, it will not work.

The exception to the above would be a class of reversible logic functions that at some point might emerge from pure theory to find practical uses in cryptography and/or quantum computing.

Theoretically, a universal computer could be made entirely out of reversible logic gates; in principle therefore any irreversible function can be replaced by a reversible function having certain nice theoretical properties like extremely low or even nonexistent power dissipation. It will certainly be interesting to see what comes of it. There are a few well-known examples of simple reversible functions: multiplication by −1, which toggles the sign of a number; the Boolean NOT (turning 0 into 1, and 1 into 0); and EXCLUSIVE OR. This last-named is a personal favorite: given two equal-length bit-patterns as inputs, XOR will yield a bit-pattern which XORed with either of the two original bit-patterns reproduces the other one. But these simple reversible functions are not sufficient for universal reversible computation.[9]

A corollary of the asymmetry of functions is that observing a function's output, even when we know its internal mechanism, doesn't allow inferring with certainty the input that caused the output. What is past is past, nor is it logically valid to adduce absent causes from present signs: a moment's reflection will reveal that any state of affairs could be a consequence of many different possible causes. How odd then, that this native forensic mode of reasoning, in real life so relied upon, should be logically invalid. Aristotle called it the "enthymeme" or "logically fallacy" of "affirming the consequent." (An unfortunate translation: logical fallacies though fallible need not always lead to false conclusions.) To affirm the consequent reverses the deductive syllogism ("modus ponens") which states, "If A implies B, and A, then B." It is to say rather, "If A implies B, and B, then A." The American philosopher C. S. Peirce thought affirming the consequent (which he termed "abduction") was after deduction and induction, the missing but vital third form of reasoning without which any account of logic or science would remain incomplete. It's what the palaeontologist does in reconstructing a whole brontosaurus from a brontosaur's toe-bone; or the detective, in reconstructing a crime. It is the fallible anti-logic, the "analogic," of sense perception, pattern recognition, diagnosis: how we read the signs and in-between the lines.[10] Computer science rediscovered abductive inference in the 1980s; it had been neglected since AI broke with cybernetics and information theory some twenty years before.

Abductive or analogical pattern-matching is easily realized by means of an inverted index, a variant form of look-up table where rather than having keys mapped to single values they are mapped to sets or lists of values. (An inverted index therefore isn't a function but rather a "relation.") Nothing too complicated, it's how a book index or search engine works. The words given in a search query will have already been associated by the search engine with lists of spidered web pages where these terms have occurred. The best matching pages are identified by superimposing the result lists belonging to the given terms, so that the more times a page is cited in the aggregated multiset, then the higher, all else being equal (indexes also employ statistical methods that assign numeric "weights" to terms and items to better reflect their probable relevance) it will be placed in the outcome.[11]

The index, as it were, "reverses time."[12] It is an imperfect, indeterminate, in logical terms strictly illegitimate one-to-many mapping that goes from a single "effect" (the input key) to the set of its multiple possible "causes" (the key's inverted file). It is a kind of abstract deconvolution, a way to tackle what physical scientists call the "general inverse problem." The evidential traces or signs of an event are convolutions (literally "enfoldings") of the event with whatever objects or medium its nth-order effects encounter and become mixed up with. The material imparts its own intrinsic bias or twist to the event record; it acts like a filter or lens. To recover an "image" of the time-and-space-distant original entails superimposing many scattered, diffuse, faint, redundant, and to unknown degree noise-corrupted[13] signals from its spreading "event-cone." A term from physical optics perfectly captures the idea: "circles of confusion." Drawn together[14] and superimposed, the circles of confusion resolve an image (doubtless rather blurry, but still useful) of the original event. (The "circles" are really cross-sectional slices of a spherical (roughly) wavefront of effects propagating outwardly in space and forward in time to intersect the plane of image formation in what I hope isn't too strained an analogy.)

Embedding Functions

Computers and software, for all that they have become ordinary parts of life and when working correctly are as much taken for granted as sewers or electricity, are scaffolded upon certain inviolable rules, "deep structures" that underlie (we are led to infer) both physical reality and the mental apparatus by whose aid we are able to recognize and grasp reality, to name and shape it. The elements of software, its functions and variables, are at bottom simple things; as equally, in the faith of scientists and philosophers, must be the elements and principles which make up the world.

But software also teaches that the simplicity is hard-won; it is hard to slow thoughts down to allow their dissection into irreducible, atomic components of structure and action that permit reconstructing them into something that behaves the way you imagined it would when you had the idea. Underwriting the ability of people to create software is a bedrock gnosis of "how things work," a kinesthetic intuition of causes and effects that is as much physical as logical. The function is a mental diagram of an ideal machine. With the development of computers, so deeply enmeshed in the semiconductor physics of the substrate, it became evident (if it wasn't before) that thought's rigging of logic—the "it-is-so"-ness of recognizing when a thing makes sense and when it doesn't, quite—is at least conditioned by the basic construction of the world; and that to know one clearly is also to know the other.[15]

Notes

1. Gertrude Stein, as quoted in William Gass, *The World Within the Word.*

2. Alfred North Whitehead, *Introduction to Mathematics.*

3. Pride of place goes to the "A-O compiler," created in 1952 for the Remington Rand UNIVAC computer by a team under Grace Hopper's admiralship. Also notworthy is Kenneth Iverson's APL, which was an early functional programming language originating in a Fortran matrix subroutine library. (K. E. Iverson, *A Programming Language.*)

4. For stacks, see Phil Koopman's definitive, *Stack Computers: The New Wave,* now available online from the author's home page.

5. No one save the mathematician or theologian could get so precise about something that by its definition is so indefinite. It's not for nothing (it was rather for aleph-null)

that the finest speculative theologist of the modern era was Georg Cantor, inventor of set theory and the transfinite numbers. (Even while his career in the higher abstraction was punctuated by periods of enforced repose in asylums for the deeply spiritually afflicted.)

6. The psychologist Roger Shepard, in an essay on the preconditions of knowing, describes how the world transduced by the sensory enfilade serves as an index into "consequential regions of psychological space" where are found and activated a suite of innate and acquired propensities and preparednesses—memories and knowledge that will likely prove equal to the circumstances at hand. Vertebrate brains seem to be organized in such a way that a high-dimensional feature vector (a "sparse population code" representing the animal's ensemble sensory nerve activity) acts as an "address" into, in effect, a very large, wet, sloppy look-up table. (R. N. Shepard, "Towards a Universal Law of Generalization for Psychological Studies.") in *Science* Vol. 237 Issue 4820.

7. Charles Babbage, *The Ninth Bridgewater Treatise.*

8. Sir Karl Popper was knighted for, among other things, having pointed out that the power of science is mostly negative, and that scientific progress proceeds by disproving erroneous theories (i.e., by modus tollens) not by proving "correct" theories true. The latter possibility obtains only in tightly circumscribed synthetic worlds like Euclidean geometry or deductive logic—or, in principle, software. Resolution theorem proving—the basis of the logic programming language Prolog—does its stuff by disproving in a reductio ad absurdum the logical complement of the proposition whose truth one wishes to prove. Obviously it can only work under the closed-world assumption that each concept has one and only one antithesis whose negation exactly reproduces and so vouchsafes true the original proposition. Full certainty can only be had in a deductive system whose logical, causal constitution has been established from the bottom up. (Descartes: "If you want to know how a body works, or a world, then build one.")

9. Pop science treatments of quantum computing (and the role of reversible functions therein) include Julian Brown, *Minds, Machines, and the Multiverse.* People who are tired of being told that quantum mechanics (and with it virtually the entire past hundred years of physics) must lie forever beyond the grasp of ordinary understanding will appreciate Carver Mead's well-credentialed demurral, *Collective Electrodynamics.*

10. On abduction: Carlo Ginzburg, "Clues: Morelli, Freud, Sherlock Holmes."

11. For best matching see Derek Robinson, "Index and Analogy: A Footnote to the Theory of Signs." The first inverted index was the Biblical concordance undertaken in 1230 by an ecclesiastical data processing department of five-hundred monks,

directed by Hugo de Sancto Caro (Hugues de Saint-Cher), a Dominican friar later made a cardinal.

12. In an intriguing if eccentric book, *Symmetry, Causality, Mind,* computer vision researcher Michael Leyton proposes that "time reversal" is the sole task undertaken by intelligence. He sees vision as a two-fold problem: first, the eye must reverse the formation of the optical image incident on the retina (a classic "inverse problem") to identify objects and the spatial relations between them; secondly, the mind must "reverse the formation of the environment"—it must adduce reasons why these objects should be where they are, and should have the forms they have, and it must ascertain as best it can the intentions or implications of these things with respect to its own needs and goals. Only then can it be in a position to decide what, if anything, to do about the situation.

13. "Noise-corrupted" is synonymous with "massively convolved with impractically many broadly diffused and attenuated traces of events that we happen not to be interested in right now."

14. "Drawn together"—see Bruno Latour's essay "Drawing Things Together" for an account of broadly analogous issues in the social production of knowledge.

15. Readers with a taste for such deliberations might enjoy following the elegant turns Paul Valery's curiosity takes in his essay, "Man and the Seashell."

■

Glitch

Olga Goriunova and Alexei Shulgin

This term is usually identified as jargon, used in electronic industries and services, among programmers, circuit-bending practitioners, gamers, media artists, and designers. In electrical systems, a glitch is a short-lived error in a system or machine. A glitch appears as a defect (a voltage-change or signal of the wrong duration—a change of input) in an electrical circuit. Thus, a glitch is a short-term deviation from a correct value and as such the term can also describe hardware malfunctions. The outcome of a glitch is not predictable.

When applied to software, the meaning of glitch is slightly altered. A glitch is an unpredictable change in the system's behavior, when *something obviously goes wrong.*

Glitch is often used as a synonym for bug; but not for error. An error might produce a glitch but might not lead to a perceivable malfunction of a system. Errors in software are usually structured as: syntax errors (grammatical errors in a program), logic errors (error in an algorithm), and exception errors (arising from unexpected conditions and events).

Glitches have become an integral part of computer culture and some phenomena are perceived as glitches although they are not glitches in technical terms. Artifacts that look like glitches do not always result from an error. What users might perceive as "glitchy" can arise from a normally working function of a program. Sometimes these might originate from technical limitations, such as low image-processing speed or low bandwidth when displaying video. For example, the codecs of some video-conferencing software, such as CU-Seeme,[1] visibly "pixelize" the image, allowing the compression of parts of the images that remain static over different frames when, for instance, the transfer speed drops.

To comply with the customary usage of "glitch" we propose to think of glitches as resulting from error, though in reality it might be difficult or impossible to distinguish whether the particular glitch is planned or results from a problem. To understand the roles glitches play in culture, knowing their origin is not of primary importance. Understanding glitches as erroneous brings more to a comprehension of their role than trying to give a clear definition that would include or subordinate encoded glitches and glitches as malfunctions.

Glitches are usually regarded as marginal. In reality, glitches can be claimed to be a manifestation of genuine software aesthetics. Let us look at machine aesthetics as formed by functionality and dysfunctionality, and then proceed to the concept of glitches as computing's aesthetic core, as marks of (dys)functions, (re)actions and (e)motions that are worked out in human-computer assemblages.

Computers do not have a recognizable or significant aesthetic that possesses some kind of authenticity and completeness. It is commonplace that the aesthetics of software are largely adopted from other spheres, media, and conventions. Thus, the desktop is a metaphor for a writing table, icons descend from labels or images of objects, while the command line interface is inherited from telegraph, teletype, and typewriter.

The aesthetics of computers that developed over a few decades from the early 1950s to the early 1980s, when they were first introduced to the public and on to the current time (consisting of dynamic menus, mouse, pointer, direct manipulation of objects on the screen, buttons, system sounds, human computer interaction models) are, in our opinion, not rich and self-sufficient enough to be called the aesthetic of the computer.

On top of that the current aesthetic of software is not complete; it does not work very well as it does not contribute enough to the computer's user-friendliness. Besides, it is a widely acknowledged problem that the customary information design principles of arranging computer data, derived from earlier conventions (such as the treelike folder structure), result in users having problem, with data archiving and the memorization of document names and locations.

Historically, the shape, style, and decoration of every new technology has been introduced in a manner owing much to the aesthetics and thinking customary of the time. Thus, when mechanism had not yet replaced naturalism as means of framing reality, Lewis Mumford argues, mechanisms were introduced with organic symbols. For instance, a typical eighteenth century automaton, "the clockwork Venus," consisted of a female mannequin resting on top of a clockwork mechanism.[2] As technology developed further, some genuine machine aesthetics were born, primarily derived from machine functionality. And it was their functionality that some avant-garde movements of the twentieth century admired in the machine. For instance, among the Russian avant-garde movements of the beginning of the twentieth century (e.g., Cubo-Futurism, Abstractionism, Rayonism, Suprematism) artists such as Mayakovsky, Gontcharova, Kandinsky, Larionov, and Malevich poeticized new machines for their speed, energy, and dynamics. The methods they used to depict movement, light, power, and speed could be regarded aesthetically as grandparents of some of today's glitches (certain correlation of color mass; unlimited diversity of colors, lines and forms; repeating geometrical structures, figures, lines, dots, etc.).

Rationalism and the precision of technical creation inspired many. Thus, Meyerhold writes: "Arts should be based on scientific grounds."[3] Russian constructivists such as Tatlin established a compositional organization based on the kinetics of simple objects and complex ideas of movement—rotating inner mechanisms and open structure, using "real" materials—all intended to function for utilitarian use. Punin writes of Tatlin's Tower: "Beneath our eyes there is being solved the most complex problem of culture: utilitarian form becomes pure creative form."[4]

Functional machines, primarily built by engineers, established strong aesthetic principles that have defined technological design for years. Functional elements are later used as nonfunctional design elements that are appreciated as "beautiful" by users not least due to the cultural memory of their origin. For instance, the curved part of the wing over the tire of some car models reproduces the guards used in horse-driven vehicles and early automobiles to protect users and vehicle from dust and to affix lights onto. It does not carry any advance in function, but is used in automobile design as a recognizable and nostalgic element.

Today, the functionality of the computer is concealed inside the gray/white/beige box that covers the cards, slots, motherboard, and wires. In modding[5] these parts are reimagined as elements of visual richness that convey a symbolism. Hardware elements are aestheticized: Users might install neon lights, weird jumbo fans and colorful wires into a transparent computer case or even build an entirely new one from scratch. Electronic boards jutting out at 90 degree angles and architectures of twisted wire are widely used, as in cinema and design, to represent *technical substances*.

By contrast, the way data is presented on a hard drive is not human-readable. It is stored in different segments of the disk and reassembled each time the documents are retrieved according to a plan kept as a separate file. Software functionality here is invisible and an interface is needed to use the machine. Modern software almost always conceals its functionality behind the window. It provides us instead with images such as a page flying from one folder to another, an hourglass, or that of a gray line gradually being filled with color.

There are moments in the history of computer technology that are rich in computer functionality producing distinct aesthetics. At such times, computer functionality reveals itself through technological limitations. Bottlenecks, such as processor speed, screen resolution, color depth, or network bandwidth—4-bit, 8-bit music, 16-color pixelized visuals, slow rendering, compressed image and video with artifacts—create an authentic computer aesthetics, that is, the aesthetics of low-tech today.

There are vast contemporary 8-bit music communities (such as Micromusic .net), based entirely on producing music on emulators or surviving models of the early home computers of the 1980s, such as Atari or Commodore. Alongside producing sine waves, the sound chips of such computers attempted to simulate preexisting musical reality: guitar, percussion, piano. Imperfect and restricted, the chips could only produce idiosyncratic, funny and easy to recognize sounds which were far from the originals. Scarcity of means encouraged a special aesthetics of musical low-tech: of coolness, romanticism and imperfection. People making 8-bit music nowadays relate back to their childhoods' favorite toys, memories that are shared by many people. Returning to a genuine computer aesthetics of obsolete technology is not a question of individual choice, but has the quality of a communal, social decision.

Functionality, as a characteristic of established machine aesthetics is always chased by dysfunctionality (if not preceded by it). Functional machines, robots, mechanized people (from Judaism's Golem,[6] Frankenstein's monster[7]) to the rebellious computers of the twentieth century) are interpreted as alien to human nature, sooner or later becoming "evil" as they stop functioning correctly. Thus, the dysfunctional mind, conduct, and vision become human, compelling, sincere, meaningful, revelatory. As aesthetic principles, chance, unplanned action, and uncommon behaviors were already central to European and Russian literature of the nineteenth century in the work of writers such as Balzac, Flaubert and Dostoyevsky.

In the technological era, society became organized according to the logic of machines, conveyor belt principles, "rationally" based discrimination theories, and war technology, with an increase in fear, frustration, refusal, and protest. As a response, errors, inconsistencies of vision, of method, and of behavior become popular modernist artistic methods used in Dadaism, Surrealism, and other art movements. One of Surrealism's declared predecessors, the Comte de Lautréamont, provided us with the lasting phrase that something could be as "beautiful as the chance encounter of a sewing machine and an umbrella on a dissection table."[8] The introduction of chance, "hasard," (fr.), subconsciousness, and irrationality into art and life was seen as being both opposed to and deeply embedded in rationality and functionality.

Dysfunctional machines are not only those that are broken (images and figures of crashed cars and other mass produced imperfections figure in the aesthetics of Fluxus and Pop Art); they are also those that do not comply with the general logic of machines, by acting irrationally and sometimes even turning into humans. Thus, at the end of the Soviet movie *Adventures of Electronic Boy* (1977), a robotic boy starts crying and this emotion symbolizes that he has become human.

A glitch is a singular dysfunctional event that allows insight beyond the customary, omnipresent, and alien computer aesthetics. A glitch is a mess that is a moment, a possibility to glance at software's inner structure, whether it is a mechanism of data compression or HTML code. Although a glitch does not reveal the true functionality of the computer, it shows the ghostly conventionality of the forms by which digital spaces are organized.

Glitches are produced by error and are usually not intended by humans. As a not-entirely human-produced reality, its elements are not one-hundred percent compatible with customary human logic, visual, sound, or behavioral conventions of organizing and acting in space. Aesthetically some glitches might inherit from avant-garde currents, but are not directly a product of the latter (figure 8). Avant-garde artists inspired or disgusted by technology and its societal influence have created a range of artistic responses, the aesthetics of which today's glitches strangely seem to comply with. A glitch reminds us of our cultural experience at the same time as developing it by suggesting new aesthetic forms.

A glitch is stunning. It appears as a temporary replacement of some boring conventional surface; as a crazy and dangerous momentum (Will the computer come back to "normal"? Will data be lost?) that breaks the expected flow. A glitch is the loss of control. When the computer does the unexpected and goes beyond the borders of the commonplace, changes the context, acts as if it is not logical but profoundly irrational, behaves not in the way technology should,

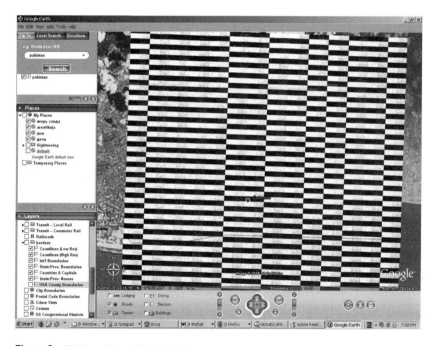

Figure 8 Glitch on *Google Earth,* 2006.

it releases the tension and hatred of the user toward an ever-functional but uncomfortable machine.

Error sets free the irrational potential and works out the fundamental concepts and forces that bind people and machines. An error [is] a sign of the absence of an ideal functionality, whether it be understood in the technical, social or economic sense.[9]

As with every new aesthetic form, glitches are compelling for artists and designers as well as regular users. Glitches are an important realm in electronic and digital arts. Some artists focus on finding, saving, developing, and conceptualizing glitches, and glitches form entire currents in sonic arts and creative music making. For example, the Dutch-Belgian group Jodi are known for their attention to all kinds of computer visual manifestations that go beyond well-known interfaces. It's enough only to look at their web-page http://wwwwwwwww.jodi.org to get a sense of their style (figure 9). On http://text.jodi.org a user browses through an endless sequence of pages that are obviously

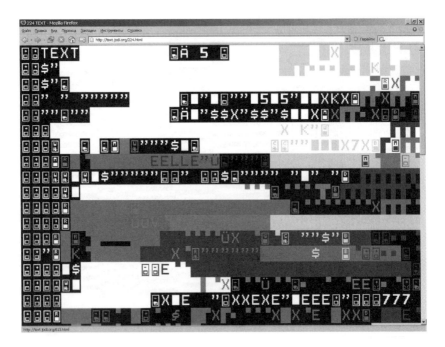

Figure 9   JODI, http://text.jodi.org.

of computer origin, and appear to be both meaningless and fascinatingly beautiful.

Video gamers practice glitching (exploiting bugs in games).[10] Game modifications by Jodi, such as *Untitled Game,*[11] as well as by other artists, such as Joan Leandre's *(Retroyou) R/C* and *NostalG*[12] are achieved by altering parts of the code of existing games (figure 10). The resulting games range from absurd environments in which cars can be driven, but with a distinct tendency to sometimes fly into outer space, to messy visual environments one can hardly navigate, but which reveal dazzling digital aesthetic qualities.

In his *aPpRoPiRaTe!* (figure 11) Sven Koenig exploits a bug found in a video player that makes a video compression algorithm display itself.[13] By deleting or modifying key frames (an encoded movie does not contain all full frames but a few key frames, the rest of the frames are saved as differences between key frames) he manages to modify the entire film without much effort. As a result

Figure 10   Jean Leandre, *(Retroyou) R/C.*

Figure 11 Stefan Koenig, *aPpRoPiRaTe!*.

we get excitingly distorted yet recognizable variants of videos popular in file exchange networks, where such algorithms are widely used. And, of course, with this much work already done for them in advance, we'll see the power of the new aesthetics of the glitch used in commercial products very soon.

Notes

1. Traces of CU-SeeMe can be found through http://archive.org by searching for http://cu-seeme.com.

2. Lewis Mumford, *Technics and Civilization*, 52–55.

3. Vsevolod Meyerhold, "Artist of the Future," in *Hermitage,* no. 6, 10.

4. Nikolay Punin, *The Memorial to the Third International,* 5.

5. See "case modification" in Wikipedia: http://en.wikipedia.org/wiki/Case_modification/.

6. For an excellent account of Golem, see: http://en.wikipedia.org/wiki/Golem/.

7. Mary Shelley, *Frankenstein.*

8. Lautréamont, *Les chants de Maldoror,* Russian edition, 55.

9. Pit Schultz, "Jodi as a Software Culture." in Tilman Baumgarten, ed. *Install.exe,* Christoph Merian Verlag.

10. See "glitch" in Wikipedia: http://en.wikipedia.org/wiki/Glitch/.

11. JODI, http://wwwwwwwww.jodi.org/.

12. Joan Leandre (Retroyou), R/C and NostalG, http://www.retroyou.org/ and http://runme.org/project/+SOFTSFRAGILE/.

13. Sven Koenig, *aPpRoPiRaTe!,* http://popmodernism.org/appropirate/.

■

Import/Export

Lev Manovich

Although "import"/"export" commands appear in most modern media authoring and editing software running under GUI, at first sight they do not seem to be very important for understanding software culture. You are not authoring new media or modifying media objects or accessing information across the globe, as in web browsing. All these commands allow you to do is to move data around between different applications. In other words, they make data created in one application compatible with other applications. And that does not look so glamorous.

But think again. What is the largest part of the economy of the greater Los Angeles area? It is not entertainment—from movie production to museums and everything in between accounts for only around 15 percent. It turns out that the largest part is import/export business, accounting for over 60 percent. A commonly invoked characteristic of globalization is greater connectivity— places, systems, countries, organizations, etc., becoming connected in more and more ways. And connectivity can only happen if you have certain level of compatibility: between business codes and procedures, between shipping technologies, between network protocols, and so on.

Let us take a closer look at import/export commands. As I will try to show, these commands play a crucial role in software culture, and in particular in media design. Because my own experience is in visual media, my examples will come from this area, but the processes I describe apply now to all media designed with software.

Before they adopted software tools in the 1990s, filmmakers, graphic designers, and animators used completely different technologies. Therefore, as much as they were influenced by each other or shared similar aesthetic sensibilities, they inevitably created different-looking images. Filmmakers used camera and film technology designed to capture three-dimensional physical reality. Graphic designers worked with offset printing and lithography. Animators worked with their own technologies: transparent cells and animation stands with stationary film cameras capable of making exposures one frame at a time as the animators changed cells and/or moved background.

As a result, twentieth-century cinema, graphic design, and animation (that is, standard animation techniques used by commercial studios) developed distinct artistic languages and vocabularies both in terms of form and content. For example, graphic designers worked with a two dimensional space; film directors arranged compositions in three-dimensional space; and cell animators worked with a "two-and-a-half" dimensional space. This holds for the overwhelming majority of works produced in each field, although of course exceptions do exist. (For instance, Oscar Fishinger made one abstract film that involved moving three-dimensional shapes, but as far as I know, this is the only time in the whole history of abstract animation where we see an abstract three-dimensional space).

The differences in technology influenced what kind of content would appear in different media. Cinema showed photorealistic images of nature, built environment, and human forms articulated by special lighting. Graphic designs featured typography, abstract graphic elements, monochrome backgrounds, and cutout photographs. And cartoons showed hand-drawn flat characters and objects animated over hand-drawn but more detailed backgrounds. The exceptions are rare. For instance, while architectural spaces frequently appear in films they almost never appeared in animated films in any detail—until animation studios started using 3-D computer animation.

Why was it so difficult to cross boundaries? In theory one could imagine making an animated film in the following way: printing a series of slightly different graphic designs and then filming them as though they were a sequence of animated cells. Or in a film, a designer could make a series of hand drawings that use the exact vocabulary of graphic design and then film them one by one. And yet, to the best of my knowledge, such a film was never made. What we find instead are many abstract animated films that reflect the styles of abstract painting. We can find abstract films, animated commercials, as well as movie titles in the graphic design style of the times. For instance, some moving image sequences made by motion graphics pioneer Pablo Ferro around 1960s display psychedelic aesthetics which can be also found in posters, record covers, and other works of graphic design in the same period.[1]

And yet, it is never exactly the same language. Projected film could not adequately show the subtle differences between typeface sizes, line widths, and grayscale tones crucial for modern graphic design. Therefore, when the artists were working on abstract art films or commercials that used design aesthetics (and most key abstract animators produced both), they could not simply expand the language of printed page into time dimension. They had to invent a parallel visual language that used bold contrasts, more easily readable forms and thick lines, which because of their thickness were in fact no longer lines but shapes.

Although the limitations in resolution and contrast of film and television image compared to that of the printed page played a role in keeping the distance between the languages used by abstract filmmakers and graphic designers for the most of the twentieth century, ultimately I do not think it was the decisive factor. Today the resolution, contrast, and color reproduction between print, computer screens, and television screens are also substantially different, and yet we often see exactly the same visual strategies deployed across these different display media. If you want to be convinced, leaf through any book or a magazine on contemporary 2-D design (i.e., graphic design for print, broadcast, and the web). When you look at a spread featuring the works of a particular designer or design studio, in most cases it is impossible to identify the origins of the images unless you read the captions. Only then do you find that this image is a poster, that one is a still from a music video, and this one is a magazine editorial.

Taschen's *Graphic Design for the 21st Century: 100 of the World's Best Graphic Designers* has several good examples.[2] Peter Anderson's images showing a heading against a cloud of hundreds of little letters in various orientations turn out to be the frames from the title sequence for a television documentary. Another of his images, which similarly contrasts jumping letters in a large font against irregularly cut planes made from densely packed letters in much smaller fonts turns to be a spread from *IT Magazine*. Since the first design was made for broadcast while the second was made for print, we would expect that the first design would employ bolder forms; however, both designs use the same scale between big and small fonts, and feature texture fields composed from text that does not need to be read. A few pages later we encounter a design by Philippe Apeloig that uses exactly the same technique and aesthetic as Anderson. In this case, tiny lines of text positioned at different angles form a 3-D shape floating in space. On the next page another design by Apeloig also creates a field in perspective made from hundreds of identical abstract shapes.

These designs rely on software's ability (or on the designer being influenced by software use and following the same logic while doing the design manually) to treat text as any graphical primitive and to easily create compositions made from hundreds of similar or identical elements positioned according to some pattern. Since an algorithm can easily modify each element in the pattern, changing its position, size, color, etc., instead of the completely regular grids of modernism we see more complex structures that are made from many variations of the same element.

Each designer included in the Taschen book was asked to provide a brief statement to accompany the portfolio of their work, and the design studio Lust provided this phrase as their motto: "Form-follows-process." So what is the nature of the design process in the software age, and how does it influence the forms we see today around us?

Everybody who is involved in design and art today knows that contemporary designers use the same set of software tools to design everything. The crucial factor is not the tools themselves but the workflow process, enabled by "import" and "export" operations.

When a particular media project is being put together, the software used at the final stage depends on the type of output media and the nature of the project. For instance, After Effects is used for motion graphics projects and video compositing, Illustrator or Freehand is for print illustrations, InDesign for graphic design, Flash for interactive interfaces and web animations, and 3DS Max or Maya for 3-D computer models and animations. But these programs are rarely used alone to create a media design from start to finish. Typically, a designer may create elements in one program, import them into another program, add elements created in yet another program, and so on. This happens regardless of whether the final product is an illustration for print, a website, or a motion graphics sequence, whether it is a still or a moving image, interactive or noninteractive, etc. Given this production workflow, we may expect that the same visual techniques and strategies will appear in all media designed with computers.

A designer can use Illustrator or Freehand to create a 2-D curve (technically, a spline). This curve becomes a building block that can be used in any project. It can form a part of an illustration or a book design. It can be imported into an animation program where it can be set into motion, or imported into 3-D program where it can be extruded in 3-D space to define a solid form.

Each of the types of programs used by media designers—3-D graphics, vector drawing, image editing, animation, compositing—excel at particular design operations, that is, particular ways of creating a design element or modifying on already existing element. These operations can be compared to the different blocks of a Lego set. While you can make an infinite number of projects out of these blocks, most of the blocks will be utilized in every project, although they will have different functions and appear in different combinations. For example, a rectangular red block may become a part of the tabletop, part of the head of a robot, etc.

Design workflow that uses multiple software programs works in a similar way, except the building blocks are not just the different kinds of visual elements one can create—vector patterns, 3-D objects, particle systems, etc.—but also various ways of modifying these elements: blur, skew, vectorize, change transparency level, spherisize, extrude, etc. This difference is very important. If media creation and editing software did not include these and many other modification operations, we would see an altogether different visual language at work today. Instead of "digital multimedia"—designs that simply combine elements from different media—we see what I call "metamedia"—the remixing of working methods and techniques of different media within a single project.

Here are a few typical examples of this media remixability that can be seen in the majority of design projects done today around the world. Motion blur is applied to 3-D computer graphics; computer generated fields of particles are blended with live action footage to produce an enhanced look; flat drawings are placed into virtual spaces where a virtual camera moves around them; flat typography is animated as though it is made from a liquid-like material (the liquid simulation coming from computer animation software). Today a typical short film or a sequence may combine many of such pairings within the same frame. The result is a hybrid, intricate, complex, and rich media language—or rather, numerous languages that share the basic logic of remixabilty.

Import/Export

The production workflow specific to the software age has two major consequences: the hybridity of media language we see today in the contemporary design universe, and the techniques and strategies used are similar regardless of the output media and type of project. Like an object built from Lego blocks today's typical design combines techniques coming from multiple media. It uses the results of the operations specific to different software programs that were originally created to imitate work with different physical media (e.g., Illustrator was created to make illustrations, Photoshop to edit digitized photographs, After Effects to create 2-D animation, etc.). While these techniques continue to be used in relation to their original media, most of them are now also used as part of the workflow on any design job.

The essential condition that enables this new design logic and the resulting aesthetic is compatibility between files generated by different programs. In other words, "import" and "export" commands of graphics, animation, video editing, compositing, and modeling software are historically more important than the individual operations these programs offer. The ability to combine raster and vector layers within the same image, to place 3-D elements into a 2-D composition and vice versa, and so on, is what enables the production workflow with its reuse of the same techniques, effects, and iconography across different media.

The consequences of this compatibility between software and file formats that was gradually achieved during the 1990s are hard to overestimate. Besides the hybridity of modern visual aesthetics and the reappearance of the same design techniques across all output media, there are also other effects. For instance, the whole field of motion graphics as it exists today came into existence to a large extent because of the integration between vector drawing software, specifically Illustrator, and animation/compositing software such as After Effects. A designer typically defines various composition elements in Illustrator and then imports them into After Effects, where they are animated. This compatibility did not exist when the initial versions of different media authoring and editing software initially became available in the 1980s. It was gradually added in subsequent software releases. But when it was achieved around the middle of the 1990s, within a few years the whole language of contemporary graphic design was fully imported into the moving image area—both literally and metaphorically.

In summary, the compatibility between graphic design, illustration, animation, and visual effects software has played the key role in shaping the visual and spatial forms of the software age. On the one hand, never before have we witnessed such a variety of forms as today. On the other hand, exactly the same techniques, compositions, and iconography can now appear in any media. And at the same time, any single design may combine multiple operations that previously only existed within distinct physical or computer media.

Notes

1. Jeff Bellantoni and Matt Woolman, *Type in Motion: Innovations in Digital Graphics*, 26–27.

2. Charlotte Fiell and Peter Fiell, eds., *Graphic Design for the 21st Century: 100 of the World's Best Graphic Designers*.

■

Information

Ted Byfield

"Information" can describe everything from a precise mathematical property of communication systems, to discrete statements of fact or opinion, to a staple of marketing rhetoric, to a world-historical phenomenon on the order of agriculture or industrialization. The frequency and disparity of its use, by specialists and lay people alike, to describe countless general and specific aspects of life, makes it difficult to analyze; no single academic discipline or method can offer an adequate explanation of the term or the concept, to say nothing of the phenomena it encompasses.

A typical approach to a problem of this kind is to address it on the level of the word as such: to gather examples of its use, codify their meanings, and arrange them into a taxonomy, whether "synchronic" (limited to a specific period—say, current usage), or "diachronic" (as they have transformed over time). This has been done, of course, with varying degrees of success. One prominent American-English dictionary defines the word in slightly less than two hundred words. These efforts are admirable, but the popularity of claims that we live in an "information society" (or even more grandly in an "information age") suggest, in their inclusiveness, that information is the sum of the word's multiple meanings. Apparently, it—the word or, more properly, the category—is *sui generis*, and in a particularly compelling way. What qualities make it so?

The word itself dates in English to the late fourteenth century, and even so many centuries ago was used in ways that mirror current ambiguities. The *Oxford English Dictionary* cites early attestations (in, among other sources, Chaucer's *Canterbury Tales*) as evidence for defining it variously as "The action of informing" and the "communication of instructive knowledge" (I.1.a); "Communication of the knowledge or 'news' of some fact or occurrence" (I.2); and "An item of training; an instruction" (I.1.b)—generally, an action in the first cases, and a thing in the last case. Even the ambiguity of whether it is singular or plural, which is still unclear, seems to date to the early sixteenth century ("an item of information or intelligence," curiously "with *an* and *pl[ural]*" [I.3.b]).

As the word came into wider use in the centuries leading up to the twentieth, it took on a variety of additional meanings. Of these, the most striking trend was its increasingly legalistic aspect. This included informal usages (for example, related to or derived from "informing" on someone [I.4]) as well as narrow technical descriptions of charges lodged "in order to the [sic] institution of criminal proceedings without formal indictment" (I.5.a) This inconsistency—in one instance referring to particular allegations of a more or less precise factual nature and, in another, to a formal description of a class or type of assertion—is still central to current usage of the word; so are connotations that information relates to operations of the state.

Yet it was in the twentieth century that the word was given decisively different meanings. The first of these modern attestations appears in the work of the British statistician and geneticist R. A Fisher. In his 1925 article, "Theory of Statistical Estimation," published in *Proceedings of the Cambridge Philosophical Society*,[1] he described "the amount of information in a single observation" in the context of statistical analysis. In doing so, he appears to have introduced two crucial aspects to "information": that it is abstract yet measurable, and that it is an aspect or byproduct of an event or process.

"Fisher information" has had ramifications across the physical sciences, but its most famous and most influential elaboration was in the applied context of electronic communications. These (and related) definitions differ from Fisher's work, but they remain much closer to his conception than to any earlier meanings.[2] Three years after Fisher's paper appeared, the American-born electronics researcher Ralph V. L. Hartley, who had studied at Oxford University at almost exactly the same time that Fisher studied at Cambridge (1909–1913) before returning to the United States, published a seminal article in *Bell System Technical Journal*.[3] In it, he built upon the work of the Swedish-American engineer Harry Nyquist (who was working mainly at AT&T and Bell Laboratories), specifically on Nyquist's 1924 paper "Certain Factors Affecting Telegraph Speed,"[4] which sought in part to quantify what he called "intelligence" in the context of a communication system's limiting factors. Hartley's 1928 article, "Transmission of Information," fused aspects of Fisher's conception of information with Nyquist's technical context (albeit without citing either of them, or any other source). In it, he specifically proposed to "set up a quantitative measure whereby the capacities of various systems to transmit information may be compared." He also added another crucial aspect by explicitly distinguishing between "physical as contrasted with psychological considerations"—meaning by the latter, more or less, "meaning." According to Hartley, information is something that can be transmitted but has no specific meaning.

It was on this basis that, decades later, Claude Shannon, the American mathematician and geneticist turned electrical engineer, made the most well known of all modern contributions to the development of the idea of information.[5] At no point in his works did he ever actually define "information"; instead, he offered a model of how to quantitatively measure the reduction of uncertainty in receiving a communication, and he referred to that measure as "information." Shannon's two-part article in 1948, "A Mathematical Theory of Communication,"[6] and its subsequent reprinting with a popularizing explanation in his and Warren Weaver's book, *The Mathematical Theory of Communication*,[7] are widely heralded as the founding moment of what has since come to be known as "information theory," a subdiscipline of applied mathematics dealing with the theory and practice of quantifying data.

Shannon's construction, like those of Nyquist and Hartley, took as its context the problem presented by electronic communications, which by definition are "noisy," meaning that a transmission does not consist purely of intentional signals. Thus, they pose the problem of how to distinguish the intended signal from the inevitable artifacts of the systems that convey it, or, in Shannon's words, how to "reproduc[e] at one point either exactly or approximately a message selected at another point." Shannon was especially clear that he didn't mean meaning:

Frequently the messages have *meaning*; that is they refer to or are correlated according to some system with certain physical or conceptual entities. These semantic aspects of communication are irrelevant to the engineering problem.[8]

In *The Mathematical Theory of Communication*, he and Weaver explained that "information is a measure of one's freedom of choice when one selects a message" from a universe of possible solutions.[9] In everyday usage, "freedom" and "choice" are usually seen as desirable—the more, the better. However, in trying to decipher a message they have a different consequence: The more freedom of choice one has, the more ways one can render the message, and the less sure one can be that a particular reproduction is accurate. Put simply, the more freedom one has, the less one knows.

Small wonder that the author of such a theory would view efforts to apply his ideas in other fields as "suspect."[10] Of course, if Shannon sought to limit the application of his "information" to specific technical contexts—for example, by warning in his popularizing 1949 book that "the word information, in this theory, is used in a special sense that must not be confused with its ordinary usage"—he failed miserably. The applications of his work in computational and communication systems, ranging from read-write operations in storage devices to the principles guiding the design of sprawling networks, have had pervasive effects since their publication."[11] Those effects offer quite enough reason for "nonspecialists" to take a strong interest in information, however it is defined; their interests, and the "popular" descriptions that result, surely carry at least as much weight as Shannon's mathematical prescription.

However disparate these prescriptions and descriptions may be, both typically have one general and essential thing in common: mediation. Where Shannon's information is an abstract measure, analogous to the negative space around a sculpture in a crate, the common experience of what is often called information is indirect, distinguished from some notional immediate or immanent experience by mediation—say, through a commodity (hardware, software, distribution, or subscription) and/or an organization (a manufacturer, a developer, or a "resource"). So, to the growing list of paradoxes that have marked information for centuries—whether it is an action or a thing, singular or plural, an informal assertion of fact or a procedure for making a formal statement, its ambivalent relationship to operations of state, and so on—we can add some modern ones: It is abstract yet measurable, it is significant without necessarily being meaningful, and, last but not least, it is everywhere and nowhere.

It's tempting to ask how a single category that has come to encompass such a babel of ideas could be very useful, of course; the underlying assumption of such a question is that a word's worth is measured by the consistency or specificity of its meanings. That assumption is false: very common words—"stuff," say, or "power"—are useful because they are *indiscriminate* or *polysemic*. But those are very different qualities[12]; for now—which may be very early in terms of historical periodization—information is (or does) both.

On the one hand, it seems to proffer an indiscriminate lumping-together of everything into a single category in common phrases such as "information society," "information age," and "information economy." And those phrases, in turn, are fairly specific compared to the wild (and wildly contradictory) implications attributed to information in commercial communications (for example, advertising and marketing). In those contexts, at one extreme, information appears as a cudgel—a driving, ubiquitous, relentless, inevitable, almost malevolent historical force that overturns assumptions, disrupts and threatens institutions, and forces adaptation. At the other extreme it appears as a carrot—an enticing, endless, immaterial garden of delights in which instantaneous access to timeless knowledge promises the opportunity of transformation for individuals and for the globe as a whole. On the other (equally woolly) hand, information is widely thought to mark a historical divide, for example, in the urban-legend-like claim that people today are exposed to more information in some small unit of time than their indeterminate ancestors were in their lifetime.[13] What remains unclear in these popular claims is whether information itself is new in the sense of a recent historical invention (akin to nuclear fission, for example) or, rather, whether its pervasiveness is new.

Even if we limit ourselves to more sober usages, we are still left with a category that variously includes assertions of specific fact or belief; some type of assertion made in a specific (for example, technical) context; a statement or instruction to be acted upon or executed; a kind of knowledge or communication, maybe vaguely related to "intelligence"; a specific communication, which, additionally, may or may not mean something; an aspect of communication that specifically means nothing; an aspect of specific or general communications that can be measured; and, more loosely, archives and catalogs, facts and factoids, static and streaming data, opinions and ideas, accounts and explanations, answers to questions; and/or virtually any combination thereof.

As noted, the theory of information has played a pivotal role in systems automation and integration, a dominant—maybe *the* dominant—development in postindustrial social and technical innovation. Given the dizzying complexity, breadth, and interdependence of these developments, a single category that provides (if only illusorily) a common reference point for myriad social actors, from individuals right up to nations, might be useful precisely because it is tautological. The reduction to a single term, which itself might mean anything or literally nothing, offers a sort of lexical symbiosis in which technical and popular usages inform each other: Technical usages derive implications of broad social relevance from popular usages, and popular usages derive implications of rigor and effectiveness from technical usages. Yet what's hardest to hear through this cacophony is what might be most useful of all: Gregory Bateson's enigmatic and epigrammatic definition of information as "the difference that make a difference."[14]

Notes

1. R. A. Fisher, "Theory of Statistical Estimation," *Proceedings of the Cambridge Philosophical Society* XXII, (1925) 709.

2. For example, Norbert Wiener, widely credited as the father of cybernetics—that is, the study of feedback systems in living organisms, machines, and organizations—noted in his 1948 book *Cybernetics* that "the definition [of information] . . . is not the one given by R. A. Fisher for statistical problems, although it is a statistical definition" (III.76).

3. V. L. Hartley, "Transmission of Information," *Bell System Technical Journal*, VII, (July 1928) 540.

4. Harry Nyquist, "Certain Factors Affecting Telegraph Speed," *Bell System Technical Journal*, Vol. 3 (April 1924), 324–346.

5. Shannon's PhD dissertation "An Algebra for Theoretical Genetics"—an application of his "queer algebra," in the words of Vannevar Bush—was written at MIT in 1940 under the direction of Barbara Burks, an employee of Eugenics Record Office at Cold Spring Harbor Laboratory; Shannon was recruited by Bell Labs to research "fire-control systems"—automated weapon targeting and activation—"data smoothing," and cryptography during World War II. See Eugene Chiu et al., "The Mathematical Theory of Claude Shannon: A Study of the Style and Context of His Work up to the Genesis of Information Theory."

6. Claude Shannon, "A Mathematical Theory of Communication."

7. Claude Shannon and Warren Weaver, *A Mathematical Theory of Communication.*

8. Ibid, 379.

9. Ibid, 99.

10. David Ritchie, "Shannon and Weaver: Unraveling the Paradox of Information," in *Communication Research*, Vol. 13 No. 2.

11. As this account suggests (and as one should expect), Shannon's work was just one result of many interwoven conceptual and practical threads involving countless researchers and practitioners working across many fields and disciplines. In the two decades that separated Hartley's 1928 article and Shannon's publications, myriad advances had already had immense practical impact—for example, on the conduct and outcome of World War II, in fields as diverse as telegraphy, radiotelegraphy, electromechanical systems automation and synchronization, and cryptography. More generally, an important aspect and a notable result of that war were the unparalleled advances in systems integration across government, industry, and academia, from basic research through procurement, logistics, and application. Shannon's work, as Voltaire might have put it, "had to be invented."

12. "There is always a moment when, the science of certain facts not yet being reduced to concepts, the facts not even being grouped together organically, these masses of facts receive that signpost of ignorance: 'miscellaneous.'" Marcel Mauss, "Techniques of the Body," in *Zone 6: Incorporations*, 454.

13. For example, "[T]oday's children . . . have access to more information in a day than their grandparents did in a lifetime" (House of Representatives, *Excellence in Teaching: Hearing Before the Committee on Education and the Workforce*, 106th Cong., 2nd Session, June 1, 2000 [Indianapolis, IN], serial no. 106–110, available at http://commdocs .house.gov/committees/edu/hedcew6-110.000/hedcew6-110.htm); "[a] person today is exposed to more information in one day than a person living in the 1700s was exposed to in an entire lifetime" ("James" of MIT's Center for Reflective Community Practice, whose "experience" was "captured" by Invent Media [n.d.], available at http://www .inventmedia.com/clients/mitfellows/james/soundfellows.html); "[t]oday's students are exposed to more information in a day than a person living in the Middle Ages was exposed to in a lifetime" ("Goal 1 Report," Technology Planning Committee, Howard County [MD] Public School System [2001], available at http://www.howard.k12.md .us/techplan/Goal1.html); "[w]ith the use of satellites, television and computers, you and I receive more information in one day of our lives than our ancestors of several generations ago used to receive in 1000 days!" (Barbara Deangelis, *Real Moments*, quoted—as

"credulously regurgitating factoids"—in *Kirkus Reviews* 1, [August 1994], available at http://www.magusbooks.com/catalog/searchxhtml/dctail_0440507294/choice_A/category_/isbook_0/catlabel_All+Magusbooks+Categories/search_Deangelis ,+Barbara/index.htm); and "a student is exposed to more information in one day than a person living in the Middle Ages was exposed to in a lifetime" (New Jersey State Department of Education, Division of Educational Programs and Student Services, Plan for Educational Technology Task Force, "Educational Technology in New Jersey: A Plan for Action" [Dec. 1992], available at http://ftp.msstate.edu/archives/nctp/new .jersey.txt). This "meme" seems to have gained currency among American educational technologists in the late 1980s through the mid-1990s.

14. Gregory Bateson, *Steps to an Ecology of Mind*, xxv–xxvi.

■

Intelligence

Andrew Goffey

Although Alan Turing's 1950 paper on "Computing Machinery and Intelligence" was not the first time humans had speculated on the question of whether or not machines can think—and whether or not that was indeed an intelligent question to ask—the famous test Turing proposed in this paper testified to the existence of an enduring problematic within which questions of machine intelligence have been framed. The Turing Test first proposed in this paper provided a staged relay of the crucial feature of the Turing machine as a universal machine—a machine that can simulate all others.

Turing sought to answer the question, "can machines think?" by asking the question: can a man pretending to be a woman in a three-way "imitation game" comprising a man, an interlocutor, and a woman (whose role is to help the interlocutor make the correct identification) be successfully replaced by a computer? That is to say, can the interlocutor, whose role is to ask the man questions, be fooled as often by a computer as by a man? Turing's answer, of course, was that this would indeed be the case in time and that an interlocutor could be fooled, to the extent that one would eventually be able to talk of machines thinking "without expecting to be contradicted."[1] It is by virtue of its programmability that the Turing machine could be made to reasonably approximate the behavior of all other machines. Turing was perfectly aware that claiming that in principle a machine could imitate a human was not the end of the story. Indeed, how one might then program a machine to do this was a much more complicated problem. Turing's provisional plan was to suggest that one might initially program the machine to imitate a child, and then subject it to a course of education, in which it would learn to follow the commands it was given.

Both the Turing test and the Turing machine are indicative of how machine intelligence has historically been conceptualized as imitation. The machine is imagined not only having an uncanny ability to mimic other machines but also to imitate humans. But the nature of the problem of machine intelligence is badly understood if the properly libidinal dimension of phenomena of imitation is overlooked. Turing's statement that "we may hope eventually that machines will compete with men in all purely *intellectual* fields"[2] (my emphasis) not only initiated a whole generation of research into the development of machines that could play chess but couldn't open a packet of crisps, but also pointed towards the dimension of rivalry which, according to anthropologist Réné Girard, underlies all phenomena of imitation.[3]

Before sketching out a definition it is useful to acknowledge the libidinal dimension to the problem of intelligence, because it offers an entry point into the analysis of the confusion and ambivalence in the relationship between humans and machines.[4] It is not just that computing science has pondered the question of whether machines might think like humans. The confusion and ambivalence is highlighted by a commonplace observation that in order to work well with computers (to program them or to use them) it is necessary to think like a machine. This, ostensibly, was the virtue of the early female programmers of computers. It is not clear whether the problem is one of machines thinking like humans or humans thinking like machines. Little wonder that Joseph Weizenbaum's 1965 AI program ELIZA became notorious for the way that it attempted to imitate a psychotherapist.[5]

A problematic of imitation is not the only way to approach the question of machine intelligence, but it does have the merit of encouraging a speculative exploration of the cultural aspects of computing. The rivalry and conflict characteristic of the libidinal underpinnings of the ways in which issues of machine intelligence have been posed tap into a far broader material and conceptual issue. Debates about the deskilling resulting from the use of computers in the workplace and about the role of information technology in shifting the composition of the workforce only make sense to the extent that machine intelligence is understood as a possible substitution for human intelligence.

That humans and machines can compete with each other for jobs is indicative of a rivalry in the purposive, command-driven, goal-oriented activity of the contemporary economy. But it is entirely debatable whether framing the issue of machine intelligence in the mirror of the human will allow us to understand what the real problem is. That machines can replace humans tells us nothing special about intelligence, particularly if this is as part of an economy that, in its entropic repetition of the eternally self-same, generally produces stupidity rather than intelligence. As critic Avital Ronell puts it, "stupidity can body-snatch intelligence, disguise itself, or, indeed, participate in the formation of certain types of intelligence with which it tends to be confused."[6]

An example will make the anthropocentric prejudices of this way of understanding intelligence more evident. In a chapter of his book, *How The Mind Works,* entitled "Thinking Machines," the psychologist Steven Pinker suggests that despite the difficulties we have in defining intelligence "we recognize it when we see it." He asks what an alien would have to do to "make us think it was intelligent."[7] We must assume, as Pinker does, that the alien actually wants to be recognized by us (a debatable assumption but one that is often made in discussions of self-other, master-slave relationships). Pinker argues that we recognize an alien as intelligent if it displays "the ability to attain goals in the face of obstacles by means of decisions based on rational (truth-obeying) rules."[8] This amounts to saying that we can recognize something as intelligent to the exact extent that it recognizes, or wants to be recognized by, us. (Presumably, if the alien didn't want recognition it wouldn't bother trying to persuade us that it was the same as us . . .). If this sounds a little complicated, it is. It summarizes the logic of alienation (or of desire in the Lacanian view). Applied to the problem of intelligence, it amounts to saying that all intelligence is alienated intelligence.

The question this entry poses, by contrast, is the following: Is it possible to arrive at an understanding of intelligence without implicitly or explicitly referring to the human as our model? Is it possible, in other words, to think of the intelligence that traverses machines and our relations with them as really alien? Let's call this conception of intelligence *machinic intelligence,* to underline simultaneously its proximity to and distance from the machine intelligence with which computing science has been preoccupied.[9] This idea is grounded in some simple conceptual observations. The first is that it is difficult to grasp the creative potential of thinking machines while one's measure of what makes them intelligent is explicitly or implicitly human. The second is that what makes intelligence interesting is that it marks something in excess of the congenitally human. This is why the new is so frequently figured in terms of the monstrous or the inhuman.[10]

Critical common sense would find the idea of an alien, machinic intelligence not only rebarbative but contradictory. Because humans program machines, machines must in principle be under the control of humans. The tacit assumption here is that it is impossible to make something autonomous. To think otherwise would be fetishism or reification and, in the case of computing, to subscribe to the dehumanizing effects of instrumental rationality. But for all its sophistication, a demystifying critique of this sort, although quite rightly pointing towards the labour of fabrication, fails to make the imaginative leap outside of the sort of human-centred thinking which views all non-human reality as purely inert, dumb mechanism until animated by human labor. And it doesn't really matter whether we think of the cultural construction of machine intelligence in a sort of historical materialist way, or in a quasi-Foucauldian way as the production of discursive rules, or, indeed, as the artifact of networks of texts and their traces: it's often enough to figure something as a cultural/historical/discursive/textual construction for the unstated inference that it is nothing but . . . to follow on quite readily.

Fortunately a conceptual framework is available to enable us to combat this false dichotomy. Calling into question the reductive implications of social construction need not imply falling back on the contrary position (that intelligence is some unproblematic and self-evidently measurable property of things—usually people—themselves). The research of actor-network theorist Bruno Latour and philosopher of science Isabelle Stengers has alerted us to the ways in which the world gets divided by scientists, technologists, and their cultural critics into the unproblematically real and the socially or culturally constructed.

In her book, *The Invention of Modern Science*, Stengers characterizes the specific event of modern science as "the invention of the power to confer on things the power of conferring on the experimenter the power to speak in their name."[11] Where we normally *see* nature "speaking for itself" or see society speaking through the scientist's erstwhile facts, Stengers and Latour encourage us to see instead a complex assemblage in which things (in this instance, scientific facts) become autonomous through a process of fabrication. Simply because there is immense labor involved in the production of a scientific fact does not mean that that is all there is to it. Andrew Pickering has suggested that the endeavor of science and technology to capture the agency of things themselves is a little like the sort of disciplinary setup explored by Michel Foucault, involving the same relationship of power and resistance.[12] That the computer scientist operates on symbols and codes or the chip designer on the properties of silicon, silicon dioxide, and so on is little different from the complex set of processes characteristic of disciplinary society. In each case the aim is to construct a co-functioning ensemble of elements that acts autonomously, in a stable and predictable fashion. Alan Turing's biographer, Andrew Hodges, provides a vivid account of Turing's attempts at constructing computers and the experimental processes of tinkering with the properties of various machinic "phyla" in order to produce a relatively stable synthesis of machine components.[13] An overheating battery on a laptop is a reminder of the fragile equilibrium, the machinic ecology, within which software operates: beyond a certain latitude of temperature variation, the machine will start to act up. This is because a computer, like pretty much anything else, is made up of a series of agents that through a process of interactive stabilization have been tamed enough to work together on their own. Most of the time, at least.

A speculative hypothesis, derived from Gilles Deleuze and Alfred North Whitehead, holding that reality is a network of events caught up in divergent and convergent series, an ensemble of contingent processes, will clarify this more general point. The autonomous agents that have been the province of Artificial Intelligence and subsequently Artificial Life research, the bots and spiders that daily scuttle around the internet, and the Java code that controls a toaster or washing machine are perfectly autonomous—both despite and because of the logic and control provided by algorithms—because they are networks of events as are we.[14] The autonomous reality of software, however, is a contingent achievement: not just because a programmer may leave bugs in code or because component elements may be faulty but because the reality within which software and hardware operates and of which it is a part is itself inherently buggy. But, of course, the issue is whether or not the reality of software is itself intelligent.

(It is worth recalling here Avital Ronell's observation that stupidity and intelligence can get mistaken for one another. A convenient myth in the world of software development holds that machines, are really just dumb and inert until they are told what to do. This is a myth, not because computers don't need to be plugged in or programmed, but because intelligence isn't something that simply comes to inform dumb matter: the programmer works within a highly complex balance of forces and a material infrastructure that is no simple tabula rasa.)

Much early AI research conceptualized intelligence in terms of the manipulation of abstract symbol systems. Robots (such as the delightful Shakey discussed by Daniel Dennett) essentially attempted to accomplish real world actions by retaining an encoded representation of the things it might find in its environment. A series of rules that followed from a set of initial axioms could then be used to build up a logical schema for an action to accomplish, given sensory input parsed in a pre-defined way. In this respect the concept of intelligence operative in AI was effectively prefigured in the research of Turing, since the purpose of the Turing machine was to mechanize the intelligent activity of a mathematician. As Robert Rosen put it, "If this aspect of human mental activity can be 'mechanized,' why not others? Why not all?"[15] To put it differently: The concept of intelligence operative in AI is closely related to the intelligence of computing, as both rely on the formal possibilities of symbol systems (and such systems have the engineering advantage of being relatively easy to implement physically).[16] It is perhaps not that surprising then that cognitive science subsequently found itself arguing, as a consequence of the success of the abstractions of symbol manipulation, that human intelligence itself was computation. But as Ed Hutchins has pointed out, "the physical symbol-system architecture [exemplified in many good old fashioned AI projects] is not a model of individual cognition. It is a model of the operation of a social-cultural system from which the human actor has been removed."[17]

Translated into the chains of formal-logical implication that symbol-system architectures cater for, it is easy to mistake the contingencies of intelligence for the epistemological problem of truth and falsity, keeping the logical form of reasoning (call it "overcoding") intact and ignoring the surplus, the excess over itself that projects the intelligent agent into futurity. Reducing that excess by attempting to make an action and its consequences deducible from an initial set of axioms, early AI quickly found that on the margins of its "microworlds"[18] the creative possibilities of programmed intelligence quickly produced machinic catatonia, the complete inability to act. The "frame problem," recurrent in AI, is a telling reminder of some of the problems inherent in a formalist, symbolic conception of intelligence. The frame problem can be glossed as concerning the knowledge needed to accomplish some task: given some identifiable sensory input ("this is a block of wood"), what part of that input gives rise to relevant logical implications ("do I need to know what type of wood it is to move it?" for example)? It is typically understood as an epistemological issue; for AI researchers part of the problem is finding criteria to determine what information is pertinent in any situation. The very fact that the matter is considered an epistemological problem is itself indicative of the assumption that intelligent activity necessarily follows some kind of formal-logical set of rules or law.

One response to this problem has been to claim that computers can't be intelligent because they are unable to recover the kind of meaning that would allow them to do what humans, with all the tacit knowledge their culture supplies, do with little difficulty. However, that, rather obviously, is to use the failings of AI and the prejudices of anthropocentric pragmatism to resolve the problem.[19]

Research in the areas of artificial life, complexity theory, and connectionism has developed a conception of intelligence supposedly capable of countering the problems that arise from unduly subsuming intelligence under a model of formal symbol manipulation. Such work follows the lead of Warren McCulloch and Walter Pitts, whose 1943 paper, "A Logical Calculus of the Ideas Immanent in Nervous Activity," thematically explored a conception of intelligence based on the idea that certain logical functions could be proved calculable by fairly simple networks of neurons.[20] In place of a brittle axiomatic/theorematic intelligence that must code in advance the territory within which it operates (by specifying what is significant and what not) these more recent kinds of research do not define in advance the salient features of the environment within which their agents operate. Repeated contact with an environment for an agent with a "plastic" cognitive system (one which is not rigidly hard-coded and is thus susceptible to modification over time) allows that agent to learn inductively about relevant features of its environment and thus to evolve appropriate responses. Neural networks, for example, will use known patterns within data to set the weights on nodes in an artificial network of software neurons in order to develop probabilistic correlations between sets of input data and likely output data. The programmer will typically randomize the weightings to all the neurons at the outset, leaving the final configuration of the network to be generated by the patterns or resonances existing in the data itself. The ability of a neural network to converge on a solution to a problem is not a formal certainty, only a likelihood deriving from a series of heuristic measures that researchers have developed.[21]

But the newer research paradigms, for all their interest in ethology, in evolutionary processes, and in intelligence as an emergent phenomenon, remain resolutely territorial: retina-scanning, handwriting recognition, or the simulation of predator-prey relationships are conspicuously bounded processes. One trains a neural network on specific, finite datasets. The ability to pattern-match more generally presupposes the existence of redundancy in the data and thus self-similarity. So, one could argue that the ability to discern redundancy in data is the ability to learn about how things imitate or repeat themselves (like the data-mining software that tells us which books we want to buy).

Both artificial intelligence and artificial life research provide us with some interesting insights into the kind of intelligence that is operative within software, but neither are well equipped to help us understand the exteriority of a kind of intelligence that exceeds both software and its human users. Our contention is that such intelligence must be understood in terms of a logic of events: It is the process-flux of events of which software is a part that bears the intelligence, not the relatively closed systems that we program and over which believe we have control.

The concept of the natal proposed by Gilles Deleuze and Félix Guattari in *A Thousand Plateaus* provides a helpful way to work through this argument. The natal "consists in a decoding of innateness and a territorialisation of learning"[22] and as such overcomes the innate-acquired dichotomy that has dogged theories of learning. Behavior or activity specified in advance (maybe in the form of specific sets of axioms or rules of inference) ceases to be entirely innate (preprogrammed), to the extent that the code that specifies it has a margin of indeterminacy—an obvious point if it is accepted that formal systems are inherently incomplete. Likewise, the learning of behavior is not a completely random process of empirical induction because it takes place within territories that constrain it in certain ways. Rodney Brooks's concept of a "subsumption architecture" (in which the order and combination of behaviors in a robot are not specified in advance but prescribed by the constraints presented by the environment) confirms this,[23] while the failings of good old-fashioned AI might be traced to its unwillingness to concede that learning only takes place because all systems are open systems (in effect, this is what the concept of the natal shows us). However, AI's emphasis on abstract symbol systems itself produces a disjunction between code and territory with its own deterritorializing effects.[24] Computer scientist Robert Rosen's argument that "there are (a) formal constructions without material counterpart, and conversely, (b) material constructions without formal counterpart" is indicative of both the decoding and deterritorializing aspects of machinic intelligence which the concept of the natal points out.[25] What this means, very crudely, is that because material reality and symbol systems do not "add up," there is an unformalized excess that undercuts our understanding of intelligence. This excess continues to undermine attempts to manage intelligence by means of coded, rationally deductible properties.

Friedrich Kittler's amusing view of computers as operating like the Lacanian unconscious, expressed best in his statement that all coding operations are ultimately "signifiers of voltage differences"[26] casts light on why machine intelligence has been and needs to be seen as a libidinal problem. If Kittler's view is followed programmable machines would be, as Turing imagined, like the child in the proverbial family triangle: in training them to do what we ask them, they internalize the (formal) law on which the desire for recognition depends and give us the answers we deserve to the questions we ask. However as Gilles Deleuze and Félix Guattari have shown, the artificial isolation of a "primal scene" (of programming, in this instance) makes it all too easy to forget the flux of events that gnaws away at the laws of formalism and that makes intelligence something in excess of the symbols that we might choose to represent it.[27]

To summarize then: In the fields of computing and cognitive science, the question of intelligence has been posed historically in terms of imitation. The reason for understanding intelligence this way, it has been suggested, derives from how machine intelligence discloses the libidinal dimension of software. Breaking out of an implicitly or explicitly human-centered understanding of machine intelligence (while also acknowledging the enormous labor that goes into constructing that intelligence) requires a theoretical framework which allows us to understand how something can be fabricated as autonomous. With this framework in place it becomes easier to understand the "intelligence" put into play by of computers and the creation of software as an alien, machinic intelligence, a fact partially grasped by AI, artificial life, and cognitive science but without the means to fully project that intelligence into a reality outside of itself.

Notes

1. Alan M. Turing, "Computing Machinery and Intelligence," *Mind*, 260.

2. Ibid.

3. See Réné Girard, *Mensonge et Vérité Romanesque*.

4. Lacan's formulation of desire as "désir de l'autre" is a way of underlining this confusion. "Désir de l'autre" can be translated as desire for the other or as the other's desire. See Jacques Lacan, *Écrits: A Selection*.

5. Weizenbaum's ELIZA is discussed in many books on AI. A brief but succinct account appears in Les Goldschlager and Andrew Lister, *Computer Science: A Modern Introduction*.

6. Avital Ronell, *Stupidity*, 10.

7. Steven Pinker, *How The Mind Works*, 60.

8. Ibid., 61.

9. Gilles Deleuze and Félix Guattari, *A Thousand Plateaus*. See also Ray Brassier, "Liquider l'homme une fois pour toutes," in Gilles Grélet, ed., *Théorie – rebellion*.

10. In addition to the work of Gilles Deleuze, writers as different as Alain Badiou and Jean-Francois Lyotard have drawn attention to the "monstrous" or "inhuman" as part of a philosophy of escaping the all too human tenets of modern nihilism. The possibility and desirability of escaping the anthropocentric prejudices of a human-centered way of thinking have been explored, in different ways, in Graham Harman, *Tool-Being* and Quentin Meillassoux, *Aprés la finitude*.

11. Isabelle Stengers, *The Invention of Modern Science*, 89.

12. Andrew Pickering, *The Mangle of Practice*.

13. See, for example, the discussion of the problems associated with using cathode ray tubes in Andrew Hodges and Alan Turing, *Alan Turing: The Enigma of Intelligence*.

14. See, for example, Gilles Deleuze, *The Fold* and Alfred North Whitehead, *Process and Reality*.

15. See Robert Rosen, "Effective Processes and Natural Law," in Rolf Herken, ed., *The Universal Turing Machine, a Half-Century Survey*, 524.

16. In addressing the problem of the limits of formalism Rosen cites Martin Davis's musings about extraterrestrial intelligence. See Rosen, "Effective Processes and Natural Law," Ibid. 524.

17. Ed Hutchins, *Cognition In The Wild,* 363.

18. See Paul Edwards, *The Closed World: Computers and the Politics of Discourse in Cold War America.*

19. Daniel Dennett, *Consciousness Explained.*

20. Warren S. McCulloch and Walter H. Pitts, "A Logical Calculus of the Ideas Immanent in Nervous Activity," in Deirdre Boden, ed., *The Philosophy of Artificial Intelligence.*

21. Simon Haykin, *Neural Networks: A Comprehensive Foundation.*

22. Gilles Deleuze and Félix Guattari, *A Thousand Plateaus*, 367.

23. Rodney Brooks, *"Intelligence Without Representation,"* 139–159.

24. This point has been made, albeit in a slightly different way, by Andy Clark in his useful overview of recent trends in cognitive science research, *Being There*, in which he describes language as the "ultimate artifact" and draws attention to the ways that as an artifact it introduces a qualitative difference into the cognitive systems of humans. See Andy Clark, *Being There: Putting Brain, Body, and World Together Again*, 193–218.

25. Robert Rosen, "Effective Processes and Natural Law," 535. A formal process with no material counterpart has a deterritorializing effect, while a material process with no formal counterpart has a decoding effect.

26. Friedrich Kittler, *Literature, Media, Information Systems*, 150.

27. Gilles Deleuze and Félix Guattari, *Anti-Oedipus.*

■
Interaction

Michael Murtaugh

Types of interaction can be categorized in a variety of ways. One popular sort of interaction consists of the user making choices, either textual or via a graphical user interface: selecting items from a menu; typing bits of information into a form; moving a mouse; clicking; double-clicking. The popularity of the web and hypertext has bound the idea of interaction to branching link structures. The word "interactive" has become so overused in relation to computing and new media that, for instance, Lev Manovich describes its use in relation to computing as "tautological" and takes care to qualify any employment of the word when unable to avoid it altogether.[1]

Interaction is also linked to a tradition of engineers, mathematicians, and software hackers looking for a way to break out of the rigidity and the strictness of their systems—out, as it were, of the black box. Interaction in the 1960s represented reaction against, and liberation from, the mainframe batch-processing computer center. It proposed a radical usage of computers: giving (untrained) groups of users "live" contact with the machine.

Input Tape

An early proponent of this new approach to computation was J. C. R. Licklider, a researcher with a background in psychoacoustics. In the 1950s Licklider had access to the TX-2, an experimental computer developed at MIT that, along with having a Cathode Ray Tube display, speaker, control knobs, and a light pen, was fully transistor-based. The TX-2 could be readily reprogrammed from its keyboard instead of requiring physical rewiring or the use of punchcards.[2]

It was on the TX-2 that Ivan Sutherland would later develop his Sketchpad program, cited by many, including Licklider, as a groundbreaking demonstration of the potential for truly interactive software.[3] Licklider describes the then "state of the art":

Present-day computers are designed primarily to solve preformulated problems or to process data according to predetermined procedures. The course of the computation may be conditional upon results obtained during the computation, but all the alternatives must be foreseen in advance. If an unforeseen alternative arises, the whole process comes to a halt and awaits the necessary extension of the program. . . . If the user can think his problem through in advance, symbiotic association with a computing machine is not necessary. . . One of the main aims of man-computer symbiosis is to bring the computing machine effectively into the formulative parts of technical problems.[4]

Licklider links interaction to a crucial shift from computer as problem-solver to computer as problem-finder or problem-explorer in a space of necessarily unforeseen possibilities.

Writing in the 1980s, cybernetician Stafford Beer describes an algorithm as "a technique, or mechanism, which prescribes how to reach a fully specified goal." He contrasts this with the idea of a heuristic (method), a word derived from the adjective meaning "to find out":

An heuristic specifies a method of behaving which will tend towards a goal which cannot be precisely specified because we know what it is but not where it is. . . . The strange thing is that we tend to live our lives by heuristics, and try and control them by algorithms. Our general endeavour is to survive, yet we specify in detail ("catch the 8.45 train," "ask for a raise") how to get to this unspecified and unspecifiable goal. We certainly need these algorithms, in order to live coherently; but we also need heuristics—and we are rarely conscious of them.[5]

Writing in the 1990s, computer science theorists Peter Wegner and Dina Goldin provide another description of an algorithm: "A systematic procedure that produces—in a finite number of steps—the answer to a question or the solution to a problem.[6]

Wegner and Goldin propose an alternative to the Turing Machine based around a unifying concept of interaction. In the classic formulation, a Turing machine is an idealized computer that reads and writes symbols from an endless tape and has a notion of "state," allowing a program written in these symbols to control the operation of the machine. The rules for this particular model dictate that once the machine begins operation, no new input may be received, and it must be guaranteed to reach a final state in a fixed amount of time. In addition, the starting state for the machine is precisely specified and must be identical each time the machine is started.

In contrast, Wegner and Goldin propose "interactive computation" based on "interaction with an external world, or the environment of the computation, during the computation—rather than before and after it, as in algorithmic computation.[7]

In one alternative model called a Persistent Turing Machine, Wegner and Goldin describe a variation on the classic Turing machine, now with tapes. The crucial differences in this model are: (1) the use of an input and an output tape to interface with the dynamic environment of the machine, (2) the provision for a work tape that remembers results from previous operation, and (3) the allowance for the machine to run continuously (no requirement to reach a final state). By writing to and subsequently reading from the environment, the potential for feedback occurs. It is, however, a noisy channel, as the environment is explicitly allowed to be unpredictable, and potentially acted upon by other processes. Allowing past operation to influence the starting state also introduces a greater degree of uncertainty. Allowing indefinite operation reflects a more heuristic-driven approach as a result may be "tended towards" without necessarily being definitively reached.

By explicitly representing a place "outside" of the machine, Wegner and Goldin show that the resulting model is more expressive, able to describe machines that are not possible to fully represent as traditional Turing machines. In addition, they show how such a model fits much more readily with the realities of contemporary computation such as operating systems, networked software, and portable devices.[8]

Wegner and Goldin point out that Turing himself acknowledged other potential models that might include human interaction (choice-machines) or other external inputs (oracle-machines).[9]

Talking to to Stuart Brand in the 1980s, Andy Lippmann, director of an early experimental videodisc called the *Aspen Movie Map*, provided the following working definition of interactivity: "Mutual and simultaneous activity on the part of both participants usually working toward some goal, but not necessarily."[10]

The *Aspen Movie Map* was an attempt to recreate the experience of exploring a city by virtually driving through the city's streets, selecting points of interest along the way to view in depth. The challenge for Lippman and the other designers of the project was to realize that goal within the extreme limitations of a static and limited storage medium.

Lippman describes five "corollaries" or properties he felt were necessary to add to this to attain true interactivity: interruptibility; graceful degradation; limited look-ahead (not pre-computed); no default pathway, and; the "impression of an infinite database."[11]

Work Tape

Surveying these different perspectives, some themes seem to emerge as central to interaction in relation to computation: liveness, plasticity and accretion, interruption and incompleteness.

Liveness

A key recurrent theme in interactivity is liveness. Licklider states that a central aim for human-computer symbiosis is "to bring computing machines effectively into processes of thinking that must go on in 'real time.'" Lippman's "limited look ahead," the importance of computational decisions happening "on the fly" is paralleled by Wegner and Goldin's notion of noncomputability, the idea that not all possible pathways can be precomputed.

The idea of the "infinite database" is the subjective counterpoint to this noncomputability and liveness of the system: the feeling that there are infinite possibilities to explore. A result of this liveness is that an interactive system is one that supports a sense of playing or performing with the system.

An important consequence of liveness is that interaction always occurs over time. In black box computation, time is neglible—the only requirement is that computation completes in a finite time. There is no sense of the "mutual" or simultaneous in algorithmic computation, all computation is completed before any results are passed on to the next process.

Interaction always involves simultaneity, as computation occurs iteratively through feedback to a shared and changing environment. Designing with interaction requires a sensitivity to the timing of the processes involved.

Plasticity and Accretion

Licklider, formulating the idea of the computer as a communication device uses the term "cooperative modeling," writing, "Creative, interactive communication requires a plastic or moldable medium that can be modeled, a dynamic medium in which premises will flow into consequences, and above all a common medium that can be contributed to and experimented with by all."[12]

Lippmann's notions of interruptibility and graceful degradation express the desire for a kind of plasticity to the experience; the participant can push without breaking the system.

The idea of malleability and plasticity connects back to the central role of persistence in Wegner and Goldin's interactive computation. The fact that the computation "holds its shape" in some sense requires that the interaction have some lasting effect (if only short-term). Interaction includes the potential for processes to improve or evolve with accretion. The lack of a fixed starting state or default pathway underscores the importance of accretion to the computation.

Interruption and Incompleteness

For Lippman, it is the potential for interruption that keeps a conversation from becoming merely a lecture. In Wegner and Goldin's interactive computation, it is in the noisy channel of the environment that interuption potentially occurs. The environment of the computation serves as the interface between the various processes, be they purely computational or the result of human intervention.

The desire for graceful degradation relates to the idea that the computation must not only be open to unpredictable input, but should use it well.

Models of the real world and even of integers sacrifice completeness in order to express autonomous (external) meanings. Incompleteness is a necessary price to pay for modeling independent domains of discourse whose semantic properties are richer than the syntactic notation by which they are modeled.[13]

The components of an interactive system are inherently incomplete. Interaction always involves a tension between autonomous operation and cross-influence of a system's parts. The challenge for authors is to design processes that tend to steer the system toward desirable states rather than hard coding those states. An interactive process exploits its environment in order to fully realize its own functionality.

Output Tape

For the software designer, programming with interaction involves seeking a kind of magical moment of transformation, a moment when one begins to get back more than what was put in; an unexpected moment when the system seems not only just to work, but to almost come to life; a moment when what had previously been a noisy mess of buggy half-working mechanisms seems to flow together and become a kind of organic whole.

The elusive chase for this kind of transformative moment is the essential reason why geeks keep banging away at their keyboards, deep into the night, deprived of sleep and propped up by caffeine and sugar and the adrenaline of the experience of feeling in contact with something larger than oneself.

Interaction rips computation out of the clean room of the algorithm and thrusts it into the tainted and unpredictable space of dynamic and shared environment.

Interaction forces a rethinking of algorithmic approaches toward those that perform a kind of dance alternating between active computation and responsive strategies to a changing environment.

Embracing interaction requires the programmer or designer to break open the black boxes of algorithmic processes and acknowledge the incompleteness of what they create in the pursuit of experiences that are playful, insightful, and potentially surprising.

Notes

1. Lev Manovich, *The Language of New Media*, 55.

2. M. Mitchell Waldrop, *The Dream Machine: J. C. R. Licklider and the Revolution that Made Computing Personal*, 142–147.

3. Ibid, 255.

4. J. C. R. Licklider, "Man-Computer Symbiosis," *IRE Transactions on Human Factors in Electronics, vol. HFE-1*, 4–11.

5. Stafford Beer, *Brain of the Firm*, 52–53.

6. Eugene Eberbach, Dina Goldin, and Peter Wegner, "Turing's Ideas and Models of Computation" 1 online version, available at http://www.cis.umassd.edu/~eeberbach/papers/eberbach_12092003.pdf.

7. Ibid, 16.

8. Peter Wegner, "The Paradigm Shift from Algorithms to Interaction: Why Interaction is More Powerful than Algorithms," *Communications of the ACM*.

9. Eberbach, Goldin, and Wegner, "Turing's Ideas and Models of Computation."

10. Stuart Brand, *The Media Lab*, 46–50.

11. Ibid.

12. J. C. R. Licklider, "The Computer as a Communications Device," *Science and Technology* (April 1968), 22.

13. Wegner, *The Paradigm Shift,* 10.

■

Interface

Florian Cramer and Matthew Fuller

The term "interface" appears to have been borrowed from chemistry, where it means "a surface forming a common boundary of two bodies, spaces, phases."[1] In computing, interfaces link software and hardware to each other and to their human users or other sources of data. A typology of interfaces thus reads:

1. hardware that connects users to hardware; typically input/output devices such as keyboards or sensors, and feedback devices such as screens or loudspeakers;
2. hardware that connects hardware to hardware; such as network interconnection points and bus systems;
3. software, or hardware-embedded logic, that connects hardware to software; the instruction set of a processor or device drivers, for example;
4. specifications and protocols that determine relations between software and software, that is, application programming interfaces (APIs);
5. symbolic handles, which, in conjunction with (a), make software accessible to users; that is, "user interfaces," often mistaken in media studies for "interface" as a whole.

While all of these categories of interface are significant in relation to computing as a whole, only the last three, (3), (4), and (5), are discussed here.

Regarding (3), software typically functions as an interface to hardware. Computer programs can be seen as tactical constraints of the total possible uses of hardware. They constrain, for example, the combination of a CPU, RAM, hard disk, mainboard, video card, mouse, keyboard, and screen with its abundant possible system states to the function of a word processor, a calculator, a video editor, etc. In other words, they interface to the universal machine by behaving as a specialized machine, breaking the former down to a subset of itself. This operation is linguistic because it reformulates the totality of available machine instructions into a new control language. This language acts as an "abstraction layer." It is either a subset of the total available instructions when it is Turing incomplete, or a redressing of them with different symbolic handles when it is Turing complete.

"User interface" and "programming interface" have not always differed. They had been identical in many operating systems and including the 8-bit home computers in the 1980s that booted into a BASIC programming language prompt, or MIT's Lisp machines, which had a Lisp programming environment as their user interface. Character-based shells such as DOS and Unix are used both as programming and user interfaces. The same is true, to a lesser degree, for graphical user interfaces when they are scriptable. But even if they are not scriptable, they still effectively act as specialized symbolic computer control languages. The distinction between a "user interface," an "Application Program Interface" (API), and a computer control language is purely arbitrary. That more complex interfaces to computer functions tend to be called "programming languages" and less complex, more specialized ones are known as "user interfaces" is simply a nomenclature arising out of convention. Since the user interface to a computer program is always symbolic, and involves syntactical and symbolic mappings for operations, it always boils down to being a formal language. To the extent that they are understood symbolically, everything that can be said about software interfaces falls under the entry on language.

Similar to both its meaning in chemistry and to the meaning of "language," "interfaces" are the point of juncture between different bodies, hardware, software, users, and what they connect to or are part of. Interfaces describe, hide, and condition the asymmetry between the elements conjoined. The asymmetry of the powers of these bodies is what draws the elements together. Unless they are savants, human users cannot quickly calculate Pi to the 100th place, or generate a model world in which the dimensions and trajectory of its every element are mapped, as a computer is able to do. In this sense the term interface emphasizes the representation or the re-articulation of a process occurring at another scalar layer, while the term language, in a computer context, emphasizes control. The condensations of computational power that computers embody and that are differently articulated by individual pieces of software. Such condensations of power are of intense fascination and generate such productivity, and, at the same time, are radically alien to most human experiences of the world. It is this alienness that allows software, particularly at moments when one is attempting to understand its workings or to program it, that engenders the delicious moments of feedback between the styles of perception and ordering, logic and calculation, between the user and the computer to be so seductive and compelling. At the same time, this initially rich engagement with an interface tends to lose its luster once users realize the limitations of the programmed system. Equally, as when software is used to monitor, queue, and structure the flow of work, the compulsion provided by an interface can be of a different kind. The asymmetric powers conjoined by means of human-machine interfaces, also find themselves arranged in other relations which themselves articulate, filter, and organize the activities modeled and modulated by the interface.

This asymmetry, while fundamental to the differences between human and machine operations, can further materialize in other levels of machine control granted to the user. While any user interface, including every programming language, mediates machine functions, the mediation can be deliberately (Turing-)incomplete or (Turing-)complete. But even the latter usage and programming interface—Unix shells or the turtle of the Logo programming language for example—like any language or instrument still impose and enhance particular workflows, thought modes, and modes of interaction upon or in combination with human users.

Asymmetry of powers is also mapped and sieved through interfaces in other ways. A search engine operates as an interface of many layers, ostensibly that between the user and the data being sought. Crucially, it also establishes an interface whereby the database can read the user, by means of records of patterns of search terms and choices. And asymmetry is not simply a means of recognizing the associations made between computers and humans. APIs, as well as protocols that operate as interfaces between computers linked over a network, also establish descriptions of operations that are allowed and assigned a priority or blocked. APIs are increasingly important to the development of networks that rely on data and software working without being constrained by hardware platform, and the formulation of the algorithms that govern their operation has become of particular interest.

Within the paradigm of "user-friendliness," that which is most easily recognizable and visible, software has been traditionally understood to place the user as its subject, and the computational patterns and elements initiated, used, and manipulated by the user as the corresponding grammatical objects. As software is diffused through urban, social, and institutional contexts, the design of interfaces and even the basic level of awareness about what does or does not constitute part of an interface, or that triggers a computational event, becomes increasingly important. Learning to recognize a human functioning as an interface to a spreadsheet, or, as in much of generic electronic art, being able to read the sensors and interaction grammars deployed in a constructed space, are increasingly useful skills as interfaces not only spread out from the screen and the keyboard, but are also designed to dissimulate their function as interfaces.

Addressing item 5 in our initial list, the user interface articulates asymmetry via different means: by the use of text; visual-spatial structuring devices such as a window and its subcomponents, timeline or button; sounds, such as system event sounds; animated representations of running data-processes such as a "loading" bar, "throbbers" (used in web browsers), spinning cursors; widgets; menus, which describe available functions; and other elements. Because such interface elements provide a mode of access to data and data structures, the ordering and occurrence of such elements are usually describable by and at a lower level designed using formalisms, context-free grammars that attempt to describe a metasyntax comprising every possible use of the computer or within a language or application. If the universal machine describes every possible rational computation, such systems set out the syntax for all possible interactions within the domain they describe. While the syntax of an interaction is logically describable, no such constraint is necessary for visual or audio elements of interface within item 5. Such interfaces, and especially the "skinning" systems that provide users with the opportunity to personalize the visual appearance of interface elements in applications or operating systems, conjoin, even if only at the representational level, formal grammars with assemblages of visual codes drawn from domains as diverse as heavy metal and manga graphics. Low-level formalisms articulated through the representational matrices of high-trash genre conventions provide a refreshing break from the pretensions of computing to objectivity.

The meshing of poetic and formal language in the area of writing known as "codeworks" explores the rich experimental and speculative potential of alphanumerical computer control languages. Other net and software artists have demonstrated how audiovisual computer control languages (user interfaces) can be a playground for subjective, ironical, and epistemological disruptions, experiments, and critique. These interventions become all the more important the more the deliberate separation between "user" and "programming" interfaces and languages is maintained.

Notes

1. According to *Webster's Ninth Collegiate Dictionary,* which dates the term to 1882.

■

Internationalization

Adrian Mackenzie

Enumerated entities are historical objects.

—HELEN VERRAN[1]

The questions of "otherness" is rarely posed in relation to software. This is because universality figures so large in software. Software makes historically and materially specific claims to universality (think of Java's "Write once, run anywhere" promise). This tends to push questions of otherness in software aside. By virtue of the notions of universality attached to numbering systems (such as decimal and binary), to computation (Universal Turing Machine), and to global technoculture itself, software seems virulently universal. When figures of otherness appear around software, they tend to be pathological. Pathological software forms such as viruses, worms, trojan horses, or even bugs are one facet of otherness marked in software. Much of the architecture and design, as well as much everyday work, pivots on security measures meant to regulate the entry and presence of these others, and at the same time to permit software to translate smoothly between institutional, political, linguistic and economic contexts.

"Greetings," "Inquiry," "Farewell": Technical Universality

Within the design and architecture of much contemporary software, different strategies of coping with otherness have developed. In the software industry, one of the main strategies for figuring others is a process known as "internationalization" or "i18n" (for the 18 letters between i and n in "internationalization"). Techniques of internationalization allow software to be readily adapted to different local conventions, customs, and languages. Take an industry standard programming language of the late 1990s, Java a product of Sun Microsystems Corporation. As a programming language and software platform, Java's claims to technical universality include cross-platform execution, numerous network programming constructs and code portability. As Sun's Java documentation states,

Internationalization is the process of designing software so that it can be adapted (localized) to various languages and regions easily, cost-effectively, and in particular without engineering changes to the software. Localization is performed by simply adding locale-specific components, such as translated text, data describing locale-specific behavior, fonts, and input methods.[2]

"Internationalized" Java software makes use of classes from the java.util package to separate universal components from local components. Local components may have linguistic, symbolic, cultural, and geographic specificities. In the tutorial on Sun's Java Tutorial site, the following code demonstrates this elementary separation:

```
import java.util.*;3
```

This sample code declares variables that hold values for "language," and "country," and it invokes classes (bundles of methods, functions, and data) that represent combinations of language and country called Locales. A Locale is used to choose appropriate resources from the ResourceBundle, a collection of language-specific property files distributed with the program. For instance, a German resource bundle might contain the following entries:

```
greetings = Hallo.
farewell = Tschüß.
inquiry = Wie geht's?
```

Java supports a standard set of locales that correlate with well-developed, affluent countries.[4] These include messages, writing systems, and symbols such as currency displayed to users, as well as more basic algorithmic processes such as counting, searching, and sorting, which often need to be internationalized. For instance, dates are formatted differently in different locales, and need to be sorted according to their format. The concept of the locale points to another key aspect of internationalization: As software is distributed globally, it has to take into account where and when it is running. Time zones form key parts of the infrastructural relations that situate software geographically. Most software needs to be able to represent where and when it is running. Time zones form part of the cross-hatched texture of actions in other spaces and times articulated in software. Additionally, practices of sorting (a key consideration in any software) shift radically between writing systems. For instance, sorting alphabetically, a straightforward task in European writing systems, cannot be taken for granted in Asian writing systems. In Java, all text characters are encoded in Unicode, a character set that represents all characters in all written languages by unique numbers (in fact, Unicode itself constitutes a primary component of present day software internationalization processes; it merits discussion in its own right[5]). In the character series for European languages, the order of Unicode characters corresponds to alphabetical order. This is not guaranteed for all languages. Sorting strings in non-European languages requires different techniques. Assumptions about order, sequence, and sorting go to the heart of the design of software. Interestingly, the closer one moves to the core of the Java programming environment, the more restricted the set of supported locales becomes. For instance, whereas Java graphic user interface components display messages in roughly a dozen different languages, the messages displayed by the Java Software Development Kit (the bundle of tools used to develop Java software) only display messages in English and Japanese.

Software for "Human Beings": Fictitious Universality

Technically universal yet abstractly local, commercial internationalization focuses on consumption and use of software, not its distribution or production. Wider distribution may be the purpose of internationalization, but the nature of distribution and production themselves does not change through techniques of internationalization, no matter how thoroughly carried through into different aspects of software. Yet distribution is perhaps the key issue in software today because changes in the nature of distribution of software change what can be done with and through software. Software is becoming social. *Ubuntu*, "Linux for Human Beings," a project supported heavily by Mark Shuttleworth, a South African entrepreneur,[6] is a Linux/GNU distribution in which internationalization of distribution itself figures centrally as part of the project. Ubuntu represents a politically progressive open source or FLOSS alternative to commercial strategies of internationalization represented by Sun's Java or various equivalents found in Microsoft's .NET, etc. The Ubuntu Manifesto states that "Software should be available free of charge, that software tools should be usable by people in their local language, and that people should have the freedom to customize and alter their software in whatever way they need."[7]

Whereas the techniques of internationalization are concerned with the cost-effective entry of products into different markets, the Ubuntu distribution makes use of the "very best in *translations and accessibility infrastructure* that the Free Software community has to offer, to make Ubuntu usable for as many people as possible." (my emphasis) The "translation and accessibility infrastructure" that the manifesto has in mind are none other than Rosetta (a web-based system for translating open source software into any language)[8] and LaunchPad (a collection of services built by Shuttleworth).[9] These software services coordinate the localization of software by allowing volunteers and other participants to supply the translation of menu items, dialogs, and other text-based elements of the user interface and help files. The distribution of Ubuntu is predicated partly on the redistribution of the work of translating to cohorts of volunteer translators who are explicitly assured that "Ubuntu will always be free of charge."[10]

Like i18n, Ubuntu assumes a great deal about the universal relevance of its code. This is a point that Soenhke Zehle has recently highlighted.[11] Code is produced for Ubuntu (and many other software projects) in technically advanced contexts in Europe, North America, India, and East Asia, and then localized for execution in less developed countries by volunteers (who themselves may or may not be local). Ubuntu introduces a multinational dimension to the internationalization of software, but the software itself remains universal in its aims and expectations because code and software themselves are presumed to be universal as text and as a practice. In this respect, no matter how distributed its production might become, and how many eyes and hands contribute to it, there is no Other figured in software because software itself now garners universality from that other universal, "human beings," free individuals who are normalized in important ways. Despite the reorganization of distribution and production to include collective modes of localization, and the corresponding overcoming of institutional, national, and economic discrimination against certain ethnic groups, the code itself makes assumptions about computing platforms, network infrastructures, information environments, and people that may not be universally relevant.

Tropically Relevant Code and Ideal Universality

Could i18n be done differently? This question touches on political struggles over the value of universals that have been at the heart of much theoretical debate in the last decade. It is difficult to articulate any viable alternative to technical universality (software that runs anywhere, as Java claims) or to fictitious universality (Ubuntu's software for human beings) because universality itself is a deeply ambiguous concept.[12] To highlight this ambiguity, I want to point out some of the underpinnings of all software: reliance on practices of numbering, enumerating, and sorting.

In volume 1 of *The Art of Computer Programming*, Donald Knuth wrote: "Computer programs usually operate on tables of information. In most cases these tables are not simply amorphous masses of numerical values; they involve important *structural relationships* between the data elements."[13] The keys terms are already highlighted by Knuth. Software never deals with amorphous masses of value, but structural relationships. The properties of these relationships, and the value accorded to different relations are not universal. They exist in particular places, histories, and contexts. The panoply of data structures, algorithms, database designs, protocols, and network topologies developed by programmers over the last fifty years attest to the singularity of these relationships. Software concatenates every single value, no matter how trivial, in relationships that are essentially social, communicative, and corporeal or living.

These relationships afford some kinds of universality and not others. To understand this, we need only turn to recent anthropological studies of mathematics. Ethnomathematics is motivated by the problem of universality and, in particular, how to make sense of different ways of dealing with unity and plurality without bogging down in relativism. It offers leads on how we might begin to think about universality more concretely and thereby begin to radicalize software internationalization. Such analysis points to forms of universality that ultimately call into question existing figures of consumer, user or human. In *Science and an African Logic*, Helen Verran writes, "numbers are located in the embodied doing of rituals with hands, eyes, and words, but if this is so, how is it that they seem to have the capacity to be definitive even in the absence of any bodily doings?"[14] Her answer to this question is highly germane to software. It pivots on the idea that certain practices transform written forms of numerals (Knuth's "numerical values") into numbers (Knuth's "structural relationships"): "Enumeration 'transforms' all numerals to numbered bodies by the very precise operation of interpellating, and likewise transforms non-enumerated bodies to enumerated."[15] That is, numerals are elements in a writing system, but numbers are things that marshal, order, and define bodies in the most general sense. The translation from inscribed numeral to embodied number occurs through practices of *enumeration* that are lived, singular, and specific.

For instance, the Yoruba numbering practices described by Verran are multi-base (base 5, base 10, and base 20). This affords highly flexible and rapid mental calculation far surpassing what can be done in base 10 mental calculation that appeared in European cultures sometime around 1300.[16] This implications of this go far: Yoruba numbers are different to European numbers in the way they deal with unity and plurality. Rather than projecting outwards in long series or sets of numbers as European practices of enumeration tend to, they incorporate inwards, in numbers nested in each other.[17] That is, numbers are generated by differing forms of number-naming that themselves stem from different bodily and linguistic practices. Distinctions between hands and feet, left and right figure directly in Yoruba multibase numbering, whereas ten fingers "are treated as a set of homogeneous elements taken as linearly related."[18]

In a less radical difference, programming languages could be analyzed in terms of their enumeration strategies and the ways they generate unities and pluralities. Lisp differs from Python by virtue of the emphasis it puts on recursion as a way of enumerating, but recursion is sometimes difficult to invoke. Python and Java make enumeration a readily available function, invoked countless times by programmers and programs. For instance, the elementary "dictionary" datatype in Python defines one-to-one relationships between keys and values[19] that allow mental operations of ordering to be merged with physical operations. Most of the fundamental data structures learned by programmers permit entities to be numbered in some way. Tables, lists, queues, arrays, and trees all offer ways of enumerating, as well as sorting, ordering, searching, and accessing. It is easy to forget that these structural relationships also interpellate bodies as subjects, citizens, inhabitants, patients, users, clients, workers, events, others, things, parts, animals, organisms, stock, sets, lives, etc. The very same construction and manipulation that transform numerals (graphic forms) into numbers (things in relations of plurality), constitute bodies in structural relationships. Interpellation is one way of theorizing the ritual hailing that brings bodies of all kinds into forms of subjecthood in relation to number. This singularizing effect is deeply embedded in the graphical writing systems on which software so heavily draws. The very existence of a numeral zero has intense cultural specificity that passes from India through Arabic to medieval Italian calculation techniques. It need only be invented in numbering systems that ill-afford mental calculation such as the base 10 systems Western cultures have long used ("Zero seems to emerge with the pressures of the graphic recording of a clumsy calculating system"[20]).

Enumeration has specificities that relate to rituals of interpellation embedded in language, gesture, and writing. This point has deep implications for what software does, and how "others" are designated and predicated in software. If these rituals differ between times and places (Verran discusses Yoruba tallying and counting practices in detail), then relations of unity and plurality differ. The general logic constantly re-enacted in elementary software constructs defined at the level of programming languages and at the level of software architectures makes particular ways of enumeration (and sorting, searching, etc.) continue to work. Although enumeration practices are usually "naturalized" (that is, taken for granted), making particular enumerations work is political: it concerns how people belong together. "In any practical going-on with numbers," writes Verran, "what matters is that they can be *made* to work, and *making* them work is a politics. Yet is a politics that completely evades conventional foundationist [that is, based on necessarily uniform ideals] analysis."[21] The universality that might be at stake here could be called "ideal" in the sense that it is "always already beyond any simple or 'absolute' unity, therefore a source of conflicts forever."[22]

Problems of Actual Internationalization

In analyzing how software moves from technical to fictitious to ideal universality, internationalization becomes increasingly problematic. The figuring of otherness becomes steadily more deeply embodied. In i18n, the local adaptations of technical universality weave software into the techno-economic realities of globalization. More recent alterations in software distribution and certain aspects of production broaden the spectrum of actors involved and begin to change the way software moves globally. Yet this occurs at a cost: It requires individuals to fit a norm of being human beings. However in ideal universality, the construct that animates internationalization is transindividual by nature. That is, it questions the given and seemingly natural rules that constitute software as a convoluted set of practices of tallying, numbering, sorting, and searching. This questioning directly concerns embodiment, power, and language. It is not easy to point to any practical instance of this questioning. The notion of an ideal universality of software might, however, frame the problem of software internationalization at a different level.

Notes

1. Helen Verran, *Science and An African Logic*.

2. Java internationalization.

3. Sun Microsystems, *After Internationalization: The Java Tutorial*.

4. See http://java.sun.com/j2se/1.5.0/docs/guide/intl/locale.doc.html.

5. Unicode Consortium, "What is Unicode?"

6. Soenhke Zehle, "FLOSS Redux: Notes on African Software Politics."

7. Canonical Ltd, The Ubuntu Manifesto.

8. Mark Shuttleworth, *Rosetta*.

9. Mark Shuttleworth, *The LauchPad Homepage.* http://www.launchpad.net/.

10. From the Ubuntu About Screen.

11. Zehle, "Floss Redux."

12. Etienne Balibar, "Ambiguous Universality."

13. Donald Knuth, *The Art of Computer Programming*, 232.

14. Verran, *Science and An African Logic*, 101.

15. Ibid, 103.

16. Brian Rotman, *Signifying Nothing: the Semiotics of Zero*.

17. Verran, *Science and An African Logic*, 65.

18. Ibid, 66.

19. Guido van Rossum, *2.3.8 Mapping Types—classdict, Python Library Reference*.

20. Verran, *Science and An African Logic*, 64; on this point, also see Rotman, *Signifying Nothing*, 60.

21. Verran, *Science and An African Logic*, 88.

22. Balibar, Universality, *Ambiguous Universality*, 72.

■

Interrupt

Simon Yuill

In the early days of modern computing, the computer would execute a single program at a time, from start to finish. This is known as "batch processing"; programs would be collected in a batch and then run one after another. By the late 1950s a new paradigm had emerged, that of interactive computing, in which the computer operator could stop and start programs and edit them on the computer itself. This required the computer processor to receive external signals while it was running. Two methods emerged for handling this: "polling" and "interrupts." In polling, the computer periodically checks to see if any external signals have arrived but the processor retains control over when they are handled. In interrupts, the signals are handled whenever they arrive, "interrupting" the processor in whatever it is doing, and giving some control over its activities to an external agent. While polling continues to be used on some simple processor devices, the interrupt enabled more sophisticated forms of interaction between a computer and the external world. It has become the basis of most operating system designs and is hardwired into many processor chips and computer boards, such as the IRQ (Interrupt ReQuest) lines, which provide the link between the central processing unit (CPU) and all kinds of external devices such as keyboards, mice, and network cards. Interrupts can also be used for handling interaction between different programs on one operating system, signalling, for example, when a program has completed. It is also used for handling errors that arise in the execution of a program, such as buffer overflows, errors in allocating memory, or attempting to divide a number by zero. The interrupt is the main mechanism through which an operating system seeks to maintain a coherent environment for programs to run within, coordinating everything external to the central processor, whether that be events in the outside world, such as a user typing on a keyboard or moving a mouse, or things outside the system's internal coherence, such as a buffer overflow or an operational error in a piece of software.[1]

The interrupt fundamentally changed the nature of computer operation, and therefore also the nature of the software that runs on it. The interrupt not only creates a break in the temporal step-by-step processing of an algorithm, but also creates an opening in its "operational space." It breaks the solipsism of the computer as a Turing Machine, enabling the outside world to "touch" and engage with an algorithm.[2] The interrupt acknowledges that software is not sufficient unto itself, but must include actions outside of its coded instructions. In a very basic sense, it makes software "social," making its performance dependent upon associations with "others"—processes and performances elsewhere. These may be human users, other pieces of software, or numerous forms of phenomena traced by physical sensors such as weather monitors and security alarms. The interrupt connects the dataspace of software to the sensorium of the world.

Within an operating system, the various kinds of interrupt signals are differentiated by an identifier, which is mapped to a short handler program by an "interrupt vector." In this way, typing on a keyboard can be handled differently from a packet arriving over the network. The notion of an interrupt vector, however, can be rethought, not only in terms of how particular external events extend into actions within the operating system, but also in terms of how the actions of a particular piece of software are themselves extended into, and are extensions of, various sorts of social actions. The interrupt vector, then, becomes a carrier through which different elements of a social assemblage are associated. The social aspect of software unfolds in the very process of making these associations. Latour describes the "social" as being the associations that link different "actors" in time and space.[3] These actors can be humans, or non-human objects. An actor is any entity that plays a significant part in the formation of associations from which the social is formed. The interrupt is one principle through which such associations can be constructed and broken. During a lecture by the philosopher Jacques Derrida, a member of the audience, the cultural theorist Avital Ronell, interjected with the question: "How do you recognize that you are speaking to a living person?" to which Derrida responded: "By the fact that they interrupt you."[4] In this sense, we could say that software's "cognition" of the social is comparable to Derrida's. Indeed, the action of interruption, of the break, is fundamental to the notion of the "gram," the mark that differentiates, upon which Derrida's grammatology, the study of the role of inscription in the construction of human social and cultural systems, is based.[5] The interrupt, therefore, is the mechanism through which the social, as a process of making and breaking associations with others, is inscribed into a piece of running software.

If software is understood as an actor in such assemblages, then the operational space in which it performs is potentially the space of an entire assemblage, one which grows and contracts as circumstances change. The combinations in which software operates are often more complex than might first be assumed. A typical piece of desktop software, such as a text editor program, operates within an assemblage that includes not only the software itself and the user but also the operating system on which the program runs, and the devices through which the user interacts with it: the mouse, keyboard, and screen. If the keyboard is removed, the text editor program becomes inoperative, even though the program itself has not been altered. Elements such as the keyboard also provide a form of liminal boundary. When we press the keyboard we are literally and consciously entering into the operational space of the software. The situation becomes more complex, however, as we start to consider the kinds of assemblage that are constituted by other forms of software, such as those in embedded devices, and the "actors" with which they operate, such as radio frequency identification tags (RFID). Whereas we might describe the operational space of software in the context of a user at a desktop system as having a liminal boundary, these other, far more distributed, forms of software operate in a much more porous situation. Liminal boundaries are those that draw a distinct line, that one can have a definite sense of crossing, of being inside and outside of. Porous boundaries are less distinct; it is harder to tell when one is inside or outside, and they may have qualities of absorbency and leakage. Some assemblages may consist of multiple operational spaces, either nested or overlapping. The interrupt can therefore be thought of, on an extended level, as the vector that not only constructs associations between actors, but also traverses varying operational spaces.

Transport systems has been one of the main fields of deployment of such porous software systems. A combination of road surface sensor systems and networked CCTV cameras, linking in various analysis tools, have brought roadways into the operational space of software such as Automated Number Plate Recognition Systems (ANPRS) and Intelligent Transportation Systems (ITS). These systems monitor traffic flow for irregular incidents such as speed violation and breakdowns, or track vehicles in Congestion Charging Zones such as that in central London.[6] The roadway itself becomes a software interface, and road-markings and traffic signs all become actors within the assemblage of the roadway's operational space. The cars traveling on the roads may contribute their own software actors, in employing intelligent braking systems, or GPS navigation consoles. Within the process of airline travel, numerous software actors enter in and out of a variety of assemblages that travelers, pilots, and other staff all, similarly, enter and exit. These include the software that manages the transport of luggage and tourists through the airport terminal, the software that analyzes x-ray scans of luggage, the passport systems that log traveler IDs, which, in turn, are often connected to automated photographic devices or biometric scanners. The interoperability of runway markings, air corridors, and control tower navigation systems, and the on-board flight controllers also play a part. On an average day, an individual in a city may connect and disconnect from numerous assemblages involving different software actors. Frequently, they are unaware of the various operational spaces that they have interrupted: using mobile phones, "smart" cards on public transport systems (such as London's Oyster card), bank autoteller machines, RFID tagged goods, or a keycode to access a building. The CCTV system of a bank, office, or housing estate may be linked up to movement analysis tools, seeking to detect a possible hold-up scenario, or irregular movement patterns among the building's occupants. The introduction of chip-carrying biometric identity cards, as is currently planned in the United Kingdom, may bring with it the ability to cross-reference these cards and the readings of CCTV facial analysis systems, linking the interruptions of human activity in urban space to singular identities, just as logging onto a computer links the interrupts of keyboard and mouse to a particular username.[7] The operational space of software extends over large physical areas in which algorithms become the arbiters of normative behavior and of inclusion and exclusion. The "Cartografiando el Territorio Madiaq" is an ongoing project to map the complex of surveillance systems, military bases, and communication infrastructures that are in place across the Strait of Gibraltar between Spain and Morocco.[8] It demonstrates the complex assemblages of actors (technological, military, and legal) that are involved in policing the Spanish borders. The play of the liminal and porous in evidence here is not only one of boundaries along the operational spaces of various software systems, but also the construction of the European Union's own political and economic boundaries which, through such surveillance, become conflated with software processes.

Porous is not the same as open. A porous surface acts as a regulatory mechanism, as the porosity of skin regulates the flow of moisture and air between the body and its environment. The systems described above create porosity in otherwise open spaces. The regulatory trajectory, however, is not exclusively one-way. In a memoir, one of the inventors of the interrupt mechanism, Edsger Dijkstra, wrote:

It was a great invention, but also a Box of Pandora. Because the exact moments of the interrupts were unpredictable and outside our control, the interrupt mechanism turned the computer into a nondeterministic machine with a non-reproducible behavior, and could we control such a beast?[9]

The interrupt increases the contingency of the environment in which a piece of software runs. In constructing associations with an "outside" it makes the operation of software more situated in that outside and, therefore, prone to the contingencies of that outside environment.[10] The interrupt transfers governance back and forth between computer and user, or other outside actors. Around every piece of software, a set of shadow practices develop that are not inscribed in the code itself, but on which its ability to act depends. Christian Heath and Paul Luff's studies of the use of software in businesses and organizations demonstrates that the software is often only effective when nested within larger structures of governance that guide the gestures of those who interact with it.[11] This combined governance of software and user environments is sharply evident in call centers, in which a hybrid software and managerial infrastructure maintains the overall mechanism.[12] What might be called "counter-interruptive" practices also develop, such as maps of CCTV and traffic cameras enabling people to plan routes that avoid them, or call center employees who trigger fake systems crashes to buy a bit of unlogged free time.[13] The transfer of governance can also be an opportunity to interrupt its initial vector and claim other possibilities.

If the interrupt teaches us anything about software, it is that software is in many cases only as effective as the people who use it, those nondeterministic machines with their complex, non-reproducible behaviors, those "others" on whom it relies—can it really control such beasts? To understand software in terms of the interrupt is to understand it in terms of its place within larger structures of social formation and governance. Software engineering is simultaneously social engineering. Software criticism, therefore, must also be simultaneously social. In critically engaging with software, we must not only map the vectors of the interrupt, but also seek to make our own interruptions, to pose questions and insert alternative vectors and practices within the assemblages it connects to.

Notes

1. The specific forms and namings of interrupts can vary on different operating systems and hardware platforms, for a detailed account of interrupt handling in Linux see Daniel P. Bovet and Marco Cesati, *Understanding the Linux Kernel*. For a comparison of interrupt systems on different processors, including those used in embedded systems, see William Bolton, *Microprocessor Systems*, and Myke Predko, *Programming and Customizing PICmicro MCU Microcontrollers*. For information on the historical development of the interrupt and comparisons to polling, see Mark Smotherman, "Interrupts"; Norman Hardy, "History of Interrupts"; Randall Hyde, "Interrupts and Polled I/O," in *The Art of Assembly Language Programming*; David A. Rusling, "Interrupts and Interrupt Handling."

2. Peter Wegner and Dana Goldin have argued that this introduces a different level of capability into computers that the Turing Machine does not allow, therefore changing the ways in which computations can be processed and assessed; see Peter Wegner and Dana Goldin, "Computation Beyond Turing Machines" and the entry on Interaction.

3. Bruno Latour, *Reassembling the Social: An Introduction to Actor-Network Theory*. Latour originally used the term "network," as in his Actor-Network Theory, but has recently shifted to "assemblage." The latter carries stronger connotations of something that is put together and taken apart and possibly quite contingent, which "network" does not convey. As it also helps keep a clearer conceptual distinction between a computer network and a social assemblage, I have used it here.

4. The event is described in Avital Ronell, *Finitude's Score: Essays for the End of the Millennium*, 3.

5. Jacques Derrida, *Of Grammatology*.

6. For an overview of such systems, see Stephen Graham and Simon Marvin, *Telecommunications and the City: Electronic Spaces, Urban Places*. One of the key algorithms used in traffic analysis is the McMaster algorithm developed at McMaster University, Toronto; see Fred L. Hall, "McMaster Algorithm."

7. Computer vision and video analysis is currently a major area in computer sciences research; example projects include: Jaime Dever, Niels da Vitoria Lobo, and Mubarak

Shah, "Automatic Visual Recognition of Armed Robbery," and Douglas Ayers and Mubarak Shah, "Monitoring Human Behavior from Video Taken in an Office Environment." Proponents of algorithmic-based facial recognition often state that it does not suffer from problems of social and cultural prejudice that human surveillance staff often bring with them. Studies of such algorithms, however, have shown that due either to the data sets on which they are trained, or empirical factors in how they operate, they may still demonstrate aspects of differential treatment for different ethnic groups, which result in racially-weighted responses; see Lucas D. Introna and David Wood, "Picturing Algorithmic Surveillance: The Politics of Facial Recognition Systems."

8. Hackitectura, *MAPA: Cartografiando el territorio madiaq.*

9. Edsger W. Dijkstra, "My Recollections of Operating System Design," 13–14. In this document, Dijkstra also discusses some of the limitations of the polling method.

10. Lucy Suchman has analyzed this aspect of computer use in detail through the concept of "situatedness" in Lucy Suchman, *Plans and Situated Actions: The Problems of Human-Machine Communication.*

11. Christian Heath and Paul Luff, *Technology in Action.*

12. A detailed account of various employees' experiences of working in call centers is provided in Kolinko, *Hotlines - Call Centre Inquiry Communism.*

13. The Institute for Applied Autonomy's *iSee* is an interactive online map of CCTV systems in central New York; it enables users to plot a path of least surveillance between two locations in the city: http://www.appliedautonomy.com/isee.html/. http://www.controleradar.org is a French website providing listings of computer-controlled road cameras across France. Kolinko, *Hotlines - Call Centre*, provides several accounts of ways in which call center employees have tried to counteract the conditions under which they work.

■

Language

Florian Cramer

Software and language are intrinsically related, since software may process language, and is constructed in language. Yet language means different things in the context of computing: formal languages in which algorithms are expressed and software is implemented, and in so-called "natural" spoken languages. There are at least two layers of formal language in software: programming language in which the software is written, and the language implemented within the software as its symbolic controls. In the case of compilers, shells, and macro languages, for example, these layers can overlap. "Natural" language is what can be processed as data by software; since this processing is formal, however, it is restricted to syntactical operations.

While differentiation of computer programming languages as "artificial languages" from languages like English as "natural languages" is conceptually important and undisputed, it remains problematic in its pure terminology: There is nothing "natural" about spoken language; it is a cultural construct and thus just as "artificial" as any formal machine control language. To call programming languages "machine languages" doesn't solve the problem either, as it obscures that "machine languages" are human creations.

High-level machine-independent programming languages such as Fortran, C, Java, and Basic are not even direct mappings of machine logic. If programming languages are human languages for machine control, they could be called cybernetic languages. But these languages can also be used outside machines—in programming handbooks, for example, in programmer's dinner table jokes, or as abstract formal languages for expressing logical constructs, such as in Hugh Kenner's use of the Pascal programming language to explain aspects of the structure of Samuel Beckett's writing.[1]

In this sense, computer control languages could be more broadly defined as syntactical languages as opposed to semantic languages. But this terminology is not without its problems either. Common languages like English are both formal and semantic; although their scope extends beyond the formal, anything that can be expressed in a computer control language can also be expressed in common language. It follows that computer control languages are a formal (and as such rather primitive) subset of common human languages.

To complicate things even further, computer science has its own understanding of "operational semantics" in programming languages, for example in the construction of a programming language interpreter or compiler. Just as this interpreter doesn't perform "interpretations" in a hermeneutic sense of semantic text explication, the computer science notion of "semantics" defies linguistic and common sense understanding of the word, since compiler construction is purely syntactical, and programming languages denote nothing but syntactical manipulations of symbols.

What might more suitably be called the semantics of computer control languages resides in the symbols with which those operations are denoted in most programming languages: English words like "if," "then," "else," "for," "while," "goto," and "print," in conjunction with arithmetical and punctuation symbols; in alphabetic software controls, words like "list," "move," "copy," and "paste"; in graphical software controls, such as symbols like the trash can.

Ferdinand de Saussure states that the signs of common human language are arbitrary[2] because it's purely a cultural-social convention that assigns phonemes to concepts. Likewise, it's purely a cultural convention to assign symbols to machine operations. But just as the cultural choice of phonemes in spoken language is restrained by what the human voice can pronounce, the assignment of symbols to machine operations is limited to what can be efficiently processed by the machine and of good use to humans.[3] This compromise between operability and usability is obvious in, for example, Unix commands. Originally used on teletype terminals, the operation "copy" was abbreviated to the command "cp," "move" to "mv," "list" to "ls," etc., in order to cut down machine memory use, teletype paper consumption, and human typing effort at the same time. Any computer control language is thus a cultural compromise between the constraints of machine design—which is far from objective, but based on human choices, culture, and thinking style itself[4]—and the equally subjective user preferences, involving fuzzy factors like readability, elegance, and usage efficiency.

The symbols of computer control languages inevitably do have semantic connotations simply because there exist no symbols with which humans would not associate some meaning. But symbols can't denote any semantic statements, that is, they do not express meaning in their own terms; humans metaphorically read meaning into them through associations they make. Languages without semantic denotation are not historically new phenomena; mathematical formulas are their oldest example.

In comparison to common human languages, the multitude of programming languages is of lesser significance. The criterion of Turing completeness of a programming language, that is, that any computation can be expressed in it, means that every programming language is, formally speaking, just a riff on every other programming language. Nothing can be expressed in a Turing-complete language such as C that couldn't also be expressed in another Turing-complete language such as Lisp (or Fortran, Smalltalk, Java . . .) and vice versa. This ultimately proves the importance of human and cultural factors in programming languages: while they are interchangeable in regard to their control of machine functions, their different structures—semantic descriptors, grammar and style in which algorithms can be expressed—lend themselves not only to different problem sets, but also to different styles of thinking.

Just as programming languages are a subset of common languages, Turing-incomplete computer control languages are a constrained subset of Turing-complete languages. This prominently includes markup languages (such as HTML), file formats, network protocols, and most user controls (see the entry "Interface") of computer programs. In most cases, languages of this type are restrained from denoting algorithmic operations for computer security reasons—to prevent virus infection and remote takeover. This shows how the very design of a formal language is a design for machine control. Access to hardware functions is limited not only through the software application, but through the syntax the software application may use for storing and transmitting the information it processes. To name one computer control language a "programming language," another a "protocol," and yet another a "file format" is merely a convention, a nomenclature indicating different degrees of syntactic restraint built into the very design of a computer control language.

In its most powerful Turing-complete superset, computer control language is language that executes. As with magical and speculative concepts of language, the word automatically performs the operation. Yet this is not to be confused with what linguistics calls a "performative" or "illocutionary" speech act, for example, the words of a judge who pronounces a verdict, a leader giving a command, or a legislator passing a law. The execution of computer control languages is purely formal; it is the manipulation of a machine, not a social performance based on human conventions such as accepting a verdict. Computer languages become performative only through the social impact of the processes they trigger, especially when their outputs aren't critically checked. Joseph Weizenbaum's software psychotherapist Eliza, a simple program that syntactically transforms input phrases, is a classical example,[5] as is the 1987 New York Stock Exchange crash that involved a chain reaction of "sell" recommendations by day trading software.[6]

Writing in a computer programming language is phrasing instructions for an utter idiot. The project of Artificial Intelligence is to prove that intelligence is just a matter of a sufficiently massive layering of foolproof recipes—in linguistic terms, that semantics is nothing else but (more elaborate) syntax. As long as A.I. fails to deliver this proof, the difference between common languages and computer control languages continues to exist, and language processing through computers remains restrained to formal string manipulations, a fact that after initial enthusiasm has made many experimental poets since the 1950s abandon their experiments with computer-generated texts.[7]

The history of computing is rich with confusions of formal with common human languages, and false hopes and promises that formal languages would become more like common human languages. Among the unrealized hopes are artificial intelligence, graphical user interface design with its promise of an "intuitive" or, to use Jef Raskin's term, "humane interface,"[8] and major currents of digital art. Digital installation art typically misperceives its programmed behaviorist black boxes as "interactive," and some digital artists are caught in the misconception that they can overcome what they see as the Western male binarism of computer languages by reshaping them after romanticized images of indigenous human languages.

The digital computer is a symbolic machine that computes syntactical language and processes alphanumerical symbols; it treats all data—including images and sounds—as textual, that is, as chunks of coded symbols. Nelson Goodman's criteria of writing as "disjunct" and "discrete," or consisting of separate single entities that differ from other separate single entities, also applies to digital files.[9] The very meaning of "digitization" is to structure analog data as numbers and store them as numerical texts composed of discrete parts.

All computer software controls are linguistic regardless of their perceivable shape, alphanumerical writing, graphics, sound signals, or whatever else. The Unix command "rm file" is operationally identical to dragging the file into the trashcan on a desktop. Both are just different encodings for the same operation, just as alphabetic language and morse beeps are different encodings for the same characters. As a symbolic handle, this encoding may enable or restrain certain uses of the language. In this respect, the differences between ideographic-pictorial and abstract-symbolic common languages also apply to computer control languages. Pictorial symbols simplify control languages through predefined objects and operations, but make it more difficult to link them through a grammar and thus express custom operations. Just as a pictogram of a house is easier to understand than the letters h-o-u-s-e, the same is true for the trashcan icon in comparison to the "rm" command. But it is difficult to precisely express the operation "If I am home tomorrow at six, I will clean up every second room in the house" through a series of pictograms. Abstract, grammatical alphanumeric languages are more suitable for complex computational instructions.[10] The utopia of a universal pictorial computer control language (with icons, windows, and pointer operations) is a reenactment of the rise and eventual fall of universal pictorial language utopias in the Renaissance, from Tommaso Campanella's "Città del sole" to Comenius' "Orbis pictus"—although the modern project of expressing only machine operations in pictograms was less ambitious.

The converse to utopian language designs occurs when computer control languages get appropriated and used informally in everyday culture. Jonathan Swift tells how scientists on the flying island of Lagado "would, for example, praise the beauty of a woman, or any other animal . . . by rhombs, circles, parallelograms, ellipses, and other "geometrical terms."[11] Likewise, there is programming language poetry which, unlike most algorithmic poetry, writes its program source as the poetical work, or crossbreeds cybernetic with common human languages. These "code poems" or "codeworks" often play with the interference between human agency and programmed processes in computer networks.

In computer programming and computer science, "code" is often understood either as a synonym of computer programming language or as a text written in such a language. This modern usage of the term "code" differs from the traditional mathematical and cryptographic notion of code as a set of formal transformation rules that transcribe one group of symbols to another group of symbols, for example, written letters into morse beeps. The translation that occurs when a text in a programming language gets compiled into machine instructions is not an encoding in this sense because the process is not one-to-one reversible. This is why proprietary software companies can keep their source "code" secret. It is likely that the computer cultural understanding of "code" is historically derived from the name of the first high-level computer programming language, "Short Code" from 1950.[12] The only programming language that is a code in the original sense is assembly language, the human-readable mnemonic one-to-one representation of processor instructions. Conversely, those instructions can be coded back, or "disassembled," into assembly language.

Software as a whole is not only "code" but a symbolic form involving cultural practices of its employment and appropriation. But since writing in a computer control language is what materially makes up software, critical thinking about computers is not possible without an informed understanding of the structural formalism of its control languages. Artists and activists since the French Oulipo poets and the MIT hackers in the 1960s have shown how their limitations can be embraced as creative challenges. Likewise, it is incumbent upon critics to reflect the sometimes more and sometimes less amusing constraints and game rules computer control languages write into culture.

Notes

1. Hugh Kenner, "Beckett Thinking," in Hugh Kenner, *The Mechanic Muse*, 83–107.

2. Ferdinand de Saussure, *Course in General Linguistics, "Chapter I: Nature of the Linguistic Sign."*

3. See the section, "Saussurean Signs and Material Matters," in N. Katherine Hayles, *My Mother Was a Computer*, 42–45.

4. For example, Steve Wozniak's design of the Apple I mainboard was considered "a beautiful work of art" in its time according to Steven Levy, *Insanely Great: The Life and Times of Macintosh*, 81.

5. Joseph Weizenbaum, "ELIZA—A Computer Program for the Study of Natural Language Communication between Man and Machine."

6. Marsha Pascual, "Black Monday, Causes and Effects."

7. Among them concrete poetry writers, French Oulipo poets, the German poet Hans Magnus Enzensberger, and the Austrian poets Ferdinand Schmatz and Franz Josef Czernin.

8. Jef Raskin, *The Humane Interface: New Directions for Designing Interactive Systems*.

9. According to Nelson Goodman's definition of writing in *The Languages of Art*, 143.

10. Alan Kay, an inventor of the graphical user interface, conceded in 1990 that "it would not be surprising if the visual system were less able in this area than the mechanism that solve noun phrases for natural language. Although it is not fair to say that 'iconic languages can't work' just because no one has been able to design a good one, it is likely that the above explanation is close to truth." This status quo hasn't changed since. Alan Kay, "User Interface: A Personal View," in, Brenda Laurel ed. *The Art of Human-Computer Interface Design*, Reading: Addison Wesley, 1989, 203.

11. Swift, Jonathan, *Gulliver's Travels*, Project Gutenberg Ebook, available at http://www.gutenberg.org/dirs/extext197/gltrv10.txt/.

12. See Wolfgang Hagen, "The Style of Source Codes."

■

Lists

Alison Adam

The list is a fundamental way of classifying and ordering information. In computing, the word refers to a data structure that is an ordered group of entities, although, as explored below, culturally, its roots are much wider. Arrays, which are multidimensional, are related to lists in that a list can be considered as a one dimensional array. Queues and stacks are special types of lists. In a queue, the element that was added to the queue first is processed first, behaving in much the same way as an orderly queue of people waiting in line for a bus. This is often described as "first in, first out," or FIFO, processing. By contrast, in a stack, the last element added to the stack is processed first—"last in, first out," or LIFO, processing. In most cultures, a stack approach to waiting in line for a bus would not be acceptable.

Lists can be present in spoken and written language. Arguably, it is the business of recording lists which marks out literate societies from preliterate societies, where knowledge was passed orally from older to younger generations.[1] A list is a form of knowledge representation that can free knowledge from the limitation of having to be passed down, through direct contact, from one generation to another. Some of the earliest evidence of written language is in the form of lists. The cuneiform tablets from around the second millennium BC contain accounting lists and lists of objects and vocabularies, lists for performing religious rituals and types of medical treatment.[2] Such lists can be lists of things, such as data or objects, they can also be lists of instructions, or we could even regard them as programs of sorts. Recipe lists detail a list of steps needed to complete a task but contain no generality nor the idea of proof; rather they contain "hard coded" steps or sequences of instructions. Lists supply knowledge or information about what exists and how to behave in the world.

The power of such lists is apparent in the fact that the kings of Mesopotamia regarded leaving a list inscribed on a tablet, after death, as insurance for an everlasting legacy. The Sumerian king list, a chronology of dynasties of Mesopotamian kings, is just such a document. It indicates a smooth succession of rulers, a successive rolling out of seamless historical epochs, but leaves out the bumpy bits of history, when rival Mesopotamian cities vied for control. In this way, lists can be a way of sanitizing and simplifying knowledge. As Geoffrey Bowker and Susan Leigh Star[3] attest, there is always a tension between attempts at universal standardization via lists and the local circumstances of their use.

List-making is often seen as a fundamental activity of modern society. Indeed Michel Foucault[4] and Patrick Tort[5] claim that the production of lists (e.g., classifications of geological specimens, languages, races, animals, and so on) is a defining feature of the development of modern science. Latour[6] argues that the main job of the bureaucrat is to construct lists that can then be shuffled around and compared. The bureaucratization of science in the nineteenth century is an important move away from science as the province of the gentleman amateur to science as bureaucratic control in the service of empire. We can then see the connection between the nineteenth-century scientific taxonomists, collecting and organizing and measuring and ordering the world, and the ancient cuneiform lists. Both tell us what the world is and how we are to behave, therefore they tell us how to order the world and how to organize work and labor. Through lists we order and control ourselves and the world we inhabit. According to Bowker and Star in describing the work of imperial taxonomists:

These diverse authors have all looked at the work involved in making these productions possible. Instead of analysing the dazzling end products of data collection and analysis—in the various forms of Hammurabi's code, mythologies, the theory of evolution, the welfare state—they have instead chosen to dust off the archives and discover piles and piles of lowly, dull, mechanical lists. The material culture of bureaucracy and empire is not found in pomp and circumstance, nor even in the first instance at the point of a gun, but rather at the point of a list.[7]

If lists are such powerful creatures, not only for representing knowledge about the world, but also for ordering and controlling the world and ourselves, it is small wonder that they hold such appeal in the design and use of programming languages.

LISP (whose name derives from "List Processor") is the prime example of a programming language that exploits the power of the list.[8] The list provides an elegant data structure for the processing of symbols, rather than numbers, which is vital for the science of artificial intelligence. Considering the requirements of a programming language that would reason about the world rather than purely crunch numbers, McCarthy, the founding father of LISP, argues: "This involved representing information about the world by sentences in a suitable formal language and a reasoning program that would decide what to do by making logical inferences. Representing sentences by list structure seemed appropriate—it still is—and a list processing language also seemed appropriate for programming the operations involved in deduction—and still is."[9]

Lists are versatile. They may order and constrain but they may also surprise. Note Jorge Luis Borges's incredible taxonomic list from an ancient Chinese encyclopaedia. This is a list of animals that is divided into "(a) belonging to the Emperor, (b) embalmed, (c), tame, (d) sucking pigs, (e) sirens, (f) fabulous, (g), stray dogs, (h) included in the present classification [*an early example of recursion?*], (i) frenzied, (j) innumerable [*potential for an infinite loop with no terminating condition?*], (k) drawn with a very fine camelhair brush, (1) *et cetera*, (m) having just broken the water pitcher, (n) that from a long way off look like flies."[10]

John Law and Annemarie Mol explain the virtues of such a list: "A list doesn't have to impose a single mode of ordering on what is included in it. Items in the list aren't necessarily responses to the same questions but may hang together in other ways . . . a list differs from a classification in that it recognizes its incompleteness. It doesn't even need to seek completeness. If someone comes along with something to add to the list, something that emerges as important, this may indeed be added to it."[11]

This applies to LISP lists. Note the example of a list of heterogeneous elements in a LISP primer:

(3 FRENCH HENS 2 TURTLE DOVES 1 PARTRIDGE 1 PEAR TREE)[12]

Note also that the list is complete—hence the parentheses—but it can be amended. We can use the CAR and CDR functions to obtain the first element of the list or the remainder of the list, respectively. (This, simply, is what these functions do.)

Lists may contain other lists.

```
((PENNSYLVANIA (THE KEYSTONE STATE))
(NEW-JERSEY (THE GARDEN STATE))
(MASSACHUSETTS (THE BAY STATE))
(FLORIDA (THE SUNSHINE STATE))
(NEW-YORK (THE EMPIRE STATE))
(INDIANA (THE HOOSIER STATE)))) [13]
```

or may even be empty (). Lists are special. AARDVARK is not the same as (AARDVARK). [14]

LISP is the second oldest programming language (after FORTRAN) still in use. McCarthy[15] attributes its longevity, in part, to its representation of symbolic information, externally by lists, and internally by list structure; LISP's programs, not just its data structures, are lists. Perhaps some of the reason for LISP's survival, through the various phases of our relationship with computers, is because, through its emphasis on the list, it captures something about the human condition and our need to make and manipulate lists to make sense of the world. The elasticity of the list, its capacity to surprise, means that LISP resists the obvious Taylorization that one might expect with such a powerful ordering and processing tool.[16] Compare the cuneiform tablets of old, and an "ancient" programming language of the modern world. LISP offers a promise of the power of both the old lists, the nineteenth-century scientific lists, and something beyond. In modern terms, this is a goal of artificial intelligence languages, of which LISP is the *lingua franca*. Lists, whether inscibed in clay, or *in silico*, represent knowledge and how we reason about knowledge.

LISP resists. Lists persist.

Notes

1. William McGaughey, "On the Cutting Edge of Knowledge: A Short History of the Most Advanced Techniques of Establishing Truth in Each Age."

2. Marc Van De Mieroop, *Cuneiform Texts and the Writing of History.*

3. Geoffrey Bowker and Susan Leigh Star, *Sorting Things Out: Classification and its Consequences,* 139.

4. Michel Foucault, *The Order of Things*.

5. Patrick Tort, *La Raison Classificatoire: Les Complexes Discursifs-Quinze Etudes*.

6. Bruno Latour, *Science in Action: How to Follow Scientists and Engineers Through Society*.

7. Bowker and Star, *Sorting Things Out,* 137.

8. John McCarthy, *LISP Prehistory—Summer 1956 through Summer 1958*.

9. Ibid.

10. Cited in Foucault, *The Order of Things,* xvi.

11. John Law and Annemarie Mol, *Complexities: Social Studies of Knowledge Practices*, 14.

12. David S. Touretzky, *COMMON LISP: A Gentle Introduction to Symbolic Computation,* 32.

13. Ibid, 49.

14. Ibid, 33.

15. McCarthy, LISP Prehistory.

16. Richard Hull, "Governing the Conduct of Computing: Computer Science, the Social Sciences and Frameworks of Computing," Accounting, Management & Information Technology 7 (1997): 213–40.

Loop

Wilfried Hou Je Bek

The symbol of the snake nibbling away at its own tail, that mythological archetype of paradoxical repetition, is only partly suitable as a metaphor for the LOOP, that gargoyle of cyclical imagination in computation. The LOOP, a "reusable pattern where the language executes part of the pattern automatically, and you supply the parts that are different"[1] is one of the ways in which programming has gusto.[2] But it is not a single minded concept; the LOOP denotes a vast chain of beings (iterators, GO TO statements with passing arguments, count-controlled loops, condition-controlled loops, collection controlled loops, tail-end recursion, enumerators, continuations, generators, Lambda forms . . .) that crowd computer science and cloud the circumstances of its miracles.

Programming is an art[3] but we talk of computer *science*; this army of engineers has, however, failed to deliver us something like a looposcope, an instrument of vision that would augment our understanding of the manmade world we are trying to manipulate into constructs of unearthly beauty. This hypothetical apparatus would, in another medium, recreate with mnemogenic rhythm the striking experience of circularity produced by the straight-line forwardism of a discrete state machine.

The LOOP is an uphill continuum of abstractions. Some key moments stand out:

1. The humble origins of the LOOP when it leaks aboveground from the patterns carved on the stone that is the hardware.
2. The LOOP logically engineered for elegance on the slab of the programming language designer.
3. The release of the LOOP in the wild where typos, logical flaws, undecidability, and sloppy implementation haunt it. The LOOP needs only one opportunity in a run-time to become infinite.

In between these inauspicious moments, in the elephantiasis of abstraction and invention, in the syntactic sugar-coated manifestations of its form, the looposcope would be an invaluable aid to call its tail from its head and track the movement of the LOOP through memory, its state permutations and its maneuvres in search space.

A read-write head lives along the infinite tape of a Turing Machine. Its behavior (the head moving back and forth, reading, writing, and erasing symbols after having been instructed to do so by symbols written on that tape) is the sum of all patterns created by the minimal instruction set that guides it. Imagine the following scenario: the head is instructed to JUMP to a certain position on the tape only to find when there another JUMP instruction telling the head to return to whence it came. There it will be instructed to go where it is now and so on and so on and so on, unconditionally and infinitely switching between states. Mostly a LOOP is merely a loop inside another. Traversing this control flow hierarchy the programmer climbs up and down, interrupting from above the loop that has become immortal below. The LOOP is a subset of all possible behavior made possible by JUMP (or BRANCH), the infinite loop is a special class within this set defined by the absence of interruption. The central position of the halting problem (the question of whether a computer given a certain input will halt, or run infinitely) in formal computation suffices to show that the LOOP is the foremost poetic entity in programming.

It is the goal of the programming language designer to provide powerful abstractions. For Alan Kay, designer of Smalltalk, these are "special ways of thinking about situations that in contrast with other knowledge and other ways of thinking critically boost our abilities to understand the world."[4] Such a statement succinctly aligns programming with the agenda of poetic theorists like Coleridge and Yeats. If we regard the loop as a species of tool for thinking about and dealing with problems of a certain nature, the sheer light-footedness of looping allows you to run away with the problem with more ease. Indeed, the debate over what constitutes the most elegant way to organize LOOPs from JUMPs is responsible for some of the most classic texts in computer science.

If you look carefully you will find that surprisingly often a GO TO statement which looks back really is a concealed FOR statement. And you will be pleased to find how the clarity of the algorithm improves when you insert the FOR clause where it belongs

writes Peter Naur of the programming language Algol-60 in 1963, a comment quoted by Donald Knuth in his partly contemplative, mostly technical "Structured Programming with GO TO Statements."[5] Here Knuth traces the accumulation of resentment against GO TO statements that created the conceptual agar on which Edsger Dijkstra's polemical "Go To Statement Considered Harmful,"[6] that grand diatribe against "spaghetti code," could proliferate with the success it did:

For a number of years I have been familiar with the observation that the quality of programmers is a decreasing function of the density of GO TO statements in the programs they produce. More recently I discovered why the use of the GO TO statement has such disastrous effects, and I became convinced that the GO TO statement should be abolished from all "higher level" programming languages (i.e., everything except, perhaps, plain machine code).[7]

The hesitant Knuth, declaring his goal to be to help bring about the mythopoetic entity "Utopia 84," the first "really good programming language," fabulates moments of problem-solving agony when his mind, directed by the habit to use GO TO, was tied behind his back without it. Then he goes on to show how in certain cases a WHILE clause causes wasted cycles on the machine: the convenience of abstraction versus the responsibility of power. How do you find out if Element Y is present in Array X? The computer scientist has various ways to find out, throwing a zoo of loops at it and see what sticks best, but the ordinary webscripter just asks the interpreter "Is Y in X?" and the answer will roll out. Yet it is the LOOP that drives Miss Algorithm, the LOOP that sustains those creatures that live out in the sun. On the other hand, "Language is Fossil Poetry"[8] and who denies the schoolboy his moment of love made sedimental.

In every programming language higher than the hardware mimetic assembly language, the LOOP haphazardly diverges into two branches: iteration, in which "a collection of instructions [is] repeated in a looping manner"; and recursion, which has "each stage of the repetition executed as a subtask of the previous stage." Even though the two are often thought of as being "equivalent in terms of computer power"[9] they are radically different in the way they "feel" to programmers. In iteration, "shape is superinduced," while recursion is "form as proceeding" as Herbert Read said (about classical vs. romantic poetry).[10] Perhaps even Coleridge's famous distinction between fancy and imagination applies here (after all, Read was only paraphrasing Coleridge). In the Coleridgian view iteration would be "the imprisonment of the thing" and recursion the "self-affected sphere of agency."

The glossary in Programming PERL[11] offers definitions for both recursion and iteration. The length of each entry is telling. Iteration is merely, "Doing something repeatedly." The entry for recursion begins: "The art of defining something in terms of itself," and ends: "[Recursion] often works out okay in computer programs if you're careful not to recurse forever, which is like an infinite loop with more spectacular failure modes." Recursion is surrounded in the programmer's mind with a nimbus of warm light captured in an oft-quoted bit of programmers' wisdom, variously attributed to L. Peter Deutsch and Robert Heller: "To iterate is human, to recurse, divine."[12]

Iteration branches off into two niche-driven subspecies canonized in most current programming languages as the primitives FOR and WHILE. Although often interchangeable, FOR is like a tourist that knows when it will be home (but with the power to RETURN earlier), WHILE is like a traveller away for as long as there is no hard reason to come back, potentially forever. Iteration requires special syntax, whereas recursion is the production of looping behavior generated by functions calling themselves. Iterations exist in a special time; recursion is behavior made up from the daily routines of life. Style, "that purification from insincerity, vanity, malignity, arrogance,"[13] is one reason for preferring one kind of LOOP, one instance of peripatetic know-how, above another. The nature of the memory to be manipulated, the way the magic carpet is folded[14] is another factor when deciding which LOOP to apply, which way to walk. Hash tables call for measures other than a one-dimensional list (Fibonacci numbers or a manifesto) or the nocturnal wandering through bi-directional structures (the world wide web or a city). Thinking in general and poetry in particular has forever been closely linked with iteration,[15] and was it not Coleridge who said that poetry is always a circuitous experience?

One aspect of the LOOP, and in many ways its defining quality, is the minimal means that result in automated infinite production. Is it when writing a simple FOR statement for the first time, counting to, say, 10 and printing to the screen at each iteration, that the novice programmer "Beheld the living traces and the sky-pointing proportions of the mighty Pan"?[16] This insight, its magic worn off in the mind of the experienced programmer as a mere fact of life, is that two simple lines of code can produce an "incantation" in which an effort as small as changing the upper limit increases the output to a "fairy-fountain" needing more time to be enacted than the computer it runs on will survive. Is it indeed not this raw force that allows permutation-sects to believe that the answer to the final riddles of the universe can be unwound by rephrasing them in a computational LOOP?

The LOOP is the powerhouse of worlds imagined in silico: the sweat-free producer of matter and time. It takes a Coleridge to do it justice.

Notes

1. Shriram Krishnamurti, *Programming Languages: Application and Interpretation*.

2. William Hazlitt, *The Spirit of the Age*.

3. Donald Knuth, *The Art of Computer Programming*.

4. Donald Knuth, Structured Programming with GO TO Statements.

5. A. C. Kay, "The Early History of SmallTalk," ACM SIGPLAN notices, Vol. 8, No. 3 (1993); available at http://gagne.homedns.org/~tgagne/contrib/EarlyHistoryST.html.

6. Edsger Dijkstra, "Go To Statement Considered Harmful."

7. Dijkstra, ibid.

8. Emerson, 'The Poet,' in Essays: Second Series, 1844.

9. J. Glenn Brookshear, *Computer Science*.

10. Herbert Read, *The True Voice of Feeling*.

11. Larry Wall, Tom Christiansen, Jon Orwant. *Programming Perl*.

12. James O. Coplien, "To Iterate is Human, to Recurse, Devine" in, C++ Report 10(7).

13. William Butler Yeats. *Synge and the Ireland of His Time*.

14. Vladimir Nabokov, *Speak Memory*.

15. See for instance, Rebecca Solnit, *Wanderlust: A History of Walking*.

16. Hazlitt, *The Spirit of the Age*.

■
Memory

Warren Sack

The following examination of computer memory closely scrutinizes the words, rhetoric, and discourse of computer science and several associated disciplines. Presupposed by this methodology of rhetorical analysis is the idea that the words employed in the design and evaluation of new technologies shape the form and function of those technologies. Of course, designers' vocabularies do not completely determine what a technology can do or how it works. After all, designers are not magicians and the activity of software design is not a form of incantation! But, many technologies were written and spoken about long before they were developed into practical, everyday things: flying machines and long distance communication are two technologies that were dreamt about long before they were implemented. Here we review a short history of the metaphors and analogies employed by philosophers, scientists, and technologists to understand memory. We will see how previous metaphors are sometimes later taken for literal truth. When metaphors become scientific models, alternative ways of thinking about the object of study become difficult. The purpose of this entry is to question the metaphors of memory taken as models and, thereby, begin to explore new ways to think about computer memory.

The act of perception stamps in, as it were, a sort of impression of the percept, just as persons do who make an impression with a seal. This explains why, in those who are strongly moved owing to passion, or time of life, no mnemonic impression is formed; just as no impression would be formed if the movement of the seal were to impinge on running water; while there are others in whom, owing to the receiving surface being frayed, as happens to the stucco on old chamber walls, or owing to the hardness of the receiving surface, the requisite impression is not implanted at all.[1]

Aristotle's image of memory is constructed from a seal that is known to work on soft wax or clay. His presupposition is that when our memories are in working order they are akin to a pliant solid, like wax, that can record the impression of a seal.

Aristotle's trope does not begin or end with him. Plato wrote of the analogy before Aristotle; and, Cicero, Quinitilian, Sigmund Freud, and Jacques Derrida explored the trope of memory-as-wax-tablet after him. Each new generation of memory theorists tends to incorporate the latest media technology to explore its similarities with human memory. Or, to phrase this point polemically, as media theorist Friedrich Kittler and his followers have done for the past couple of decades, "Media, then, are [at] the end of theory because in practice they were already there to begin with."[2]

Historically, theorists have not always been clear about when their references to media technology are metaphorical and when they are literal. Derrida, for example, closely scrutinizes Freud's mixed and unstated metaphors about memory.[3] But, many of today's memory theorists quite clearly state that what others might take to be a metaphor, they take to be a literal truth. Contemporary theorists compare human memory and computer memory. Cognitive scientists who explore this analogy believe that humans and machines are two species of the same genus; in the words of computer scientist and economist Herbert Simon, humans and computers are "symbol systems."[4] Thus, cognitive scientists hypothesize that human memory is not akin to computer memory, it is virtually the same thing as computer memory. Or, to put it a different way, the hypothesis is that computer memory is not just one possible model of human memory, it is the best model of memory.

This belief, that the computer is the best model of the object of study, is not unique to cognitive science. It is an operating principle in molecular biology, operations research, neuro-psychology, immunology, game theory, economics, and many other sciences. Historian of science Philip Mirowski calls this literal belief in computation one of the defining characteristics of a "cyborg science," a science that does not use the computer as an analogy but which uses it as a simulacrum of the object of study.[5] For example, Howard Gardner, in his overview and introduction to cognitive science, states that one of the paramount features of cognitive science is this belief:

There is the faith that central to any understanding of the human mind is the electronic computer. Not only are computers indispensable for carrying out studies of various sorts, but, more crucially, the computer also serves as the most viable model of how the human mind functions.[6]

The first set of models devised by cognitive psychologists to explain the structure and dynamics of human memory recapitulated many architectural aspects of then-contemporary computational hardware. For example, the model of Richard Atkinson and Richard Shiffrin[7] included a "short-term store," a "long-term store," "buffers," "slots," and a hypothesis that information processing for storing and retrieving items from memory was a sequential (rather than a parallel) operation. These are architectural details that one can also identify with the computers of that time (i.e., the 1960s). As work in this area developed, the memory models began to look less and less like then-contemporary computer hardware, but they are still frequently phrased in terms that would allow one to implement them in software.

What makes this tight coupling between human memory and computer memory seem plausible? Why might computer memory be seen as "the most viable" model of human memory? To untangle this belief of cognitive scientists it is necessary to remember that before computers were machines they were people, usually women. For over two hundred years, these women—these computers—worked together in groups compiling tables of statistics, tables of trigonometric functions, tables of logarithms. For example, computers worked together in 1757 to calculate the return trajectory of Halley's comet.[8]

When the machines we now call computers were first designed, they were designed to do the work of a human computer. In 1936, Alan Turing designed a machine that could do the work of a human computer. In his paper he writes of "computers" but when he does he is referring to those people who held the job of computer. Turing himself did not go so far as to say that his machine has memory, but he almost does. His mathematical paper is based on an extended analogy between a machine and a person, that is, a human computer. Turing explains how his machine might remember what it is doing and what it is to do next by extending the analogy like this:

It is always possible for the computer to break off from his work, to go away and forget all about it, and later to come back and go on with it. If he does this he must leave a note of instructions . . . explaining how the work is to be continued. . . . We will suppose that the computer works by such a desultory manner that he never does more than one step at a sitting. The note of instructions must enable him to carry out one step and write the next note. Thus the state of progress of the computation at any stage is completely determined by the note of instructions and the symbols on the tape.[9]

Part of Turing's accomplishment was to show that these so-called "notes," the mnemonics for remembering what to do next, could, in general, always consist of a series of integers written on a paper tape. So from Aristotle's seals we have moved to a newer technology of bureaucracy, namely numbered paper forms.

During the World War II Turing's mathematical, theoretical machines became practical. The first computers had to be "set up" for each new problem of calculation. "Set up" entailed plugging and unplugging cables and setting hardware switches. By the end of the war, it became clear to J. Presper Eckert, John Mauchly, and John von Neumann that the memory of the computer could be used to store a program as well as data and that the program could be specified to automatically set up the computer to solve a new problem. Once the so-called "stored-program" memory was implemented computers could be programmed rather than "set up."[10]

These first computers were implemented in vacuum tubes and electronics and, from then on, the term "computer" meant a machine, not a human being. Ten years after Turing's publication there existed machines that were called "computers" and these computers were said to have memories.[11] Since many of the designers and builders of these first computers were engineers; and, since engineers had been writing, at least since the end of the a nineteenth century of the "magnetic memory" of iron;[12] and, since the physical substrate of early computer's "memories" was ferromagnetic,[13] this usage of the term "memory" to refer to the storage capacity of the computer is perhaps not so surprising. What is surprising is what happened next in the scientific world. Remember that social science, especially psychology, in the United States was dominated by behaviorism for most of the first half of the twentieth century. As Sherry Turkle puts it,

As recently as the 1950s behaviorism dominated American academic psychology, its spirit captured by saying that it was permissible to study remembering but considered a violation of scientific rigor to talk about "the memory." One could study behavior but not inner states.

Turkle argues that

The computer's role in the demise of behaviorism was not technical. It was the very existence of the computer that provided legitimation for a radically different way of seeing mind. Computer scientists had, of necessity, developed a vocabulary for talking about what was happening inside their machines, the "internal states" of general systems. If the new machine "minds" had inner states, surely people had them too. The psychologist George Miller, who was at Harvard during the heyday of behaviorism, has described how psychologists began to feel embarrassed about not being allowed to discuss memory now that computers had one . . . The computer presence relegitimated the study of memory and inner states within scientific psychology.[14]

What Turkle leaves out of her short history is that in 1956, when George Miller and his colleagues were founding the discipline of cognitive psychology, it had only been a few years since computers were not machines, but people. In other words, contemporary, cognitive science work on memory is based— ironically enough—on a willful amnesia of recent history and thus on a circularity: computer memory seems to be a good model of human memory because computer memory was modeled on human memory!

Here is the best analogy to the current situation that exists in many academic disciplines, many "cyborg sciences," that human thinking, memory, and decision making can be "modeled" by computer programs. This situation would be like discovering a painted portrait of a specific man and then spending the rest of one's professional life commenting on how uncanny it was that the portrait seemed to look like a human being.

The human that serves as the model for these cyborg sciences is culturally coded in a very specific manner. The human is, as Turing's analogy makes clear, not just any human. He—for, despite the fact than many human computers were women, it is usually a "he" in this technical literature—is a bookkeeper, accountant, or bureaucrat:

We may compare a man in the process of computing a real number to a machine which is only capable of a finite number of conditions . . . The machine is supplied with a "tape" (the analogue of paper) running through it, and divided into sections (called "squares") each capable of bearing a "symbol." At any moment there is just one square . . . which is "in the machine." We may call this square the "scanned square." The symbol on the scanned square may be called the "scanned symbol." The "scanned symbol" is the only one of which the machine is, so to speak, "directly aware." However, by altering its m-configuration the machine can effectively remember some of the symbols which it has "seen" (scanned) previously.[15]

Here then is the true picture of the "human" that is the model for computer memory: he is a bureaucrat squirreling around in the back office, shuffling through stacks of gridded paper, reading, writing, and erasing numbers in little boxes. This Bartleby-the-Scrivener is the man so many cyborg scientists would like to portray or recreate as an assemblage of computational machinery.

Equipped with a clear picture of whose memory computer memory is designed to resemble, it becomes possible to parse the technical literature on computer memory. The technical literature is completely preoccupied with the management and allocation of memory. Memory in the technical literature is not Marcel Proust's lost aristocratic memories of, for instance, eating scallop-shell-shaped, lemon-and-butter-flavored cakes (madeleines) as a child. No, this technical literature is filled with the memories of bureaucrats: numbers, lists, tables, cells, and segments. Even the computer science literature on narrative memories boils down to a set of techniques for fitting stereotypical stories into preconceived grids.[16]

Memory, of this bureaucratic, gridded kind, is a major area of work in hardware and software research and development. It is easy to see the grid when examining hardware. For example, contemporary, dynamic random access memory (DRAM) consists of a matrix of capacitors—which either hold (1) or do not hold (0) a charge—wired together in rows and columns. At the lower levels of software (i.e., in the memory management routines of operating systems, programming languages, etc.) memory is represented as a vector (i.e., a fixed length sequence of integers) or a matrix (i.e., a vector of vectors) that can be indexed by row and column.

If one reads the canonical texts of undergraduate, computer science education one finds passages like this are ubiquitous to the writings about computer memory:

Memory is an important resource that must be carefully managed. . . . The part of the operating system that manages memory is called [outrageous as it may seem!] the memory manager. Its job is to keep track of which parts of memory are in use and which parts are not in use, to allocate memory to processes when they need it and deallocate it when they are done, and to manage swapping between main memory and disk when main memory is not big enough to hold all of the processes.[17]

The function of a memory manager is akin to an accountant preparing taxes on his desk. If we understand his desk to be analogous to main memory and his file drawers to be like the computer's disk, then "memory allocation" is akin to assembling together the files and folders for a given account and finding space for them on the desk; "swapping" is like moving files and folders onto the desk from the file cabinets or, vice versa. The "resource" to be "managed" is the working space on the desk. Files and folders can be stacked, heaped, moved off the desk into file cabinets (i.e., onto disk), etc.

Undergraduate computer science students learn in their first or second year of studies the exact definitions and typical implementations of software analogs of "files," "folders," or "directories"; "stacks," "heaps," and "lists"; and the "recycling" or "garbage collection" of memory. Any adequate, introductory textbook on data structures and algorithms can provide the exact definitions of these "memory structures" and their associated operations.[18]

That these operations correlate almost exactly with what the bureaucrat does with his file cabinets, desk, and trash can is no coincidence. Neither is it a coincidence that these same operations are the ones available to today's computer users, whose graphical user interfaces are based on the so-called "desktop metaphor." The metaphors of the desk, the trash can, and the mind-numbing operations of office work and bureaucracy are built right into the foundations of the computer and its user interface. Even a quick skim through the seminal, foundational texts of graphical user interface design, especially those of Douglas Engelbart, make it clear that shuffling through, stacking, listing, and filing were the ideals of "memory" and "thought" admired and implemented by the founders of computer science and interface design.[19]

Of course, not all computing can be understood as office work. Rather, all computing is deeply rooted in the metaphors and pragmatics of bureaucracy; just as it is also intertwined with a genealogy of military thinking and materiel.[20] When these genealogies of software are forgotten, one loses sight of the highly particular and ultimately idiosyncratic images of memory and reasoning that are reified in the design and design principles of software.

Computer science's notion of "memory," that is, the "memory" of software and hardware, is not necessarily "worse" than that of other fields that investigate the issue of memory. But, computer science's working theories of memory are very specific and idiosyncractic to the concerns of bureaucracy, business and the military. This is largely because funding for computer science has come from these sources.

Juxtaposition with very different images of memory help one to imagine alternatives to the "closed world"[21] conditions that contemporary computational models circumscribe. For example, Marcel Proust's image of memory does not provide a better model of memory than the computer model, but it does provide a different model: a contrasting image that can be seen to highlight issues, ideas, and materialities uncommon to the military-(post)industrial technologies of memory:

And suddenly the memory revealed itself. The taste was that of the little piece of madeleine which on Sunday mornings at Combray . . . when I went to say good morning to her in her bedroom, my aunt Léonie used to give me, dipping it first in her own cup of tea or tisane. . . . when from a long-distant past nothing subsists, after the people are dead, after the things are broken and scattered, taste and smell alone, more fragile but more enduring, more unsubstantial, more persistent, more faithful, remain poised a long time, like souls, remembering, waiting, hoping, amid the ruins of all the rest; and bear unflinchingly, in the tiny and almost impalpable drop of their essence, the vast structure of recollection.[22]

Notes

1. Aristotle, *On Memory and Reminiscence*.

2. Geoffrey Winthrop-Young and Michael Wutz, "Translator's Introduction: Friedrich Kittler and Media Discourse Analysis," in Friedrich Kittler, *Gramophone, Film, Typewriter*, xx.

3. Jacques Derrida, "Freud and the Scene of Writing," in *Writing and Difference*, translated by Alan Bass.

4. Herbert A. Simon, *The Sciences of the Artificial*.

5. Philip Mirowski, *Machine Dreams: Economics Becomes a Cyborg Science*, 14.

6. Howard Gardner, *The Mind's New Science: A History of the Cognitive Revolution*, 6.

7. Richard Atkinson and Richard Shiffrin, "Human Memory: A Proposed System and Its Control Processes," in K. W. Spence and J. T. Spence, eds., *The Psychology of Learning and Motivation: Advances in Research and Theory, Volume 2*.

8. David Grier, *When Computers Were Human*, 19.

9. Alan Turing, "On Computable Numbers with an Application to the *Entscheidungsproblem*."

10. Paul E. Ceruzzi, *A History of Modern Computing*, 20–21.

11. Oxford English Dictionary, example from entry for "memory": "1945 J. P. ECK-ERT et al. Descr. ENIAC (PB 86242) (Moore School of Electr. Engin., Univ. Pennsylvania) iii. 1 The memory elements of the machine may be divided into two groups the 'internal memory' and the 'external memory.'"

12. Oxford English Dictionary, examples from entry for "memory": "1887 Jrnl. Soc. Telegr. Engin. 16 523 No matter how treated, a piece of soft iron has a 'magnetic memory.' 1935 Proc. Royal Soc. A. 149 72 The [magnetic] field..is to be regarded as 'frozen in' and represents a permanent memory of the field which existed when the metal was last cooled below the transition temperature."

13. The ENIAC used core memory: "Magnetic core memory, or ferrite-core memory, is an early form of computer memory. It uses small magnetic ceramic rings, the cores, to store information via the polarity of the magnetic field they contain. Such memory is often just called core memory, or, informally, core." Wikipedia: http://en.wikipedia.org/wiki/Core_memory; see also, Ceruzzi, *A History of Modern Computing,* 49–50.

14. Sherry Turkle, "Artificial Intelligence and Psychoanalysis: A New Alliance," *Daedalus* 17, 1 (Winter 1988).

15. Turing, "On Computable Numbers," 231.

16. Message Understanding Conference Proceedings (MUC-7), available at http://www.nlpir.nist.gov/related_projects/muc/proceedings/muc_7_toc.htm/ (last accessed April 9, 2006).

17. Andrew S. Tanenbaum, *Operating Systems: Design and Implementation*, 191.

18. For example, Alfred V. Aho, Jeffrey D. Ullman, and John E. Hopcroft, *Data Structures and Algorithms.*

19. Douglas Engelbart, "Augmenting Human Intellect: A Conceptual Framework," Summary Report for SRI Project No. 3578; see, especially, p. 56. Also, available online at http://www.bootstrap.org/augdocs/friedewald030402/augmentinghumanintellect/3examples.html#A.3 (consulted on April 9, 2006).

20. Manuel De Landa, *War in the Age of Intelligent Machines.*

21. Paul Edwards, *The Closed World: Computers and the Politics of Discourse in Cold War America.*

22. Marcel Proust, *Remembrance of Things Past. Volume 1: Swann's Way: Within a Budding Grove*, translated by C. K. Scott Moncrieff and Terence Kilmartin, 50.

■

Obfuscated Code[1]

Nick Montfort

Although conventional wisdom holds that computer programs must be elegant and clear in order to be admirable, there are unusual counterexamples to this principle. In the practice of obfuscated programming, the most pleasing programs are held to be those that are concise but which are also dense and indecipherable, programs that run in some sort of surprising way.[2] Obfuscated code demonstrates that there are other aesthetic principles at play besides those "classical" ones that have been most prominent in discussions of programming aesthetics by programmers[3] and critics.[4]

A popular form of programming related to obfuscation was already in evidence by the beginning of the 1980s. This was the practice of writing one-line BASIC programs, undertaken by people who, for the most part, were not professional programmers, but who had started programming during the home computing boom. These recreational one-liners work in some amusing way, sometimes even implementing a simple interactive game. The following program, for instance, when run on a Commodore 64, displays random mazes:

```
10 PRINT CHR$(109+RND(1)*2); : GOTO 10
```

This is accomplished by simply printing one of two graphic characters at random, "\" or "/", and then, without printing a linebreak, jumping back to the start of the line. The idea of the one-liner is not original to the home computer era and BASIC; in a 1974 talk, Donald Knuth pointed out a precedent in APL programming and noted he enjoyed writing programs that fit on a single punched card.[5] But the one-liner became widespread as BASIC gained popularity, and some one-line BASIC programs (on systems that permit lines longer than eighty characters) became quite intricate and elaborate. A small but reasonably complete implementation of *Tetris* was done in one line of BBC

Micro BASIC in 1992,[6] and a one-line BASIC spreadsheet program has been posted on Usenet.[7] One-line BASIC programs were often printed in magazines and keyed in by users. Code compression, rather than obfuscation for its own sake, was emphasized, but presentations of these programs sometimes asked the reader to figure out what they did, indicating that these programs were puzzling and challenging to decipher.

This puzzle aspect highlights the two main "readers" for a computer program: on the one hand, the human reader who examines the code to understand how it works, and how to debug, improve, or expand it; on the other, the computer, which executes its statements or evaluates its functions by running the corresponding machine code on its processor. A program may be clear enough to a human reader but may have a bug in it that causes it not to run, or a program may work perfectly well but be hard to understand. Writers of obfuscated code strive to achieve the latter, crafting programs so that the gap between human meaning and program semantics gives aesthetic pleasure.

Obfuscated programming is institutionalized today not in microcomputer magazines but online, where programs are exchanged and contests are hosted. The International Obfuscated C Code Contest has been held eighteen times since the first contest ran in 1984, back when one-line BASIC programs were still in vogue. Only small, complete C programs can be entered in the IOCCC. The contest's stated goals include demonstrating the importance of programming style "in an ironic way" and illustrating "some of the subtleties of the C language."[8] There is also an obfuscated Perl contest, run annually by *The Perl Journal* since 1996, but the most visible tradition of Perl obfuscation is seen in short programs that print "Just another Perl hacker," which are called JAPHs. In early 1990, Randal Schwartz began the tradition of writing these programs by including them in his signature when posting on comp.lang.perl.

Some sorts of obfuscation techniques are common to IOCCC entries and JAPHs and may be used in just about any programming language. Even assembly language allows the free naming of variables and labeling of particular instructions, so that these names can be used meaningfully and can help people better understand programs. Wherever such names can be freely chosen, they can be selected in a meaningless or even a deceptive way, as when num or count is used to store something other than a number, or when x and y appear together in a program to mislead the reader into thinking they are Cartesian coordinates. Since variable names are usually case-sensitive, there are additional possibilities for confusion. In C, where no special character is used to indicate a variable, programs take advantage of this and of the case-sensitivity of variable names to name some variables o and O, inviting additional confusion with the number zero. This play, which can be called *naming obfuscation*, shows one very wide range of choices that programmers have. By calling attention to this, naming obfuscation demonstrates that everything about a programmer's task is not automatic, value-neutral, and disconnected from the meanings of words in the world.

Another obfuscation technique takes advantage of curiosities in syntax to make it seem that some piece of data—for instance, a string that is being assigned to a variable—is actually part of the program's code. Alternatively, something that appears to be a comment, and thus to have no effect on the program's workings, may actually be part of the code, or vice-versa. This *data/code/comment confusion* is invited by flaws or curiosities in a language's specification, but can be accomplished in several different languages, including C and Perl.

There are also obfuscations that appear more prominently in one language than in another. In C, a[b] and b[a] have the same meaning, which is not the case when accessing array elements in other languages. An obfuscator working in C, however, can choose the more confusing of the two. Other languages do not define the addition of strings and numbers, or they define it in a way that seems more intuitive, at least to beginning programmers. But C, by giving the programmer the power to use pointers into memory as numbers and to perform arithmetic with them, particularly enables *pointer confusion*. By showing how much room there is to program in perplexing ways—and yet accomplishing astounding results at the same time—obfuscated C programs comment on particular aspects of that language, especially its flexible and dangerous facilities for pointer arithmetic.

Perl does not invite this sort of obfuscation, but does allow for several others. There are a dazzling variety of extremely useful special variables in Perl, which are represented with pairs of punctuation marks; this feature of the language merits an obfuscation category of its own. Perl's powerful pattern-matching abilities also allow for cryptic and deft string manipulations. The name Perl is sometimes said to stand for "Practical Extraction and Report Language," but "Pathologically Eclectic Rubbish Lister" is sometimes mentioned as another possible expansion. The language is ideal for text processing, which means that short messages (such as "Just another Perl hacker,") can be printed out in many interesting ways, sometimes using little-known sorts of *pattern-matching obfuscation*.

This JAPH, posted by Randal Schwartz on April 18, 1990, provides a short example that can be explicated in some depth:

```
$_=",rekcah lreP rehtona tsuJ";s/.$/eval 'print $&',""/e while
length
```

Like most such programs, this one prints "Just another Perl hacker,"—the comma at the end is traditional—and does so in a curious way. There are only two statements in this one-line program, separated by a semicolon. The first statement puts a string with the reverse of this message into $_, the Perl special variable for the current line. The second command is the interesting one; it is a substitution operation of the form s/**FIND**/**REPLACE**/e which is called implicitly on $_. The e after the final slash means that the result will be evaluated as a Perl expression. The "while length" at the very end results in this substitution being repeatedly called, iteratively, as long as there is something left in $_. Since one character is removed from the string on each pass, the following substitution operation is called once for each character in the string:

```
s/.$/eval 'print $&',""/e
```

The effect of this is to take the last character in the current line—"J" will therefore be selected first—and prepare a string to contain it. The first such string that is built is "eval 'print_,"""". This string is evaluated as a Perl expression, which results in "eval" executing its own Perl program to print the character "J". Since this mini-program returns no value, the letter selected is replaced with nothing, and the string is diminished in length.

There would be nothing very interesting about simply reversing a string and then printing it out, or about starting at the end of a string and printing it back-to-front one character at a time, although it might be interesting to see one of these processes coded up in a single, short statement. Here, a single statement does all of this and more. The statement creates a string that, when evaluated as an expression, executes a very short program to print a character. This statement also removes that last character from the current line and then continues processing the shorter line.

A repository of JAPHs is available online[9] and explications of several have been provided.[10] An explication of an introductory obfuscated C program[11] is also available.

Recent IOCCC programs include a racing game in the style of Pole Position, a CGI-enabled web server, and a program to display mazes whose code is itself in the shape of a maze. Obfuscated code in Perl as well as C often spells out a name in large letters or assumes the form of some other ASCII art picture. This is a type of *double coding*; more generally, *multiple coding* can be seen in "bilingual" programs, which are valid computer programs in two different programming languages. Double coding in natural languages is exemplified by the sentence "Jean put dire comment on tape," which is grammatical English and grammatical French ("Jean [male name] is able to say how one types"), although each word has a different meaning in each language. Harry Mathews contributed to further French/English double coding by assembling the Mathews Corpus, a list of words which exist in both languages but have different meanings.[12] In programming, an important first step was the 1968 *Algol* by Noël Arnaud, a book of poems composed from keywords in the Algol programming language.[13] Perl poetry is a prominent modern-day form of double-coding, distinguished from obfuscated programming as a practice mainly because it is not as important in Perl poetry that the program function in an interesting way; the essential requirement is that the poem be valid Perl.

Interestingly, it is not the case that languages typically despised by hackers—for instance, COBOL and Visual Basic—are the main ones used in obfuscation. Many Perl hackers and C coders who write obfuscated programs also use those languages professionally and find it enjoyable to code in those languages. They generally do not find it fun to program in COBOL or Visual Basic, however, even to comment negatively on these languages. In addition to making fun of some "misfeatures" or at least abusable features of languages, obfuscated code shows how powerful, flexible programming languages allow for creative coding, not only in terms of the output but in terms of the legibility and appearance of the source code.

All obfuscations—including naming obfuscations as well as language-specific ones, such as choosing the least well-known language construct to accomplish something—explore the *play* in programming, the free space that is available to programmers. If something can only be done one way, it cannot be obfuscated. It is this play that can be exploited to make the program signify on different levels in unusual ways.

The practice of obfuscated programming, like the kindred practice of developing weird programming languages, is connected to certain literary and artistic traditions. The practice suggests that coding can resist clarity and elegance to strive instead for complexity, can make the familiar unfamiliar, and can wrestle with the language in which it is written, just as much contemporary literature does. Another heritage is the tradition of overcomplicated machinery that has manifested itself in art in several ways. Alfred Jarry's 'Pataphysics, "the science of imaginary solutions," which involves the design of complicated physical machinery and also the obfuscation of information and standards, is one predecessor for obfuscated programming. There are also the kinetic installations of Peter Fischli and David Weiss and the elaborate apparatus seen in their film *The Way Things Go* (1987–1988), as well as the earlier visual art of Robert Storm Petersen, Heath Robinson, and Rube Goldberg. These depictions and realizations of mechanical ecstasy comment on engineering practice and physical possibility, much as obfuscated coding and weird languages comment on programming and computation. Such "art machines" anticipate obfuscated programs by doing something in a very complex way, but also by actually doing *something* and causing a machine to work.

Obfuscated code is intentionally difficult to understand, but the practice of obfuscated programming does not oppose the human understanding of code. It darkens the usually "clear box" of source code into something that is difficult to trace through and puzzle out, but by doing this, it makes code more enticing, inviting the attention and close reading of programmers. There is enjoyment in figuring out what an obfuscated program does that would not be found in longer, perfectly clear code that does the same thing. While obfuscation shows that clarity in programming is not the only possible virtue, it also shows, quite strikingly, that programs both cause computers to function and are texts interpreted by human readers. In this way it throws light on the nature of all source code, which is human-read and machine-interpreted, and can remind critics to look for different dimensions of meaning and multiple codings in all sorts of programs.

Notes

1. Parts of this article are based on a paper entitled "A Box Darkly" that Michael Mateas and I presented at Digital Arts and Culture 2005.

2. There is also a practice of making one's code difficult to understand or reverse-engineer for commercial purposes, to keep competitors or clients from understanding one's proprietary programs. Despite some similarities in what is done in this case, this practice seems to have no aesthetic principle behind it and no important relationship to obfuscated programming as described here.

3. For example, Donald E. Knuth, "Computer Programming as an Art," in *Literate Programming*, 1–16.

4. For example, Maurice J. Black, "The Art of Code," Ph.D. Dissertation, University of Pennsylvania (2002).

5. Knuth, "Computer Programming as an Art."

6. David Moore, "Rheolism: One Line Tetromino Game," available at http://www.survex.com/~olly/dsm_rheolism/ (accessed July 1, 2001).

7. Mark Owen, "BASIC Spreadsheet." Quoted in C. D. Wright, "One Line Spreadsheet in BASIC," post to comp.lang.functional. Message-ID: <D01s7J.LK3@cix.compulink.co.uk> (November 29, 1994).

8. Landon Curt Noll, Simon Cooper, Peter Seebach, and Leonid A. Broukhis. "The International Obfuscated C Code Contest," available at http://www.ioccc.org/main.html/.

9. JAPHs, available at http://www.cpan.org/misc/japh/.

10. See Teodor Zlatanov, "Cultured Perl: The Elegance of JAPH"; Abigail, "JAPHs and Other Obscure Signatures"; and, Mark-Jason Dominus, "Explanation of japh.pl"

11. Michael Mateas and Nick Montfort, "A Box Darkly: Obfuscation, Weird Languages and Code Aesthetics."

12. Harry Mathews and Alistair Brotchie, *Oulipo Compendium.*

13. Ibid.

■

Object Orientation

Cecile Crutzen and Erna Kotkamp

Data and Data Processing

In the twentieth century, data and the processing of data formed the basis of the computer science discipline. The syntax and physical form of the presentation of information was the primary focus of the field. The semantics of information was and should be coupled in an unambiguous manner to the syntax of the information. Computer science was seen as responsible not for the content of information but only for its processing.[1] Consequently, great efforts went into developing the architectures of logic-based subsystems in information systems. In these subsystems the data structure, processing structure, and medial presentation of information are inscribed. Information and the processing of information are transformed into mathematical expressions and procedures constructed in such a manner that they can be translated into the physical structures of machinery, which can, in turn, process and save this translated information. Interactions between software and hardware are modeled as causal procedures linking senders to receivers where the actions (messages) of the sender are the impulses for the (re)actions of the receivers, the point being that there should be a univocal connection between impulse and action. (Inter)action in these subsystems is always structured and planned.

Ready-Made Action

At the end of the last century a shift took place from the processing of information to ready-made (inter)actions offered to humans. These actions were to replace or enhance human actions, such as calculating, text and image editing, and playing. Within the computer science discipline the conception continues that the handling of information by people and the way people interact can only concern the discipline in as far as it concerns theories, methods, and techniques that have a generically formalizable character.

However, this exclusion of the ambiguity of human acting did not prevent computer scientists from interfering in human activity. On the contrary, the modeling and construction of many complex interaction patterns between humans is still based on the same transmission model used for the representation of data-exchange between artificial senders and receivers.

This focus on generalizing information, communication, and interaction in computer science pushes the multiform character of individuality and the specificity of human interaction into the background. The exploration of the object-oriented approach is a significant example of this. With this example we analyze the approach as a specific methodology rather than the programming practice itself.

Object-Oriented Programming

Object-oriented programming (OOP) started out in the 1960s with the programming language Simula developed by Ole-Johan Dahl and Kristen Nygaard.[2] In OOP, objects are the basic elements of its ontology. Software is structured as a collection of objects that work together. These objects relate to and act upon each other and the interaction between these objects, the sending of messages (message passing), is the core of this programming paradigm.

The difference between OOP and other programming paradigms is that within OOP, data and the operations that can manipulate this data are placed in one object instead of being separated. This created a break with the paradigm of procedural programming, which was at that time heavily used. Within procedural programming software behavior is defined by procedures, functions, and subroutines. In OOP these behaviors are contained in the methods of the objects. A method is a basic property of an object class. It is hidden in the object itself.[3] Methods can only invoked by sending an appropriate message to the object.[4]

Object-Oriented Approach

Nowadays, object-oriented programming is not only used for developing and producing software and hardware; object orientation (OO) has also become a methodology and theory for interpretation, representation, and analysis of worlds of human interaction with which the computer interfaces: the object-oriented approach.[5] OO is used for the representation of the dynamics of interaction worlds, leading us beyond the data-oriented approach and making room for the opportunity to discuss the character of human behavior. (OO is often used, for instance, in Graphic User Interfaces.) Because human behavior is not predictable and is itself situated in the interaction, OO only discloses planned action. Within the ontology of OO, the real world can be described as an interaction world. In this world, humans or other entities can only act if a predefined plan exists and its execution conditions are satisfied.

Because data and manipulation are contained within the object, changes in interaction are only possible if preprogrammed within the object. Interaction and the representation of interaction are located within the objects instead of on a procedural level. The "change of change" is impossible. Within the ontology of OO the behavior of humans can only be represented as frozen in routine acting. With abstraction tools in OO such as classification, separation, and inheritance, the process of real world analysis is colonized.

Colonization of Analysis

This colonization from ICT-system realization into world analysis is dictated by analyzing subjects' focus on the avoidance of complexity and ambiguity, by selecting the documents, texts, tables, and schemes in the analyzed domain that are the most formalized and hence closest to the syntactical level of object-oriented programming languages. Natural language in the domain is transformed into a set of elementary propositions. As a result hierarchical structures and planned behaviors are highlighted, and ad hoc (inter)actions are obscured.

This use of OO as a methodology in informatics is exemplary for the ontological and epistemological assumptions in the discipline: Not only is it possible to "handle the facts" but also to handle and therefore control real behavior itself. The expert users of the object-oriented approach strongly suggest that with OO the total dynamics of reality can be represented objectively in artificial objects.

Feminist theories provide arguments for doubting the assumptions within the OO approach. They question how these approaches are always based on the same illusions of objectivity and neutrality of representation: the veiling of power and domination by its translation into something "natural and obvious." Retaining OO as a methodology means to only use it again for the purpose for which it was originally meant: the programming and production of software. Software production based on the OO approach (not to be confused with OO Programming) results in the predictable and planned interaction of artificial actors; it cannot be the foundation for the analysis and representation of human behavior.

However, a total rejection of OO cannot be the answer to these doubts. The presence of OO-based products enforces the disclosure of some unwanted consequences of OO. In the OO methodology ambiguity and doubt are invisible but not absent.

Fear

In software and hardware products constructed through the OO approach, the fear of doubt is embedded and transferred into the interaction worlds of which they are part. The goal of software engineering is to produce unambiguous software that masters complexity. Based on the principles of controlling complexity and reducing ambiguity within software, software engineers try to tame the complexity and ambiguity of the real world. Abstraction activities, a fundament of most modeling methods such as generalization, classification, specialization, division, and separation, are seen as unavoidable for the projection of dynamic real world processes into ready-to-hand modeling structures and for the production of ready-made acting. Abstractions are simplified descriptions with a limited number of accepted properties. They rely on the suppression of a lot of other aspects of the world. Hoare suggests: "Abstraction arises from recognition of similarities between certain objects, situations or processes in the real world and the decision to concentrate upon these similarities and to ignore for the time being the differences."[6] These structures and modeling methods necessitated a search for the similarities of human actors, situations, processes, and events, ignoring their differences.

According to Coyne, the academic world:

expects that once we get beneath the surface, we can find out what things have in common and thereby understand them better. Phenomena are abstracted so that they are describable in the same way. . . . This interest in similarity is evident in the quest for the structures underlying language and social practices (as in structuralism). It is also evident in the concern in design fields, such as architecture, with identifying typologies, generic forms and ordering principles.[7]

Invisibility

OO representations create prefabricated and generic ready-made actions. Ready-made actions are designed on base of searches for similarity. Differences, which are not easy to handle, or may not be relevant in the view of the observer and modeler, will be neglected and suppressed. Within the OO approach a real world phenomenon can only have a representation within the world of artificial objects when it fits into an object class. The sequence in the modeling process—first classification and then instantiation—renders some phenomena incomplete or not represented at all. They are made invisible for the users of the ready-made action of the implemented objects. This concept of classes has the same effect as the concept of laws, about which Evelyn Fox Keller noted: "Such laws imply an a priori hierarchy between structuring principle and structured matter that suggests a striking resemblance to laws of authoritarian states."[8] The class structure will suppress "listening to the material itself."[9] According to Susan Leigh Star, in the making and modeling process of our technological environment, there will be a "tempering of the clutter of the visible" by the creation of invisibles: "Abstractions that will stand quietly, cleanly and docilely for the noisome, messy actions and materials."[10]

Ambiguity

The models produced by computer scientists using the OO approach as methodology for interpreting and analyzing human behavior leave no room for negotiation or doubt. Models translated into ready-made products, interaction, and communication are only defined on a technical and syntactical level. But the same models are also used on a semantic and pragmatic level to construct the planned and closed interaction of humans. The semantic and pragmatic ambiguities, which occur in "being-in-interaction," are ignored. Ambiguity is seen as troublesome and inconvenient and thus has to be prevented and "dissolved" at the technical and syntactical level.[11] In the making process, these views on (inter-)action are embedded in the artificial product. But they are also frozen into the routines of computer scientists and into their products, which they use themselves and which they apply and feed back into the computer science domain. In the main, computing professionals do not design but use established methods and theories. They focus on security and non-ambiguity and are afraid of the complex and the unpredictable.[12] The methodical invisibility of the representation of ready-made interaction is based on the planned cooperation between software and hardware. It could close the design options of users resulting in design activities that are locked into the frame of pre-established understanding.

Doubt

In spite of the OO approach the pre-established meanings established by the software designers are not the final meanings of a system. On the contrary, these methodical invisibilities have the potential to create doubt, and this could be a starting point for the process of changing the meaning of ready-made interaction. Users are experts at escaping from rigidly planned interaction; they determine usability in their own interaction world. In this way, methodical invisibility can lead to "playful exploration and engagement."[13] Systems, which are in this sense actable, can be successful, because they can "be perceived and enacted in very different ways by different people in different situations, if the users can find the keys for this disclosure."[14] Doubt leading to exploration and change is, according to Heidegger, the essence of technology; it is not simply a means to an end, it is a way of revealing the world we live in.[15]

However, is this change of meaning still possible? It requires the blowing up of the pre-established conditions for change embedded in OO-products. Users slide unnoticed into a state of fearfulness about changing their habits because this might disturb the surrounding pre-planned acting. Our society is forcing us into using specific tools, because a lot of other tools have disappeared; they did not fit into the digital lifestyle of our society.

Are we still allowed to have doubt and is doubt not becoming the unwelcome intruder, which hinders us in exploiting the unintended opportunities of ready-made action? Is it still true that tools challenge us to interact with our environments? Are we still in the position to create an interactive environment if we are not skilled computer scientists?

Notes

1. There have been serious moves toward modeling the semantics of natural language in artificial intelligence, cognitive science, and computational linguistics, translating meaning into a logical structure and relating that to syntax.

2. Ole-Johan Dahl, *The Birth of Object Orientation: The Simula Languages.*

3. A class is a set of objects that share a common structure and a common behavior. The covering up of data types and methods is called encapsulation. This is the enclosing of programming elements inside larger, more abstract entities; the classes.

4. Matt Weisfeld, "Moving from Procedural to Object-Oriented Development."

5. For the OO (Object Orientation) approach see: Grady Booch, *Object-Oriented Analysis and Design, with Applications*; Ivar Jacobson, Magnus Christerson, Patrik Jonsson, and Gunnar Övergaard, *Object-Oriented Software Engineering: A Use Case Driven Approach*; James R. Rumbaugh, Michael R. Blaha, William Lorensen, Frederick Eddy, and William Premerlani, *Object-Oriented Modeling and Design*.

6. O. Dahl and E. Dijkstra, C. A. R. Hoare, *Structured Programming*. Cited in Grady Booch, *Object Oriented Design, with Applications*, 39.

7. Richard Coyne, "Heidegger and Virtual Reality: The Implications of Heidegger's Thinking for Computer Representations."

8. Evelyn Fox Keller, *Reflections on Gender and Science*.

9. Ibid.

10. Susan Leigh Star, "Invisible Work and Silenced Dialogues in Knowledge Representation."

11. See Cecile Crutzen, "Giving Room to Femininity in Informatics Education." Alan Davis gives an example of this fear of ambiguity: "As systems become more complex however, it becomes increasingly difficult to explain behavior in an unambiguous manner. . . . one of the reasons for this ambiguity is the inherent ambiguity in any natural language. . . . A model simply provides us with a richer, higher level, and more semantically precise set of constructs than the underlying natural language. Using such a model reduces ambiguity, makes it easier to check for incompleteness, and may at times improve understandability." Alan M. Davis, *Software Requirements: Objects, Functions and States*, 213–214.

12. See Cecile Crutzen and Jack F Gerrissen, "Doubting the OBJECT World" and Cecile Crutzen, *Interactie, een wereld van verschillen. Een visie op informatica vanuit genderstudies*.

13. Phoebe Sengers and Bill Gaver, "Designing for Interpretation." In sociological studies of technology many examples have been generated proving that users escape from the pregiven meaning of technological products, such as Nelly Oudshoorn and Trevor Pinch, eds., *How Users Matter*.

14. P. Béguin and P. Rabardel, in "Designing for Instrument Mediated Activity," call this "catacresis." The term "catacresis" is borrowed from linguistics and rhetoric, where it refers to the use of a word in place of another, or in a way that goes beyond

its normal meaning. The idea is also employed in the field of instrumentation for the using of one tool in place of another, or the using of tools to carry out tasks for which they were not designed.

15. Martin Heidegger, *Die Technik und die Kehre*.

■

Perl

Geoff Cox and Adrian Ward

Perl (an acronym for "Practical Extraction and Report Language") is a programming language, first developed for Unix by Larry Wall in 1987 as an open source project to build on the capabilities of the "awk" utility.[1] Wall required a language that combined the quickness of coding available in "shell" (or awk) programming, with the power of advanced tools like "grep" (without having to resort to a language like C, C++ or assembly). Perl therefore lies somewhere between low-level programming languages and high-level programming languages. It combines the best of both worlds in being relatively fast and unconstrained: "Perl is easy, nearly unlimited, mostly fast, and kind of ugly."[2]

Perl uses a highly flexible syntax that gives programmers greater freedom of expression than many other languages.[3] Its concise regular expressions allow complex search and modify operations to be encoded into dense operators. This makes Perl particularly difficult to read (or ugly) for those unfamiliar with its form, however the syntax is really relatively simple, and carries its own particular aesthetic attractions.

Perl programs are generally stored as text source files, which are compiled into virtual machine code at run-time. There is a distinction between the program that interprets, compiles, and executes Perl code (perl) and the language name (Perl). In reference to other Open Source projects that embrace obfuscation, it should never be an acronym (PERL) despite the documentation clearly stating it stands for both Pathologically Eclectic Rubbish Lister and Practical Extraction and Report Language. Perl programs are usually called "Perl scripts" and, due to the interpreted nature of the language, are ideal for rapid development and reworking of code. Changes can be made and the code retried very swiftly, which has led to Perl being favored in diverse scenarios requiring complex yet quick solutions. In addition, Perl is particularly useful as "glue code" and for mixed-language script programming. Perhaps this is what the artist Harwood was thinking about in his "porting" of William Blake's poem *London* (1792) into *London.pl* (2002). This is more than simply a formal exercise. In both the original Blake version and Harwood's adaptation, statistics and the modulation of populations are used for social comment, but in the Perl version material conditions are registered more overtly as both form and content. The politics of Blake's poem describing the social conditions of London are translated to a contemporary cultural and *technical reality in which people* are reduced to data:[4]

```
local %DeadChildIndex;


# The Data for the DeadChildIndex should be structured as follows:


# %{DeadChildIndex} => {
#       IndexValue => {
#               Name        =>   " Child name If known else undefined ";
#               Age         =>   " Must be under 14 or the code will throw an
#                                exception due to $COMPLICITY";
#               Height      =>   "Height of the child"
#               SocialClass =>   "RentBoy YoungGirl-Syphalitic-Innoculator
#                                CrackKid WarBeatenKid ForcedFoetalAbortion
#                                Chimney-Sweeps UncategorisedVictim "
#       }, As many as found
# }
```

In terms of the application of Perl for social comment, Harwood is extending an established aesthetic practice referred to as "perl poetry" that emphasizes the point that code is not merely functional but can have expressive or literary qualities too.[5] Take, for example the winner of The Perl Poetry Contest of 2000 by Angie Winterbottom:

```
if ((light eq dark) && (dark eq light)
    && ($blaze_of_night{moon} == black_hole)
    && ($ravens_wing{bright} == $tin{bright})){
 my $love = $you = $sin{darkness} + 1;
};
```
[6]

Poetry is analogous to code in that it is both written and spoken or read and executed.[7] There are accepted techniques for reading code, and Winterbottom's poem relies on her choice of spatial arrangement and the syntactic understanding of the language itself. Only a programmer familiar with hash tables would understand that "`$blaze_of_night{moon} == black_hole`" can be read as "The moon, a black hole in the blaze of night."

Interpreted scripting languages such as Perl appear to hold more open-ended creative possibilities that emphasize process rather than end-product, if only because access to the source code is so readily available, and because quite often part of using a Perl script entails reading its source—this is true regardless of whether dealing with Perl poetry or in a conventional functional deployment.

Programming with Perl emphasizes material conditions, which evokes how N. Katherine Hayles, in *Writing Machines*, stresses materiality in relation to writing.[8] She describes the mixed (semiotic) reality that literature engenders—between the reality literally at hand, the one evoked through imagination, and the situation to which it applies—as a play of signification in other terms. In addition to the writer and reader, there are other players involved in the production of a text or program that include those who participate in the development of the programming language, other software developers, the engineers who design the machines on which the program runs, the factory workers who build these machines, the technicians who maintain them, and so on.[9] All these players are situated in the material world and the social relations that arise from this.

Materiality expressed in this way follows a critical modernist tradition that brings into view the technical apparatus or writing machine that produces it—this is familiar to an analysis focused on cultural production such as literary criticism. Hayles goes further than this, and to this wider context, adds the materiality of the text itself to the analysis in a similar way to those who consider code to be material. In this way, it is the materiality of writing itself that is expressed through the relationship between natural language and code—one, code, tended towards control and precision, the other, language, tending toward free form and expression.[10] This is particularly evident in "codework" (such as Harwood's above) and other examples that combine so-called natural and artificial languages that play with signification. In such examples, meaning and authorship remain in question.[11]

Working with code goes further than this. The execution of code engages materiality and imagination through the possible and often unpredictable actions that result. The materiality therefore requires attention to the technical apparatus, but also to the program—the activity of programming and the activity of the program once executed. Perl is a useful tool in this respect. It remains free and transparent; and because it does not require compiling in order to run it is impossible to make an opaque binary. If installed and run, it can always be turned back into source code. Perl is an open source project, emerging out of a Unix-inspired culture of sharing.[12]

In the lecture "Perl, the first postmodern computer language," Larry Wall is keen to point out that modernist culture was based on "or" rather than "and," something he says that postmodern culture reverses.[13] But this position appears to disregard a critical modernist tradition that would emphasize issues of materiality, reflexivity, and transparency of production. For instance, Marshall Berman's argument, in *All That Is Solid Melts into Air*, posits that dialectical thinking asserts "and-both" over "either-or." Berman is skeptical of claims about change if they do not embrace contradiction. His position is informed by a dialectical understanding of modernity representing a transitional state between the old and the new—modernity remains an "incomplete project."[14] Berman suggests that it is our thinking about modernity that has stagnated. He says:

Modernity is either embraced with a blind and uncritical enthusiasm, or else condemned . . . in either case, it is conceived as a closed monolith, incapable of being shaped or changed . . . Open visions of modern life have been supplanted by closed ones, Both/And by Either/Or.[15]

In claiming "AND has higher precedence than OR does," Wall is focusing on the eclecticism of Perl and how algorithms can be expressed in multiple ways that express the style of the programmer. Both of these operators are fundamental to Boolean logic and hence applying precedence to one over another appears to be contradictory.[16] However, Perl embraces this sort of peculiarity, and this is how it extends the possibilities of coding beyond simply functional intentions. The extent to which Perl gets (mis)used might point out how contemporary software practices focus more on diversity and recapitulation than innovation and optimisation. This resonates in Wall's claim that one of Perl's features is to focus attention not so much on the problem but on the person trying to solve the problem, on the creativity of the programmer: "It doesn't try to tell the programmer how to program."[17]

```perl
$wall {modernism } = 'or';
$wall {postmodernism} = 'and';

$berman{modernism} = 'both/and';
$berman{postmodernism} = 'either/or';

if ($wall {modernism || $berman {postmodernism}) {
 if ($wall {postmodernism} && $berman {modernism}) {
  $wall {modernism) = &condemn($berman {postmodernism}); #closed
  $wall {postmodernism) = &embrace($berman {modernism}); #open
 }
}
print "Wall: '$wall{postmodernism}'\n";
print "Berman: '$berman{modernism}'\n";

sub embrace {
 return $_[0]; #blind and uncritical enthusiasm
}

sub condemn {
 undef $_[0]; #blind and uncritical condemnation
}
```

In this way, rather than Perl being condemned as the first postmodern computer language, the preference for the connective "and" as opposed to "or" is in keeping with critical practices that promote the development of new forms of expression that preserve contradiction.[18] The suggestion is that Perl is not only useful on a practical level but that it also holds the potential to reveal some of the contradictions and antagonisms associated with the production of software.

Notes

1. Larry Wall, "Perl, the First Postmodern Computer Language," available at http://www.wall.org/~larry/pm.html/ (interestingly, Wall's background is in linguistics).

2. Randall L. Schwartz and Tom Phoenix, *Learning Perl,* 4.

3. For instance, Perl Mongers is a loose association of international Perl User Groups, http://www.pm.org, and discussions take place at The Perl Monastery, http://www.perlmonks.org; see also *The Perl Journal,* http://www.tpj.com/.

4. Florian Cramer has written a feature on Harwood's *London.pl* on the Runme software art repository, http://www.runme.org/feature/read/+londonpl/+34/.

5. An early example of literature using the Perl programming language is Sharon Hopkins's 1992 paper, "Camels and Needles: Computer Poetry Meets the Perl Programming Language," in *The Perl Review,* Vol. 0, Issue 1 (1991), available at http://www.theperlreview.com/Issues/The_Perl_Review_0_1.pdf. It was first presented at the Usenix Winter Technical Conference in 1992.

6. Kevin Meltzer, "The Perl Poetry Contest," in *The Perl Journal,* Vol. 4, Issue 4 (2000), available at http://www.tpj.com. The original poem by Edgar Allan Poe reads: "If light were dark and dark were light/The moon a black hole in the blaze of night/A raven's wing as bright as tin/Then you, my love, would be darker than sin." This example was previously cited in Geoff Cox, Alex McLean, and Adrian Ward, "The Aesthetics of Generative Code," *Generative Art 00* conference, Politecnico di Milano, Italy (2001), available at http://www.generative.net/papers/aesthetics/index.html.

7. This statement reflects our previous collaborative essay (with Alex McLean), "The Aesthetics of Generative Code."

8. N. Katherine Hayles, *Writing Machines.*

9. Ibid., 6.

10. See Florian Cramer for more on this relation, in "Ten Theses About Software Art" (2003), available at http://cramer.plaintext.cc:70/all/10_thesen_zur_softwarekunst/.

11. The materiality of text or code is verified by the property rights exerted on it—intellectual property would even cast ideas as material objects in this respect.

12. Perl is, by and large, an all-inclusive implementation of Unix and the GNU utilities. See Eric S. Raymond, *The Art of UNIX Programming.*

13. Wall, "Perl, the First Postmodern Computer Language."

14. Incompleteness is the character that Jürgen Habermas assigns to modernity, emphasizing its transitory, elusive, ephemeral, dynamic qualities, in "Modernity—An Incomplete Project," 5.

15. Marshall Berman, *All That Is Solid Melts Into Air: the Experience of Modernity,* 24.

16. Following Boolean logic, data follows both an arithmetical and logical binary form, as a set of choices between two conditions. It can also be extended to include more complex and conditional formations such as "or," "and," "not," as well as rules about consistency, implication, and contradiction.

17. Wall, "Perl, the First Postmodern Computer Language."

18. For example, Florian Cramer's "and.pl"

```
open(THIS, 'and');open
(THAT, ">>and") ;while (<THIS>) {print$_; print THAT"#$_"};
"#to"; close (THIS);
```

■

Pixel

Graham Harwood

Nowadays, all well-fed people are expected to take pictures, in the same way that everyone is expected to speak. Pixels, bitmaps, digital cameras, phone cameras, closed circuit television cameras, and scanners litter our homes, offices, and landfill sites. At the MediaShed, a center for free media at the mouth of the Thames (Southend-on-Sea, UK) we have been given fifteen scanners, four digital cameras and twenty graphics cards in two months as people upgrade to the next level of seeing machine.

One possible explanation for this glut of constructed seeing and its associated problems of heavy metal waste, of cheap labor, and environmental damage, might be the continuation of a historical preoccupation with both the splitting of light into its constituent parts and the moving of light from one place to another. This can be seen in the historic formulation of perspective by the artist-technologists Filippo Brunelleschi and Leone Battista Alberti in the fifteenth century and with Newton's use of a prism to split white light into its constituent colors in the seventeenth century.

While there are many threads in the story of the quantification of vision resulting in the pixel, I have chosen to draw a line from perspective as a technical progenitor.

Creating an enchanting image of a technique at work, the fifteenth-century architect Filippo Brunelleschi is said to have demonstrated the principle of central perspective by depicting the Baptistry as seen through the door of the Florentine cathedral.[1] He placed a net over an entrance, thus forming a grid, and then drew the intersecting lines he saw. In each cell of this net he constructed a sample of the light visible from a central point. Brunelleschi's net has evolved into a system in which the light intensities at each point of a far finer grid of photosensitive cells are recorded.

The algorithm to render perspective relies on the fact that light normally propagates along straight lines. We can therefore work out, for any object in space, which light rays from its surface will reach a given point. This knowledge allows anyone who learns the method to achieve a repeatable result. In addition to showing how lines of light radiate from objects, perspective sets up rules by which they can be shown to converge at a point. In this way it creates the position of a witness outside the frame of the picture, a position by which the scene can be interrogated. This position can only be occupied by a mechanism or person endowed with the correct procedures of interpretation. Such a systematization of sight sets in play a skepticism of non-verifiable personal perception. It sets up a mechanics of vision relying on self-correction and verification: logical procedures employed in today's seeing machines.

With the dual—and not entirely uncontradictory—ascents of science and capitalism as explanatory and organizing principles, picturing, with its inheritance from perspective has tended to become synonymous with possession. This can account for much of the mechanical seeing and picture processing habits that we see around us. While this understanding is useful, in an age of binary rationalism we still find ourselves trying to explain the irrational and mesmerising hold that pictures have over our imagination.

Pixels first appeared at Princeton's Institute for Advanced Study in New Jersey in 1954.[2] At that time the word "pixel" simply described the glowing filaments of the machine's vacuum memory registers. The term later gained use in image processing to describe the raster elements in a screen or image, as "picture elements," descendents of the squares of light caught in Brunelleschi's net. Alongside the growth in use of the term, we have learned to shape our pixels to better reflect the world, even as we spent the last 50 years re-ordering the world to more closely approximate those phosphorescent dots. The pixel has become both a mirror and a lens, reflecting and shaping the realities of its own making.

It is useful in this inquiry to see the picture element or pixel as the basic unit of programmable color in our seeing machines. Logical as well as physical, organized clusters of pixels enable us to dive through our screens and stand in the position occupied by the lens. Each pixel is formed from a set of three separate channels of red, green, and blue visual data that overlap on our monitors to form a convincing speck of colored light. The pixel usually consists of a structure of one to eight bits for each of its red, green, and blue component values of light. According to its scientific figuration, light is an electromagnetic wave or signal from a source that is made out of one or more frequencies. The human eye is sensitive to a very narrow band of frequencies, namely the frequencies between 429 terahertz (THz) and 750 THz. This is the same sensitivity range as a charge coupled device (CCD) or a complementary metal oxide semiconductor (CMOS) chip found in our digital cameras.

Digital cameras sample light from a particular position, that of the lens. This involves converting the signal from the continuous light we see to the discrete quantities of light recorded in bitmaps. The fineness of the grid by which a recording is made is the picture resolution. Quantization, converting the amplitude of the signal from a continuous and infinite range of values to a finite set of discrete values, can be thought of as setting the bit-depth of the picture, establishing subtle or visibly discontinuous gradations of light. Pixels can be square, hexagonal, rectangular, or irregularly shaped, but given that each pixel has boundaries they require a process by which the world is chopped up into chunks that conform to those boundaries and is still visually meaningful. Discretization is part of the process by which color and light values are allocated to a pixel. It consists of sorting values, evaluating a cut-point where a value changes or merges, and setting the intervals between samples and value setting. Each of these stages require algorithms that shape the resulting pictures, and the speed of their processing. The development of discretization largely follow the path of a closer fit between data and its algorithmic processing.

Light discharged by pixels, themselves organized and stored as bitmaps, falls on the retina of the eye. Agitated by small electrical charges, the monitor pours light at an imagined viewer. At a biological level this is experienced through electromagnetic waves making contact with the retina, lined with two types of photosensitive cells. These photoreceptors are known as rods and cones. The rods only detect whether or not light is present. They are sensitive to the whole spectrum at once but only in terms of brightness or "luminence." Cones are sensitive only to certain frequencies: red, green, and blue, values of "chrominance." In this way, the pixel on a screen models the component light values held within the cells of the eye.

Bitmaps allow pixels to coagulate into pictures. They can be thought of as containers for holding discrete values of red, green, and blue light or as sets of visual data, usually rectangular in form, that reflect the underlying 2-D mathematical arrays that hold the derived variables of light. Bitmaps hold visual data in cells based on a Cartesian (x,y) grid that allows individual pixels to be filtered, manipulated, and sent to the framebuffer for display. When you need to make a print for Nan's birthday your personal printer reinterprets the bitmap as a series of commands to use certain inks in a set order. For monitors, the same set of electrical impulses are interpreted to set specified intensities of chrominence and luminence.

A seeing machine's ultimate goal is the natural and effortless sampling of reality as representation. As an information system, it is a neutral carrier of your pictures characterized by a very low signal-to-noise ratio. The construction of a neutral carrier allows for the transmission of pictures as equally neutral numerical values and helps us enjoy all forms of self-surveillance fun with minimal loss of quality. The conception of neutrality is transferred from the device and onto the programmers and engineers who develop the software and hardware, leaving them too as mere vessels for the message, whatever it may be.

As with their ancestor, perspective, today's binary seeing machines, have managed to convince us that *now* we really can possesses an infallible method of representation: a system for the automatic and mechanical production of truths about the material world. That is, if we buy the new 15-megapixel cellphone with the Adobe plug-ins that will no doubt be available next year. Or was that last year? Aided by the political and economic ascendance of Western systems of objectification and piggy-backing on photography's history, artificial seeing has conquered the world of representation.

We now have, not two eyes, but as many as we can afford. We enjoy using our computers to process the pictures and leave them around on our hard drives or pop them up on the web for mum or aunty to have a look at. Digital imaging products with feature-lists such as wi-fi LAN support enabling wireless transfer, shooting and printing, super-bright 2.5-inch LCD monitors,

D-Lighting improving images recorded with unsatisfactory exposure, and face-priority auto focus that can pinpoint a human face in the shot and provide sharp focus accordingly, make it irresistible!

No matter whether it is a monitor, camera, printer, or the screen of a mobile phone, the output device is always an attempt to reflect or transmit light to the retina of a viewer. The viewer in turn, mesmerized by the light, enters commands that again shine onto the retina. In this way the pixel and its attendant soft and hardware systems can be seen as an element in a net drawn up by the social, economic and cultural re-ordering of the variables of ambient light. Such a net is made possible by reducing the spectrum of light to a set of repeatable tasks, as analyzed by the linguistic tools of code, made possible by contemporary hardware environments. This is now the natural mode of representation in most rich countries and through it we enjoy our neutral appropriation of the pixel's reality.

Nowadays, all well-fed people are expected to take pictures in the same way that everyone is expected to speak. Over the past twenty years the pixel has gone from being a blocky grid-like thing to achieving the ever-higher resolutions that we expect. Seen from some future water-table polluting slag-heap of heavy metals made from last year's cast-off monitors, printers, and scanners, the pixel will glint and wink at us, the guiding light in the reordering of our individual and collective sight, reduced to the soft/hardware systems that are used to record, judge, display, and manipulate the ambient variables of light.

Notes

1. W. J. T. Mitchell, *The Language of Images*, 193–196.

2. See Richard F. Lyon, "A Brief History of 'Pixel'"; and, Andrew Zolli, "Pixelvision: A Meditation."

■
Preferences / settings / options / control panels

Søren Pold

If, as Umberto Eco pointed out in 1994, the contemporary graphical user interface (GUI) inherited its icons and user-friendly behavior from counter-reformation Catholicism, then the preferences palette is both its most holy place and a critical corner in the contemporary graphical user interface.[1] The preferences palette presents a peephole into the area behind the scenes, the backstage area where the representation that is presented to the human user is produced.[2] In the "preferences," "settings," "options," or "control panels," all similar places in different software, it is possible to manipulate the very staging of the interface, its colors, language, interaction menus, file handling, auto functions, warning messages, security levels, passwords, cooperation with other software, networks, peripherals, and so on. It is here that the software and the interface are configured and increasingly personalized to match with individual needs and aesthetic taste through skins, sounds, themes, etc. As such, it is here that the aesthetics and the functionality—together with issues around the construction of user behaviours and the use of software as self-representation—are negotiated or perhaps clash.

Preferences came out of parameters and configuration files. Parameters are ways of specifying characteristics when calling certain functions my in, for example, command line interfaces such as DOS or Unix.[3] A configuration file is a file that contains configuration instructions for the software. MS-DOS had a configuration file called "config.sys" that describes how the computer is configured in respect to devices, drives, memory locations, etc. In the era of MS-DOS, advanced users could not resist experimenting with the config.sys file, which often led to crashing the system if they were not sufficiently skilled. When software became further commodified and marketed to ordinary consumers, the software interfaces increasingly included preference palettes and menus. Since then preferences have grown and now often include several sub-screens. Today GUI systems like Microsoft Windows still have settings and configuration files kept in a "registry." It can be edited, but this is often reserved for system administrators and advanced users, and it is more or less off limits to the normal user. The registry stores the configurations that the user has made in the various preferences palettes.[4]

In general, the preferences regulate three spheres around the software interface: functionality, power relations, and aesthetics. Functionality concerns issues such as compatibility, file placement, plug-ins and extensions, peripherals, and cooperation with other software, whereas management of administrative rights, security and passwords, levels of insight into technical codes, and configurations are more related to the power relations between the software and the user.[5] Seen from the point of view of aesthetics, the preferences often control skins, themes, and sounds, which are related to a superficial aesthetic, the "look-and-feel" of the software where the user—perhaps aided by themes from various websites—is free to change the appearance into, for example, something that relates to sci-fi fantasy worlds, popular icons, games, or the appearance of other operating systems.

But there is more to aesthetics than surface. The preferences set up and negotiate an equivalent to the contract that a theatre audience or a reader adhere to when entering a fictional representation: a mental, cultural contract negotiating one's expectations and how one is supposed to act and react in the representational space. The relations between the software's senders[6] and receiver(s) or user(s) are defined, most often within very strict limits. Normally, it is only possible to change certain things and change them the way the senders have prefigured, and often one cannot find the setting that controls an annoying feature one wants to get rid of. As a result one becomes irritatingly aware of the fact that the interface is structured around principles set up by the sender(s): I see what I may change and to what other options; and sometimes I can even see as a dimmed option representing something that I cannot change, something that can only be changed by higher powers in the hierarchy controlling the software, that is, the technical department. Preferences regulate the contract between the producers, the machine and its software environment, and what I as a user prefer, thus my preferences are not purely mine, but highly negotiated in this software hierarchy. Recently one can even see so-called "parental controls" pop up (e.g., in the internally released Windows Longhorn 4015) that limit the user. In the early 1990s Apple marketed At Ease, a simplified interface with limited possibilities.[7] It becomes clear that the preferences control a power hierarchy, and the user's fiddling around with them is a way of both realizing and compensating for this.

In this sense, the software user as a character with certain rights, abilities, and limits is constructed here. This construction of the user has become more and more dynamic and cybernetic; the software automatically models itself on (its model of) the user. Software increasingly constructs dynamic models of its user and customizes itself accordingly; for example, it stores traces of user behavior such as last opened documents, commonly used functions, and menus, cookies, caches, and histories of internet behavior. In this sense, software aims at automatically changing some settings according to user behavior, such as the personalized menus in Microsoft software, in which only frequently used menu items are initially shown, or the way most web browsers remember and suggest URLs and most email clients store and suggest email addresses. Some of these traces are to some extent open for reconfiguration for the advanced user; at least the user might be able to delete them. Still it highlights how "my" preferences on my personal computer become some sort of automated autobiography within the medium of software, on my personal computer becomes a cybernetic mirror of me.[8]

Preferences, and the way they negotiate the representational levels of the software interface, present the software as a functional tool directed toward a specified task, delimited by the sender of the software and often by traditional notions of the task from earlier software and pre-digital tools. Most word processors such as Microsoft Word (figure 12), for example, are directed toward a specific kind of formal, technical, and business-related writing, which is supposed to be printed on pages, and to already look "printed" when you write. Of course this does not mean it cannot be used for other more creative or literary kinds of writing, but it does not encourage or suggest it, and sometimes it even tries to direct the writing toward more formal writing styles, for example, suggesting bullets, numbering, footnotes, and certain spelling and grammar corrections, while it never advances more creative elements of writing. This will often drive the user to the preferences in order to reconfigure the software toward his or her writing style to avoid disturbing interferences from the software. Most of these things can be switched off with some fiddling, but traditional software is still built to be a relatively neutral tool for a specific domain, and lets the user work on the domain or the content while the tool is mostly fixed within the borders delimited by the preferences. Microsoft Word is not suitable for producing experimental electronic literature that engages with new digital forms of writing—like hypertext, generative and dynamic texts—but mainly for producing documents modeled on traditional document formats like letters, reports, and (academic) books. Furthermore, Word is not directed toward writing code, not even HTML code, although it does

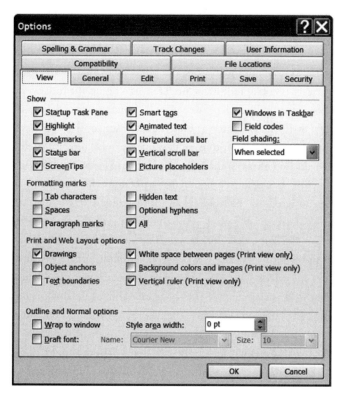

Figure 12 Microsoft *Word 2002* (2001).

allow its user to save his or her document as web page. One could argue that Word promotes an office perspective on writing, a typographical writing that has not taken the various digital developments of writing fully into account.[9]

Software is generally presented as a tool for use in a specific way, often modeled on previous media,[10] and notwithstanding the possibilities to change the superficial aesthetics and the autobiographical elements; it is not presented as a media for expression or for developing new kinds of use. Software thus does not have meaning but function. As a consequence, most software studies have, until now, been usability studies.

Meanwhile, as already suggested, a closer look reveals that function and meaning are closely interwoven. Although there are good functional reasons for letting the user change various preferences, most of us engage in this also because of aesthetic reasons or taste and issues of self representation: We do not like the sounds, colors, short-cuts, interruptions, defaults—in general how the software represents itself and operates—we want to change this in order to personalize the software and become sophisticated users.[11] According to popular knowledge among system administrators, the preferences are the first thing to delete when software is corrupted; users' preferences clog up the functionality of the software—it would be easier if we were all confined to the defaults of Apple or Microsoft. Still, the trend toward letting the user control the superficial aesthetics can be seen as a symptom users wanting to become more than plain users. Users want to contribute, change, get more insight, etc.; they get annoyed by being reduced to default users. In fact we change the defaults in order to see and re-negotiate how the software and its senders have confined us.

The preferences palette gives a glimpse of the staging of the software interface. In order to make some defaults changeable, the software has to make them explicit. The preferences palette is where the common, everyday user—with no access to or knowledge of code—can make his mark and play around with the representational machinery of the software. And while this playing around is often aesthetisized—as in skins, themes, etc., which do not influence the workings of the software—or commodified as in third party extensions and plug-ins, it still bears witness to the fact that software is more than a standard tool with standard uses, and that users are by instinct fighting against being standardized according to typical functionalistic values.

Notes

1. Umberto Eco, "La bustina di Minerva."

2. Brenda Laurel presented the theatrical perspective on the computer and its interface in *Computers as Theatre*.

3. For example, in DOS you can call the copy function with the parameter "/v" in order to add a controlling of the copied files, along with the source and destination of the copying as parameters. Thus a typical command to copy a text file from the disk drive to the hard drive and control the copying will be "copy a:\readme.txt c:/v." This way of using parameters stems from programming, where subroutines in a program are often called with some parameters and variables.

4. In Unix environments configurations are stored in so-called dot files (because they start with a ".", which hides the file from casual listing), that are editable and exchanged.

Examples may be found on the web at websites such as "dotfiles" (http://dotfiles.com/) (see "Configuration file" from Wikipedia, http://en.wikipedia.org). Even though Open Source software builds on an open access to the source code and thus also its configurations, much Open Source software imitates the way preferences are implemented in commercial GUI software.

5. See Matthew Fuller, *Behind the Blip: Essays on the Culture of Software*.

6. The sender of a piece of software is some combination of the company behind the software and the local technical department controlling the configuration of the software, for example, in large institutions and companies—that is, all the people and institutions that produce and control the software. Only rarely is software presented with a naming of its authors or developers; more often the CEO stands in for the large group of developers engaged (such as Steve Jobs, Bill Gates. . .).

7. Marcin Wichary, GUIdebook, *Graphical User Interface Gallery*.

8. The artist group 0100101110101101.org put their personal Linux computer on-line (from 2000–2003) in their "real-time digital self-portrait," "Life Sharing," so that users could read their files, settings, emails, etc. (archived at http://www.0100101110101101 .org/home/life_sharing/; (last accessed March 20, 2006). Their comments on the project included: "Whoever works with a computer on a daily basis, at least for a few years, will soon realise that his own computer resembles more and more to its owner. You share everything with your computer: your time (often even for 13 hours a day), your space (desktop), your culture (bookmarks), your personal relationships (e-mails), your memories (photos archives), your ideas, your projects, etc. To sum up, a computer, with the passing of time, ends up looking like its owner's brain. It does it more and better than other more traditional media, e.g. diaries, notebooks, or, on a more abstract level, paintings and novels. If you accept the assumption of a computer being the thing that gets closer to your brain, you will also assume that sharing your own computer entails way more than sharing a desktop or a book, something we might call life_sharing" (retrieved March 20, 2006 from http://209.32.200.23/gallery9/lifesharing/). The obvious next thing would be to steal somebody's identity by stealing their preferences (which of course already happens with cookies, data mining, phishing, etc.) or buy some important person's preferences in order to explore and experience his personality . . .

9. See Olav W. Bertelsen, and Søren Pold, *Criticism as an Approach to Interface Aesthetics;* and Matthew Fuller, *Behind the Blip*.

10. Another good example of this is Adobe Photoshop, which is directed toward the old medium of photography, now digitized, and not toward more generative images in the manner of Adrian Ward's software art works Auto-Illustrator or Auto-Shop. Available at http://www.auto-illustrator.com/, http://www.signwave.co.uk/go/products/autoshop.

11. When presenting with a computer to an audience, it is striking how many presenters avoid the default design templates, desktop settings, and some even the most common presentation software packages (such as Microsoft PowerPoint), perhaps in order to avoid being seen as default standard users. This is evidence of the increasing role that software plays for self-presentation and appearance.

■

Programmability

Wendy Hui Kyong Chun

According to the *Oxford English Dictionary*, programmability is "the property of being programmable"—that is, capable of being programmed.[1] Although the term "program," as both noun and verb, predates the modern digital computer, programmability and programmable do not, and the digital computer has changed the meanings of the word "program." The definition of program, the noun, not only includes "a descriptive notice, issued beforehand of any formal series of proceedings" and a "broadcast presentation treated as a single item for scheduling purposes" but also "a series of coded instructions, which when fed into a computer will automatically direct its operation in carrying out a specific task."[2] Program, the verb, includes "to arrange by or according to a programme," and "to broadcast," as well "to express (a task or operation) in terms appropriate to its performance by a computer or other automatic device; to cause (an activity or property) to be automatically regulated in a prescribed way."[3] Combined with the fact that "stored program" has become synonymous with von Neumann architecture, these definitions make it appear that programs are native to computers. Programs, however, were not always programs.

As David Alan Grier, among others, has argued, the term program did not stabilize until the mid-1950s.[4] According to Grier, the verb "to program" is probably the only surviving legacy of the ENIAC—the first working electronic digital computer and the immediate precursor to those using stored programs. Importantly, the ENIAC's "master programmer" was not a person, but a machine component, responsible for executing loops and linking sequences together.[5] That is, the master programmer handled the "program control" signal that each unit produced after it successfully executed a function. This use of "program" stems from electronics engineering, where a program signal is any signal corresponding to speech, or other activity, and stresses program as a thing that is transmitted, rather than a thing responsible for execution. As computers became machines, programmers became human and programming became functionally equivalent to the process of "setting up" the ENIAC— the physical act of wiring the machine for a particular problem.[6] Indeed, this "setting up" (once considered "operating" the machine) has been retroactively classified as "direct programming"; Grier argues that the term "program" was favored over the term "planning" (then in use in numerical methods) in order to distinguish machine from human computing. Although this process of setting up the machine seems analogous to the same process on contemporaneous analog machines, there is an important difference between them, for programmability marks the difference between digital and analog machines. This is not to say that analog machines are not programmed, but that what is meant by programming is significantly different. Programming an analog computer is descriptive; programming a digital one is prescriptive.

To program an analog machine, one connects the units and sets the values for amplification and attenuation, as well as the initial conditions. That is, one assembles the computer into an analog of the problem to be solved or simulated. As Derek Robinson argues: "while a digital computer can simulate feedback processes by stepwise iteration . . . analog computers embody dynamic feedback fundamentally. The "computation" takes place at all points in the circuit at the same time, in a continuous process. Circuits are systems of circular dependencies where effects are fed back to become the causes of their own causes."[7] That is, analog computers perform integration directly and can be used "generatively." Digital computers, on the other hand, employ numerical methods. They break down mathematical operations, such as integration, into a series of simple arithmetical steps. To do so, they must be programmable; that is, they must be able to follow precisely and automatically a series of coded instructions. Although one would think that the breakdown of mathematical operations into a series of arithmetical ones would induce more errors than direct integration, this is not usually so. The programmability and accuracy of digital computers stems from the discretization (or disciplining) of hardware.

Since analog computers produce signals that simulate the desired ones, they are measured rather than counted. The accuracy of the result is thus affected by noise and its precision by the sensitivity of the measuring instrument. In contrast, digital computers count rather than measure, and they do so by rendering analog hardware (vacuum tubes, transistors, etc.) signal magnitudes into discrete units. By translating a certain quantity into a value (5V into 1; 0V into 0), they can greatly reduce the effects of noise, and thus essentially build a system in which one step can predictably lead to another. As Alan Turing and von Neumann both acknowledged early on, there are no "discrete" or digital machines; there are only continuous machines that in Turing's words can be "profitably thought of as being discrete state machines," machines in which, "given the initial state of the machine and the input signals it is always possible to predict all future states." This, he argues, "is reminiscent of Laplace's view that from the complete state of the universe at one moment of time, as described by the positions and velocities of all particles, it should be possible to predict all future states."[8] Again, reasonably accurate results depend on the design of hardware in specific ways: on timing gates carefully so that gate delays do not produce significant false positives or negatives; on signal rectification; and on designs that cut down on cross-talk and voltage spikes. Without this disciplining of hardware, digital computers—or digital-analog hybrids—could not be (however inadequately or approximately) universal mimics, or Turing complete.

This "return to Laplace" and the desire for programmability (and programs as we now know them) was arguably predated by work in mid-twentieth-century genetics. Most famously, Erwin Schrodinger, drawing from the work of contemporaneous researchers in biology and chemistry, posited the existence of a genetic code-script in his 1944 *What is Life?*[9] Schrodinger posits this code-script as the answer to the challenge human genetics presents to statistical physics, namely, given that statistical physics shows that Newtonian order only exists at large scales, how is it possible that the barely microscopic chromosomes guarantee the orderly succession of human characteristics? Also, given the second law of thermodynamics, how does life maintain order in this sea of disorder? Given how microscopic the chromosomes are, Schrodinger argues that they must be an aperiodic crystal code-script, a code-script—not unlike Morse code—that determines the entire pattern of an individual's future development and of its functioning in the mature state. Thus the code-script is a seemingly impossible return to Laplace. Schrodinger writes, "in calling the structure of the chromosome fibres a code-script we mean that the all-penetrating mind, once conceived by Laplace, to which every causal connection lay immediately open, could tell from their structure whether the egg would develop, under suitable conditions, into a black cock or into a speckled hen, into a fly or a maize plant, a rhododendron, a beetle, a mouse or a woman."[10] Importantly, software—which was not foreseen by computing pioneers—and not DNA would come to fulfill Schrodinger's vision of a code-script as "architect's plan and builder's craft in one."

Just as Schrodinger links programmability to an all-penetrating mind, programmability is linked to the feelings of mastery attributed to programming, its causal pleasure.[11] As Edwards has argued, "programming can produce strong sensations of power and control" because the computer produces an internally-consistent if externally incomplete microworld, "a simulated world, entirely within the machine itself, that does not depend on instrumental effectiveness. That is, where most tools produce effects on a wider world of which they are only a part, the computer contains its own worlds in miniature. . . In the microworld, as in children's make-believe, the power of the programmer is absolute."[12] This power of the programmer, however, is not absolute and there is an important difference between the power of the programmer/programming and the execution of the program. Alan Turing, in response to the objection that computers cannot think because they merely follow human instructions, wrote, "machines take me by surprise with great frequency."[13] This is because the consequences of one's programs cannot be entirely understood in advance. Also, as Matthew Fuller has argued in his reading of Microsoft Word, there is an important gap between the program and the experience of using it. The mad attempt to prescribe and anticipate every desire of the user produces a massive feature mountain whose potential interaction sequences mean that a user's actions cannot be completely determined in advance: the more features a program provides, the more possibilities for the user to act unpredictably.[14]

Importantly, programmability is being attacked on all sides: from quantum computers that are set up rather than programmed (in the sense currently used in software engineering) to "evolutionary" software programs that use programmable discrete hardware to produce software generatively.[15] This apparent decline in programmability is paralleled in new understandings of genomics that underscore the importance of RNA (the same portion of DNA can transcribe more than one protein)—biology and computer technology are constructed metaphorically as two strands of a constantly unravelling double helix. This seeming decline, however, should not be taken as the death knell of programmability or control, but rather the emergence of new forms of control that encourage, even thrive on, limited uncertainty.[16]

Notes

1. Oxford English Dictionary Online (2006). http://www.oed.com/.

2. Ibid.

3. Ibid.

4. David Grier, "The ENIAC, the Verb 'to program' and the Emergence of Digital Computers," 51.

5. H. H. Goldstine and A. Goldstine, "The Electronic Numerical Integrator and Computer (ENIAC)," 10–15.

6. For more on this see Wendy Hui Kyong Chun, "On Software, or the Persistence of Visual Knowledge."

7. Derek Robinson, presentation at Software Studies Symposium, Piet Zwart Institute, Rotterdam, 2006.

8. Alan M. Turing, "Computing Machinery and Intelligence."

9. Erwin Schrodinger, *What is Life?*

10. Schrodinger, Ibid.

11. Chun, Ibid.

12. Paul Edwards, "The Army and the Microworld: Computers and the Politics of Gender Identity," 108–109.

13. Turing, Ibid.

14. Matthew Fuller, "It Looks Like You're Writing a Letter," in Behind the Blip, essays on the culture of Software.

15. For more on this see, N. Katherine Hayles, *My Mother was a Computer*; Julian Dibbell, "Viruses Are Good For You"; Jussi Parikka, "The Universal Viral Machine."

16. See Wendy Hui Kyong Chun, *Control and Freedom*.

■

Sonic Algorithm

Steve Goodman

Contemporary sound art has come under the influence of digital simulations. These simulations are based on artificial life models, producing generative compositional systems derived from rules abstracted from actual processes occurring in nature. Yet taking these intersections of algorithms and art, divorced from a wider sonic field can be misleading. With their often arbitrary, metaphorical transcodings of processes in nature into musical notation, uncritical transpositions of artificial life into the artistic domain often neglect the qualitative, affective transformations that drive sonic culture. With care, however, we can learn much about the evolution of musical cultures from conceptions (both digital and memetic) of sonic algorithms—on the condition that we remember that software is never simply an internally closed system, but a catalytic network of relays connecting one analog domain to another. Here, the computing concept of the abstract machine attains a wider meaning, corresponding to the immanent forms that also pattern non-computational culture. For this reason, an analysis of the abstract culture of music requires the contextualization of digital forms within the contagious sonic field of memetic algorithms as they animate musicians, dancers and listeners.

An algorithm is a sequence of instructions performed in order to attain a finite solution to a problem or complete a task. Algorithms predate digital culture and are traceable in their origins to ancient mathematics. Whereas a computer program is the concretization or implementation of an assemblage of algorithms, the algorithm itself can be termed an abstract machine, a diagrammatic method that is programming language independent. Abstract machines are "mechanical contraptions [that] reach the level of abstract machines when they become mechanism-independent, that is, as soon as they can be thought of independently of their specific physical embodiments"[1] thereby intensifying the powers of transmission, replication and proliferation. This quality of algorithms is crucial to software-based music, with key processes distilled to formalized equations that are generalizable, transferable, reversable, and applied. "Coupled with software (or mechanism or score or programme or diagram) that efficiently exploits these ideas, the abstract machine begins to propagate across the technological field, affecting the way people think about machines and eventually the world."[2] The affective power of the sonic algorithm is not limited to the morphology of music form. Leaking out of the sterile domain of the digital sound lab and across the audio-social field, these abstract machines traverse the host bodies of listeners, users, and dancers, producing movements and sensations, before migrating back to the vibratory substrate.

If, as Gottfried Leibniz proposed, all music is "unconscious counting,"[3] then clearly, despite its recent popularity, algorithmic music composition cannot be considered the exclusive domain of computing. It should instead be placed in an historical context of experiments with, for example, out of phase tape recorders, where tape loops already constituted "social software organized to maximize the emergence of unanticipated musical matter."[4] As Michael Nyman has outlined, bottom-up approaches to musical composition take into account the context of composition and production as a system, and are "concerned with actions dependent on unpredictable conditions and on variables which arise from within the musical continuity."[5] Examples from the history of experimental music can be found in the oft-cited investigations of rule-centered sonic composition processes in the exploration of randomness and chance, such as John Cage's use of the I Ching, Terry Riley's "In C," Steve Reich's "It's Gonna Rain" and "Come Out," Cornelius Cardew's "The Great Learning," Christian Wolff's "Burdocks," Frederic Rzewski's "Spacecraft," and Alvin Lucier's "Vespers."[6] In this sense, as Kodwo Eshun argues, the "ideas of additive synthesis, loop structure, iteration and duplication are pre-digital. Far from new, the loop as sonic process predates the computer by decades. Synthesis precedes digitality by centuries."[7]

Recent developments in software music have extended this earlier research into bottom-up compositional practice. Examples centering around the digital domain include software programs such as Supercollider, MaxMsp, Pure Data, Reactor and Camus,[8] which deploy mathematical algorithms to simulate the conditions and dynamics of growth, complexity, emergence, and mutation of evolutionary algorithms and transcode them to musical parameters. The analysis of digital algorithms within the cultural domain of music is not limited to composition and creation. Recent Darwinian evolutionary musicology has attempted to simulate the conditions for the emergence and evolution of music styles as shifting ecologies of rules or conventions for music-making. These ecologies, it is claimed, while sustaining their organization, are also subject to change and constant adaption to the dynamic cultural environment. The suggestion in such studies is that the simulation of complexity usually found within biological systems may illuminate some of the more cryptic dynamics of musical systems.[9] Here, music is understood as an adaptive system of sounds used by distributed agents (the members of some kind of collective; in this type of model, typically, none of the agents would have access to the others' knowledge except what they hear) engaged in a sonic group encounter, whether as producers or listeners. Such a system would have no global supervision. Typical applications within this musicological context attempt to map the conditions of emergence for the origin and evolution[10] of music cultures modeled as "artificially created worlds inhabited by virtual communities of musicians and listeners. Origins and evolution are studied here in the context of the cultural conventions that may emerge under a number of constraints, for example psychological, physiological and ecological."[11] Eduardo Miranda, despite issuing a cautionary note on the limitations of using biological models for the study of cultural phenomena,[12] suggests that the results of such simulations may be of interest to composers keen to unearth new creation techniques. He asserts that artificial life should join acoustics, psychoacoustics, and artificial intelligence in the armory of the scientifically upgraded musician. According to Miranda, software models for evolutionary sound generation tend to be based on engines constructed around cellular automata or genetic algorithms.

Cellular automata were invented in the 1960s by von Neumann and Stanislaw Ulam as simulations of biological self-reproduction.[13] Such models attempted to explain how an abstract machine could construct a copy of itself automatically. Cellular automata are commonly implemented as an ordered array or grid of variables termed cells. Each component cell of this matrix can be assigned values from a limited set of integers, and each value usually corresponds with a color. On screen, the functioning cellular automata is a mutating matrix of cells that edges forward in time at variable speed. The mutation of the pattern, while displaying some kind of global organization, is generated only through the implementation of a very limited system of rules that govern locally. Heavily influential to generative musicians such as Brian Eno, the most famous instantiation of cellular automata is John Conway's Game of Life (1967). Game of Life has recently been implemented in the software system CAMUS, whereby the emergent behaviors of cellular automata are developed into a system that transposes the simple algorithmic processes into musical notation. The rules of the Game of Life are very simple. In the cellular grid, a square can be either dead or alive. With each generation, or step of the clock, the squares change status. A square with one or zero neighbors will die. A square with two neighbors will survive. A square with three neighbors becomes alive if not already, and a square with four or more neighbors will die from overcrowding. The focus of such generative music revolves around the emergent behavior of sonic lifeforms from their local neighborhood interactions, where no global tendencies are preprogrammed into the system.

As in the case of cellular automata and artificial neural networks, models based around genetic algorithms transpose a number of abstract models from biology, in particular the basic evolutionary biological processes identified in particular by Darwin[14] and updated by Dawkins.[15] These algorithms are often used to obtain and test optimal design or engineering results out of a wide range of combinatorial possibilities. Simulations so derived allow evolutionary systems to be iteratively modeled in the digital domain without the inefficiency and impracticality of more concrete trial and error methods. But, as Miranda points out, by abstracting from Darwinian processes such as natural selection based on fitness, crossover of genes, and mutation, "genetic algorithms go beyond standard combinatorial processing as they embody powerful mechanisms for targeting only potentially fruitful combinations."[16] In practice, genetic algorithms will usually be deployed iteratively (repeated until fitness tests are satisfied) on a set of binary codes that constitute the individuals in the population. Often this population of code will be randomly generated and can stand in for anything, such as musical notes. This presupposes some kind of codification schema involved in transposing the evolutionary dynamic into some kind of sonic notation, which, as Miranda points, out will usually seek to adopt the smallest possible "coding alphabet." Typically each digit or cluster of digits will be cross-linked to a sonic quality such as pitch, or specific preset instruments as is typical in MIDI. This deployment consists of three fundamental algorithmic operations, which, in evolutionary terms, are known as recombination (trading in information between a pair of codes spawning offspring codes through combining the "parental" codes), mutation (adjusting the numerical values of bits in the code, thereby adding diversity to the population) and selection (choosing the optimal code based on predetermined pre-coded fitness criteria or subjective/aesthetic criteria). One example of the application of genetic algorithms in music composition is Gary Lee Nelson's 1995 project *Sonomorphs*, which used

genetic algorithms to evolve rhythmic patterns. In this case, the binary-string method is used to represent a series of equally spaced pulses whereby a note is articulated if the bit is switched on . . . and rests are made if the bit is switched off. The fitness test is based on a simple summing test; if the number of bits that are on is higher than a certain threshold, then the string meets the fitness test. High threshold values lead to rhythms with very high density up to the point where nearly all the pulses are switched on. Conversely, lower threshold settings tend to produce thinner textures, leading to complete silence.[17]

In summary, then, the development of artificial life techniques within music software culture aims to open the precoded possibilities of most applications to creative contingency.[18] The scientific paradigm of artificial life marks a shift from a preoccupation with the composition of matter to a focus on the systemic interactions between the components out of which nature is under constant construction. Artificial life uses computers to simulate the functions of these actual interactions as patterns of information, investigating the global behaviors that arise from a multitude of local conjunctions and interactions. Instead of messy biochemical labs deployed to probe the makeup of chemicals, cells, etc., these evolutionary sonic algorithms instantiated in digital software take place in the artificial worlds of the CPU, hard disk, the computer screen, and speakers. However, with an extended definition of an abstract machine, sonic algorithms beyond artificial life must also describe the ways in which software-based music must always exceed the sterile and often aesthetically impoverished closed circuit of digital sound design. With non-software musics, such abstract machines leak out in analog sound waves, sometimes laying dormant in recorded media awaiting activation, sometimes mobilizing eardrums and bodies subject to coded numerical rules in the guise of rhythms and melodies. The broader notion of the abstract machine rewrites the connection between developments in software and a wider sonic culture via the zone of transduction between an abstract sonic pattern and its catalytic affects on a population. By exploring these noncomputational effects and the propagation of these sonic algorithms outside of digital space, software culture opens to the outside that was always within.

Notes

1. Manuel De Landa, *War in the Age of Intelligent Machines*, 142.

2. Kodwo Eshun, "An Unidentified Audio Event Arrives from the Post-Computer Age," in Jem Finer, ed., *Longplayer*, 11.

3. Gottfried W. Leibniz, *Epistolae ad diversos*, 240.

4. Eshun, "An Unidentified Audio Event Arrives from the Post-Computer Age," 11.

5. Michael Nyman, *Experimental Music: Cage & Beyond.*

6. David Toop, "Growth and Complexity," in *Haunted Weather.*

7. Eshun, "An Unidentified Audio Event Arrives from the Post-Computer Age," 11.

8. Supercollider (http://www.audiosynth.com/), MaxMsp (http://www.cycling74.com/), Pure Data (http://puredata.info/), Reactor (http://www.native-instruments.com), Camus (http://website.lineone.net/~edandalex/camus.htm).

9. See, for example, Peter Todd, "Simulating the Evolution of Musical Behavior," 361–389.

10. Eduardo Miranda, *Composing Music with Computers*, 139–143, points to four mechanism in origins and evolution useful for modeling musical systems:

a. transformation and selection (should preserve the information of the entity): improve components of ecosystem evolution of music subject to psychophysiological constraints rather than biological needs (i.e., survival); exceptions are bird song and mate attraction
b. co-evolution: pushes the whole system (of transformations and selections) toward greater complexity in a coordinated manner, e.g., musical styles co-evolve with music instruments/ technologies.
c. self-organization: coherence ingredients include (1) a set of possible variations, (2) random fluctuations, and (3) a feedback mechanism.

d. level formation: formation of higher level compositional conventions, e.g., abstract rules of rhythm e.g. metre and a sense of hierarchical functionality.

11. Miranda 2001, 119.

12. Miranda is particularly cautious of linear, progressive models of evolution:

> Evolution is generally associated with the idea of the transition from an inferior species to an superior one and this alleged superiority can often be measured by means of fairly explicit and objective criteria: we believe, however, that this notion should be treated with caution . . . with reference to prominently cultural phenomena, such as music, the notion of evolution surely cannot have exactly the same connotations as it does in natural history: biological and cultural evolution are therefore quite different domains. Cultural evolution should be taken here as the transition from one state of affairs to another, not necessarily associated with the notion of improvement. Cultural transition is normally accompanied by an increase in the systems' complexity, but note that "complex" is not a synonym for "better." (140)

13. E. F. Cood, *Cellular Automata.*

14. Charles Darwin, *The Origin of Species*, 1859.

15. Richard Dawkins, *The Blind Watchmaker*, 1986.

16. Eduardo Miranda, *Composing Music with Computers*, 131.

17. Ibid., 136.

18. See Peter Todd, "Simulating the Evolution of Musical Behavior," and Eleonora Bilotta, Pietro Pantano, and Valerio Talarico, "Synthetic Harmonies: An Approach to Musical Semiosis by Means of Cellular Automata."

Source Code

Joasia Krysa and Grzesiek Sedek

```
/ Barszcz C recipe
*
* string based cooking
*
* Copyleft (C) 2006 Denis "Jaromil" Rojo
* for the barszcz project (currently unfinished)

#include <stdio.h>
#define ingredient char
#define tool char

#define few     3
#define some    5
#define pinch   1
#define plenty 8
#define one     1

#define soft_cooked 5

ingredient **take(int quantity, ingredient **ingr) {
     int c;
     int len = strlen(ingr) +10;
     ingredient = malloc( (quantity+1) * sizeof(*ingredient));
     for(c = 0; c < quantity; c++)
            ingredient[c] = malloc(len * sizeof(ingredient));
     ingredient[c+1] = NULL;
     return ingredient;
}
```

In *The Art of Computer Programming* Donald Knuth equates programming and recipes in a cookbook as a set of instructions to follow. Algorithms, much like cooking recipes, provide a method, a set of defined formal procedures to be performed in order to accomplish a task in a finite number of steps.[1] Examining the source code of a particular program reveals information about the software in much the same way as the ingredients and set of instructions of a recipe reveals information about the dish to be prepared. The analogy is rather straightforward perhaps but reveals something of the interests involved in the preparation, execution, and consumption of the work.[2] The importance of source code for the description of software is that, alongside computer commands, it also usually provides programmers' comments—that is, a documentation of the program including a detailed description of its functionality and user instructions.[3] Furthermore, the importance of source code is that any modifications (improvements, optimizations, customizing, or fixes) are not carried out on compiled binary code (object code or machine code) but on the source code itself. The significance of this is that the source code is where change and influence can be exerted by the programmer. In the example of recipes, further descriptions are provided in the accompanying narrative. Although recipes are clearly not reducible to code—and vice versa—the analogy emphasizes that both programming and cooking can express intentionality and style.

Source code (usually referred to as simply "source" or "code") is the uncompiled, non-executable code of a computer program stored in source files. It is a set of human readable computer commands written in higher level programming languages. Defined by a higher level of abstraction from machine language they share some of the characteristics of natural language, for instance, rules of syntax. When compiled, the source code is converted into machine executable code (binary), a series of simple processor commands that operate on bits and bytes. The process of compiling is twofold: the source code is converted into an executable file either automatically by a compiler for a particular computer architecture and then stored on the computer, or executed on the fly from the human readable form with the aid of an interpreter. In principle, any language can be compiled or interpreted and there are many languages such as Lisp, C, BASIC, Python, or Perl that incorporate elements of both compilation and interpretation.[4] In the history of computation, programs were first written and circulated on paper before being compiled in the same way as recipes were written and shared before being compiled in cookbooks. The first case of an algorithm written for a computer is credited to Ada Lovelace. It interpreted Charles Babbage's Analytical Engine (of 1835) not merely as a calculator but as a logic machine capable of arranging and combining letters and other symbolic systems.[5] The source code of a modern digital computer derives from the further adaptation (in the 1940s) of Babbage's ideas.[6] What came to be known as the "von Neumann architecture" is important as it presented a single structure to hold both the set of instructions on how to perform the computation and the data required or generated by the computation; it demonstrated the stored-program principle that has led to development of programming as separate from hardware design. Remington Rand's UNIVAC (Universal Automatic Computer, 1951) was one of the first machines to combine electronic computation with a stored program and capable of operating on its own instructions as data.[7] With a stored-program computer, a sequence of instructions that might be needed more than once could be stored. The computer could store the sequence in memory and insert the sequence into the proper place in the program as required. By building up a library of frequently used sequences, a programmer could write a complex program more efficiently.[8] In *A History of Modern Computing*, Paul E. Ceruzzi explains this development, from building up libraries of subroutines, then getting the computer to call them up and link them together to solve a specific problem, to a more general notion of a high-level computer language with the computer generating fresh machine code from the programmer's specifications.[9]

The principle of re-using or sharing code relies on storing collections of code lines, or functions, in "libraries." The function or subroutine, often collected into libraries, is a portion of code within a larger program, which performs a specific task and is relatively independent of the remaining code. A subroutine is often coded so that it can be executed several times or from several places during a single execution of the program. It can be adapted for writing more complex code sequences, and is thereby a labor-saving programming tool and an important mechanism for sharing and re-using code.[10] An early example of a community-based library of subroutines was SHARE (1955), a repository for shared use developed by a group of IBM users. More recently, the principle of sharing source code is instantiated in online repositories (such as *Source-Forge, Freshmeat,* or *Code Snippets*.) Other tools including source code search engines that index programming code and documentation are also available from open-source repositories (for instance, *Koders, Krugle, Codefetch,* and *Codase*).[11] Online code repositories are often used by multi-developer projects to handle various versions and to enable developers to submit various patches of code in an organized fashion. CVS, a version control system commonly used in open source projects, is an important management mechanism that allows several developers to work on the same files both simultaneously and remotely. It allows the recording of individual histories of sources files and documents while storing the code on a single central server.[12]

There are other examples that extend the online repository model to the cultural realm. For instance, *Perlmonks.org* is a repository, discussion forum, and learning resource for the Perl community that also provides an online platform for presenting Perl poetry and obfuscated code. Another example is *Sweetcode.org*, which presents a themed and contextualized (reviewed) systematic selection of links to innovative free software.[13]

In *Free Software, Free Society*, Richard Stallman suggests that the sharing of software is as old as computing, just as the sharing of recipes is as old as cooking.[14] However, the reverse of this analogy holds too. As much as recipes can be shared (open) they can also be kept secret (closed) in the same way as software licensing reinforces two radically opposite models of production, distribution, and use of software—"open source" and "closed source." In general terms, under open source conditions, source code is included with a particular software package to allow its viewing and further modifications by the user (i.e., source code distributed under the terms of licenses such as BSD, GNU/GPL, MIT), whereas a proprietary model of closed source prevents its free distribution and modification, and software is released as already compiled binary code (e.g., software distributed under the Microsoft EULA [End User License Agreement]).[15] However, the politics of open source are much more complex. A further distinction is made between Open Source Software and Free Software within the free software community to articulate different ideological positions in relation to open source—emphasizing respectively either its development methodology or the ethical and social aspect of the "freedom" of software.[16] More currently, the term FLOSS has been used as a more generic term to refer to Free, Libre, and Open Source Software.

The idea of source code, and indeed the open source model, extends beyond programming and software. For instance, Knuth points to creative aspects of programming alongside technical, scientific, or economic aspects, and says that writing a program "can be an aesthetic experience much like composing poetry or music."[17] Source code can be considered to have aesthetic properties; it can be displayed and viewed.[18] It can be seen as not only as a recipe for an artwork that is on public display but as the artwork itself—as an expressive artistic form that can be curated and exhibited or otherwise circulated.[19] For example, the activity of obfuscating code (making source code deliberately hard to read and understand), while in more general usage serves the purpose of protecting software applications from reverse engineering, might also be seen as creative practice in itself. An executable function is combined with an aesthetic quality of the source code through "simple keyword substitution, use or non-use of whitespace to create artistic effects, to clever self-generating or heavily compressed programs."[20] The software art repository Runme.org lists obfuscated code under the category of "code art" alongside code poetry, programming languages, quines, and minimal code.[21] In the context of programming, the creative aspects are also registered in competitions such as the International Obfuscated C Code Contest, in which "The aims of the contest are to present the most obscure and obfuscated C program, to demonstrate the importance of ironic programming style, to give prominence to compilers with unusual code and to illustrate the subtleties of the C language."[22]

The excerpt of source code at the beginning of this entry is from a longer program and part of the *Barszcz.net* project. An online repository and a platform for presenting and sharing barszcz soup recipes in the form of source code written in a number of programming languages, the project brings together cooking recipes and source code in a literal sense.[23] In a wider cultural context, this exemplifies a general way of thinking about source code as an open model for creative practice; it can be used to encourage collaboration and further development of existing work on the level of contribution, manipulation, and recombination, and can be released under the same or similar licenses in the public domain.

```
/* reminder about things we can do in the kitchen:
* peel, wash, chop, cook */

beetroots = wash( beetroots );
cabbage = chop( cabbage );

cooking = 0;
do {

        cook( beetroots );
        cook( cabbage );
        cook( carrots );
        cook( parsnips );
```

```
} while( cooking < soft_cooked);

exit(1);
}
```

Notes

1. Donald Knuth, *The Art of Computer Programming, Vol. 1, "Fundamental Algorithms,"* 8.

2. The metaphor is also used by the Belgian artists group Constant in their project *Cuisine Interne Keuken* (2004) to examine the economics of the internal organization of the cultural system and the workplace—a system that consists of components (ingredients), tools (utensils), and work and creation processes (recipes). Available at http://www.constantvzw.com/cn_core/cuisine/.

3. Paul E. Ceruzzi, in *A History of Modern Computing,* 92–93, points to some earlier examples of programs such as COBOL that had "the ability to use long character names that made the resulting language look like ordinary English." Thus the program was self-documenting—instructions were sufficient descriptions for both machine and humans and programmer's comments were not required.

4. "For instance the 'compiler' for a bytecode-based language translates the source code into a partially compiled intermediate format, which is later run by a fast interpreter called a virtual machine. Some 'interpreters' actually use a just-in-time compiler, which compiles the code to machine language immediately before running it." http://en.wikipedia.org/wiki/Programming_language.

5. J. David Bolter, *Turing's Man,* 33.

6. Although the stored-program principle is commonly credited to John von Neumann for his "First Draft of a Report on the EDVAC" (1945), he was not the sole creator of "von Neumann Architecture." According to Paul E. Cerruzi in *A History of Modern Computing,* 21–22, it was J. Presper Eckert and John Mauchly who first conceived of the idea (in 1944).

7. UNIVAC was designed by Eckert and Mauchly (Ceruzzi, *A History of Modern Computing,* 20).

8. Ceruzzi, *A History of Modern Computing,* 84.

9. Ibid, 108.

10. Knuth, *The Art of Computer Programming,* 182.

11. Examples cited: *SourceForge* http://sourceforge.net/; *Freshmeat* http://freshmeat .net/; *CodeSnippets* http://www.bigbold.com/snippets/; *Koders* http://www.koders.com/; *Krugle* http://www.krugle.com/; *Codefetch* http://www.codefetch.com/; *Codase* http:// www.codase.com/.

12. CVS developed from an earlier versioning system, RCS, and is similar to other packages such as PRCS, and Aegis. See http://www.nongnu.org/cvs/.

13. Examples cited are *PerlMonks.org* (http://perlmonks.org) and *Sweetcode.org* (http:// www.sweetcode.org/). One of the developers of the *Runme* software art repository, Alex McLean, described Sweetcode.org as "perhaps the closest thing to an art gallery for the free software community, and indeed one of the inspirations for Runme.org." See http://runme.org/feature/read/+sweetcode/+45/.

14. Richard Stallman, "GNU Project," in Joshua Gay, ed., *Free Software, Free Society: Selected Essays of Richard M. Stallman,* 31–39.

15. Examples cited: BSD (Berkeley Software Distribution) http://www.bsd.org/; GPL (General Public License) http://www.gnu.org/; GNU/Linux project http://www.kernel .org/; MIT OpenCourseWare http://ocw.mit.edu/; and Microsoft End User License Agreement http://msdnaa.oit.umass.edu/Neula.asp. For an extensive list of licenses see: http://www.opensource.org/licenses/ or http://www.fsf.org/licensing/licenses/.

16. Richard Stallman, "Why Free Software is Better than Open Source," in Joshua Gay, ed., *Free Software, Free Society: Selected Essays of Richard M. Stallman*, 55–60. Also see Free Software Foundation http://www.fsf.org/ and Open Source Initiative http:// www.opensource.org.

17. Donald Knuth, *The Art of Computer Programming, Vol. 1, "Fundamental Algorithms,"* v.

18. Describing an example of a music application, Geoff Cox said "In this area of soft- ware arts practice programmers make music in keeping with the expressive qualities of live performance, by using interpreted scripting languages (such as perl) and coding in real-time with the source code on public display." Geoff Cox, "Software Actions," in Joasia Krysa, ed., *Curating Immateriality: DATA Browser 03,* 76.

19. The phenomenon of computer viruses demonstrates the aesthetization of code quite explicitly. For the purpose of art, harmful properties of viruses are typically removed and viruses are exhibited as aesthetic systems. For example, the notorious work "biennale.py," a computer virus programmed in Python by the artist collective [epidemiC] and net art group 0100101110101101.org, operated with the sole purpose being "to survive" by acting upon its exhibition context of the 49th Venice Biennale. It was subsequently included along with other examples in *I Love You* (2002), a larger show dedicated to phenomena of computer viruses in artistic context. See Alessandro Ludovico, "Virus Charms and Self-Creating Codes," in Franziska Nori, ed., *I love you: computerviren, hacker, kultur, exhibition catalogue* 40.

20. See http://www.wikipedia.org/wiki/Obfuscated_code/.

21. See http://www.runme.org/categories/+code_art/.

22. See http://www.digitalcraft.org/iloveyou/c_code.htm/.

23. In culinary terminology "Barszcz" [English: Borscht] refers to a traditional Eastern European speciality soup of red beetroot that comes in many regional varieties. See http://www.barszcz.net/.

■

System Event Sounds

Morten Breinbjerg

"System event sounds" is the term for unique sounds assigned to program events such as Windows Logon, Windows Logoff, Close Window, Exit Windows, New Mail Notification, etc. Every day we expose ourselves to these sounds; they form the soundscape of our computers. It is reasonable to assume that the startup tone of *Windows XP* is the most frequently played musical composition we have. In nature sounds occur only when different parts of matter interact.[1] The sounds in our computer however are not a consequence of such interaction. No matter interacts, at least not on the level of human perception, since only small electrical signals are exchanged in electronic circuits. But these patterns of exchange sometimes call out a designed sound to inform us of the state of our computer (battery is low), comment on the action performed (print complete), and/or signify the connection to a larger network outside of our machine (you've got mail). These designed sounds are supposed to help make the computer and the actions performed more understandable and thereby contribute to the efficiency of use. I call this way of using sound "semiotic."

Sounds are also used other ways: to evoke emotions, to signify the quality of the software or the values characteristic of the companies producing it; or to create an ambience, a more ambiguous and subjective space of interpretation, (as in the music of the *Windows* startup sound, the soundscapes of internet pages, and the virtual spaces of computer games). This manner of using sound I call "aesthetic."

In this text I will concentrate solely on the aesthetic use of sounds in the *Microsoft Windows* operating system. My purpose is to outline how system event sounds and especially the *Windows* startup sound are designed to evoke emotional response and also how system event sounds enter into a broader cultural context, regulating social behavior.

The Semiotic Use of Sound

Talking about the semiotic use of sound in operating systems or individual programs like Microsoft Word I refer to the intention of unambiguous communication. Sound is applied as yet another layer of semiosis in order to make the software comprehensible and to reduce the time and energy spent. Its function is to denote the actions being performed, as direct feedback when pushing a button, or as information on background processes being initiated or completed. The way sound is used corresponds to everyday listening, that is, hearing sounds as indexes to events taking place.

One advantage of sound is that, due to the nature of aural perception, sound information can be processed while other types of events are taking place, as opposed to the one-at-a-time modus of focused visual perception. Hence the sound information of incoming mail can be perceived instantaneously without (necessarily) interrupting the typing of a letter or some other task being performed.

How sounds are used and for what reasons vary in different programs but, in general, sound occurs when the user acts on the computer, when there is a change of state in the computer system, or when automated procedures are being carried out. Sound functions in this way to provide immediate feedback on actions performed or initiated, or to warn of disallowed actions, critical changes in the state of the computer, and of actions needed. In short, system event sounds indicate actions needed, performed, initiated, or completed, whether these actions are carried out by the user or the computer.

The system event sounds of *Windows XP* are mostly symbolic, although some can be characterized as iconic. The icon is a type of sign that resembles the object signified, while the symbol is a sign that represents its object purely by convention.

The sound of a piece of paper being crumpled up following the "empty recycle bin" command is a well known auditory icon. The sound of a switch when you navigate the forward or backward button from within a given brief-case window is another. Although both sounds are iconic, the first is special since it relates to the semantics of the action performed. The crumpling sound is a strong analogy to the intention of throwing away paper. The sound of a switch however, does not relate to the intention of navigating back and forth. Here the iconic analogy is purely the sound of something being activated.

System event sounds are typically short pitched sounds or short melodic phrases that are synthetic in nature although many of them have a bell-like, or even piano-like character. As symbols they bear no resemblance to the function they represent and therefore it takes time to learn which function they address. Nevertheless, some of them are value-laden because they attribute an emotional state to the action being performed; this lies beyond simple feedback information and beyond the semantics of the action.

The Aesthetic Use of Sound

Consider the two sounds that in many cases alert users to the state of the battery. The first is a "low battery" warning, the other, if no action has been taken, is a "critical battery" warning. The first is a single percussive sound and the second, more critical one is a deep-pitched, rhythmic figure of a repeated unison note (da dam). The sound provides us with a simple feedback response that demands our attention. Perhaps, or hopefully, we will learn that it refers to the critical state of the battery (its semantic content). But even before we reach that conclusion, the deep and insistent rhythm of the sound evokes a male stereotype communicating authority and strength. The sound signifies not only the purely objective information, that the battery is running out of power, but the potential catastrophe of this fact. As such it presents itself as a warning.

The logon and logoff sounds of *Windows XP* are additional examples of sounds that express emotional states beyond the context-specific semantics of the action (log on/log off). The two sounds mirror each other, since it is the same melody played forward (logon) and backward (logoff). The logon melody is a rising interval of a fifth with a small string sound crescendo played an octave lower than the first note of the interval. The logoff melody is a descending interval of a fifth with a string sound played an octave above the first note of the interval. The most characteristic feature of the two melodies is the upward and downward movement. From the theory of metaphorical projection[2] we know that the up/down dichotomy is used as a metaphorical projection across many domains.[3] Up (rising, ascending, etc.) is good, while down (descending, falling, etc.) is bad, as when we speak of a person as a rising or falling star. To stand up demands energy (force), activity, and intentionality and when you stand, your body is ready to act. To sit down you just let go. It demands no energy since the body has a natural tendency to collapse. The ascending logon melody is perceived as the positive energized action and the descending logoff as the negative one. So what does the logon sound signify? It tells us that we have pushed the button and are about to log on to the operating system of *Windows*. It also indicates that the computer has been activated, that it is about to stand up, forceful and ready.[4]

The power of music to express emotional states is generally accepted. Writers of the Attic period such as Plato and Aristotle in, respectively, *The Republic* and *Politics* talked about the power of music and sound to control the emotions of (young) people, warning against the seductive power of certain keys. In the so called "affektenlehre" of the Baroque period, music theorists tried to describe and categorize the affective connotations of scales, rhythms, and instruments; Italian theorist Geoseffe Zarlino's asserted that it was well known that the harmony of major and minor represent joy and sadness. Although we know that we should be cautious about such assertions, we must acknowledge that music, especially film and theater music, draws heavily on stereotypes and heuristic rules of ascending and descending melodies of slow and fast, straight and syncopated rhythms, etc. In fact these media have stereotyped these ways of hearing and comprehending. As such, the immediate understanding of the "critical battery" sound as a warning and the experience of the logon sound as a positive action is due to both innate experiences of music and cultural ways of listening. By discussing these natural and cultural aspects of perception and understanding, we have entered the realm of aesthetics. Here we are confronted with a much more ambiguous and subjective interpretation, built upon the connotative power of sound and music.

In continuing the discussion we must move beyond the semiotic interest of traditional human-computer interaction design and start to discuss how system event sounds:

1. are employed to express and brand the qualities of the product and/or the values of those who produce as well as those who use it, more than just to assist us in navigating the virtual space of our computer. Sound can be a brand, sound can be retro, sound can denote style, etc.
2. force our attention by representing the voice of our computer, as it explains it needs ("my power is low") or communicates something that slipped our attention ("someone just mailed you"). As such the sounds of our computer regulate social behavior.

Let us continue by discussing the aesthetic function of the startup sound of the *Windows* operating system and see what values are reflected in the sound. The startup sound signifies that the operating system is starting up, in much the same way that the toolbar click sound of *Microsoft Word* indicates that you did push a button. But this simple information feedback is neither the sole nor the most important reason why the sound is there. The startup sound introduces the world opening up in front of us and, as such, is an overture to the *Windows XP* experience. Compare this to the simple stereotypical fanfare (ta-da) first used as a startup sound in *Windows 3.1*.

A fanfare is a short trumpet or horn sound played in the low natural tones of the instrument in a major triad. A fanfare is traditionally used for ceremonial purposes, to state an occasion and to draw the listener's attention, such as when an important person arrives. The sound of the trumpet is loud and powerful and the trumpet often has the function of marking power and status such as that associated with kingship. The fall of the Walls of Jericho under the sound of trumpets as described in the Old Testament is probably the most famous allegory that refers to the trumpet.

It is doubtful that Microsoft designed a fanfare based on its historical use in occidental music or with the intention to signify the culturally defined values inherited with the sound of trumpets. However, we do know that Microsoft does consider the cultural value and the importance of the startup sound as a brand; they not only used Brian Eno as the composer of the *Windows 95* startup sound, but also recently engaged Robert Fripp, another famous experimental rock musician, to compose and play the sounds for *Windows Vista*.

In an interview[5] Brian Eno explained that Microsoft presented him with a list of the adjectives (inspiring, optimistic, futuristic, sentimental, emotional, etc.) that they wanted the sound to reflect. He composed eighty-four different pieces of music, from which they chose one.

The one chosen (the "Microsoft Sound") is an ascending melody that can be divided into three phrases all played on a bell or harp-like instrument. The first is an interval of a fifth, the second a short arpeggio, and the third a repeating lapping interval of a fifth. Underneath the last phrase a string sound slowly appears. The direction of the melody is clear although a bit hesitant as it strives upward. The harmony never resolves but includes a subtle minor second at the end that shrouds the sound in mystery despite the generally warm and easy feel of the melody. The Microsoft Sound is a gentle and much more elegant melody than the simple fanfare of *Windows 3.1*. The melody has the positive movement upwards, but not in any insistent or aggressive way. It signifies calmness and gentleness as it unfolds. The instrumentation is also significant; the harp (if we agree on the idea that it sounds like one) gives the melody a lyrical touch. In romantic music the harp is, by convention, a symbol of beauty and harmony. As a more general symbol the harp is like a ladder. It leads to the world beyond, to a new ontological level. But the mystery invoked by the minor second and the unresolved harmony indicates that there is more than meets the eye. As such the Microsoft Sound invites or perhaps even rouses us to dive into the Microsoft world which reveals the full potential of the machine.

The commission of Brian Eno was well conceived. Brian Eno is famous for playing keyboards in the experimental rock group Roxy Music in the early 1970s and for developing the concept of ambient music, as well as for experimenting with generative and aleatoric principles of composition inspired by John Cage and Steve Reich, among others. He is well known as producer of Talking Heads, David Bowie, and U2. Furthermore, Brian Eno not only makes music but also publishes theoretical work and as such belongs to the intelligentsia of rock and electronic music. With his background Microsoft not only hired a competent musician, they hired a cultural icon.

By means of the use of sound, the computer is given a voice and thereby the ability to contact and communicate with its user and the world around it. In short it comes alive. Three interesting aspects can be drawn from this Tamagotchi-like nature of the computer. First, the computer uses sound to draw our attention the same way that the sound of a telephone or an alarm does. Our responses to these sounds are part of our social behavior: consider how the cell phone distracts us with its ring tone, even in inappropriate situations. Second, the computer is able to communicate the nature of its own state, for example: "I am running out of power" meaning that we have to interfere if we want to avoid loosing our data or continue working. The ability to communicate the possibility of its own ruin, thereby commanding us to act, is remarkable and unique for a tool; not many tools interfere with our social behavior in this way. Third, by the use of sound the computer not only communicates with the user, it announces its presence within a larger context and exposes the actions of its user. We (shamefully) recognize this when sound reveals that we are checking our email at a meeting or booting up our computer during a talk.

System event sounds as aesthetic objects have become a part of broader culture outside the control of Microsoft. Allowing for personalization, system event sounds can be modified or even replaced. Not surprisingly all kinds of funny sounds from *Star Trek, The Simpsons,* and the like can be downloaded from the internet, and used to brand ourselves. System event sounds are themselves also used as material for music compositions like the "Windows Noises" of Clown Staples.[6] Hence system event sounds, as with all digital material, are edited and mixed, downloaded and distributed. As aesthetic objects, system event sounds have themselves equally become part of a culture (and of a new billion dollar industry) of sharing, buying, managing, recording, and downloading.

Notes

NB: The system event sounds discussed in this article, can all be heard at, Marcin Wichary, "GUIdebook, Graphical User Interface Gallery," available at http://www.guidebookgallery.org/sounds/.

1. W. W. Gaver, "What in the World Do We Hear?: An Ecological Approach to Auditory Event Perception."

2. George Lakoff and Mark Johnson, *Metaphors We Live By.*

3. The theory of metaphorical projection is laid out by Mark Johnson in collaboration with George Lakoff. The theory basically states that the metaphor is a fundamental cognitive structure rooted in our bodily experience of the world. Our bodily experience and our spatial and temporal orientation develop into patterns of recognition that structure the way we perceive and understand the world around us. Johnson calls these patterns "Image Schemata." There are many different schemata but here I refer to the

schemata of movement and force to suggest why different system event sounds are designed the way they are and how we interpret them. Ibid.

4. In "What's in those video games?" Ulf Wilhelmsson used the theory of metaphorical projection to analyze the function of sound in *Pac-Man* and other videogames.

5. Joel Selvin, "Chronicle Pop Music Critic."

6. See Clown Staples, available at http://www.geocities.com/clownstaples/.

■

Text Virus

Marco Deseriis

> Would you offer violence to a well intentioned virus on its slow road to symbiosis?
> —WILLIAM S. BURROUGHS[1]

On April 17, 2001, an alarmed email message was sent from an unknown location in Brazil. Within a few days the message was bouncing frantically through mailing lists, Usenet groups, and the private mailboxes of thousands of users in many countries. One of the English versions of the message read:

Dear All: We received a virus on a message. I followed the instructions below . . . located the virus and was able to delete it. The bad news is that you probably have it, as you are in My Address book! More bad news is that my anti virus program did not detect this virus. The virus lies dormant for 14 days and then "kills" your hard drive.

Here is what to do. If you follow the instructions and then see that you have the virus, you need to send a similar e-mail to everyone in your address book.

Remove the virus by following these steps:

1. Go to "Start." Then to "Find" or "Search."
2. In the "Search for files or folders" type sulfnbk.exe—this is the name of the virus.
3. If your search finds this file, it will be an ugly blackish icon that will have the name sulfnbk.exe. DO NOT OPEN IT! If it does not show up on your first "Search," try a "New Search."
4. Right click on the file—go down to "Delete" and left click.[2]

Each text had slightly different features. One version warned "The virus HIDES in the computer for 2 weeks and then DAMAGES THE DISC IRREPARA- BLY." Another added that the latent phase of the virus had a specific dead- line: "It will become active on June 1, 2001. It might be too late by then. It wipes out all files and folders on the hard drive."[3] Although not all of the ver- sions considered Sulfnbk.exe a lethal threat, most of them referred to the help- lessness of standard antivirus software to detect it.

It took a few days to realize that Sulfnbk.exe was not a virus, but in fact a regular Windows utility to restore long file names if they become damaged or corrupted. As a result, the same gullible users who had erased the file on their machine had to recover it from a Windows installation disc and to forward an apologetic message explaining how to do this.

In the next few weeks various experts tried to analyze the case. Some ar- chived it as an ordinary email hoax. Others, perhaps more accurately, read the Sulfnbk.exe frenzy as an urban legend or a "self-fulfilling mass hysteria."[4] As a matter of fact, the alarm took off a few weeks after the first detection of the Magistr virus, a real mass-mailing email spreading as an .exe attachment and in- fecting any 32-bit Windows portable executable file. The experts argued that as Sulfnbk was probably one of the infected executables, "Someone who fell victim to Magistr mistakenly thought that the host file was the culprit and decided to warn others about it."[5]

In other words, the hoax was not planned by anyone but was one of the by- products of virus paranoia (the other major one being the prosperity of anti- virus software companies). The episode could be dismissed as an accident if the same cycle had not repeated itself a year later, targeting another Windows utility—*Jdbgmgr.exe*, a file with a teddy bear icon used in Java environments. Even in this case it was hard to say whether the hoax was planned or was a pos- sible "spin-off" of the Magistr virus.

In the impossibility of ascertaining their origins, such hoaxes appear as epi- phenomena of a machinic system characterized by a high level of commixture of natural language and computer code. In fact, it is precisely in the moments in which users delete what is supposed to be a virus that they become the virus of their own operating systems. It is precisely in the moments in which users try to help other people that they behave like worms within a distributed sys- tem. To be sure, the users correctly decode the alert messages in natural lan- guage, but being unable to grasp the meaning of computer code they behave, de facto, as machines that mechanically perform instructions.

By adopting this inverted perspective, we can thus read the alert message as a set of formal instructions (1. Go to Start, etc.), that are unambiguous enough to be executed by a human recipient or a machine.[6] From this angle, the Sulfnbk type of email hoax is nothing more than a manually-driven virus in which humans and machines exchange roles.

Far from being a novelty, this process of inversion has deep roots, as shown by the etymology of the word "hoax." The term derives from hocus pocus, a formula used by magicians (such as abracadabra or sim sala bim) that by transmuting an "h" into a "p" epitomizes the act of transformation itself. Some trace the origin of the expression to the Roman Catholic Eucharist, when in the moment of lifting the wafer the priest utters "hoc est enim corpus meum" or "hoc est corpus" (this is the body) to enact the transubstantiation of the wafer into the body of Jesus.

Although not everybody agrees on the etymology of the term,[7] what is relevant to us is that hocus pocus is a performative speech act that has the power of enacting and producing that which it names, rather than merely representing it.[8] However, in the context of a church or of a show, the priest and the magician reenact a discursive practice cemented by long tradition, whereas the text virus lacks apparently such tradition. Nevertheless, the text virus is socially recognized as such only after an antivirus firm categorizes it as such. By archiving, labeling, and rating viruses and hoaxes, antivirus firms set a tradition and enact the same preservative function of the clergy. My argument here is that this categorization freezes the ever-sliding nature of (machinic) writing, and prevents us from discovering the power of this ambivalence.

In order to articulate this thesis, I have to step back to the *Phaedrus*, the famous Platonic dialogue in which Socrates denounces writing as a mnemonic device that, far from empowering memory, will make humans even more forgetful. What disturbs Socrates most (according to Plato and "retraced" by Derrida) is the fact that writing is a supplement that, circulating randomly without its father, cannot be interrogated, and thus diverts us from the search for truth:

And once a thing is put into writing, the composition, whatever it may be, drifts all over the place, getting into the hands not only of those who understand it, but equally of those who have no business with it; it doesn't know how to address the right people, and not address the wrong. And when it is ill treated and unfairly abused it always needs its parent to come to its aid, being unable to defend or attend to its own needs.[9]

For this reason writing is a *pharmakon*—a Greek term that stands both for medicine and poison—an errant simulacrum of a living discourse that comes from afar and whose effects are unknown to those who take it.[10] Adopting a familial metaphor, Plato portrays writing as the patricidal son who has the ability to imitate and thus replace his father, that is, the only authority that can authenticate with his living presence the truthfulness and property of speech.[11]

Now the analogies with our text virus are apparent. Devoid of a specific origin, the alert message "drifts all over the place," appearing to the end user as a drug that will prevent a disease from taking over his machine. But, in fact, the drug is a poison, and only the second message, containing the instructions on how to restore the file, will be the remedy for the self-inflicted damage. Equally, if we consider Magistr as a parent of Sulfnbk.exe and Jdbgmgr.exe (the two are labeled as viruses after infection by Magistr) we can see how the user has exchanged the offspring for the progenitor, and, in the impossibility of deciding who is the real impostor, has killed them both.

Thus, with machinic writing, we arrive at a curious inversion of the genealogic relation described by Plato: This time it is the parent who has the power to master (or to "magistr") the offspring in order to spread through the system. However, the user cannot read this genealogy insofar as she or he ignores the underlying grammar and even the alphabet of the machinic environment.

This metaphor is quite literal, as it points us back to another major historic leap—the introduction of the phonetic alphabet in the West. After the Greeks inherited the alphabet from the Phoenicians, they elaborated a set of twenty-four characters in which each letter represented a consonant or a vowel.

Although the utter simplicity of this sound-based technical innovation represented a major shift from the complex logographic systems based on hundreds of signs, the Semitic and Phoenician aleph-beth was still based on the pictographic glyph. For instance the first letter, aleph, was represented by a symbol whose shape stylized an "ox" (aleph is also the ancient Hebrew word for ox). The Greeks simply turned the symbol onto its head and so created the "A." The letter mem, that means "water" in Hebrew, was drawn by the Phoenicians as a series of waves. The Greeks rendered it more symmetrical transforming it into our "M." The letter qoph, "monkey" in Hebrew, was a circle intersected by a long tail. The Greek "Q" still retains a sense of that image.

By making the characters suitable for the needs of the hand and the eye, that is, by making them more rational, the Greeks removed from the alphabet all the references to sensible phenomena. As David Abram points out, the pictographic glyph still referred to an external and animated world of which it was the static image; for the Greeks "a direct association is established between the pictorial sign and the vocal gesture, for the first time completely bypassing the thing pictured."[12]

In this way, a self-referential system is set in motion whose dynamics are exclusively determined by the interplay of the grammatical and phonetic rules governing a specific language.

This self-reflexivity implies, following the linguist Ferdinand de Saussure, the arbitrariness of the relation between signifier and signified and is a cornerstone for the semiotic reading all the systems of signs, including games, signposts, maps, genomes, etc. Computer code is no exception and its origin is based on an invention that is conceptually no different that the shift from pictographic to phonetic literacy.[13]

In 1937, Claude Shannon showed that a schema of relays and switching circuits could be easily translated into algebraic equations and binary arithmetic.[14] Abstracted from their iconic counterparts, the operators of Boolean calculus could now be used for controlling the flow of electricity inside computers.[15]

Initially computers had to be rewired constantly by human agents. In 1948, the manual task of plugging and unplugging cables was deviated by embedding a set of sixty stored instructions in the memory of the ENIAC. In a certain sense, software was born and the introduction in 1949 of assembly language simplified the work of the programmer by translating the machine language into a set of human-readable notations.[16]

The subsequent movement toward higher-level programming made the code even closer to natural language, but at the same time obfuscated the machine behind layers and layers of code. Revising Derrida we can say that it is the double translation of a relay scheme into a string of 0s and 1s and of that string into a word that constitutes "the prior medium in which opposites are opposed, the movement and the play that links them among themselves, reverses them or makes one side cross over into the other."[17] A "love letter" can kill your hard drive. A patch is a virus. A remedy is a poison.

Thus, in a machinic environment the hoax constantly redoubles the acts of magic through which programmers translated one language into another after they lost their respective parents (the external world for the alphabet, the machine for code). Both orphans, the two systems can now exchange their functions and look for a different destiny. But to express its virtuality, machinic writing constantly struggles with the gatekeepers that try to disambiguate it and reinscribe it in a proper and productive system of signification.

Notes

1. William S. Burroughs, *The Electronic Revolution*, Expanded Media Edition, 7.

2. This is an abridged version. The full version can be found on the Symantec web site: http://www.symantec.com/avcenter/venc/data/sulfnbk.exe.warning.html.

3. Ibid.

4. Among those there is Vmyths.com, a website not sponsored by antivirus companies.

5. http://urbanlegends.about.com/library/blsulfnbk.htm/.

6. Florian Cramer, "Concepts, Notations, Software, Art."

7. For an exhaustive explanation of the origins of the term, see Craig Conley, *Magic Words: A Dictonary*, available at http://www.blueray.com/magic/magicwords/index.php?p=177/.

8. John Austin, *How to Do Things with Words*; John Searle, *Speech Acts: An Essay in the Philosophy of Language*.

9. Plato, *Phaedrus* (275d–e).

10. On the concept of writing as a simulacrum or supplement, see Jacques Derrida, *Dissemination*, 108–110.

11. Ibid., 80–81. In Plato's Greece, the juridical personality was centered around the property-owning male. This property is made of himself, his land, wife, children, household, animals, produce, etc. Contrary to the Sophists, who write and sell speeches to the emerging class of the money-bearing democrats, the aristocrat speaks always in the name of his property. He can lose his property, be exiled from the city, and hence lose his citizenship. Thus, value cannot be detached from the person who is giving the speech. Writing for Plato displaces this genealogical relationship and threatens the ideal of the old agricultural society.

12. David Abram, *The Spell of the Sensous*, 100–101.

13. The magnitude of such a shift was firstly noted by Eric Havelock: "The invention of the Greek alphabet, as opposed to all previous systems, including the Phoenician, constituted an event in the history of human culture, the importance of which has not as yet been fully grasped. Its appearance divides all pre-Greek civilizations from those that are post-Greek." Eric Havelock, "The Preliteracy of the Greeks," 369.

14. Claude E. Shannon, *A Symbolic Analysis of Relay and Switching Circuits.*

15. Manuel De Landa, *War in the Age of Intelligence Machines*, 145–146.

16. Wendy Hui Kyong Chun notes how during World War II the ENIAC was re-wired by the Women's Royal Naval Service (Wrens), women with some background in mathematics who physically plugged and unplugged cables at the orders of a male programmer. After the war, this manual task was removed by directly embedding the physical settings into the computer memory. This migration of knowledge dramatically decreased the time necessary for programming while increasing the time necessary for computation. The next step was to enable the computer to not only read instructions, but to write its own instructions by using "interpreters, assemblers, compilers and generators—programs designed to operate other programs, that is, automatic programming." (Mildred Koss). Wendy Hui Kyong Chun, "On Software, or the Persistence of Visual Knowledge."

17. Derrida, *Dissemination*, 127.

■

Timeline (sonic)

Steve Goodman

A common feature of all time-based media, the timeline typically stratifies the on-screen workspace into a metric grid, adjustable in terms of temporal scale (hours / minutes / seconds / musical bars or frames / scenes). With sonic timelines, zooming in and out, from the microsonic field of the sample to the macrosonic domain of a whole project, provides a frame for possible sonic shapes to be sculpted in time.

As an antidote to the digital philosophies of computer age, hype, many media philosophers have been reassessing the analog ground upon which digital technology is built. They are, questioning temporal ontologies, which emphasize the discreteness of matter via a spatialization of time (in the composition of the digital) in favor of a refocus on the continuity of duration. Typical objections to the ontology of the digital temporality share much with the philosophy of Henri Bergson. In Bergson's philosophy of duration, he argues that the spatialization of time belies the "fundamental illusion" underpinning Western scientific thought. Bergson criticized the cinematographic error of Western scientific thought,[1] which he describes as cutting continuous time into a series of discreet frames, separated from the temporal elaboration of movement, which is added afterward (via the action, in film, of the projector) through the perceptual effect of the persistence of vision. Yet sonic time plays an understated role in Bergson's (imagistic) philosophy of time, being often taken as emblematic of his concept of duration as opposed to the cinematographic illusion of consciousness. In *Time & Free Will* he uses the liquidity of the sonic, "the notes of a tune, melting, so to speak, into one another" as exemplifying that aspect of duration that he terms "interpenetration."[2]

The sequencer timeline is one manifestation of the digital coding of sound, which, while breeching Bergson's spatialization of time taboo—an intensive sonic duration is visualized and therefore spatialized—has opened a range of possibilities in audiovisual production. The timeline traces, in Bergsonian terms, an illusory arrow of time, overcoding the terrain of the sequencing window from left to right. As with European musical notation's inheritance from written text, digital audio software sequencers have inherited the habit of left-to-right visual scanning. The timeline constitutes the spatialization of the clock into a horizontal time-coded strip that stretches from left to right across the screen, constituting the matrix of the sequencing window across which blocks of information are arranged. The sonic becomes a visualization in terms of a horizontally distributed waveform spectrograph, or sonic bricks. The temporal parts and the whole of a project are stretched out to cover an extensive space.

A temporal sequence of sounds suddenly occupies an area of the computer screen. What is opened up by this spatialization is the ease of temporal recombination. That marker of the transitory present, the cursor, and its ability to travel into the future and past (the right or left of the cursor) melts what appears, at least within the Bergsonian schema, to be the freezing of audio time into spatialized time stretches, instead of intensive durations. This arrangement facilitates nonlinear editing by establishing the possibility of moving to any point, constituting the key difference between nonlinear digital editing

Timeline (sonic)

and analog fast forwarding and rewinding. The timeline pivoting around the cursor, marker of the transitory present, distributes the possible past (left of the cursor) and future (to the right of the cursor) of the project.

Aside from its improvement of the practicalities of editing and the manipulation of possibility, the digital encoding of sonic time has opened an additional sonic potential in terms of textural invention, a surplus value over analog processing. While the temporal frame of the timeline in digital applications makes much possible, a more fundamental temporal potential of sonic virtuality is locatable in the apparently un-Bergsonian realm of digital sampling, known as discrete time sampling.[3] At a fundamental level, in its slicing of sonic matter into a multiplicity of freeze frames, digital samples treat analog continuity as bytes of numerically coded sonic time and intensity, grains which may or may not assume the consistency of tone continuity, the sonic equivalent of the persistence of vision.

Warning against the conceptual confusion of virtual potential with actual digital possibility, Brian Massumi notes that, despite the hype of the digital revolution, "sound is as analog as ever, at least on the playback end . . . It is only the coding of the sound that is digital. The digital is sandwiched between an analog disappearance into code at the recording and an analog appearance out of code at the listening end."[4] Yet, perhaps in the timestretching function a machinic surplus value or potential is opened in sonic time.

In contrast to the Bergsonian emphasis on continuity in duration, in the 1940s, the elementary granularity of sonic matter was noted by physicist Dennis Gabor, dividing time and frequency according to a grid known as the Gabor matrix. Prising open this quantum dimension of sonic time opened the field of potential, which much more recently became the timestretching tool within digital sound editing applications.[5] The technique "elongates sounds without altering their pitch, demonstrates how the speed at which levels of acoustic intensity are digitally recorded (around 44,000 samples/second) means that a certain level of destratification is automatically accomplished. Since magnitudes (of acoustic intensity) are all that each sample bit contains, they can be manipulated so as to operate underneath the stratification of pitch/duration which depends on the differentiation of the relatively slow comprehensive temporality of cycles per second."[6]

The technique referred to as time-stretching cuts the continuity between the duration of a sonic event and its frequency. In granular synthesis, discreet digital particles of time are modulated and sonic matter synthesized at the molecular level. In analog processing, to lower the pitch of a sound event adds to the length of the event. Slow down a record on a turntable for example, and a given word not only descends in pitch but takes a longer time to unfold. Or allocate a discreet sampled sound object to a zone of a midi keyboard; the difference between triggering the sample using one key, and moving to a key one octave down doubles the time of the sound, and halves its pitch. Timestretching, however, facilitates the manipulation of the length of a sonic event while maintaining its pitch, and vice versa. Timestretching, a digital manipulation process common to electronic music production is used particularly in the transposing of project elements between one tempo (or timeline) and another, fine tuning instruments, but also as a textural effect producing temporal perturbations in anomalous durations and cerated consistencies.

Notes

1. Henri Bergson, *Creative Evolution*, 322.

2. Henri Bergson, *Time and Free Will: An Essay on the Immediate Data of Consciousness*, 100.

3. Ken C. Pohlmann, *Principles of Digital Audio*, 21–22.

4. On the difference between the possible and potential (or virtual) see Brian Massumi, "The Superiority of the Analog," in *Parables for the Virtual*, 138.

5. Curtis Roads, *Microsound*, 57–60; and, Dennis Gabor, "Acoustical Quanta and the Theory of Hearing."

6. Robin Mackay, "Capitalism and Schizophrenia: Wildstyle in Effect," 255.

■

Variable

Derek Robinson

To be is to be the value of a bound variable.
—WILLARD VAN ORMAN QUINE[1]

You can be anything this time around.
—TIMOTHY LEARY[2]

There is a distinction to be made between the variables employed by programmers and those employed by scientists, engineers, and mathematicians.
Not that one can't straightforwardly write a program that uses computer-type
variables to implement statistical algorithms. Nor is it hard to find a general
logical definition good for both types. But it would not reveal the pragmatic,
historical, and subcultural reasons why the word "variable" means different
things to the programmer and the statistician (even if the latter's data analysis
is likely performed with software written by the former). The root of the difference is that a programmer's variables are implemented on a computer, which
means they must concretely exist in a computer's memory, in accordance with
whose concreteness they must be named, ordered, addressed, listed, linked,
counted, serialized, unserialized, encoded, decoded, raveled, and unraveled;
how this happens bears little resemblance to algebraic symbols scratched on a
chalkboard.

The programmer's variable is a kind of box; its name is the label written on
the lid. To open the box, accomplished by the magical act of reciting its name
in a prepared context, is to be granted access to what has been put "inside" it:
the variable's value—one datum. Or say, what it denotes, what it "means,"
under a hugely impoverished notion of meaning that analytical philosophers
spent much of the past century trying to shoehorn thought and language into.
Cavils aside, it's in good part due to their efforts that there appeared in that
century's middle third, the new science of computation.

A variable is a box stripped of sides, top, and bottom, abstracted away from
geometry and physics, of no especial size or shape or color nor situated—so
far as the programmer who conjures it needs to know or worry about—in any
particular place. It's like there's always a spare pocket available any time there's
something to be kept track of, and all it costs is to think up a name for it. (And
then to remember what the name was; sadly not always so easy.) The passed

buck of reference, the regressus of signs, begins and ends in the blank affect-less fact of the unfilled vessel, an empty signifier that awaits only assignment to contain a content. (In the upside-down tree-universe of Lisp, all termini point to "NIL.")

High-level computer languages relieve programmers of worrying about where values are kept in the computer's address space or how to liberate the lo-cations they've occupied when they're no longer needed (this is done with a bit of legerdemain called garbage collection). In reality the variable is situated in a reserved area of physical memory called the Symbol Table. What is recorded in the Symbol Table is just the variable's name, paired with a pointer (a number understood as an address), which points to the location of some other cell that's allocated on demand from a heap of memory locations not currently claimed. Since all this takes place in a computer, naturally there are further layers of in-direction and obliqueness between how a program accesses the variable's value and its extra-symbolic physical existence as an elaborate roundelay of trapped charges in doped silicon or mottles of switchable ferromagnetic domains on a spinning metal oxide-coated plastic disk.

The variable's role is as an index that points to something, somewhere. C. S. Peirce, grandfather of semiotics, once defined a sign as "a lesser that contains a greater."[3] Like a magical Arabian Nights tent, it appears bigger on the in-side than its outside. One hears an echo of Turing's poser: "How can 2.5 kilo-grams of grey-pink porridge contain a whole universe?" (A hint: The finger points out of the dictionary.) A variable is a marker, a token, or placeholder staking out a position within a formal conceptual scheme. As Alan Kay[4] re-marked, "The fundamental meaning of a mark is that it's there." An empty slot awaiting instantiation by being "bound" to a specific value, to be provided by someone's fingers at keyboard and mouse, or by some sensed, measured, electronically amplified, transduced, encoded alteration in the fabric of things happening elsewhere.

Some variables don't vary. A "constant" is a mnemonic stand-in conscripted simply because names are easier for people to remember and recognize than numbers. At bottom this is what any variable is: a name standing for a number that is interpreted as an address that indexes a memory location where a pro-gram is directed to read or write a sequence of bits. Electronic sensors attached to a computer are de facto variables registering external events in a set-aside range of addresses that act as portholes to view sampled digital representations of the changing voltages provided by the sensor.

In the Forth programming language, variables don't even need names. They can be values placed on top of a data stack as arguments to functions that apply operations to them and leave the results on top of the stack as arguments for subsequent functions. The necessity to name is here obviated by the specificity of place. (Forth has named variables too, but to actually use them is regarded as unsporting.) The Unix operating system has its own unnamed variables, called "pipes," for chaining together sequences of code, turning outputs into inputs, to engineer ad hoc assembly-lines of textual filters and transformers. It is this brilliant concept to which Unix owes much of its enduring success.[5]

An especially important use of variables is as arguments passed to a function subroutine. Instances of argument names found in the function body will be automatically replaced by the values of the variables that were provided when the function was invoked. Instances of argument names occurring within a function's scope act like pronouns referring to the place and time in the executing program where the arguments were last assigned values. They are pseudonyms, aliases, trails of breadcrumbs that point back up the "scope chain" of nested execution contexts. (A function "A" called from another function "B" will acquire any variable bindings found in the scope of B; likewise if B was itself called from a function "C," the latter's bindings become a tertiary part of the context of A.) In object-oriented languages there is a special argument or keyword named "this" or "self," which is used within class definitions to enable object instances at runtime to reference themselves and their internal states.[6]

The single most critical constraint on a variable's use is that it, and its every instance, must be uniquely determined in the context or "namespace" of its application, if it is to serve naming's ambition of unambiguous indication. This isn't as uncomplicated as it might seem. Namespaces are easily entangled, and before too long even 64 bits of internet addressing (allowing for 2^{64} or some 18 sextillion different designations) won't suffice to insure uniqueness. (Bruce Sterling is good on the implications of this stuff, and Mark Tansey has made a nice picture.[7]) However all that turns out, beyond the onomastic imperative of having to be uniquely determined within a context, a variable can denote, refer to or stand in place of anything that people are capable of apprehending, conceiving, and representing as a "thing."

Pronouncing upon the thingness of things has historically been considered the special preserve of philosophers, but programmers, being the practical engineering types that they are, simply had to get on with the job. The things represented in software in one way or another all ultimately reduce to patterns of series of on-and-off switches, zeros and ones. No bit-pattern can represent anything without a program to interpret it. The meanings plied through natural language may, they say, be subject to the drift and swerve of an indefinitely deferred semiosis, but software's hermeneutic regress must finally bottom out. It's interpreters all the way down—then it's just bits.[8]

Under the hood, variables are arranged so that a specific pattern of 0s and 1s can be interpreted as a character string (and then as a word, or as several) in one context, a series of numbers, part of a picture, or maybe some music in another context. All of these pieces of information can be connected with some person, some object, or some more abstract category, and stored in a database somewhere. Ultimately they're all bits, and what software does is make sure that what one expects to find when one asks for something, and what one does find are one and the same. (Deliberately or accidentally incurred or induced violations are collected and swapped by connoiseurs of "glitch art" and "data bending.")[9]

Some things are fairly easily resolved. Numbers, still software's main stock in trade, are in the computer usually as integers (counting numbers, without decimal points) from a range between a fixed minimum and maximum (e.g., the 256 counting numbers from −128 to +127) or they are "floating point" numbers—a type of scientific notation (with exponents and mantissas) for representing non-integer values (with decimal points), which can be much larger or much smaller than integers. Alphanumeric characters have several different UTF-standardized 8-, 16-, or 32-bit-long character codes for specifying any graphic symbol used in any human language.

In the grand architectural design of Sir Tim Berners-Lee's Semantic Web, the bottomless puddle of the thingness of things is neatly sidestepped by dictating that things referenced must have URIs ("Uniform Resource Indicators," like web addresses). As long as URIs can be resolved into properly formatted truthful representations of information that people care to assert and are willing to stand by then automated proof procedures can be applied to them. Presumably, at the terminal node of the implied indefinitely extended and ramifying series of assertions asseverating the trustworthiness of other asseverations, we shall arrive at a planet-sized AI and either all our troubles are over, or they've just begun.[10]

The recent rise of markup languages[11] like HTML, CSS, XML, XSL, or SVG is recognition that in many applications, once the data have been properly set up, the ordinary kind of programming that relies on IF-THEN conditions to alter execution flow isn't much needed. The data organization can look after the heavy lifting. Markup languages conform to the abstract data type known as "trees," branching geneologies whose member "nodes" (which can also be trees) are accessed via parent and sibling relations. Trees resemble the table of contents in a book. They are usually implemented using "list" data structures, although how these lists are implemented under the hood isn't important, as long as the lists behave like lists so that trees (and other things) created out of lists will behave like trees (or the other things).[12]

Data structures are compound, multicellular super-variables. Their purpose is to make it easy to arrange logical aggregations of data in ways that make it easy to carry out complex operations on their members. Apart from lists, whose cells can be grown and pruned and grafted in near-organic profusion, core data structures provided in most programming languages include character strings, linear arrays indexed by the counting numbers (used to make 2-D or higher dimensional data tables), and associative arrays: look-up tables whose cells are indexed with arbitrary symbols as the keys (internally turned into addresses by a hashing function,[13] or stuffed into lexicographic trees perhaps). The devil's in the details. Get the data structures right—picture and populate them, imagine traversals and topologies, strike a truce between redundancy and compression, cut a deal with the coder's old familiar foes of Time and Space, "solve et coagula," and mind the gap—and everything else will follow.

If computers can be made to agree on how data shall be represented and interpreted, encoded and decoded, then data can be shared between them the way audio, video, and text files are shared, and many different programs written in different languages running on different computer platforms can co-operatively behave as one very large distributed computer running one very large distributed program. The web is such a thing, and has gradually (if one can call the delerious growth of the past ten years gradual) been awaking to the fact. Mundane attention to marshaling and unmarshaling complex data structures in accordance with commonly agreed dialects and schemas (provision of which is the purpose of the Extensible Markup Language, XML, whose authors had the foresight to see that a data format for specifying data formats would be a good idea) is already rewriting the conduct of commercial life. A spirit of openness and peer collaboration is blowing even through hidebound proprietary holdouts like academic publishing; we await Silent Tristero's Empire and the Brittanica's demise.[14]

Notes

1. W. V. O. Quine (1939), "Designation and Existence." This phrase ("To be is to be the value of a bound variable") became a motto of Quine's, and through him, of mid-century Anglo-American analytical philosophy generally. (Reprinted in H. Feigl, and W. Sellars, *Readings in Philosophical Analysis.*

2. Dr. Timothy Leary, *You Can be Anyone This Time Around.*

3. For a summary of C. S. Peirce's philosophy of the sign, see Umberto Eco's *Semiotics and the Philosophy of Language.*

4. Alan Kay coined the term "object-oriented," headed the Learning Systems Group at Xerox PARC in the 1970s (which developed the now ubiquitous bit-mapped graphical desktop metaphor), invented the "Dynabook," and was the model for (obscure computer geek trivia alert) the Jeff Bridges video game programmer hero in the 1982 Disney film "Tron" (Kay's wife wrote the screenplay).

5. For Forth, see Leo Brodie's *Thinking Forth*, widely regarded as one of the best books about programming for anyone who programs in any language; a free PDF of the 2004 revision is available at the author's website. The Unix philosophy is summarized by Doug McIlroy (inventor of pipes) as follows: 1. Write programs that do one thing well; 2. Write programs that work together; 3. Use text streams as a universal interface.

6. For more information on scope, binding, and reference, see Harold Abelson, Gerald Jay Sussman, *The Structure and Interpretation of Computer Programs.* (A free online version can be found at the book's MIT Press website.)

7. Brian Cantwell Smith's *On the Origin of Objects* plumbs software's ontology very deeply and very densely (however it's only recommended for people not put off by infinite towers of procedural self-reflection).

8. Bruce Sterling would be the well-known science fiction writer, astute cognizer of past and present trends, peripatetic blogger, afficionado and sometime teacher of contemporary design. Recently he authored a book, *Shaping Things,* about "spimes," his neologism for a new category of post-industrially fabricated semi-software objects. Mark Tansey paints large monochromatic post-modern puzzle pictures in the high style of mid-twentieth-century illustration art. The painting referred to shows the crouching figure of (we assume) an archaeologist, bent over a small object, likely a

rock, in a desert landscape that contains many widely scattered small rocks. It has the enigmatic title, "Alain Robbe-Grillet Cleansing Everything in Sight."

9. See "Glitch," this volume.

10. Dieter Fensel, et al., *Spinning the Semantic Web*. An authoritative and up-to-date source is the World Wide Web Consortium: http://www.w3.org/.

11. Markup languages like XML acronymically descend from a typesetting language for IBM computer manuals called SGML, dating from a time (circa 1966) when IBM stood second only to the Jehovah's Witnesses as the world's biggest publisher of print materials. See Yuri Rubinsky, *SGML on the Web*.

12. John McCarthy, *LISP 1.5 Programmer's Manual*. For non-tree data structures implemented using lists, see Ivan Sutherland's *Sketchpad: A Man-Machine Graphical Communication System*—this was the first object-oriented program, the first computer aided design program, and the first "constraints-based" programming system. Utterly revolutionary at the time, it still rewards a look. In 2003 an electronic edition was released on the web.

13. Hash functions are numerical functions for mapping arbitrary character data regarded as numbers to pseudo-random addresses within a predefined range. Their great virtue is constant-time access, unlike tree-based structures. The data stored in hashtables are (obviously) unordered, however.

14. Jon Willinsky, *The Access Principle: The Case for Open Access to Research and Scholarship*. Silent Tristero is implicated in the secret sixteenth-century postal service around whose continued existence or lack thereof the plot of Thomas Pynchon's novel *The Crying of Lot 49* revolves; elements of Pynchon's baroque conspiracy are borrowed from the Rosicrucian Brotherhood, an actual sixteenth-century conspiracy whose Invisible College perhaps only existed as carefully planted and cultivated rumors. (A mailing list of the name is frequented by white-hatted hacker types; with luck and unbending diligence in the pursuit of the art an invitation one day may arrive in your mailbox.)

■
Weird Languages[1]

Michael Mateas

Programming languages are often seen as a given an immutable logic within which everyday coding practice takes place. Viewed in this light, a programming language becomes a tool to be mastered, a means to an end. The practice of writing obfuscated code (see Montfort in this volume) exploits the syntactic and semantic play of a language to create code that, often humorously, comments on the constructs provided by a specific language. But the constructs and logics of languages are themselves contingent abstractions pulled into being out of the space of computational possibility, and enforced and maintained by nothing more than programs, specifically the interpreters and compilers that implement the languages.

In the field of "weird" or "esoteric" languages,[2] programmers explore and exploit the play that is possible in programming language design. Weird programming languages are not designed for any real-world application or normal educational use; rather, they are intended to test the boundaries of programming language design itself. A quality they share with obfuscated code is that they often ironically comment on features of existing, traditional languages.

There are literally dozens, if not hundreds of weird languages, which comment on many different aspects of language design, programming history, and programming culture. A representative selection is considered here, with an eye toward understanding what these languages have to tell us about programming aesthetics.

Languages are considered in terms of four dimensions of analysis: (1) parody, spoof, or explicit commentary on language features, (2) a tendency to reduce the number of operations and strive toward computational minimalism, (3) the use of structured play to explicitly encourage and support double-coding, and (4) the goal of creating a puzzle, and of making programming difficult. These dimensions are not mutually exclusive categories, nor are they meant to be exhaustive. Any one weird language may be interesting in several of these ways, though one particular dimension will often be of special interest.

INTERCAL is the canonical example of a language that parodies other programming languages. It is also the first weird language, and is highly respected in the weird language community. It was designed in 1972 at Princeton University by two students, Don Woods and James Lyon. (Later, while at

Stanford, Woods was the co-author of the first interactive fiction, *Adventure*.)
The explicit design goal of INTERCAL is

to have a compiler language which has nothing at all in common with any other major
language. By "major" we meant anything with which the author's were at all familiar,
e.g., FORTRAN, BASIC, COBOL, ALGOL, SNOBOL, SPITBOL, FOCAL, SOLVE,
TEACH, APL, LISP and PL/I.[3]

INTERCAL borrows only variables, arrays, text input/output, and assignment from other languages. All other statements, operators, and expressions
are unique (and uniquely weird). INTERCAL has no simple "if" construction
for doing conditional branching, no loop constructions, and no basic math operators—not even addition. Effects such as these must be achieved through
composition of non-standard and counterintuitive constructs. In this sense
INTERCAL also has puzzle aspects.

However, despite the claim that this language has "nothing at all in common with any other major language," INTERCAL clearly spoofs the features
of contemporaneous languages, combining multiple language styles together
to create an ungainly, unaesthetic style. From COBOL, INTERCAL borrows
verbose, English-like constructs, including optional syntax that increases the
verbosity; all statements can be prepended with PLEASE. Sample INTERCAL
statements in this COBOL style include FORGET, REMEMBER, ABSTAIN
and REINSTATE. From FORTRAN, INTERCAL borrows the use of optional
line numbers, which can appear in any order, and the DO construct, which in
FORTRAN is used to initiate loops. In INTERCAL, however, every statement
must begin with DO. Like APL, INTERCAL makes heavy use of single characters with special meaning, requiring even simple programs to be liberally
sprinkled with non-alphanumeric characters. INTERCAL exaggerates the worst
features of many languages and combines them together into a single language.

Thirty-three years after its conception, INTERCAL still has a devoted following. Eric Raymond, the current maintainer of INTERCAL, revived the
language in 1990 with his implementation C-INTERCAL, which added the
COME FROM construct to the language—the inverse of the much-reviled
GO TO.

While parody languages comment on other programming languages, languages in the minimalist vein comment on the space of computation. Specifically, they call attention to the very small amount of structure needed to create

a universal computational system. A "system" in this sense can be as varied as a programming language, a formal mathematical system, or physical processes, such as one embodied in a machine. Universal computation was discovered by Alan Turing and described in his 1937 investigation of the limits of computability, "On Computable Numbers."[4] A universal system can perform any computation that it is theoretically possible to perform; such a system can do anything that any other formal system is capable of doing, including emulating any other system. This property is what allows one to implement one language, such as Perl, in another language, such as C, or to implement an interpreter or compiler for a language directly in hardware (using logic gates), or to write a program that provides a virtual hardware platform for other programs (as the *Java Virtual Machine* does). Universality in a programming language is obviously a desired trait, as it means that the language places no limits on the processes that can be specified in the language.

Minimalist languages strive to achieve universality while providing the smallest number of language constructs possible. Such languages often strive for syntactic minimalism, making the textual representation of programs minimal as well. Minimal languages are sometimes called Turing Tarpits, after epigram 54 in Alan Perlis' Epigrams of Programming: "54. Beware the Turing tar-pit in which everything is possible but nothing of interest is easy."[5]

Brainfuck is an archetypically minimalist language, providing merely eight commands, each represented by a single character. These commands operate on an array of 30,000 byte cells initialized to 0. The commands are:

>   Increment the pointer (point to the memory cell to the right)
<   Decrement the pointer (point to the memory cell to the left)
+   Increment the byte pointed to
−   Decrement the byte pointed to
.   Output the byte pointed to
,   Accept a byte of input and write it into the byte pointed to
[Jump forward to the corresponding] if pointing to 0
]   Jump back to the command after the corresponding [if pointing to a nonzero value.

A Brainfuck program which prints out the string "Hello World," follows.

```
+++++++++[>++++++>+++++++++++>+++>+<<<<]>++.>+.+++++++..+++.>++.«+
+++++++++++++.>.+++.------.--------.>+.>.
```

Some weird languages encourage double-coding by structuring the play within the language such that valid programs can also be read as a literary artifact. Double-coding is certainly possible in languages such as C and Perl, and in fact is an important skill in the practice of obfuscated programming. But where C and Perl leave the space of play relatively unstructured, forcing the programmer to shoulder the burden of establishing a double-coding, structured play languages, through their choice of keywords and their treatment of programmer-defined names (i.e., variable names), support double coding within a specific genre of human-readable textual production. The language Shakespeare exemplifies this structured play aspect.

Here is a fragment of a Shakespeare program that reads input and prints it out in reverse order:

```
[Enter Othello and Lady Macbeth]

Othello:
You are nothing!


             Scene II: Pushing to the very end.

Lady Macbeth:
Open your mind! Remember yourself.


Othello:
You are as hard as the sum of yourself and a stone wall. Am I as
horrid as a flirt-gill?


Lady Macbeth:
If not, let us return to scene II. Recall your imminent death!


Othello:
You are as small as the difference between yourself and a hair!
```

Shakespeare structures the play of the language so as to double-code all programs as stage plays, specifically, as spoofs on Shakespearean plays. This is done primarily by structuring the play (that is, the free space) that standard languages provide in the naming of variables and constants. In standard languages, variable names are a free choice left to the programmer, while numeric constants (e.g., 1) are either specified by the textual representation of the number, or through a name the programmer has given to specific constants. In contrast, Shakespeare Dramatis Personae (variables) must be the name of a character from a Shakespeare play, while constants are represented by nouns. The two fundamental constants in Shakespeare are -1 and 1. The nouns recognized by the Shakespeare compiler have been divided into positive, negative, and neutral nouns. All positive (e.g., "lord," "angel," "joy") and neutral (e.g., "brother," "cow," "hair") nouns have the value 1. All negative nouns (e.g., "bastard," "beggar," "codpiece") have the value -1. Constants other than -1 and 1 are created by prefixing them with adjectives; each adjective multiplies the value by 2. So "so sorry little codpiece" denotes the number -4.

The overall structure of Shakespeare follows that of a stageplay. Variables are declared in the Dramatis Personae section. Named acts and scenes become labeled locations for jumps; "let us return to scene II" is an example of a jump to a labeled location. Enter and exit (and exeunt) are used to declare which characters (variables) are active in a given scene; only two characters may be on stage at a time. Statements are accomplished through dialog. By talking to each other, characters set the values of their dialog partner and themselves, compare values, execute jumps, and so forth.

In a programming language, keywords are words that have special meaning for the language, indicating commands or constructs, and thus can't be used as names by the programmer. An example from C is the keyword "for," used to perform iteration; "for" cannot be used by the programmer as the name of a variable or function. In standard languages, keywords typically limit or bound play, as the keywords are generally not selected by language designers to facilitate double-coding. This is, in fact, what makes code poetry challenging; the code poet must hijack the language keywords in the service of double-coding. In contrast, weird languages that structure play provide keywords to facilitate the double-coding that is generally encouraged by the language.

Another language, Chef, illustrates different design decisions for structuring play. Chef facilitates double-coding programs as recipes. Variables are declared in an ingredients list, with amounts indicating the initial value (e.g., 6 oz. of red salmon). The type of measurement determines whether an ingredient is wet or dry; wet ingredients are output as characters, dry ingredients are output as numbers. Two types of memory are provided—mixing bowls and baking dishes. Mixing bowls hold ingredients that are still being manipulated, while baking dishes hold collections of ingredients to output. What makes Chef particularly interesting is that all operations have a sensible interpretation as a step in a food recipe. Where Shakespeare programs parody Shakespearean plays, and often contain dialog that doesn't work as dialog in a play ("you are as hard as the sum of yourself and a stone wall"), it is possible to write programs in Chef that might reasonably be carried out as a recipe. Thus, in some sense, Chef structures play to establish a triple-coding: the executable machine meaning of the code, the human meaning of the code as a literary artifact, and the executable human meaning of the code as steps that can be carried out to produce food.

A number of languages structuring play have been based on other weird languages. Brainfuck is particularly popular in this regard, spawning languages such as FuckFuck (operators are replaced with curse words) and Cow (all instructions are the word "moo" with various capitalizations).

Languages that have a puzzle aspect explicitly seek to make programming difficult by providing unusual, counterintuitive control constructs and operators. While INTERCAL certainly has puzzle aspects, its dominant feature is its parody of 1960s language design. Malbolge, named after the eighth circle of hell in Dante's *Inferno*, is a much more striking example of a puzzle luaguage. Where INTERCAL sought to merely have no features in common with any other language. Malbolge had a different motivation, as author Ben Olmstead writes:

It was noticed that, in the field of esoteric programming languages, there was a particular and surprising void: no programming language known to the author was specifically designed to be difficult to program in . . .

Hence the author created Malbolge. . . . It was designed to be difficult to use, and so it is. It is designed to be incomprehensible, and so it is. So far, no Malbolge programs have been written. Thus, we cannot give an example.[6]

Malbolge was designed in 1998. It was not until 2000 that Andrew Cooke, using AI search techniques, succeeded in generating the first Malbolge program, the "hello, world!" program—actually, it prints "HEllO WORld"—that follows:

```
(=<`$9]7<5YXz7wT.3,+O/o'K%$H"'~D|#z@b=`{^Lx8%$Xmr kpohm-
kNi;gsedcba`_^]\[ZYXWVUTSRQPONMLKJIHGFEDCBA
@?>=<;:9876543s+O<oLm
```

The writing of more complex Malbolge programs was enabled by Lou Scheffer's cryptanalysis of Malbolge in which he discovered "weaknesses" that the programmer can systematically exploit:

The correct way to think about Malbolge, I'm convinced, is as a cryptographer and not a programmer. Think of it as a complex code and/or algorithm that transforms input to output. Then study it to see if you can take advantage of its weaknesses to forge a message that produced the output you want.[7]

His analysis proved that the language allowed for universal computation. The "practical" result was the production of a Brainfuck to Malbolge compiler.

What makes Malbolge so difficult? Like many minimalist languages, Malbolge is a machine language written for a fictitious and feature-poor machine, and thus gains some difficulty of writing and significant difficulty of reading from the small amount of play provided to the programmer for expressing human, textual meanings. However, as Olmstead points out, the mere difficulty of machine language is not enough to produce a truly devilish language. The machine model upon which Malbolge runs has the following features that contribute to the difficulty of the language: a trinary, rather than binary, machine model, minimalism, counterintuitive operations, indirect instruction coding (the meaning of a program symbol depends on where it sits in memory), and mandatory self-modifying code (code mutates as it executes, so it never does the same thing twice). These factors account for the two years that passed before the first Malbolge "hello, world" program appeared.

By commenting on the nature of programming itself, weird languages point the way toward a refined understanding of the nature of everyday coding practice. In their parody aspect, weird languages comment on how different language constructions influence programming style, as well as on the history of programming language design. In their minimalist aspect, weird languages comment on the nature of computation and the vast variety of structures capable of universal computation. In their puzzle aspect, weird languages comment on the inherent cognitive difficulty of constructing effective programs. And in their structured play aspect, weird languages comment on the nature of double-coding, how it is that programs can simultaneously mean something for both the machine and for human readers.

All of these aspects are seen in everyday programming practice. Programmers are extremely conscious of language style, of coding idioms that not only "get the job done" but do it in a way that is particularly appropriate for that language. Programmers actively structure the space of computation for solving specific problems, ranging from implementing sub-universal abstractions such as finite-state machines for solving problems such as string searching, up to writing interpreters and compilers for custom languages tailored to specific problem domains, such as Perl for string manipulation. All coding inevitably involves double-coding. "Good" code simultaneously specifies a mechanical process and *talks about* this mechanical process to a human reader. Finally, the puzzle-like nature of coding manifests not only because of the problem solving necessary to specify processes, but because code must additionally, and simultaneously, make appropriate use of language styles and idioms, and structure the space of computation. Weird languages thus tease apart phenomena present in all coding activity, phenomena that must be accounted for by any theory of code.

Notes

1. Parts of this article are based on a paper ("A Box Darkly: Obfuscation, Weird Languages and Code Aesthetics") that Nick Montfort and I presented at *Digital Arts and Culture 2005*.

2. "Esoteric" is a more common term for these languages, but it is a term that could apply to programming languages overall (most people do not know how to program in any language) or to languages such as ML and Prolog, which are common in academia but infrequently used in industry. A better designation might be *art languages*. However, while such languages are undoubtedly a category of software art, developers of these languages do not use this term themselves, and it seems unfair to apply the term "art," with all of its connotations, to their work. The term "weird" better captures the intention behind these languages, and is used at times by the language designers themselves.

3. Donald Woods and James Lyon, *The INTERCAL Programming Language Revised Reference Manual*. 1st ed. (1973). C-INTERCAL revisions, L. Howell and E. Raymond, (1996).

4. Alan M. Turing, "On Computable Numbers, with an Application to the Entscheidungsproblem. A Correction," from *Proceedings of the London Mathematical Society*, Ser. 2, Vol. 43, 1937.

5. Alan Perlis, "Epigrams on Programming."

6. Ben Olmstead, *Malbolge*, available at http://www.antwon.com/other/malbolge/malbolge.txt 1998/.

7. Lou Scheffer, *Introduction to Malbolge*, available at http://www.lscheffer.com/malbolge.html/.

Bibliography

0100101110101101.org. Life_Sharing, 2000–2003. Available http://www
.0100101110101101.org/home/life_sharing/ (accessed March 20, 2006).

Abbate, Janet. *Inventing the Internet.* Cambridge, MA: The MIT Press, 2000.

Abendsen, Hawthorne, *The Grasshopper Lies Heavy.*(n.d.).

Abigail. "JAPHs and Other Obscure Signatures," presentation slides, 2000–2001.
Available at http://www.foad.org/%7Eabigail/Perl/Talks/Japhs/.

Abelson, Harold, and Gerald Jay Sussman with Julie Sussman. *Structure and Interpretation of Computer Programs*, 2nd ed. Cambridge, MA; The MIT Press, 1996.

Abram, David. *The Spell of the Sensuous.* New York: Vintage Books, 1996.

Agre, Philip. *Computation and Human Experience.* Cambridge: Cambridge University
Press, 1997.

Aho, Alfred V., Jeffrey D. Ullman, and John E. Hopcroft. *Data Structures and Algorithms.* Boston, MA: Addison-Wesley, 1983.

Alexander, Christopher, et al. *A Pattern Language: Towns, Buildings, Construction.* New
York: Oxford University Press, 1977.

Anderson, David P. BOINC: A System for Public-Resource Computing and Storage," 5th IEEE/ACM International Workshop on Grid Computing, Pittsburgh, PA (November 8, 2004). See also http://boinc.berkeley.edu/.

Apple Computer, Apple Human Interface Guidelines, Apple Computer Inc., Cupertino, CA (2006). Retrieved March 20, 2006 from http://developer.apple.com/documentation/UserExperience/Conceptual/OSXHIGuidelines/.

Aristotle. *On Memory and Reminiscence.* Translated by J. I. Beare. eBooks@Adelaide, The University of Adelaide Library, Adelaide, 2004. Available at http://etext.library.adelaide.edu.au/a/aristotle/memory/memory.zip/.

Artificial Paradises. Available at http://www.1010.co.uk/ap0202.html/.

Ashby, W. Ross. *Introduction to Cybernetics*, 2nd ed. London: Chapman and Hall, 1957.

Ascher, Marcia and Robert Ascher. *Code of the Quipu: A Study in Media, Mathematics, and Culture.* Ann Arbor: University of Michigan Press, 1980.

Atkinson, Richard, and Richard Shiffrin. "Human Memory: A Proposed System and Its Control Processes." In K. W. Spence and J. T. Spence, eds., *The Psychology of Learning and Motivation: Advances in Research and Theory, Volume 2*. New York: Academic Press, 1968.

Auden, W. H. *The Dyers Hand*. London: Faber, 1955.

Austin, John. *How to Do Things with Words*, edited by J. O. Urmson. Oxford: Clarendon Press, 1962.

Axelrod, Robert. *Structure of Decision*. Princeton: Princeton University Press, 1976.

Ayers, Douglas D., and Mubarak Shah, "Monitoring Human Behavior from Video Taken in an Office Environment," *Image and Vision Computing*, vol. 19, issue 12, 1 (2001), 833–846.

Babbage, Charles. *The Ninth Bridgewater Treatise*, 2nd ed. London: John Murray, 1838.

Francis Bacon, *The Advancement of Learning, Second Book*. Available at Renascence Editions, an online repository of works printed in English between the years 1477 and 1799, University of Oregon, http://darkwing.uoregon.edu/~rbear/adv2.htm/.

Balibar, Etienne, "Ambiguous Universality," *Differences: A Journal of Feminist Cultural Studies* 7(1)(1995), 48–74.

Barnsley, Michael. *Fractals Everywhere: The First Course in Deterministic Fractal Geometry.* New York: Academic Press, 1988.

"Barszcz." Available at http://www.barszcz.net/.

Basel Action Network. Available at http://www.ban.org/.

Bataille, Georges, Isabelle Woldberg, and Lain White. *Encyclopaedia Acephalica.* London: Atlas Press, 1995.

Bateson, Gregory. *Steps to an Ecology of Mind.* New York: Ballantine Books, 1972.

Beer, Stafford. *Brain of the Firm*, 2nd ed. Chichester, UK: John Wiley & Sons, 1981.

Béguin, P., and P. Rabardel. "Designing for Instrument Mediated Activity," *Scandinavian Journal of Information Systems* 12, 2000, 173–193. Available at http://www.daimi.au.dk/~olavb/sjis12/7-PB_p173-190.PDF (accessed April 23, 2006).

Bellantoni, Jeff, and Matt Woolman. *Type in Motion: Innovations in Digital Graphics.* London: Thames and Hudson, 2000.

Benjamin, Walter. *Illuminations. Essays and Reflections.* Edited and with an Introduction by Hannah Arendt. New York: Shocken, 1969.

Bergson, Henri. *Creative Evolution.* Translated by Arthur Mitchell. London: MacMillan, 1911.

Bergson, Henri. *Time and Free Will: An Essay on the Immediate Data of Consciousness.* Translated by F. L. Pogson. New York: Harper & Brothers, 1960.

Berman, Marshall. *All That Is Solid Melts Into Air: The Experience of Modernity.* London: Verso, 1999.

Bertelsen, Olav W., and Søren Pold. "Criticism as an Approach to Interface Aesthetics." In *Proceedings of the third Nordic conference on Human-Computer Interaction*, Tampere, Finland, ACM Press, 2004.

Bertin, Jacques. *Graphics and Graphic Information Processing*. Berlin and New York: Walter de Gruyter, 1981.

Bijker, Wiebe E., Thomas P. Hughes, and Trevor Pinch, eds. *The Social Construction of Technological Systems: New Directions in the Sociology and History of Technology*. Cambridge, MA: The MIT Press, 1987.

Bilotta, Eleonora, Pietro Pantano, and Valerio Talarico. "Synthetic Harmonies: An Approach to Musical Semiosis by Means of Cellular Automata." In Bedau, Mark A. et al. eds., *Artificial Life VII Proceedings of the Seventh International Conference on Artificial Life*. Cambridge, MA: The MIT Press, 2000.

Black, Maurice J. *The Art of Code*. Ph.D. Dissertation, University of Pennsylvania, 2002.

Blackmore, Susan. *The Meme Machine*. Oxford: Oxford University Press, 2000.

Blum, B. I. "Free-Text Inputs to Utility Routines," *Communications of the ACM*, vol. 9, issue 7 (July 1966).

Bolter, J. David, and Richard Grusin. *Remediation: Understanding New Media*. Cambridge, MA: The MIT Press, 1999.

Bolter, J. David. *Turing's Man*. Chapel Hill, NC: University of North California Press, 1984.

Bolton, William, *Microprocessor Systems*. Harlow, UK: Longman Pearson Education, 2000.

Booch, Grady. *Object-Oriented Analysis and Design, with Applications*. 2nd ed. Redwood City, CA: Benjamin/Cummings, 1994.

Bovet, Daniel P., and Marco Cesati. *Understanding the Linux Kernel*. Sebastopol, CA: O'Reilly, 2001.

Bowker, Geoffrey C., and Star, Susan L. *Sorting Things Out: Classification and Its Consequences*. Cambridge, MA: The MIT Press, 1999.

Brand, Stuart. *The Media Lab*. London: Penguin, 1987.

Brassier, Ray. "Liquider l'homme une fois pour toutes." In Gilles Grélet, ed., *Théorie—rébellion*. Paris: L'harmattan, 2005.

Brodie, Leo. *Thinking Forth*. Englewood Cliffs, NJ: Prentice-Hall, 1984.

Brooks, Rodney. "Intelligence Without Representation," *Artificial Intelligence Journal* (47) (1991), 139–159. Available at http://people.csail.mit.edu/brooks/papers/representation.pdf/.

Brookshear, J. Glenn. *Computer Science*. Redwood City, CA: Benjamin/Cummings, 1994.

Brown, Julian. *Minds, Machines, and the Multiverse*. New York: Simon & Schuster, 2000.

Bruhn, Henning. "Periodical States and Marching Groups in a Closed Owari." 2005, preprint, available at http://www.rpi.edu/~eglash/isgem.dir/texts.dir/clowari.pdf/.

Burroughs, William S. "The Discipline of DE" In *Exterminator!* London: Corgi Books, 1976.

Burroughs, William S. *The Electronic Revolution*. Bonn: Expanded Media Edition, 1991.

Camara, Gilberto. "Open Source Software Production: Fact and Fiction." In MUTE, vol. 1, issue 27 (Winter/Spring 2004), 74–79.

Campbell-Kelly, Martin. *From Airline Reservations to Sonic the Hedgehog: A History of the Software Industry*. Cambridge, MA: The MIT Press, 2004.

Campbell, Lewis, and William Garnet. *Life of James Clerk Maxwell*. London: Macmillan, 1882.

Canonical Ltd., The Ubuntu Manifesto, available at: http://www.ubuntu.com.

Card, Stuart, Jock Mackinlay, and Ben Schneiderman, eds. *Readings in Information Visualization: Using Vision to Think*. San Francisco: Morgan Kaufmann, 1999.

Ceruzzi, Paul E. *A History of Modern Computing*. Cambridge, MA: The MIT Press, 1998.

Chaitin, Gregory, "Elegant LISP Programs." In Cristian Calude, ed., *People and Ideas in Theoretical Computer Science*. Singapore: Springer Verlag, 1998.

Chaitin, Gregory. "Epistemology as Information Theory: From Leibniz to Omega." *Alan Turing Lecture on Computation and Philosophy, E-CAP'05, European Computing and Philosophy Conference*, Malarden University, Vasterås, Sweden, June 2005.

Chaitin, Gregory, *Meta Maths. The Quest for Omega.* London: Atlantic Books, 2006.

Chen, Chaomei. *Information Visualisation*, 2nd ed. Heidelberg: Springer, 2004.

Chiu, Eugene, Jocelyn Lin, Brok McFerron, Noshirwan Petigara, and Satwiksai Seshasai. "The Mathematical Theory of Claude Shannon: A Study of the Style and Context of His Work up to the Genesis of Information Theory," submitted for The Structure of Engineering Revolutions (MIT course 6.933J/STS.420J), n.d.

Chun, Wendy Hui Kyung. "On Software, or the Persistence of Visual Knowledge," *Grey Room 18* (Winter 2005), 26-51.

Chun, Wendy Hui Kyung. *Control and Freedom.* Cambridge, MA: The MIT Press, 2006.

Chun, Wendy Hui Kyung, and Thomas Keenan, eds. *New Media, Old Media.* New York: Routledge, 2005.

Clark, Andy. *Being There: Putting Brain, Body, and World Together Again.* Cambridge, MA: The MIT Press, 1997.

Clown Staples. Available at http://www.geocities.com/clownstaples/.

Codase available at http://www.codase.com/.

Codefetch, available at http://www.codefetch.com/.

Code Snippets available at http://bigbold.com/snippets/.

Coleman, Biella. "The Politics of Survival and Prestige: Hacker Identity and the Global Production of an Operating System." Masters Thesis, University of Chicago, 1999. Available at http://healthhacker.org/biella/masterslongversion.html.

Colemann, Biella. "High-Tech Guilds in the Era of Global Capital." Available at http://www.healthhacker.org/biella/aaapaper.html, undated.

Computer-Human Interaction in Southern Africa. CHI-SA, 2006. Cape Town, South Africa, ACM Press, 2006, 69–74.

Conley, Craig. *Magic Words: A Dictonary.* Available at http://www.blueray.com/magic/magicwords/index.php?p=177/.

Constant. *Cuisine Interne Keuken,* 2004. Available at http://www.constantvzw.com/cn_core/cuisine/.

Cood, E. F. *Cellular Automata.* London: Academic Press, 1968.

Coplien, James O. "To Iterate is Human, to Recurse, Divine" *C++ Report* 10(7), July August (1998), 43–51.

Cotton, C. M. *Ethnobotany: Principles and Applications.* New York: John Wiley & Sons, 1996.

Cox, Geoff, Alex McLean, and Adrian Ward. "The Aesthetics of Generative Code," *Generative Art 00* conference, Politecnico di Milano, Italy, 2001. Available at http://www.generative.net/papers/aesthetics/index.html/.

Cox, Geoff. "Software Actions." In Joasia Krysa, ed., *Curating Immateriality: DATA Browser 03.* New York: Autonomedia, 2006.

Coy, Wolfgang. *Aufbau und Arbeitsweise von Rechenanlagen: Eine Einführung in Rechner-architektur und Rechnerorganisation für das Grundstudium der Informatik,* 2nd revised and expanded edition. Wiesbaden: Braunschweig, 1992.

Coyne, Richard. "Heidegger and Virtual Reality: The Implications of Heidegger's Thinking for Computer Representations." In *Leonardo: Journal of the International Society for the Arts, Sciences, and Technology* vol. 27 no. 1, (1994), 65–73.

Cramer, Florian. "and.pl." Available at http://cramer.plaintext.cc:70/poems/and/.

Cramer, Florian. "Commentary on London.pl." *Runme* software art repository, available at http://www.runme.org/feature/read/+londonpl/+34/.

Cramer, Florian. "Concepts, Notations, Software, Art" (2002). Available at http://userpage.fu-berlin.de/~cantsin/homepage/writings/software_art/concept_notations/concepts_notations_software_art.html.

Bibliography

Cramer, Florian. "Ten Theses About Software Art" (2003). Available at http://cramer .plaintext.cc:70/all/10_thesen_zur_softwarekunst/.

Crawford, Chris. *The Art of Computer Game Design.* Berkeley: McGraw-Hill/Osborne, 1984.

Crowston, Kevin, and James Howison. "The Social Structure of Open Source Software Development Teams" (2003). Available at http://crowston.syr.edu/papers/icis2003sna .pdf/.

Crutzen, Cecile. "Giving Room to Femininity in Informatics Education." In A. F. Grundy, D. Köhler, V. Oechtering, and U. Petersen, eds., *Women, Work and Computerization: Spinning a Web from Past to Future.* Berlin: Springer-Verlag, 1997, 177–187.

Crutzen, Cecile. and Jack F. Gerrissen. "Doubting the OBJECT World." In Ellen Balka and Richard Smith, eds., *Women, Work and Computerization: Charting a Course to the Future.* Boston: Kluwer Academic Press, 2000, 127–136.

Crutzen, Cecile. *Interactie, een wereld van verschillen. Een visie op informatica vanuit genderstudies* (2000). Thesis, Open Universiteit Nederland, Heerlen.

Dahl, Ole-Johan. *The Birth of Object Orientation: The Simula Languages*, 2001. Available at http://heim.ifi.uio.no/~olejohan/birth-of-oo.pdf (accessed April 24, 2006).

Darwin, Charles. *The Origin of Species.* London: Murray, 1859.

Davis, Alan M. *Software Requirements: Objects, Functions and States.* Englewood Cliffs, NJ: Prentice Hall, 1993.

Dawkins, Richard. *The Blind Watchmaker.* London: Penguin, 1986.

De Landa, Manuel. *War in the Age of Intelligent Machines.* New York: Swerve Editions, 1991.

Deleuze, Gilles. *Foucault.* Paris: Minnit, 1986.

Deleuze, Gilles, and Félix Guattari. *A Thousand Plateaus*, 2nd ed. Translated by Brian Massumi. London: Continuum, 2004.

Deleuze, Gilles, and Félix Guattari. *Anti-Oedipus*, 2nd ed. Translated by Robert Hurley, Mark Seem, and Helen R. Lane. London: Continuum, 2004.

Deleuze, Gilles. *The Fold*. Translated by Tom Conley. London: Continuum, 2006.

Dennett, Daniel. *Consciousness Explained*. London: Penguin, 2004.

Derrida, Jacques. *Of Grammatology*. Baltimore and London: Johns Hopkins University Press, 1976.

Derrida, Jacques. "Freud and the Scene of Writing." In *Writing and Difference*. Translated by Alan Bass., Chicago: University of Chicago Press, 1978.

Derrida, Jacques. *Dissemination*. Translated by Barbara Johnson. Chicago: University of Chicago Press, 1981.

Dever, Jaime, Niels da Vitoria Lobo, and Mubarak Shah. "Automatic Visual Recognition of Armed Robbery," *IEEE International Conference on Pattern Recognition, Canada*, (2002), 451–455.

Dibbell, Julian. "Viruses Are Good For You." In Wendy Hui Kyong Chun and Thomas Keenan, eds., *New Media, Old Media*. London: Routledge, 2005, 219–232.

Dick, Philip K. *The Man in the High Castle*. New York: Putnam, 1962.

Digitalcraft, 'Obfuscated Code,' available at http://www.digitalcraft.org/iloveyou/c-code.html.

Dijkstra, Edsger, W. "Go To Statement Considered Harmful," *Communications of the ACM*, vol. 11, no. 3 (1968), 147–148.

Dijkstra, Edsger W. "My recollections of operating system design" (2000–2001). Handwritten memoir, pp. 13–14, available as an electronic document, EWD1303, from the Dijkstra archives: http://www.cs.utexas.edu/users/EWD/transcriptions/EWD13xx/EWD1303.html and http://www.cs.utexas.edu/users/EWD/ewd13xx/EWD1303.PDF/.

Dominus, Mark-Jason. "Explanation of japh.pl" (October 31, 2000). Available at http://perl.plover.com/obfuscated/solution.html/.

Eberbach, Eugene, Dina Goldin, and Peter Wegner. "Turing's Ideas and Models of Computation." In Christof Teuscher, ed., *Alan Turing: Life and Legacy of a Great Thinker*. Berlin: Springer, 2004.

Eco, Umberto. "La bustina di Minerva," *Espresso* (September 30, 1994). Translation available at http://www.themodernword.com/eco_mac_vs_pc.html/ (accessed March 27, 2006).

Eco, Umberto. *Semiotics and the Philosophy of Language*. Bloomington: Indiana University Press, 1983.

Edwards, Paul. *The Closed World: Computers and the Politics of Discourse in Cold War America*. Cambridge, MA: The MIT Press, 1996.

Edwards, Paul. "The Army and the Microworld: Computers and the Politics of Gender Identity," *Signs* 18:1 (1990).

Eglash, Ron. "Culturally Situated Design Tools." Available at: http://www.rpi.edu/~eglash/csdt.html/.

Eglash, Ron. "Geometric Algorithms in Mangbetu Design." In *Mathematics Teacher*, v. 91 n. 5 (May 1998), 376–381.

Eglash, Ron. *African Fractals: Modern Computing and Indigenous Design*. New Brunswick, NJ: Rutgers University Press, 1999.

Eglash, Ron, and J. Bleecker. "The Race for Cyberspace: Information Technology in the Black Diaspora," *Science as Culture*, vol. 10, no. 3 (2001).

Eglash, Ron, Jennifer L. Croissant, Giovanna Di Chiro, and Rayvon Fouche, eds. *Appropriating Technology: Vernacular Science and Social Power*. Minneapolis: University of Minnesota Press, 2004.

Emerson, Ralph Waldo. "The Poet." In *Essays: Second Series*, 1866.

Engelbart, Douglas. "Augmenting Human Intellect: A Conceptual Framework." *Summary Report for SRI Project No. 3578,* Stanford Research Institute, Stanford, CA (1962). Available at http://www.bootstrap.org/augdocs/friedewald030402/augmentinghuman intellect/3examples.html#A.3 (accessed on April 9, 2006).

Eshun, Kodwo. "An Unidentified Audio Event Arrives from the Post-Computer Age." In Jem Finer, ed., *Longplayer*. London: Artangel, 2001.

Eriksson, Inger V., Barbara A. Kitchenham, and Kea G. Tijdens. *Women, Work and Computerization: Understanding and Overcoming Bias in Work and Education*. Amsterdam: Elsevier Science Publishers, 1991.

"Facsimile & SSTV History." Available at http://www.hffax.de/html/hauptteil_fax history.htm.

Fensel, Dieter, James Hendler, Henry Lieberman, and Wolfgang Wahlster. *Spinning the Semantic Web*. Cambridge, MA: The MIT Press, 2003.

ffmpeg, *FFMPEG Multimedia System*. Available at http://ffmpeg.sourceforge.net/index.php/ (accessed Feb 4, 2006).

Fiell, Charlotte, and Peter Fiell, eds. *Graphic Design for the 21st Century: 100 of the World's Best Graphic Designers*. Cologne: Taschen, 2003.

Fisher, R. A. "Theory of Statistical Estimation," *Proceedings of the Cambridge Philosophical Society*, vol. XXII, no. 709 (1925).

Fleischmann, Kenneth R. "Exploring the Design-Use Interface: The Agency of Boundary Objects in Educational Technology," Doctoral dissertation, dept of STS, Rensselaer Polytechnic Institute, 2004.

Flusser, Vilém. "Curie's Children: Vilém Flusser on an Unspeakable Future," *Artforum* (March 1990).

Foucault, Michel. *The Order of Things*. London and New York: Routledge, 1980.

Foucault, Michel. *The Archaeology of Knowledge*. Translated by Alan Sheridan Smith. London: Routledge, 1989.

Freshmeat. Available at http://freshmeat.net/.

Fuller, Matthew. *Behind the Blip: Essays on the Culture of Software*. New York: Autonomedia, 2003.

Fuller, Matthew. *Media Ecologies: Materialist Energies in Art and Technoculture.* Cambridge, MA: The MIT Press, 2005.

Fuller, Matthew. "It Looks Like You're Writing a Letter," *Telepolis* (March 7, 2001). Available at http://www.heise.de/tp/r4/artikel/7/7073/1.html/ (last accessed March 29, 2006).

Fuller, Matthew. *Softness, Interrogability, General Intellect, Art Methodologies in Software.* Digital Research Unit, Huddersfield University, Huddersfield, 2006.

Gabor, Dennis. "Acoustical Quanta and the Theory of Hearing," *Nature* 159(4044) (1947), 591–594.

Gardner, Howard. *The Mind's New Science: A History of the Cognitive Revolution.* New York: Basic Books, 1985.

Gass, William. *The World Within the Word.* New York: Knopf, 1978.

Gaver, W. W. "What in the World Do We Hear?: An Ecological Approach to Auditory Event Perception," *Ecological Psychology*, 5(1) (1993), 1–29.

Gay Joshua. *Free Software, Free Society: Selected Essay of Richard M. Stallman.* Boston, MA: GNU Press, Free Software Foundation, 2002.

Geus, Aart J. de. "To the rescue of Moore's Law," keynote address, *20th Annual Custom Integrated Circuits Conference*, Santa Clara, CA, May 11-14, 2000.

Ghosh, Rishab Aiyer. "Clustering and Dependencies in Free/Open Source Software Development: Methodology and Tools," *First Monday*, 8(4) (April 2003).

Gilder, George. "The Information Factories," *Wired* vol. 16, no 10. pp. 178–202, Oct. 2006.

Ginzburg, Carlo. "Clues: Morelli, Freud, Sherlock Holmes." In Umberto Eco and Thomas Sebeok, eds., *The Sign of Three.* Bloomington: Indiana University Press, 1983.

Girard, Réné. *Mensonge et vérité romanesque.* Paris: Hachette, 1999.

Goldschlager, Les, and Andrew Lister. *Computer Science: A Modern Introduction*, 2nd ed. Hemel Hempstead: Prentice-Hall, 1988.

Goldstine, H. H., and A. Goldstine. "The Electronic Numerical Integrator and Computer (ENIAC)," *IEEE Annals of the History of Computing*, 18:1 (Spring 1996), 10–15.

Goodman, Nelson. *Languages of Art, an approach to a theory of Symbols,* Indianapolis: Hackett Publishing Company, 1976.

Goriunova, Olga and Alexei Shulgin eds. *Read Me 1.2 Festival*, catalogue, Moscow 2002. Also online at http://www.macros-center.ru/read_me/.

Goriunova, Olga and Alexei Shulgin eds. *Read Me 2.3 Reader, about software art*. Nordic Institute for Contemporary Art, Helsinki, 2003.

Goriunova, Olga and Alexei Shulgin eds. *Read_Me, Software Art and Cultures, edition 2004*. Århus: University of Århus Press, 2004.

Graham, Stephen, and Simon Marvin. *Telecommunications and the City: Electronic Spaces, Urban Places.* London: Routledge, 1996.

Brassier, Ray. "Liquider l'homme une fois pour toutes." In Gilles Grélet, ed., *Théorie—rébellion.* Paris: L'harmattan, 2005.

Grassmuck, Volker. "Das Ende der Universalmaschine." In Claus Pias, ed., *Zukünfte des Computers*. Zürich-Berlin: Diaphanes, 2005.

Greenpeace, *Green My Apple Campaign*. Available at http://www.greenmyapple.org/.

Grier, David. *When Computers Were Human*. Princeton, NJ: Princeton University Press, 2005.

Grier, David. "The ENIAC, the Verb 'to program' and the Emergence of Digital Computers," *IEEE Annals of the History of Computing* 18:1 (Spring 1996).

Grune, Dick. *Concurrent Versions System*. Amsterdam: Vrije Universiteit. Available at http://www.cs.vu.nl/~dick/CVS.html#History/.

Gumbrecht, Hans Ulrich and K. Ludwig Pfeiffer, eds., *Materialities of Communication*. Translated by William Whobrey, Stanford, CA: Stanford University Press, 1994.

Habermas, Jürgen. "Modernity—An Incomplete Project" (1980). In Hal Foster, ed., *Postmodern Culture*. London: Pluto Press, 1991.

Hacker, Sally L. *Doing it the Hard Way*.

Hackitectura. *MAPA: Cartografiando el territorio madiaq* (2004). Available at http://mcs. hackitectura.net/tiki-index.php?page=MAPA%3A+cartografiando+el+territorio+ma diaq (accessed March 14, 2006).

Hagen, Wolfgang. "The Style of Source Codes." In Wendy Hui Kyong Chun and Thomas Keenan, eds., *New Media, Old Media*. New York: Routledge, 2005.

Hall, Fred L. *McMaster Algorithm* (2000). Available at http://www.mcmaster.ca/ graduate/flhall/macalg.html (accessed March 14, 2006).

Hankins Thomas and Robert Silverman. *Instruments and the Imagination*. Princeton: Princeton University Press, 1995.

Hansen, H. R. and W. H. Janko, eds. *Dikussionspapiere zum Tatigkeitsfeld Informations verarbeitung unde Informationswirtschaft*.

Haraway, Donna. Lecture, UCSC, 1992.

Hardwick, M. Martin, David L. Spooner, Tom Rando, and K.C. Morris. "Sharing Manufacturing Information in Virtual Enterprises," *Communications of the ACM*, vol. 39, no. 2 (February 1996).

Hardy, Norman. *"History of Interrupts"* (2005). Available at http://www.cap-lore .com/Hardware/int.html/ (accessed March 14, 2006).

Harman, Graham. *Tool-Being*.

Hartley, V. L. "Transmission of Information," *Bell System Technical Journal*, vol. VII, no. 540 (July 1928).

Harwood, Graham. *Lungs: Slave Labour*. 2005. Permanent collection, ZKM, Karlsruhe, Germany. Available at http://www.mongrel.org.uk/lungs/.

Hashagen, Ull and Rául Rojas, eds., *The First Computers: History and Architecture*. Cambridge, MA: The MIT Press, 2000.

Havelock, Eric. "The Preliteracy of the Greeks," *New Literary History*, vol. 8, no. 3 (1977), 369–91.

Haykin, Simon. *Neural Networks. A Comprehensive Foundation.* Hemel Hempstead: Prentice-Hall, 1998.

Hayles, N. Katherine. *My Mother Was a Computer.* Chicago: The University of Chicago Press, 2006.

Hayles, N. Katherine. *Writing Machines.* Cambridge, MA: The MIT Press, 2002.

Hazlitt, William. *The Spirit of the Age* (1825). Project Gutenburg, available at http://www.gutenberg.org/etext/11068/.

Heath, Christian, and Paul Luff. *Technology in Action.* Cambridge: Cambridge University Press, 2000.

Heidegger, Martin. *Die Technik and die Kehre.* Stuttgart: Günther Neske, 1962.

Heilbron, J. H. *Electricity in the 17th and 18th Centuries.* Berkeley: University of California Press, 1979.

Heims, Steve. *The Cybernetics Group.* New York: Basic Books, 1980.

Herken, Rolf, ed. *The Universal Turing Machine: A Half-Century Survey.* Oxford: Oxford University Press, 1988.

Hertzfeld, Andy. *Revolution in The Valley.* Sebastapol, CA: O'Reilly, 2004.

Hillis, W. Daniel. *The Pattern on the Stone.* London: Phoenix, 2001.

Hiltzik, Michael. Dealers of Lightning, *Xerox PARC and the Dawn of the Computer Age.* New York: HarperBusiness, 1999.

Hodges, Andrew, and Alan Turing. *The Enigma of Intelligence.* London: Unwin, 1985.

Hopkins, Sharon. "Camels and Needles: Computer Poetry Meets the Perl Programming Language." In *The Perl Review*, Vol. 0, Issue 1 (1991). Available at http://www.theperlreview.com/Issues/The_Perl_Review_0_1.pdf/.

Hull, Richard. "Governing the Conduct of Computing: Computer Science, the Social Sciences and Frameworks of Computing." *Accounting, Management & Information Technology*, 7 (4) (1997), 213–240.

Hutchins, Ed. *Cognition in the Wild*. Cambridge, MA: The MIT Press, 1995.

Huws, Ursula. *The Making of a Cybertariat: Virtual Work in a Real World*. London: Merlin, 2003.

Hyde, Randall. "Interrupts and Polled I/O." In *The Art of Assembly Language Programming*. San Francisco: No Starch Press, 2003. Available at http://courses.ece.uiuc .edu/ece390/books/artofasm/CH03/CH03-6.html#HEADING6-15 (accessed March 14, 2006).

Innis, Harold A. *Empire and Communications*, 2nd ed. Toronto: University of Toronto Press, 1972.

Introna, Lucas D., and David Wood. "Picturing Algorithmic Surveillance: The Politics of Facial Recognition Systems." In, Norris, McCahill, and Wood, eds., *Surveillance and Society, CCTV Special*, 2 (2/3), 177–198. Available at http://www.surveilllance-and-society .org/cctv.htm/.

ISO/IEC 11172-1:1993.

ISO/IEC 13818-1, I. I. Information technology—Generic coding of moving pictures and associated audio information: Systems (1995).

ISO/IEC 13818-2 Information technology—Generic coding of moving pictures and associated audio information: Video, 1995.

Iverson, K. E. *A Programming Language*. New York: John Wiley & Sons, 1962.

Jacobson, Ivar, Magnus Christerson, Patrik Jonsson, and Gunnar Övergaard. *Object-Oriented Software Engineering: A Use Case Driven Approach*. Reading, MA: Addison Wesley, 1992.

JAPHs. Available at http://www.cpan.org/misc/japh/.

The Jargon File. Available at http://www.dourish.com/goodies/jargon.html/.

JODI, http://wwwwwwwww.jodi.org/.

JODI, untitled game, http://text.jodi.org/.

Johnson, Jeff, and Teresa L. Roberts, "The Xerox Star: A Retrospective," *IEEE Computer* (September 1989), 11–29.

Johnson, Steven. *Interface Culture: How New Technology Transforms the Way We Create and Communicate*. San Francisco: HarperEdge, 1997.

Kahn, David. *The Codebreakers: The Story of Secret Writing*, 9th ed. New York: Simon and Schuster, 1979.

Kamppuri, Minna, Matti Tedre, and Markku Tukiainen. "Towards the Sixth Level in Interface Design: Understanding Culture." In Darelle van Greunen, ed., *Proceedings of the CHI-SA 2006, 5th Conference on Human Computer Computer-Human Interaction in Southern Africa*. CHI-SA, 2006 Cape Town, South Africa, ACM Press, 2006, 69–74.

Kare, Susan. "Design Biography." Available at http://www.kare.com/design_bio.html/.

Kay, Alan C. "The Early History of SmallTalk,". *ACM SIGPLAN notices*, vol. 8, no. 3 (1993). Available at http://gagne.homedns.org/~tgagne/contrib/EarlyHistoryST.html/.

Kay, Alan. "User Interface: A Personal View." In Brenda Laurel, ed., *The Art of Human-Computer Interface Design*. Reading, MA: Addison-Wesley, 1990.

Keller, Evelyn Fox. *Reflections on Gender and Science*. New Haven, CT: Yale University Press, 1985.

Kennedy, Bill. "Two Old Viruses," *The Risks Digest,* vol. 6, issue 53, March 1988.

Kenner, Hugh. "Beckett Thinking." In Hugh Kenner, *The Mechanic Muse*. Oxford: Oxford University Press, 1987, 83–107.

Kidd, Eric. "More Debugging Tips." Addenda to a webpage by Bram Cohen, "Aesthetics of Debugging," posted December 17, 2000. Available at http://advogato.org/article/215.html/.

Kirschenbaum, Matthew G.C., "Virtuality and HTML: Software Studies after Manovich," *Electronic Book Review*. 8/29/2003.

Kittler, Friedrich. *Literature, Media, Information Systems*. Amsterdam: G&B Arts International, 1997.

Kittler, Friedrich. "Universities: Wet, Hard, Soft, and Harder," *Critical Inquiry*, Vol. 31, issue 1 (Autumn 2004), 244–255.

Knuth, Donald. *Literate Programming*. Stanford, CA: Center for the Study of Language and Information, Stanford University Press, 1992.

Knuth, Donald E. "Computer Programming as an Art." In *Literate Programming*. Stanford, CA: Center for the Study of Language and Information, 1992, 1–16.

Knuth, Donald. *The Art of Computer Programming*, vols. 1-3, 3rd ed. Reading, MA: Addison Wesley, 1997.

Knuth, Donald. "Structured Programming with GO TO Statements" (1974). Available at http://pplab.snu.ac.kr/courses/adv_p104/papers/p261-knuth.pdf/

Koch, Stefan, and Georg Schneider. "Results from Software Engineering Research into Open Source Development Projects Using Public Data." In H. R. Hansen and W. H. Janko, eds. *Dikussionspapiere zum Tatigkeitsfeld Informationsverarbeitung unde Informationswirtschaft*, Nr. 22. Vienna: Wirtschaftsuniversitat, 2000.

Koders. Available at http://www.koders.com/.

Koenig, Sven. *aPpRoPiRaTe!* Available at http://popmodernism.org/appropirate/.

Kolinko, *Hotlines: Call-Centre, Inquiry, Communism*. Oberhausen: Kolinko, 2002. Also available at http://www.prol-position.net/.

Koopman, Phil. *Stack Computers: The New Wave*. Chichester, UK: Ellis Horwood, 1989.

Kowalski, Robert. "Algorithm = logic + control." *Communications of the ACM*, 22(7) (1979): 424–435.

Krishnamurti, Shriram. *Programming languages: Application and Interpretation* (2006). Available at http://www.cs.brown.edu/~sk/Publications/Books/ProgLangs/.

Krysa, Joasin, ed., *Curating Immateriality: Data Browser 03*, New York: Autonomedia, 2006.

Krugle. Available at http://www.Krugle.com/.

Lacan, Jacques. *Écrits. A Selection.* Translated by Alan Sheridan. London: Routledge, 2001.

Lakoff, George, and Johnson, Mark. *Metaphors We Live By.* Chicago: University of Chicago Press, 1981.

Lampson, Butler W. "Hints for Computer System Design," *Proceedings of the Ninth ACM Symposium on Operating Systems Principles.* New York: ACM Press, 1983.

Lange, Thomas. "Helmut Hoelzer, Inventor of the Electronic Analog Computer." In Ull Hashagen and Rául Rojas, eds., *The First Computers: History and Architecture.* Cambridge, MA: The MIT Press, 2000.

Latour, Bruno. *Science in Action: How to Follow Scienists and Engineers Through Society.* Milton Keynes: Open University Press, 1987.

Latour, Bruno, E. Hermant, et al. *Paris Ville Invisible.* Paris Le Plessis-Robinson, La Dâecouverte; Institut Synthâelabo pour le progrâes de la connaissance, 1998. Available at http://www.ensmp.fr/~latour/virtual/#.

Latour, Bruno. *Reassembling the Social: An Introduction to Actor-Network Theory.* Oxford: Oxford University Press, 2005.

Latour, Bruno. "Drawing Things Together." In Michael Lynch and Steve Woolgar, eds., *Representation in Scientific Practice.* Cambridge, MA: The MIT Press, 1990.

Laurel, Brenda. *Computers as Theatre.* Reading, MA: Addison-Wesley, 1997.

Lautréamont. *Les chants de Maldoror*, Russian edition: Lotreamont, *Pesni Maldorora*, Moscow, Ad Marginem, 1998. English edition: Comte de Lautremont, *Maldoror*, translated by Alexis Lykiard. Boston: Exact Change Press, 1993.

Law, John, and Annemarie Mol, eds. *Complexities: Social Studies of Knowledge Practices.* Durham, NC: Duke University Press, 2002.

Leandre, Joan. *(Retroyou), R/C and NostalG.* Available at http://www.retroyou.org/ and http://runme.org/project/+SOFTSFRAGILE/.

Leary, Timothy. *You Can be Anyone This Time Around.* Rykodisc, 1992. (CD re-issue of the original vinyl release from 1970.)

Leibniz, Gottfried Wilhelm. *Epistolae ad diversos,* vol. 2. Translated by Chr. Kortholt. Leipzig, 1734.

Levy, Steven. *Insanely Great: The Life and Times of Macintosh.* London: Penguin, 1994.

Leyton, Michael. *Symmetry, Causality, Mind.* Cambridge, MA: The MIT Press, 1992.

Licklider, J. C. R., "Man-Computer Symbiosis," *IRE Transactions on Human Factors in Electronics, volume HFE-1,* (1960) 4–11. Available at http://memex.org/licklider.pdf/.

Licklider, J. C. R. "The Computer as a Communications Device," *Science and Technology* (April 1968). Available at http://memex.org/licklider.pdf/.

Lineback, Nathan. "GUI Gallery." Available at http://toastytech.com/guis/index.html/ (accessed March 7, 2006).

Ludovico, Alessandro. "Virus Charms and Self-Creating Codes." In Franziska Nori, ed., *I love you: computerviren, hacker, kultur*, exhibition catalogue. Frankfurt: Museum für Angewandte Kunst, 2002.

Lyon, Richard F. "A Brief History of 'Pixel.'" Reprint, paper E1 6069-1, *Digital Photography II, IS&T/SPIE Symposium on Electronic Imaging*, San Jose, CA (January 2006).

Mackay, Robin. "Capitalism and Schizophrenia: Wildstyle in Effect." In Keith Ansell Pearson, ed., *Deleuze and Philosophy: the Difference Engineer*, London: Routledge, 1997.

Mackay, Robin. "Capitalism and Schizophrenia: Wildstyle in full effect." In Keith Ansell Pearson, ed. *Deleuze and Philosophy: The Difference Engineer.* New York: Routledge, 1997, 247–269.

MacKenzie, Donald, and Judy Wajcman, eds. *The Social Shaping of Technology*, 2nd ed. Milton Keynes: Open University Press, 1999.

Madey, Gregory, Vincent Freeh, and Renee Tynan. "Modeling the Free/Open Source Software Community: A Quantitative Investigation." In Stefan Koch, ed., *Free/Open Source Software Development,* 203–220. Hershey, PA: Idea Group Publishing, 2003.

Manovich, Lev. *The Language of New Media.* Cambridge MA: MIT Press, 2001.

Massumi, Brian. "The Superiority of the Analog." In *Parables for the Virtual*. Durham: Duke University Press, 2002.

Mateas, Michael, "Procedural Literacy: Educating the New Media Practitioner." In *On The Horizon, Special Issue: Future of Games, Simulations and Interactive Media in Learning Contexts*, vol. 13, n. 1 (2005). Also available at http://www.lcc.gatech.edu/~mateas/publications/MateasOTH2005.pdf/.

Mateas, Michael, and Nick Montfort, "A Box Darkly: Obfuscation, Weird Languages and Code Aesthetics." In *Proceedings of the 6th Digital Arts and Culture Conference*, IT University of Copenhagen (Dec 1–3, 2005), 144–153. Available at http://nickm.com/cis/a_box_darkly.pdf/.

Mathews, Harry and Alistair Brotchie, *Oulipo Compendium,* London: Atlas Press, 1998.

Mauss, Marcel. "Technqiues of the Body." In *Zone 6: Incorporations*. New York: Zone Books, 1992.

McCarthy, John, *LISP Prehistory—Summer 1956 through Summer 1958* (1996). Available at http://www-formal.stanford.edu/jmc/history/lisp/node2.html/.

McCarthy, John. *LISP 1.5 Programmer's Manual*. Cambridge, MA: The MIT Press, 1962.

McCormick, Bill H., Tom A. DeFanti, and Maxine Brown. "Visualisation in Scientific Computing," *Computer Graphics*, 21 (November 1987).

McCulloch, Warren S., and Walter H. Pitts. "A Logical Calculus of the Ideas Immanent in Nervous Activity." In Deirdre Boden, ed., *The Philosophy of Artificial Intelligence*. Oxford: Oxford University Press, 1990.

McGaughey, William. "On the Cutting Edge of Knowledge: A Short History of the Most Advanced Techniques of Establishing Truth in Each Age" (2005). Available at http://worldhistorysite.com/cuttingedge.html.

Mead, Carver. *Analog VLSI and Neural Systems*. Milton Keynes, UK: Addison-Wesley, 1989.

Mead, Carver. *Collective Electrodynamics*. Cambridge, MA: The MIT Press, 2000.

Meadows, Donella, Dennis L. Meadows, and Jørgen Randens. *The Limits to Growth*. New York: Signet Books, 1972.

Meadows, Donella, Dennis L. Meadows, and Jørgens Randers, *The Limits to Growth*.

Meillassoux, Quentin. *Aprés la finitude.*

Meltzer, Kevin. "The Perl Poetry Contest." In *The Perl Journal*, vol. 4, issue 4, (2000). Available at http://www.tpj.com/.

Message Understanding Conference Proceedings (MUC-7). Available at http://www-nlpir.nist .gov/related_projects/muc/proceedings/muc_7_toc.html/ (accessed April 9, 2006).

Meyerhold, Vsevolod. "Artist of the Future." In *Hermitage*, no. 6 (1922).

Meiksins Wood, Ellen. *The Origins of Capitalism: A Longer View*, London: Verso, 2002.

Miranda, Eduardo R. *Composing Music with Computers*. Woburn, MA: Focal Press, 2001.

Mirowski, Philip. *Machine Dreams: Economics Becomes a Cyborg Science*. Cambridge: Cambridge University Press, 2002.

Mitchell, W. J. T. *The Language of Images*. Chicago: Chicago University Press, 1974.

Moore, David. "Rheolism: One Line Tetromino Game." Available at http://www.survex .com/~olly/dsm_rheolism/ (accessed July 1, 2001).

Mumford, Lewis. *Technics and Civilization*. New York: Harbinger, 1963.

Myers, Christopher R. "Software Systems as Complex Networks: Structure, Function, and Evolvability of Software Collaboration Graphs," *Physical Review* E 68, 046116, 2003.

Nabokov, Vladimir. *Speak Memory*. New York: Putnam, 1966.

Nake, Frieder. *Der Computer als Automat, Werkzeug und Medium und unser Verhältnis zu ihm*. Bremen: Universität Bremen, 2000.

Nietzsche, Friedrich. *The Gay Science*. Translated by Walter Kaufmann. New York: Vintage, 1974.

Nold, Christian. "Greenwich Emotion Map," 2006. Available at http://www.emotion map.net.

Noll, Landon Curt, Simon Cooper, Peter Seebach, and Leonid A. Broukhis. "The International Obfuscated C Code Contest" (2005). Available at http://www.ioccc.org/main .html/.

Ludovico, Alessandro. "Virus Charms and Self-Creating Codes." In Franziska Nori, ed., *I love you: computerviren, hacker, kultur*, exhibition catalogue. Frankfurt: Museum für Angewandte Kunst, 2002.

Nyquist, Harry. "Certain Factors Affecting Telegraph Speed," *Bell System Technical Journal*, 3 (April 1924), 324–346.

Nyman, Michael. *Experimental Music: Cage & Beyond.* Cambridge: Cambridge University Press, 1999.

Odum, E. P., and H. T. Odum. *Fundamentals of Ecology*. Philadelphia: W. B. Saunders Co., 1953.

Odum, Howard. *Systems Ecology.* Wiley, 1983.

Okanoya, Kazuo. "Finite-State Syntax in Bengalese Finch Song: From Birdsong to the Origin of Language." Third Conference on Evolution of Language, April 3–4, Paris 2000. Available online at http://www.infres.enst.fr/confs/evolang/actes/_actes52.html/.

Olmstead, Ben. *Malbolge* (1998). Available at http://www.antwon.com/other/malbolge/ malbolge.txt/.

Olson, Harry F. *Dynamical Analogies,* 2nd ed. New York: Van Nostrand, 1958.

Olson, Harry F. *Music, Physics and Engineering*. New York: Dover Books, 1967.

Oudshoorn, Nelly, and Trevor Pinch, eds. *How Users Matter*. Cambridge, MA: The MIT Press, 2003.

Owen, Mark. "BASIC Spreadsheet." Quoted in C. D. Wright, "One line spreadsheet in BASIC," post to comp.lang.functional. Message-ID: <D01s7J.LK3@cix.compulink .co.uk> (November 29, 1994).

Oxford English Dictionary. Available at: http://www.oed.com/

Parikka, Jussi. "The Universal Viral Machine," *CTheory*. Available at http://www
.ctheory.net/articles.aspx?id=500/ (accessed April 13, 2006).

Pascual, Marsha. "Black Monday, Causes and Effects" (1998). Available at http://www
.ncs.pvt. k12.va.us/ryerbury/pasc/pasc.htm/.

Paynter, Henry, ed. *A Palimpsest on the Electronic Analog Art.* Geo. A. Philbrick Researches Inc., 1955.

Peitgen, Hans Otto, and Peter Richter. *The Beauty of Fractals: Images of Complex Dynamical Systems.* Berlin: Springer Verlag, 1985.

Peltier, Thomas R. "The Virus Threat," *Computer Fraud & Security Bulletin,* June 1993,
p. 15.

Perlis, Alan. "Epigrams on Programming," *SIGPLAN Notices*, 17(9), (September
1982). Available at http://www.bio.cam.ac.uk/~mw263/Perlis_Epigrams.html/.

Petersen, Jonas & Hansen, Jens Hofman. "MacLab Danmark." Available at http://www
.maclab.dk/ (accessed March 7, 2006).

Pias, Claus, ed. *Zukunfte des Computers.*

Pickering, Andrew. *The Mangle of Practice: Time, Agency, and Sciences.* Chicago: University of Chicago Press, 1995.

Pinker, Steven. *How The Mind Works.* London: Penguin, 1988.

Pohlmann, Ken C. *Principles of Digital Audio.* New York: McGraw-Hill, 1992.

Pold, Søren. "Interface Realisms: The Interface as Aesthetic Form," *Postmodern* Culture
15(2). Available at http://muse.jhu.edu/journals/postmodern_culture/v015/15.2pold
.html/ (accessed March 7, 2006).

Popper, Karl. "Science as Falsification." In *Conjectures and Refutations.* London: Routledge and Kegan Paul, 1963, pp. 33-39.

Popper, Karl. *The Logic of Scientific Discovery.* London: Routledge, 2003.

Powell, Barry B. *Homer and the Origin of the Greek Alphabet.* Cambridge: Cambridge University Press, 1991.

Predko, Myke. *Programming and Customizing PICmicro MCU Microcontrollers.* New York: McGraw-Hill, 2001.

Proudhon, Pierre-Joseph. *What is Property? An Inquiry into the Principle of Right and of Government.* Translated by Benjamin R. Tucker. New York: Dover, 1970.

Proust, Marcel. *Remembrance of Things Past. Volume 1: Swann's Way: Within a Budding Grove.* Translated by C. K. Scott Moncrieff and Terence Kilmartin. New York: Vintage, 1970.

Punin, Nikolay. *The Memorial to the Third International.* Petersburg: ISO NKP Department Press, 1920.

Pynchon, Thomas. *Gravity's Rainbow.* New York: Viking, 1973.

Pynchon, Thomas. *The Crying of Lot 49.* New York: Lippincott, 1966.

Quine, W. V. O. "Designation and Existence." In Herbert Sellars Feigl Wilfried Sellars Feigl, eds., *Readings in Philosophical Analysis.* New York: Appleton-Century Crofts, 1949.

Raskin, Jef. *The Humane Interface: New Directions for Designing Interactive Systems.* Reading, MA: Addison-Wesley, 2000.

Raymond, Eric S. *The Art of UNIX Programming.* Boston, MA: Addison-Wesley, 2004.

Read, Herbert. *The True Voice of Feeling.* New York: Pantheon Books, 1953.

Reimer, Jeremy. "A History of the GUI." (May 5, 2005). Available at http://arstechnica.com/articles/paedia/gui.ars (accessed March 7, 2006).

Riepl, Wolfgang. *Das Nachrichtenwesen des Altertums: Mit besonderer Rücksicht auf die Römer* (1913). Reprint, Darmstadt, 1972.

Ritchie, David. "Shannon and Weaver: Unraveling the Paradox of Information," *Communication Research*, vol. 13, no. 2 (April 1986), 278–298.

Roads, Curtis. *Microsound.* Cambridge, MA: The MIT Press, 2001.

Robinson, Derek. "Index and Analogy: A Footnote to the Theory of Signs," *Rivista di Linguistica 7:2*, Pisa (1995).

Rogers, Everett M. *Diffusion of Innovations*, 5th ed. New York: Free Press, 2003.

Ronell, Avital. *Stupidity.* Chicago: University of Illinois Press, 2003.

Ronell, Avital. *Finitude's Score: Essays for the End of the Millennium.* Lincoln: University of Nebraska Press, 1994.

Rosen, Robert. "Effective Processes and Natural Law." In Rolf Herken, ed., *The Universal Turing Machine: A Half-Century Surveys.* Oxford: Oxford University Press, 1988.

Rossum, Guido van. 2.3.8 Mapping Types—classdict. *Python Library Reference*, Python Software Foundation 2006. Available at: http://docs.python.org/lib/lib.html/.

Rotman, Brian. *Signifying Nothing: The Semiotics of Zero.* Stanford, CA: Stanford University Press, 1987.

Rubinsky, Yuri. *SGML on the Web.* New York: Prentice-Hall, 1997.

Rumbaugh, James R., Michael R. Blaha, William Lorensen, Frederick Eddy, and William Premerlani. *Object-Oriented Modeling and Design.* Englewood Cliffs, NJ: Prentice-Hall, 1991.

RunMe, software art repository. Available at http://www.runme.org/.

Rusling, David A. "Interrupts and Interrupt Handling." In *The Linux Kernel* (1999). Available at http://www.tldp.org/LDP/tlk/dd/interrupts.html/ (accessed March 14, 2006).

Sabel, Charles, and Michael Piore. *Dialog on Flexible Manufacturing Networks.* Durham, NC: Southern Technology Council, 1990.

Sack, Warren. "Aesthetics of Information Visualization" In Paul Christiane, Victoria Vesna, Margot Lovejoy eds. Context Providers, Minneapolis: University of Minnesota Press, 2007.

Saussure, Ferdinand de. "Chapter I: Nature of the Linguistic Sign," from *Course in General Linguistics*. Translated by Wade Baskin. In *The Norton Anthology of Theory and Criticism*. New York: Norton, 2001, 964–966.

Scaife, Mike and Yvonne Rogers, "External Cognition how do graphical representations work?," *International Journal of Human-Computer Studies*, vol. 45, no. 2, 185–213.

Scheffer, Lou. *Introduction to Malbolge*. Available at http://www.lscheffer.com/malbolge.htm/.

Scheutz, Matthias, ed. *Computationalism: New Directions*.

Sloman, Aaron, "The Irrelevance of Turing Machines to AI," in Matthias Scheutz, ed., *Computationalism: New Directions*, 87–127.

Schrödinger, Erwin. *What is Life?* Available at http://home.att.net/~p.caimi/schrodinger.html/ (accessed March 29, 2006).

Schultz, Pit. "Jodi as a Software Culture." In Tilman Baumgarten, ed. *Install.exe / Jodi*, Christoph Merian Basel: Verlag, 2002.

Schwartz, Hillel. *The Culture of the Copy: Striking Likenesses, Unreasonable Facsimiles,* 223.

Schwartz, Randall L., and Tom Phoenix. *Learning Perl*. Sebastapol, CA: O'Reilly, 2001.

Searle, John. *Speech Acts: An Essay in the Philosophy of Language*, Cambridge: Cambridge University Press, 1969.

Selvin, Joel. "Chronicle Pop Music Critic," *San Francisco Chronicle* (Sunday, June 2, 1996).

Sengers, Phoebe, and Bill Gaver. "Designing for Interpretation," *Proceedings of Human-Computer Interaction International*, 2005. Available at http://cemcom.infosci.cornell.edu/papers/sengers-gaver.design-for-interpretation.pdf/ (accessed April 24, 2006).

Shannon, Claude E. "An Algebra for Theoretical Genetics." PhD dissertation, MIT, 1940.

Shannon, Claude E. *A Symbolic Analysis of Relay and Switching Circuits.* Cambridge, MA: Massachusetts Institute of Technology, Department of Electrical Engineering, 1940.

Shannon, Claude E. "A Mathematical Theory of Communication," *Bell System Technical Journal* v. 27, (July 1948) 379–423 and (October 1948) 623–656. Available at http://cm.bell-labs.com/cm/ms/what/shannonday/paper.html/.

Shannon, Claude E., and Warren Weaver. *A Mathematical Theory of Communication.* Urbana: University of Illinois Press, 1949.

Shannon, Claude E. *Ein/Aus: Ausgewählte Schriften zur Kommunikations- und Nachrichtentheorie.* Edited by Friedrich Kittler et al. Berlin: Brinkmann U. Bose, 2000.

Shapiro, Fred R. "Origin of the Term Software: Evidence from the JSTOR Electronic Journal Archive." *IEEE Annals of the History of Computing* 22 (April–June, 2000): 69. Available at http://computer.org/annals/an2000/pdf/a2069.pdf/.

Shelley, Mary. *Frankenstein, or, The Modern Prometheus.* London: Lackington, Allen & Co., 1818.

Shepard, R. N. "Towards a Universal Law of Generalization for Psychological Studies." Plenary Lecture to the Cognitive Science Society, Ann Arbor, 1987. Also in *Science,* vol. 237, issue 4820, 1317–1323.

Schneiderman, Ben. *Leonardo's Laptop: Human Needs and the New Computing Technologies.* London: The MIT Press, 2002.

Shuttleworth, Mark. *Rosetta,* (Software) 2006.

Shuttleworth, Mark. *The LauchPad Homepage,* 2006 available at http://www.launchpad.net/.

Siegert, Bernhard. "Der Untergang des römischen Reiches." In *Paradoxien, Dissonanzen, Zusammenbrüche. Situationen offener Epistemologie,* eds. Hans Ulrich Gumbrecht and K. Ludwig Pfeiffer. Frankfurt/M. 1991, pp. 495-514. In English as "The Fall of The Roman Empire," In Hans Ulrich Gumbrecht and K. Ludwig Pfeiffer, eds., *Materialities of Communication.* Translated by William Whobrey, Stanford, CA: Stanford University Press, 1994.

Silicon Valley Toxics Coalition. Homepage available at http://www.svtc.org/.

Simon, Herbert A. *The Sciences of the Artificial*, 3rd ed. Cambridge, MA: The MIT Press, 1996.

Slade, Robert. "History of Computer Viruses" (1992). Available at http://www.cknow .com/articles/6/1/Robert-Slade&%2339%3Bs-Computer-Virus-History/.

Sloman, Aaron, "The Irrelevance of Turing Machines to AI," in Matthias Scheutz, ed., *Computationalism: New Directions*, 87–127.

Smith, Brian Cantwell. *On the Origin of Objects*. Cambridge, MA: The MIT Press, 1998.

Smith, S. W. *The Scientist and Engineer's Guide to Digital Signal Processing*. San Diego: California Technical Publishing, 2001.

Smotherman, Mark. "Interrupts" (2004). Available at http://www.cs.clemson.edu/ ~mark/interrupts.html/ (accessed March 14, 2006).

Solnit, Rebecca. *Wanderlust: A History of Walking*. London: Verso, 2000.

SourceForge. Available at http://sourceforge.net/

Spolsky, Joel, ed. *The Best Software Writing 1: Selected and Introduced by Joel Spolsky*. Berkeley: Apress, 2005.

Stallman, Richard. "GNU Project." In Joshua Gay, ed., *Free Software, Free Society: Selected Essays of Richard M. Stallman*. Boston, MA: GNU Press, Free Software Foundation, 2002, 31-39.

Stallman, Richard. "Why Free Software is Better than Open Source." In Joshua Gay, ed., *Free Software, Free Society: Selected Essays of Richard M. Stallman*. Boston, MA: GNU Press, Free Software Foundation, 2002, 55-60.

Star, Susan Leigh. "Invisible Work and Silenced Dialogues in Knowledge Representation." In Inger V. Eriksson, Barbara A. Kitchenham, Kea G. Tijdens, *Women, Work and Computerization: Understanding and Overcoming Bias in Work and Education*. Amsterdam: Elsevier Science Publishers, 1991, 81-92.

Stengers, Isabelle. *The Invention of Modern Science*. Translated by Daniel W. Smith. Minneapolis: University of Minnesota Press, 2000.

Stengers, Isabelle. *Penser avec Whitehead*. Paris: Seuil, 2002.

Stephenson, Neal. *In the Beginning was the Command Line*. New York: Avon Books, 1999.

Sterling, Bruce. *Shaping Things*. Cambridge, MA: The MIT Press, 2005.

Stone, Allucquére Rosanne. "Will The Real Body Please Stand Up?: Boundary Stories About Virtual Cultures." In Michael Benedikt, ed., *Cyberspace: First Steps*. Cambridge, MA: The MIT Press, 1991.

Suchman, Lucy. *Plans and Situated Actions: The Problems of Human-Machine Communication*. Cambridge: Cambridge University Press, 1987.

Suetonius Tranquillus, Caius. *Vitae Caesarum*, I 56, 6 and II 86.

Sukenick, Ronald. *Narralogues: Truth in Fiction*. Albany, NY: State University of New York Press, 2000.

Sulfnbk Virus. See http://www.symantec.com/avcenter/vcnc/data/sulfnbk.exe. Also see http://urbanlegends.about.com/library/blsulfnbk.htm/.

Sun Microsystems. *After Internationalization, The Java Tutorial*. (2006).

Suetonius, *The Twelve Caesars*. Translated by Robert Graves. London: Penguin, 2003.

Sutherland, Ivan. *Sketchpad: A Man-Machine Graphical Communication System*, PhD thesis, MIT, 1963.

Swift, Jonathan, *Gulliver's Travels,* Project Gutenberg Ebook, available at http://www.gutenberg.org/dirs/etext97/gltrv10.txt/.

Symantec website. Available at http://www.symantec.com/avcenter/venc/data/sulfnbk.exe.warning.html/.

Tanenbaum, Andrew S. *Operating Systems: Design and Implementation*. Englewood Cliffs, NJ: Prentice-Hall, 1987.

Tedre, Matti, Erkki Sutinen, Esko Kähkönen and Piet Kommers. "Is Universal Usability Universal Only to Us?" *On-line proceedings of the ACM conference CUU2003*, Vancouver BC, Canada (November 10–11, 2003).

Tedre, Matti, Erkki Sutinen, Esko Kähkönen and Piet Kommers. "Ethnocomputing: ICT in Social and Cultural Context," *Communications of the ACM*, vol. 49 no. 1, 126–130.

Tergan, Sigmar-Olaf, and Tanja Keller, eds. *Knowledge and Information Visualisation: Searching for Synergies (Lecture Notes in Computer Science)*. Berlin and Heidelberg: Springer-Verlag, 2005.

Teuscher, Christof, ed. *Alan Turing: Life and Legacy of a Great Thinker*. Berlin: Springer, 2004.

Thompson, Ken. "Reflections of Trusting Trust," *Communications of the ACM*, vol. 27, issue 8 (August 1984).

Todd, Peter. "Simulating the Evolution of Musical Behaviour." In Walling, Nils L., Björn Merker, and Steven Brown, eds., *The Origins of Music*. Cambridge, MA: The MIT Press, 2000.

Toop, David. *Haunted Weather*. London: Serpents Tail, 2005.

Tort, Patrick. *La Raison Classificatoire: Les Complexes Discursifs-Quinze Etudes*. Paris: Aubier, 1989.

Touretzky, David *COMMON LISP: A Gentle Introduction to Symbolic Computation*. Redwood City, CA: Benjamin/Cummings, 1990.

Tuck, Mike. "The Real History of the GUI," (August 13th 2001). Available at http://www.sitepoint.com/print/real-history-gui/ (accessed March 7, 2006).

Tufte, Edward. *Visual Explanations*. Cheshire, CT: Graphics Press, 1997.

Tukey, John W. "The Teaching of Concrete Mathematics." *American Mathematical Monthly* no. 65 (January, 1958): 1–9.

Turkle, Sherry. "Artificial Intelligence and Psychoanalysis: A New Alliance," *Daedalus*, vol. 17, no. 1 (Winter 1988).

"Two Old Viruses," *The Risks Digest,* Vol. 6, Issue 53 (March 1988), available at http://catless.ncl.ac.uk/risks.

Alan M. Turing. *Intelligence Service: Schriften.* Edited by Bernhard Dotzler and Friedrich Kittler. Berlin: Brinkmann U. Bose, 1987.

Alan M. Turing. *The Essential Turing.* Edited by Jack Copeland. Oxford: Oxford University Press, 2004.

Alan M. Turing. "Intelligent machinery." In *Machine Intelligence 5.* Edited by Bernhard Meltzer and Donald Michie. North Holland: Elsevier, 1970.

Alan M. Turing, "Computing Machinery and Intelligence," *Mind,* no. 59 (October 1950), 433, 460.

Alan Turing. "On Computable Numbers with an Application to the *Entscheidungsproblem*," *Proceedings of the London Mathematical Society,* ser. 2. vol. 42 (1936–1937), 253.

Ulanowicz, Robert. *Growth & Development: Ecosystems Phenomenology.* New York: Springer, 1986.

Unicode Consortium. "What is Unicode?" Available at http://www.unicode.org/standard/WhatIsUnicode.html/ (accessed on April 21, 2006).

Urban Legends. Available at http://urbanlegends.about.com/library/blsulfnbk.htm/.

Valery, Paul. "Man and the Seashell." In *Paul Valery: An Anthology.* Princeton, NJ: Princeton University Press, 1977.

Van De Mieroop, Marc. *Cuneiform Texts and the Writing of History.* New York and London: Routledge, 1999.

Verran, Helen. *Science and an African Logic.* Chicago: The University of Chicago Press, 2001.

Vesisenaho, Mikko, et al. "Contextualizing ICT in Africa: The Development of the CATI Model in Tanzanian Higher Education," *African Journal of Information and Communication Technology* 2(2) (June 2006) 88–109.

Virus Myths. Available at http://www.vmyths.com/ (accessed on April 21, 2006).

von Neumann, John. "First Draft of a Report on the EDVAC," 1945.

Waldby, Catherine, *The Visible Human Project: Informatic Bodies and Posthuman Medicine.* New York: Routledge, 2000.

Waldrop, M. Mitchell. *The Dream Machine: J. C. R. Licklider and the Revolution that Made Computing Personal.* London: Penguin, 2001.

Wall, Larry. "Perl, the First Postmodern Computer Language" (1999). Available at http://www.wall.org/~larry/pm.html/.

Wall, Larry, Tom Christiansen, and Jon Orwant, *Programming Perl.* Sebastopol CA: O'Reilly, 2000.

Ward, Adrian. *Signwave Auto-Illustrator* (2000–2002). Available at http://www.auto-illustrator.com/.

Ware, Colin, *Information Visualization: Perception for Design.* San Francisco: Morgan Kaufmann Publishers, 2000.

Wark, McKenzie. *A Hacker Manifesto.* Cambridge, MA: Harvard University Press, 2004.

Weber, Max. *The Protestant Ethic and the Spirit of Capitalism.* London: Allen and Unwin, 1930.

Webster's Ninth Collegiate Dictionary, Springfield MA: Merriam-Webster, 1983.

Wegner, Peter. "The Paradigm Shift from Algorithms to Interaction: Why Interaction is More Powerful Than Algorithms," *Communications of the ACM*, vol. 40 no. 5 (May 1997), 81–91. Available at http://www.cs.brown.edu/people/pw/papers/ficacm.ps/.

Wegner, Peter, and Dana Goldin. "Computation Beyond Turing Machines" (2002). Available at http://www.cs.brown.edu/people/pw/.

Weisfeld, Matt. "Moving from Procedural to Object-Oriented Development" (2004). Available at http://www.developer.com/design/article.php/3317571 (accessed April 22, 2006).

Weizenbaum, Joseph. "ELIZA—A Computer Program for the Study of Natural Language Communication between Man and Machine." In *Communications of the ACM*, vol. 9, no. 1 (January 1966), 36–45.

Whitehead, Alfred North. *Introduction to Mathematics*. London: Williams and Norgate, 1911.

Whitehead, Alfred North. *Process and Reality*. New York: Free Press, 1978.

Whitehead, Alfred North. *Science and the Modern World*. New York: Free Press, 1997.

Wichary, Marcin. *GUIdebook, Graphical User Interface Gallery*. Available http://www.guidebookgallery.org/ (accessed March 7, 2006).

Wiener, Norbert. *Cybernetics, or Control and Communication in Animals and Machines*. Cambridge, MA: The MIT Press, 1948.

Wigner, E. P. "The Unreasonable Effectiveness of Mathematics in the Natural Sciences," *Communications in Pure and Applied Mathematics 13:1*, 1960.

Wikipedia, the free encyclopedia, available at http://wikipedia.org/.

Wilhelmsson, U. "What's in those video games?" In *Proceedings of Computer Games & Digital Textualities*, IT University of Copenhagen (2001), 44–54.

Williams, Raymond. *Keywords: A Vocabulary of Culture and Society*. London: Fontana, 1976.

Willinsky, Jon. *The Access Principle: The Case for Open Access to Research and Scholarship*. Cambridge, MA: The MIT Press, 2005.

Winthrop-Young, Geoffrey, and Michael Wutz. "Translator's Introduction: Friedrich Kittler and Media Discourse Analysis." In Friedrich Kittler, *Gramophone, Film, Typewriter*. Stanford, CA: Stanford University Press, 1999.

Witherspoon, Gary, and Glen Peterson. *Dynamic Symmetry and Holistic Asymmetry in Navajo and Western Art and Cosmology*. New York: Peter Lang Publishing, 1995.

Wittgenstein, Ludwig. *Philosophical Investigations*. Translated by G. E. M. Anscombe. Oxford: Blackwell, 1953.

Wolfram, Stephen, *A New Kind of Science*, Champaign, IL: Wolfram Media, 2002. Also available at http://www.wolframscience.com/nksonline/toc.html/.

Woods, Donald, and James Lyon. *The INTERCAL Programming Language Revised Reference Manual*, 1st ed. (1973). C-INTERCAL revisions, Louis Howell and Eric Raymond (1996).

World Wide Web Consortium. Available at http://www.w3.org/.

Yeats, William Butler. *Synge and the Ireland of His Time.* Shannon: Irish University Press, 1970. Project Gutenburg, available at http://www.gutenberg.org/etext/8557/.

Youngblood, Gene. *Expanded Cinema*. New York: E. P. Dutton, 1970.

Zaslavsky, Claudia. *Africa Counts: Number and Pattern in Africa Culture.*

Zehle, Sehle. "FLOSS Redux: Notes on African Software Politics." *Mute,* vol. 3, no. 06 (2005). Available at http://www.metamute.org/en/FLOSS-Redux-Notes-on-African-Software-Politics/ (accessed on April 21, 2006).

Zlatanov, Teodor. "Cultured Perl: The Elegance of JAPH." In *Developer Works: IBM's Resource for Developers* (1 July 2001). Available at http://www.128.ibm.com/developer-works/linux/library/l-japh.html.

Zolli, Andrew. "Pixelvision: A Meditation," *Core77*, undated. Available at http://www.core77.com/reactor/opinion_06.03.asp/.

About the Contributors

Alison Adam is Professor of Information Systems at the University of Salford, UK. Her research interests are in gender and information systems, AI, and computer ethics. Recent books include *Artificial Knowing: Gender and the Thinking Machine* (Routledge, 1998) and *Gender, Ethics and Information Technology* (Palgrave, 2005).

Morten Breinbjerg is Associate Professor at the Institute of Aesthetic Disciplines, Multimedia Studies, University of Aarhus, Denmark, and holds a PhD in Computer Music Aesthetics. His research covers digital culture, media and aesthetics, interface studies of music software, and game audio.

Ted Byfield is Associate Chair of the Parsons School of Design, co-editor of ICANN Watch, and was the 2002 Journalism Fellow of the Design Trust for Public Space. He has worked for a decade as a freelance nonfiction editor with an emphasis on cultural, intellectual, and technological history. He co-moderates the Nettime mailing list and co-edited its book of proceedings, *Readme!* (Autonomedia, 1999). His writings have appeared in several languages in technical, political, and cultural journals, and he has spoken on the same range of subjects in the US and throughout Europe. He currently works as a consultant and/or advisor for several commercial and noncommercial organizations.

Wendy Hui Kyong Chun is Associate Professor of Modern Culture and Media at Brown University. She has studied both Systems Design Engineering and English Literature, which she combines and mutates in her current work on digital media. She is author of *Control and Freedom: Power and Paranoia in the Age of Fiber Optics* (The MIT Press, 2006), and co-editor (with Thomas Keenan) of *New Media, Old Media: A History and Theory Reader*

(Routledge, 2005). She is currently working on a monograph entitled *Programmed Visions: Software, DNA, Race* (forthcoming from the MIT Press, 2008).

Geoff Cox is an artist, teacher, and projects organizer as well as currently lecturer in Computing at University of Plymouth, UK. He co-edited "Economising Culture" and "Engineering Culture" as part of the DATA browser series (Autonomedia, 2004, 2005). He is also a trustee of Kahve-Society and the UK Museum of Ordure. For more information see http://www.anti-thesis.net/.

Florian Cramer is a Berlin-based independent researcher in Comparative Literature, and a writer on literature, the arts, and computing. His most recent publication is "*Words Made Flesh: Code, Culture, Imagination*," on the cultural history of software. For more information see http://pzwart.wdka.hro.nl/mdr/research/fcramer/wordsmadeflesh/ and http://cramer .plaintext.cc:70/.

Cecile Crutzen is Associate Professor of the School of Informatics of the Open University of the Netherlands. Her domain is "People, Computers, and Society." Her research field is the interaction between Gender Studies and Computer Science, specifically regarding interaction and e-learning.

Marco Deseriis (a.k.a. Snafu) is a PhD student in the Department of Culture and Communication at New York University. In 2003 he co-authored *L'Arte della Connessione* (Milan: Shake Editions) with Giuseppe Marano. As a networker, he manages the Italian node of The Thing (thething.it) and organizes Dina (d-i-n-a.net), an international festival of guerrilla communication and culture jamming. He is also a translator and a freelance journalist who contributes to various magazines distributed with *La Repubblica*.

Ron Eglash holds a B.S. in Cybernetics, an M.S. in Systems Engineering, and a PhD in History of Consciousness, all from the University of California. A Fulbright postdoctoral fellowship enabled his field research on African ethnomathematics, which was published by Rutgers University Press in 1999 as *African Fractals: Modern Computing and Indigenous Design*. He is now Associate Professor of Science and Technology Studies at Rensselaer Polytechnic Institute. Recent essay titles include "The Race for Cyberspace: Information Technology in the Black Diaspora" (*Science as Culture*), and "Race, Sex and Nerds: From Black Geeks to Asian-American Hipsters" (*Social Text*). His current project, funded by the NSF, HUD, and the Department of Education, translates the mathematical concepts embedded in cultural designs of African, African American, Native American, and Latino communities into software design tools for secondary school education. The software is available online at http://www.rpi.edu/~eglash/csdt.html.

Matthew Fuller is David Gee Reader in Digital Media at the Centre for Cultural Studies, Goldsmiths College, University of London. He is author of *ATM; Behind the Blip: Essays on the Culture of Software; Media Ecologies: Materialist Energies in Art and Technoculture* and has worked in groups such as I/O/D and Mongrel.

Andrew Goffey is Senior Lecturer in Media, Culture, and Communication at Middlesex University, London. He researches in and writes about the zones of interference between philosophy, science, and culture, edited the "Contagion and the Diseases of Information" issue of *Fibreculture* (http://www.fibreculture.org/), and co-edited the "Biopolitics" issue of *CultureMachine* (http://www.culturemachine.net/).

Steve Goodman is Program Leader of the MA Sonic Culture at the University of East London. He is currently writing a book on sonic warfare, and has published widely on sound, cybernetic culture, and philosophies of affect. He runs the record label Hyperdub (www.hyperdub.net), and under the name Kode9 (www.kode9.com), has released music on labels such as Rephlex, Tempa, and his own imprint, Hyperdub.

Olga Goriunova is a new media researcher, teacher, and organizer. She is a co-creator of the Readme software art festival series (Moscow 2002, Helsinki 2003, Aarhus 2004, Dortmund 2005), and a co-organizer of Runme.org software art repository (http://runme.org/). She is currently completing her PhD in Media Lab, University of Industrial Arts and Design, Helsinki, Finland.

Graham Harwood is the artistic director of the UK artist group Mongrel (http://www.mongrel.org.uk/). His main interests are in the networked image and in helping other people set things up for themselves. He currently lives at the mouth of the Thames with Matsuko Yokokoji, also a member of Mongrel, and their son Lani, where they are helping to set up a free media space, mediashed.org, for local people. For more information see http://www.scotoma.org/.

Wilfried Hou Je Bek is an independent social fiction worker whose projects can be found at www.socialfiction.org.

Friedrich Kittler is Professor of Media History and Aesthetics at Humboldt University-Berlin's Institute for Aesthetics. He is the author of numerous books and articles; those that have been translated into English are currently: *Discourse Networks 1800/1900; Literature, Media, Information Systems; Gramophone, Film, Typewriter.*

Erna Kotkamp is ICT Coordinator and a junior teacher/researcher for the Institute of Media and Representation at Utrecht University. She combines technical ICT skills with academic research to compare the methodology and design process of educational software in open source vs. proprietary software from a gender perspective.

Joasia Krysa is an independent curator and lecturer in Art and Technology at the University of Plymouth, UK. She established the curatorial research project, KURATOR, http://www.kurator.org/, in 2005 and currently co-organizes the Curatorial Network (with Arts Council England, South West), http://www.curatorial.net/. Recent projects include the conference "Curating, Immateriality, Systems" (London: Tate Modern, 2005) and the edited book Curating Immateriality (DATA Browser 03, Autonomedia, 2006; http://www.data-browser.net/).

Adrian Mackenzie is at the Institute for Cultural Research, Lancaster University, where he researches in the area of technology, science, and culture using approaches from cultural studies, social studies of technology, and critical theory. He has published several monographs on technology, including *Transductions: Bodies and Machines at Speed* (London: Continuum, 2002); *Cutting Code: Software and Sociality* (New York: Peter Lang, 2006), and articles on technology, digital media, science, and culture.

Lev Manovich <www.manovich.net> is the author of *Soft Cinema: Navigating the Database* (The MIT Press, 2005), and The Language of New Media (The MIT Press, 2001), which is hailed as "the most suggestive and broad ranging media history since Marshall McLuhan." He is a professor of Visual Arts of the University of California, San Diego <visarts.ucsd.edu> and a director of The Lab for Cultural Analysis at California Institute for Telecommunications and Information Technology <www.calit2.net>.

Michael Mateas's work explores the intersection between art and artificial intelligence, forging a new art practice and research discipline called Expressive AI. He is a faculty member at the University of California at Santa Cruz. Prior to moving to UCSC, he held a joint appointment in the College of Computing and the school of Literature, Communication, and Culture at the Georgia Institute of Technology. With Andrew Stern he developed the interactive drama Facade, an AI-based first-person, real-time, interactive story (www.interactivestory.net). Michael received his BS in Engineering Physics from the University of the Pacific, his MS in Computer Science from Portland State University, and his PhD in Computer Science from Carnegie Mellon University.

Nick Montfort is a PhD candidate at the University of Pennsylvania. He writes and programs interactive fiction, is a poet, and has collaborated on a variety of digital literary projects. He is author of *Twisty Little Passages: An Approach to Interactive Fiction* and co-editor of *The New Media Reader,* both published by the MIT Press in 2003.

Michael Murtaugh is a lecturer in the MA Media Design program of the Piet Zwart Institute, Willem de Kooning Academie Hogeschool Rotterdam. He also works as a freelance designer and programmer focusing on tools for reading and writing. Links and information about his work are available online at http://www.automatist.org/.

Jussi Parikka is senior lecturer in media studies at Anglia Ruskin University, Cambridge, UK. He has a PhD in Cultural History from the University of Turku, Finland. Parikka is the author of *Digital Contagions. A Media Archaeology of Computer Viruses* (2007) and several essays in English and Finnish on digital culture. A co-edited volume (with Tony Sampson) titled *The Spam Book: On Viruses, Spam and Other Anomalies from the Dark Side of Digital Culture* is forthcoming in 2008. In addition, he is now working on a book on "insect media." Parikka's homepage is at http://users.utu.fi/juspar.

Søren Pold is Associate Professor of Digital Aesthetics at Institute of Aesthetic Disciplines/Multimedia, University of Aarhus, Denmark. He has published in Danish and English on digital and media aesthetics from the nineteenth-century panorama to the interface. He established the Digital Aesthetics Research Centre (http://www.digital-aestetik.dk/) at Aarhus University in 2002; in 2004 he co-organized the Read_me festival on software art; and currently he is in charge of the research project, "The Aesthetics of Interface Culture" (http://www.interfacekultur.au.dk), supported by the Danish Research Agency. His latest book is "*Ex Libris—Medierealistisk litteratur—Paris, Los Angeles & Cyberspace*" (in Danish), which deals with relationships between literature, media, and urbanity. See http://www .bro-pold.dk/ for more information.

Derek Robinson lives in a cheap hotel in Vancouver, BC, where he enjoys puttering about with books and computers and ideas. In 2000 he wrote the second in-browser WYSI-WYG HTML editor, in Javascript (the first was by Tim Berners-Lee, written in Objective-C for the NeXT computer in 1991), in partial atonement for a season as Stockholm's least-ept Linux sysadmin. He taught Integrated Media at the Ontario College of Art in Toronto from 1986 to 1998. He publishes sparingly, although in 1995 an essay, "Index and Analogy: A Footnote to the Theory of Signs," appeared in *Rivista di Linguistica,* and in 1993 a novel algorithm for feature discovery in very large databases was presented before the International Joint Congress of A.I., Special Workshop on AI and the Genome. He's a slow learner.

Warren Sack is a software designer and media theorist whose work explores theories and designs for online public space and public discussion. Before joining the faculty at the University of California, Santa Cruz in the Film & Digital Media Department, Warren was an assistant professor at UC Berkeley, where he directed the Social Technologies Group.

He has also been a research scientist at the MIT Media Laboratory, and a research collaborator in the Interrogative Design Group at the MIT Center for Advanced Visual Studies. He earned a BA from Yale College and an SM and PhD from the MIT Media Laboratory. He is currently an assistant professor in the Film and Digital Media Department; affiliated faculty with the Computer Science Department; and, a member of the graduate faculty for the Digital Arts / New Media MFA Program (housed jointly by the Arts Division and the School of Engineering) at the University of California, Santa Cruz. For more information see http://people.ucsc.edu/~wsack/.

Grzesiek Sedek is an Open Source and Linux enthusiast. He has been working on system programming, multimedia, video, animation, e-commerce, B2B integration, and network security. He currently works at Wimbledon School of Art and is actively involved in the development of the MARCEL high bandwidth network. His other interests include music, performance, and interactive installation.

Alexei Shulgin is an artist, theorist, musician, curator, and photographer; his works include Form Art (1997), FU-FME (1999), and the world's first cyberpunk rock band 386 DX (1998 – onwards). Alexei is a co-organizer of Runme.org software art repository (2003) and a co-curator of the Readme software art festivals (Moscow 2002, Helsinki 2003, Aarhus 2004, Dortmund 2005). His recent works include the conceptual VJ tool WIMP, Super-I-Real Virtuality system and Electroboutique (http://www.electroboutique.com/). For more information see http://www.easylife.org/.

Matti Tedre is a researcher at the Department of Computer Science, University of Joensuu, Finland. His PhD dissertation on the topic "Social Studies of Computer Science" will be published in August 2006. His M.Sc thesis on the topic "Ethnocomputing" was published in May 2002. For more information see http://www.tedre.name/.

Adrian Ward is a software artist, programmer, systems administrator, and lecturer. Since 1999, his London-based company, Signwave UK (http://www.signwave.co.uk/), has existed as a mere excuse for him to do some fun things with software. He is the author of, among other things, Autoshop and Auto-Illustrator, the latter of which co-won the 2001 Transmediale Software Art award. He continues to collaborate with artists, musicians and academics in exploring new realms for software. Please see http://www.adeward.com/ for more information.

Richard Wright is an artist who has been working in digital moving image and software-based practice for nearly twenty years. Films include *Heliocentrum* (1995)—a cross between a political documentary and a seventeenth-century rave video—and *LMX Spiral* (1998)—a conceptual music video about the eighties. Recent work includes *The Bank of*

Time (2001)—a BAFTA nominated online screensaver—and *Foreplay* (2004)—a porn film without the sex. Currently in production is *The Mimeticon*—a visual search engine that exploits the interdependence of image and text through the history of the Western alphabet. For more information see http://www.futurenatural.net.

Simon Yuill is an artist based in Glasgow, Scotland, where he is part of the Chateau Institute of Technology. Projects include: spring_alpha (http://www.spring-alpha.org), the Social Versioning System (http://www.spring-alpha.org/svs), slateford (http://www.slateford.org), and Your Machines (http://www.yourmachines.org).

Index

CD-disc, 76
CDR (Compact Disc-Recordable), 176
Cellular automata, 98, 231–232
Ceruzzi, Paul E., 238
  A History of Modern Computing, 238
CGI (Common Gateway Interface), 197
Chaitin, Gregory, 88–89
Charge Coupled Device (CCD), 215
Chaucer, William, 126
  Canterbury Tales, 126
Chef, 271–272
Chen, Chaomei, 81
Chomsky, Noam, 57–58
Cicero, 41, 184
Cipher, 42
Circuit(s), 21, 23–24, 26, 27, 110, 225,
  233, 243, 254
COBOL, 197, 268
Codase, 238
Code(s), 6, 23, 33, 40–46, 50–51, 64–68,
  71, 75, 81, 86, 87–88, 91, 101–104,
  111, 114, 117, 119, 136, 138–139,
  152, 154, 156, 165, 172–173, 181,
  182, 193–195, 197–198, 207, 209,
  217, 219, 220, 222, 232, 236–240,
  251, 254, 262, 271, 273, 274
Codec(s) [MPEG-1, MPEG-2, MPEG-4,
  H.263, H.264, theora, dirac, DivX,
  XviD, MJPEG, WMV, RealVideo,
  VLC , DVB, AtsC, AVC, MP3],
  48–50, 52–54
Code condenser, 43
Codefetch, 238
Code Snippets, 238
Codex Lustinianus, 41
Codex Theodosius, 41
Coleridge, Samuel Taylor, 180–183
Colossus computer, 22
Comenius, 172
  Orbis Pictus, 172

Complementary Metal Oxide Semicon-
  ductor (CMOS), 215
Computational offloading, 82
Computing Machinery and Intelligence,
  132
Commodore, 113, 193
Concurrent Versions System (CVS),
  64–66, 68, 238
Conservation laws, 25
Conway, John, 231
Cooke, Andrew, 272
Cooperative modeling, 146
Copy Protection Technical Working
  Group, 75
Corpus Iuris, 41
Coy, Wolfgang, 40
Coyne, Richard, 203
Cow, 272
CP command, 72
Cratchit, Bob, 70
Cron, 5
Crutchfield, James, 60
CSS (Cascading Style Sheets), 73, 263
Cubo-Futurism, 112
Culturally Situated Design Tools, 95
CU-Seeme, 111
Cybernetics, 26, 107, 220
Cyborg science, 185, 188

Dadaism, 114
Dahl, Ole-Johan, 201
Darwin, Charles, 26, 232
Darwinian (evolution), 60, 230
Data mining, 80
Dato, 70
Data table, 80
Data visualization, 78, 84
Dawkins, Richard, 72, 232
Deleuze, Gilles, 18, 136, 139–140
Dennett, Daniel, 137

Tamagotchi, 248

Tansey, Mark, 262

Taschen, 121–122

Tatlin, 112

Taylorization, 177

TEACH, 268

Telos, 26

Tetris, 193

Tinguely, Jean, 102
 Homage to New York, 102

Tort, Patrick, 175

Tool Kit, 90

Trac, 65

Theodosius, Imperator, 41

Thomson, 75

Thompson, Ken, 71

Thorton, Don, 99

Thousand Plateaus, A, 139

Tufte, Edward, 79

Tukey, John W., 2

Turing, Alan Mathison, 5, 16, 43–45,
 91, 132–133, 136–137, 140, 145,
 150–151, 170, 186–188, 226–227,
 261, 269

Turing machine(s), 16–17, 41, 43, 45,
 57, 75, 132–133, 137, 144–145, 153,
 162, 180

Turing Tarpits, 269

Turing Test, 132–133

Turkle, Sherry, 187–188

TX-2, 143

U2, 248

Ubuntu Manifesto, 155–156

Ulam, Stanislav, 231

Unconscious counting, 230

Unicode, 155

UNIVAC (Universal Automatic Computer), 22, 238

Universal Code Condensers, 43

UNIX, 5, 61, 65, 72, 150–151, 169,
 171, 207, 210, 218, 262

Untitled Game, 117

URI (Uniform Resource Indicator), 263

URL (Uniform Resource Locator), 220

UTF (Unicode Transformation Format),
 263

Utopia, 84, 181

Verran, Helen, 157–159
 Science and an African Logic, 157

Viacom, 75

Viete, François, 42–43

Visualization in Scientific Computing
 (ViSC), 78–79

Visual Basic, 197

Virus, 250–254

VLSI (Very Large Scale Integrated) circuit, 27

Volta, 24

Wall, Larry, 207, 210

Ward, Adrian, 36

Ware, Colin, 79, 81

Watt, James, 26

Way Things Go, The, 198

Weaver, Warren, 127–128

Web 2.0, 60

Wegner, Peter, 144–147

Weiss, David, 198

Weizenbaum, Joseph, 133, 170

Whitehead, Alfred North, 19, 101, 136

Wigner, Eugene, 25

Wiki, 66

Wikipedia, 49, 62

Williams, Raymond, 9
 Keywords, 9

Windows Longhorn 4015, 219

Windows Media Player, 84

Windows Vista, 247

LEONARDO

Roger F. Malina, Executive Editor
Sean Cubitt, Editor-in-Chief

The Global Genome: Biotechnology, Politics, and Culture, Eugene Thacker, 2005

Media Ecologies: Materialist Energies in Art and Technoculture, Matthew Fuller, 2005

Art Beyond Biology, edited by Eduardo Kac, 2006

New Media Poetics: Contexts, Technotexts, and Theories, edited by Adalaide Morris and Thomas Swiss, 2006

Aesthetic Computing, edited by Paul A. Fishwick, 2006

Digital Performance: A History of New Media in Theater, Dance, Performance Art, and Installation, Steve Dixon, 2006

MediaArtHistories, edited by Oliver Grau, 2006

From Technological to Virtual Art, Frank Popper, 2007

META/DATA: A Digital Poetics, Mark Amerika, 2007

Signs of Life: Bio Art and Beyond, Eduardo Kac, 2007

The Hidden Sense: Synesthesia in Art and Science, Cretien van Campen, 2007

Closer: Performance, Technologies, Phenomenology, Susan Kozel, 2007

Video: The Reflexive Medium, Yvonne Spielmann, 2007

Software Studies: A Lexicon, edited by Matthew Fuller, 2008